INTERNATIONAL LAW IN THE MIDDLE EAST

International Law in the Middle East

Closer to Power than Justice

JEAN ALLAIN
Queen's University, Belfast

ASHGATE

Published by
Ashgate Publishing Limited
Gower House
Croft Road
Aldershot
Hants GU11 3HR
England

Ashgate Publishing Company
Suite 420
101 Cherry Street
Burlington, VT 05401-4405
USA

Ashgate website: http://www.ashgate.com

British Library Cataloguing in Publication Data
Allain, Jean, 1965-
    International Law in the Middle East : closer to power than
    justice
    1. United Nations - Middle East 2.International law - Middle
    East 3.Law enforcement - Middle East 4.Middle East -
    History - 20th century 5.Middle East - Foreign relations
    I. Title
    341'.0956

Library of Congress Cataloging-in-Publication Data
Allain, Jean, 1965-
    International law in the Middle East : closer to power than justice / Jean Allain.
        p. cm.
    Includes bibliographical references and index.
    ISBN 0-7546-2436-6
    1. Middle East--International status. 2. International law--Middle East. 3.
Kurds--Legal status, laws, etc. 4. Self-determination, National. I. Title.

    KZ4272.A435 2004
    341.26--dc22

2004005410

ISBN 0 7546 2436 6

Printed in Great Britain by Antony Rowe Ltd, Chippenham, Wiltshire

Contents

Table of Cases

II. Arbitrations

III. Adjudication before Other *Fora*

List of Maps

Preface

International Law in the Middle East demonstrates how international law has been interpreted and applied in the region in a qualitatively different manner that weighs in closer to power than to justice. By considering the historical evolution of the modern Middle East and demonstrating the way in which fundamental precepts of international law have been manipulated, abused, disregarded, and violated; a fundamental understanding emerges as to why an international rule of law has never truly taken hold in the region. The lack of legitimacy felt for international law in the Middle East is to be understood by the manner in which the fundamental building blocks of international relations—self-determination, the prohibition on the use of force, respect for human rights—have been disregarded so as to achieve outcomes sought by those who have had the power to dictate such results. As a result, the Middle East has emerged as the underclass of the international system, wherein law is utilized in an instrumental manner: in formative instances, the region has been witness to an international law that has been arbitrary in its interpretation, selective in its application, and punitive in its enforcement.

In seeking to demonstrate the qualitative exceptionalism of international law in the Middle East, this study first considers the plight of Kurds to demonstrate the failings of positive international law to provide even limited protection which might be afforded under the rubrics of 'self-determination'. The inability of the Westphalian State-system to accommodate the aspirations of Kurdish self-determination has relegated the various Kurdish minorities found in Middle East States to a life of oppression, which on notable occassions has taken on genocidal overtones. Despite having been promised the established of a Kurdish State when the map of the modern Middle East was being drawn at the Paris Peace Conference of 1918, Kurdish desires—unlike those of Eastern European States—would never materialize despite the Wilsonian conception of self-determination having been established as one of the Fourteen Points ending the First World War. While self-determination would come to be recognized as a principle by the United Nations Charter and later, through its use as the intellectual engine of decolonization, as a legal right, the right of self-determination would be defined in such a limited manner as to effectively exclude Kurds. The result of this denial of Kurdish self-determination, which is manifest in more than eighty years of persecution, is most vividly made evident by considering, as this study does, the cases of Iraqi and Turkish Kurds.

The study then moves to consider the underlying theme regarding the application and interpretation of international law in the Middle East. The manner in which the Suez Canal was governed during the British occupation of Egypt (1882–1956) demonstrates, in no uncertain terms, the manner in which the 1888 Constantinople Convention, meant to govern the free passage of all ships through the Canal, was interpreted not in line with the dictates of international law, but in the imperial interest of the British. Likewise, an examination of the evolution of the move toward the creation of the State of Israel shows the manner in which Western States, with the British at the forefront, were unwilling to apply international law where Palestine was concerned. In supporting the Zionist aspirations of European Jewry, Arthur Balfour would explain Great Britain's guiding principle, 'in the case of Palestine we deliberately and rightly decline to accept the principle of self-determination [...] our policy is that we regard Palestine as being absolutely exceptional'.

The third chapter considers the effective abandonment of Palestinian Refugees, forced to flee their homes as a result of the establishment of the State of Israel in 1948–49. An examination of the plight of Palestinian Refugees demonstrates clearly that international law, without the will of an international community to ensure its application through enforcing its dictates is akin to water on paper. Such lack of enforcement has manifested itself, where Palestinian Refugees are concerned, not only in the denial of their right to return, but also in their systematic loss of the legal protection afforded to all other recognized refugees. The issue of enforcement is also central to the following chapter, which examines acts of aggression which transpired in the region over the period 1980–90. Going beyond the lack of enforcement of international law, this chapter considers the selective manner in which the United Nations Security Council has dealt with invasion and occupation in the region; be it through passive neglect as was witnessed during the Iran-Iraq War; by active neglect during the occupation of Lebanon by Israel; or by bringing to bear the most comprehensive measures ever instituted in an attempt to restore peace and security in the wake of the Iraqi invasion of Kuwait in 1990. Through such a consideration, it becomes apparent that there exists a gap between law on the books and law in its application, which, from the perspective of those in the Middle East, weighs in, more often than not, on the side of the powerful and to the detriment of the weak.

Much in the same way that the underclass of a society sees law as being arbitrarily applied and enforced, it also bears witness to the punitive nature of law. Chapter 6 considers the manner in which the UN Security Council went beyond simply punitive measures in enforcing its sanctions regime against Iraq. The sanctions, although *prima facie* legal, had by the manner in which they were applied, breached the *jus cogens* imperative against the committing of crimes against humanity. As a result of the hundreds of thousands of deaths they caused in Iraq, these sanctions demonstrate a clear manifestation of the instrumental value that international law has taken in the Middle East; used to perpetuate the interests of the strong at the expense of the local population. As the following chapter makes plain, that international law is to be used as a tool and meant to serve the interest of the powerful at the expense of the weak has not been lost on authoritarian rulers in the region, who have internalized this lesson, and have, in the case of Egypt and Syria, been able to maintain their rule over their respective State apparatuses through the imposition of perpetual states of emergency. Under such regimes, a fundamental mutation of the relationship between the executive and judicial branch has taken place wherein a parallel system of 'justice' has emerged which is rife with the arbitrary nature of lawlessness, which is manifest—in the most obvious manner—in the systematic use of torture.

The solution to the exceptional nature of the application and interpretation of law in the region is not to be found within the domain of international law *per se*. As this study demonstrates, the most relevant issues are political in nature—when one moves from law on the books to the application and interpretation of law on the ground. The role to be played by the international jurist, as the concluding chapter seeks to demonstrate, is to move beyond the mainstream discourse of war and lawlessness, which has been the primary narrative of the evolution of the modern Middle East, and seek to highlight instances where international law has been effective in, for instance, settling disputes by peaceful means. In this manner, by seeking to demonstrate instances of peaceful co-existence through the recourse to an international rule of law, jurists can call on States to seek to establish the legitimacy of international law as it is played out in the region; thus creating a normative framework of peaceful co-existence and adjusting the balance closer to justice and away from power politics.

Acknowledgements

This study has its genesis in my taking a post at the American University in Cairo (AUC). By both moving to the region to teach and through the unflagging support of the University, I have been able to devote my time, in a relatively leisurely manner, to bring to bear my understanding of international law on the Middle East.

With this as my starting point, I would like to thank the people up the chain of command at the University: Enid Hill and Dan Tschirgi, each in their role as Chair of the Department of Political Science; Cynthia Nelson and Nicholas Hopkins during their individual tenure as the Dean of the School of Social Sciences and Humanities; and Tim Sullivan as Provost. I would especially like to emphasize the role which Enid Hill and Tim Sullivan played in nurturing my academic career; I have a sense that they acted as *éminences grises*, in looking out for me and making my stay at AUC so comfortable.

I would like to acknowledge the Research Grants that the University provided me during the summers of 2001 and 2002 to conduct research in Geneva and The Hague. In Geneva, I undertook research into Kurdish and Palestinian questions at the United Nations Library and the Archives of the League of Nations, located side-by-side at the *Palais des Nations*. While in Geneva, I was received by Daniel Warner and Vera Gowlland at *HEI* (the Graduate Institute of International Studies, University of Geneva), as a Fellow in their Program for the Study of International Organizations, which provided me with access to both the HEI Library and to the resources *aux Palais des Nations*. It was, indeed, nice to return to the friendly confines of the Villa Barton and enjoy the luxury of days spent on the banks of Lac Leman. Although it took some time to get settled into the rhythm of *le Palais*, the Library and the Archives proved indispensable to understanding both the disappearance of a Kurdish State and the issues surrounding the creation of the State of Israel and the exodus of a large percentage of Palestinians which was its consequence.

During the summer of 2002, I was received as a Fellow of the T.M.C. Asser Institute, which granted me office space and a place to hang my hat while in The Hague. The Peace Palace Library, which was the focal point of my previous work—which is manifest in the publication *A Century of International Adjudication: The Rule of Law and its Limits*—remains the eminent resource center for working in the area of international law. The Peace Palace Library, like the International Court of Justice and the Permanent Court of Justice, is in the midst of being woken up from its slumber by the increase recourse of States to adjudication. I was pleasantly surprised over the summer as to the extent that each has taken up the challenge of increased attention with rigour and determination. I would like to thank those at the Asser Institute who hosted me while in The Hague. I would like also to thank Andreas O'Shea and Tim Sullivan for having commented on the manuscript and acknowledge the time spent with Eugene O'Sullivan and John

Ackerman, be it travelling through the Dutch countryside by bicycle, or evenings spent engrossed in discussing the birthing process of international criminal law as it is transpiring before the ICTY.

I would like to acknowledge with appreciation the course reductions provided by the American University in Cairo which allowed me the time to draft various chapters on the manuscript during 2001 and 2002. The time proved indispensable in allowing me to climb the steep learning curve regarding the evolution of the modern Middle East. Further, I would mention that the Library of the American University in Cairo has a premiere collection of works on the Middle East. At no time during my research did I come up against a title which I was interested in consulting which was not available amongst the stakes of the AUC Library.

I would like to thank the Rare Books and Special Collection Library of the American University in Cairo for allowing me to use the images which make up the background of the front and back covers of this work. The first image, representing power, is a general view of the main door of the Sultan Hasan Mosque, which was later taken to the Mosque of Al Muayyad. Malik Sultan (1336–1362 A.D.) was the 19th Mamluk Sultan of Egypt, who reigned from: 1347–1351 and from 1354–1362. This image is taken from an original photograph by K.A.C. Creswell, and comes via the Creswell Photographic Archives of Rare Books and Special Collection Library.

The image which appears on the back cover represents justice; it is taken from a panel of the inner face of the bronze-plated door of the Mausoleum of Imam al-Shafi (767–820 A.D.). Al-Shafi was an Islamic jurist whose teaching led to the creation of the *Shafi* School of jurisprudence of Sunni Islam. The door is now located in the Museum of Islamic Art, Cairo. The image is taken from Hoda Batanouni's *Catalogue of Mamluk Doors with Metal Revetments*, Thesis for the Master of Arts Degree, American University in Cairo, 1975, Part B, Catalogue Number XII (a).

I would be remiss in not mentioning Michael Lattanzi who attended most of my Lecture Series in 2001, and who engaged me in an on-going dialogue on both the law, but more specifically, on my narrative of the Middle East, from which I gained immensely.

Finally, I would like to acknowledge and thank with love and devotion Gina Bekker for having put up with me during the times of intense writing where my single-mindedness was overbearing and during my absences from Cairo and our time spent apart.

Athenians: Then we on our side will use no fine phrases saying, for example, that we have a right to our empire because we defeated the Persians, or that we have come against you now because of the injuries you have done us—a great mass of words that nobody will believe. And we ask you on your side not to imagine that you will influence us by saying that you, though a colony of Sparta, have not joined Sparta in the war, or that you have never done us any harm.

Instead we recommend that you should try to get what is possible for you to get, taking into consideration what we both really do think; since you know as well as we do that, when these matters are discussed by practical people, the standard of justice depends on the equality of power to compel and that in fact the strong do what they have the power to do and the weak accept what they have to accept.

Melians: Then in our view (since you force us to leave justice out of the account and to confine ourselves to self-interest)—in our view it is at any rate useful that you should not destroy a principle that is to the general good of all men—namely, that in the case of all who fall into danger there should be such a thing as fair play and just dealing, and that such people should be allowed to use and to profit by arguments that fall short of a mathematical accuracy. And this is a principle which affects you as much as anybody, since your own fall would be visited by the most terrible vengeance and would be an example to the world.

Thucydides
History of the Peloponnesian War, 431 B.C.
(The Melian Dialogue)

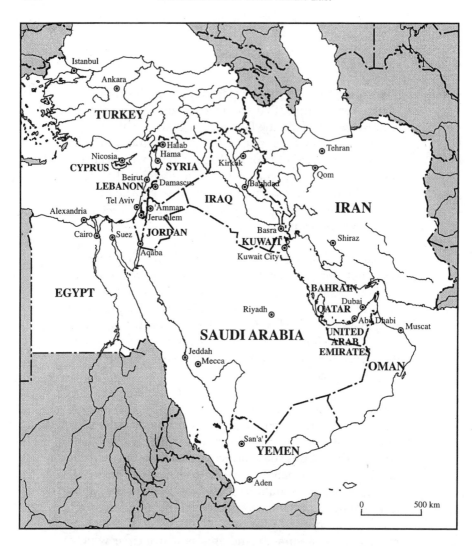

The Middle East

Introduction

Where international law in the Middle East is concerned, it is impossible to escape the simple fact that law on the books and law in practice do not equate. Much as the underclass in a domestic legal system feels the punitive, repressive, and selective nature of law, so too does the local population of the Middle East experience international law not as a shield but as a sword. As a result, international law in the Middle East lacks legitimacy. When this lack of legitimacy in superimposed on one of the most militarised regions of the world, the result is a powder keg with an extremely short fuse. As the various undertakings of international law are the only limitations to which sovereign States have consented, in their interaction on the international plane, the de-legitimization of international law means that very few constraints exist on State actions in the Middle East. As a result, the history of the modern State system in the Middle East is one of lawlessness, where, as like in the times of the Peloponnesian War, the powerful dictate and the 'weak accept what they have to accept'.

This study examines the Middle East through the lens of international law. It seeks to understand the qualitatively different manner in which international law is applied in this region of the world. Taking as a basis that law, in its *ideal* state, is meant to produce a just society, but realizing that law is ultimately a social construct—having travelled through a political process in its formulation, development, and finally in its application—means that law can never be divorced from its relationship to power. Thus, while international law may be perceived in the Western world as being neutral and benign, as a legitimate means of regulating and maintaining international order, in the Middle East it is understood to be little more than a tool of the powerful, used for coercion and oppression. With this as its starting point, this study seeks to demonstrate how, when placed on a scale; international law in the Middle East weighs in more on the side of power than on the side of justice.

In many ways, this study seeks to bring out the human experience of people in the Middle East, to examine the application and interpretation of international law from a Middle Eastern perspective. As a result, the study is informed by Orientalism and the realization that international law has been a main tenet of the Orientalist project. That international law has also played its part in the 'long and slow process of appropriation by which Europe, or European awareness of the Orient, transformed itself from being textual and contemplative into being administrative, economic, and even military'[1]. In other words, the achievements of Orientalism, as Edward Said argues, was to develop through nineteenth century European studies and writings that projected the East as backward, degenerate, and uncivilised, thus giving justification for European colonial and imperial ventures.

---

[1]   Edward Said, *Orientalism: Western Conceptions of the Orient*, 1995, p. 209.

International law, in the guise of the League of Nations' Mandate system, the Constantinople Convention of 1888, and even in the UN Security Council sanctions regime, has been a major factor in turning the 'Orient from alien into colonial space'[2]. Throughout this study, a recurring theme is the manner in which international law has been manipulated to meet the requirements, not of the local inhabitants, but the interests of Western powers.

A further stream of discourse flowing through this work is centred on the *Third World Approach* to international law, wherein previously suppressed narratives of history are brought to the fore to allow for an expanded space in which international law can be considered and critiqued. Thus, new historical veins are mined, and those facts are placed against the international legal standards of the day to seek to challenge the dominant discourse and to demonstrate the manner in which international law was been used and abused. Karin Mickelson explains:

> identifying a Third World approach as a theoretical position within international legal discourse means reclaiming a voice that has long been there, but to which very little serious attention has been paid. It is essential to bear in mind that the Third World approach to international law must be seen as lying at the intersection of two different discourses. One is the discourse of traditional international law and international legal scholarship. Here it is part of the story of the development of international law. The other discourse is that of decolonization: the full, broad panoramic view of a history of oppression and transformation. Here it can be seen as part of the story of anti-colonial and post-colonial struggle. In some ways, a Third World approach to international law is the untold part of both these stories. That which has remained somewhat marginal, while not entirely overlooked[3].

In some ways this task of focusing on suppressed narratives, has been quite easy; for instance, with respect to the plight of Palestinian refugees, as the 'new historiography' movement in Israel has fundamentally rewritten the history of the forced transfer and expulsion of Palestinians during the consolidation of the State of Israel during the period of 1947–49[4]. In other instances it has meant piecing together from various sources, threads which, when brought together, form a coherent narrative to which legal standards of the day are applied. This is made most evident with respect to the issue of Kurdish self-determination where sources are typically broken down on the Statist lines: thus, narratives exist regarding Iraqi-Kurds or Turkish-Kurds but seldom is the meta-narrative available, and rarely is it considered from an international law perspective.

---

[2]   *Id.*, p. 210.
[3]   Karin Mickleson, 'Rhetoric and Rage: Third World Voices in International Legal Discourse', *Wisconsin International Law Journal*, Vol. 16, 1998, pp. 361–362. See also Christopher Weeramantry and Nathaniel Berman, 'The Grotius Lecture Series', *American University International Law Review*, Vol. 14, 1999, pp. 1516–1569; and Antony Anghie, 'Finding the Peripheries: Sovereignty and Colonialism in Nineteeth-Century International Law', *Harvard International Law Journal*, Vol. 40, 1999, pp. 1–80.
[4]   See the chapter entitled 'The New Historiography: Israel and its Past' in Bennis Morris, *1948 and After: Israel and the Palestinians*, 1994 and more generally Eugene Rogan and Avi Shalim (eds.), *The War for Palestine: Rewriting the History of 1948*, 2001.

When these two streams converge—the subjugation of 'other' through the Orientalist project and the raising of suppressed narratives—what emerges is a sense that international law in the Middle East has been applied and interpreted in a qualitatively different manner. Even if one were to apply a purely positivist interpretation of the law: that international law is simply what States say it is. Even against this standard, the application of international law in the Middle East fails[5]. By a lack of objectivity—a common standard, uniformly applied—, in its application, international law in the Middle East loses any semblance of regulating the region in a *just* manner. This lack of impartiality which contributes to seeing a qualitatively different manner of application of international law in the region is manifest in the various issues examined in this study: in the imperial attitude which Great Britain maintained in controlling the Suez Canal and in its disregard of international law in supporting Zionism as part of its imperial policy in Palestine; in the lack of enforcement of legal obligations as toward Palestinian Refugees and the selective enforcement of the prohibition against aggression during the 1980s; in the punitive character of international law with respect to United Nations sanctions imposed on Iraq; in the ability of Egypt and Syria to maintain perpetual states of emergency. In all these cases, the law on the books dictates one outcome, while the reality of the Middle East has, in effect, created another.

The ramifications of this lack of impartial application of international law in the Middle East are that it is instrumental in nature and simply another political tool of statecraft to be used by the strong as against the weak. This alignment of international law in the Middle East closer to power than justice means that it loses much of its independence from international politics. No longer can one clearly attribute, in this region, a set of principles that should be acted upon—a normative framework. Instead of overriding legal principles—acting in good faith, the exclusion of the unilateral projection of uses of force, the peaceful settlement of disputes, etc—, the region is left to its own devices. In an anecdotal manner, this is best exemplified by the reaction to Boutros Boutros-Ghali's claim, when he was acting as the Egyptian Minister of State for Foreign Affairs in 1978, that the forcing down of a Kenyan civilian airliner, in retaliation for the storming of an Egyptian plane in Nairobi, was tantamount to piracy. The Egyptian prime minister at the time, Mahduh Salim, rebuked him, stating, 'Dr. Boutros, forget that you were a professor; international problems are not handled by international law'[6]!

Scope of Study

The 'Middle East' is a construct—more a thing of the imagination than a geographic location. The term 'Middle East' is purported to have been coined by the American naval officer and historian Alfred Thayer Mahan 'in 1902 to

---

[5]   See 'Bentham, Austin, and Classical Positivism' in M.D.A. Freeman, (ed.) *Lloyd's Introduction to Jurisprudence*, 1994, pp. 205–228.
[6]   Boutros Boutros-Ghali, *Egypt's Road to Jerusalem: A Diplomat's Story of the Struggle for Peace in the Middle East*, 1997, p. 64.

designate the area between Arabia and India'[7]. Yet, if anything, the hard core of the Middle East has re-centred itself on what used to be known, as recently as the late 1940s as the Near East[8]. Today, it appears clear which States are part of the hard core of the Middle East (one may say that the spin of the Middle East is to be found on the North-South, Jerusalem-Mecca, Axis); thus West to East: Libya, Egypt, Saudi Arabia, Yemen, Israel, Jordan, Syria, Lebanon, Oman, United Arab Emirates, Bahrain, Qatar, Kuwait, and Iraq. Beyond that, opinions vary. Are Iran or Turkey to be included? Neither is ethnically Arab. What of Tunisia, Algeria, and Morocco? All are members of the League of Arab States, but they have traditionally been considered as forming the Magreb, and look north to the Mediterranean and France. The unifying factors, to use a broad brush, are related to the Muslim religion, which allowed for Arab conquest and settlement. This, coupled with a common past under the dominance of the Ottoman Turks from 1500 till the end of the First World War, seems to centre the Middle East on more than simple geography. This study follows the same logic, as it focuses on issues related to the hard core of the Middle East, but venture off the beaten path in several instances where there is interplay between the core and the peripheries.

This interplay between the hard core of the Middle East and the peripheries comes into focus in the opening chapter, which examines the denial of Kurdish self-determination. 'Kuridstan', those areas which are predominantly inhabited by this, the third-largest ethnic group in the Middle East, consisting of nearly thirty million people, is subsumed into six existing State, only two of which can be considered as being part of the hard core of the Middle East. Chapter 1 considers the plight of the Kurdish people in the wake of the First World War and the creation of the modern Middle East. By studying the denial of Kurdish self-determination, two fundamental understandings emerge. The first, that the claim of self-determination for the Kurdish people, justly conceived, requires addressing. Second, that positive international law regarding self-determination has been established in such narrow terms that it fails to accommodate the aspirations of Kurdish people.

Justly conceived, the case for Kurdish self-determination is a strong one. Having been promised an independent State at the 1918 Paris Peace Conference, Kurdish aspirations of statehood would slowly wither; by 1920, the stillborn Treaty of Sèvres failed to provide for a Kurdish State, instead it called for local autonomy with a pledge to move toward statehood. Yet this was not to be, as Mustapha Kemal would rally Turkish forces to fight on, re-writing the peace by way of the 1923 Treaty of Lausanne. That agreement witnessed the demise of any Kurdish self-determination, with the only question of consequence remaining being whether the oil rich Kurdish province of Mosul would be attached to Turkey or the newly

---

[7]   David Fromkin, *A Peace to End All Peace: Creating the Modern Middle East, 1914–1922*, 1989, p. 224; citing Bernard Lewis, *The Middle East and the West*, 1968. See also a chapter devoted to the issue in Bassam Tibi, *Conflict and War in the Middle East: From Interstate War to New Security*, 1998, pp. 43–60.

[8]   Consider the full name of the relief agency for Palestinian Refugees—UNRWA—the United Nations Relief and Works Agency for Palestine Refugees in the Near East.

created State of Iraq. But the case of Kurdish self-determination does not only lie in the fact that the rug was pulled out from underneath its move toward statehood; it also has a basis in the manner in which Kurdish people have been treated as a minority in the newly created States of the modern Middle East. For more than eighty years, the plight of the Kurdish people, to a greater or lesser extent, has been that of the repression of their collective identity at the hand of States that have sought to establish a homogenous nationalist culture based on things 'Turkish', 'Iraqi', or 'Syrian', and so on.

Despite the case in favour of Kurdish self-determination built in Chapter 1, the current reality is that positive international law does not find room to accommodate such aspirations. The gap between self-determination in its *ideal* state and self-determination as *law* is such that States have so narrowly construed it that today it is, for all intents and purposes, no longer applicable. The movement of self-determination as a concept put forward by the then President of the United States, Woodrow Wilson; to assist in settling nationalist claims after the First World War, to its inclusion into the Charter of the United Nations as a principle; through its acceptance as a legal right during the decolonization process, has been one of continuous narrowing so that today, as a legal right, it is on the verge of disappearing. In essence, the right of self-determination in international law does not apply to the Kurdish people, as the Kurds fail in their ability to be slotted into any of the three categories that would allow them to invoke such a right. The Kurds are neither a colonised people, living under a racist regime, nor are they under the yoke of an alien occupation.

The inability of international law to accommodate the aspirations of the Kurdish people demonstrates that there are *lacunae* in positive international law that have had a detrimental effect on the people of the Middle East. Beyond the failings of positive international law to provide enough space for Kurdish aspirations, this study considers the manner in which positive international law— law on the books—has been applied in a qualitatively different manner in the Middle East. Chapter 2 considers the legacy of European imperialism *qua* colonialism as it has been played out with respect to the evolution of the legal regime governing the Suez Canal. What emerges is a sense of the manner in which European States were unwilling to see the norms of international law respected beyond their shores, where imperial imperatives and interests trumped the requirements of conduct established by international law. Though the maritime powers of the late 1800s were prepared to sign an international agreement regulating transit through the Suez Canal, Great Britain effectively suspended the coming into force of the 1888 Constantinople Convention by attaching a reservation meant to allow for the compatibility of that instrument's provisions with its occupation of Egypt.

The exceptionalism of the application of international law that has transpired with respect to events in the Middle East is manifest in the fact that it took the *Entente Cordiale* of 1904 between France and Great Britain—wherein they agreed to settle their outstanding claims with regard to Morocco and Egypt—to allow for the coming into force of the Constantinople Convention. Yet the 1904 agreement simply allowed Great Britain to consolidate its control of the Suez Canal and to treat it as an imperial asset. In this manner, Great Britain did not feel compelled to follow the dictates of the Convention; instead, it governed the Canal in line with its national interest. Thus, it allowed Italy to utilise the Canal in pursuit of its campaign against Abyssinia despite Italy having been branded the aggressor by the League of Nations. Britain then turned face and excluded Italy from transiting the Isthmus of Suez, as it would the Central Powers and later Axis Powers during the two World Wars; this effectively opened the Suez Canal to enemy attack. Despite the prohibitions against the use of force introduced in the Charter of the United Nations, Britain would maintain its imperial attitude toward 'its' Canal, in the wake of Egyptian independence, as it masterminded a tripartite aggression with France and Israel against Egypt. Despite Egypt being well within its legal right to nationalise the Suez Canal Company, Great Britain was prepared to forgo the fundamental building block of the international system—the prohibition against aggression—so as to attempt to re-establish its privileged position in the Middle East.

The attitude of European Powers during the evolution of the legal regime of the Suez Canal is indicative of the qualitative exceptionalism by which international law is applied in the Middle East. That is to say, that where the interests of European Powers collided with their obligations under international law, more often then not, they did not let those obligations limit their actions, instead they were willing to forgo the standards of behaviour established by international law. This willingness to forgo legal obligations is brought home again in Chapter 3 where consideration is given to the manifest disregard for international law demonstrated by Britain in support of Zionist policies in Palestine. With the acquiescence of the leading States during the inter-War years, Britain as part of its greater imperial aims, allowed Zionist policies to emerge in Palestine in clear disregard for the dictates of international law. With Britain willing to give voice to the Balfour Declaration from 1920–23, despite not having settled the peace with Turkey meant that Britain was in violation, in Palestine, of the laws of occupation. Under the 1907 Convention regarding the Law and Customs of War, Great Britain had a legal obligation as the belligerent occupier to maintain the *status quo* in Palestine while awaiting a final peace with the successor of the Ottoman Empire. From the 1920 San Remo Conference—which determined that Britain would gain the League of Nations' Mandate for Palestine—onward, Britain no longer felt compelled to heed the dictates of the laws of occupation, instead treating Palestine as territory under its possession. Thus, from 1920 until the ratification of the peace with Turkey, Britain violated the laws of occupation by supporting its various Zionist policies in Palestine. After 1923, Britain received the seal of approval of the League of Nations to continue such policies as it was granted a Mandate for Palestine that incorporated the Balfour Declaration in its preamble.

Yet, the Mandate for Palestine was at variance with the obligations under Article 22 of Covenant of the League of Nations, which required that Britain ensure the 'well-being and development' of Palestinian people thus forming 'a sacred trust of civilization' between itself and the inhabitants of the mandated territories. Yet this was not to be as Britain forewent the interests of the local population so as to accommodate the wishes and aspirations of European Jewry to establish a national home in the shadow of biblical Mount Zion. The imposing of Zionist policies meant that by the end of the Mandate for Palestine and the proclamation of the State of Israel in 1948, a critical mass of Jewish immigrants had established themselves in Palestine. The ability of Israelis to fight off the challenge by Arab States in 1948, coupled with the recognition by key States of the international community meant that Israel had constituted itself as an independent State. While the establishment of the State of Israel as a member of the international community of States transpired well within the boundaries of international law, the alignment of international law closer to power than justice meant that Britain's support for Zionism, as part of its imperial aims, could be undertaken in clear disregard for the principles and the wording of various international instruments. Beyond the imposition of the State of Israel on the Middle East, the events of 1948 would have a further consequence on the region as nearly a million Palestinians would be made stateless as Israel sought to consolidate its territorial gains.

Chapter 4 takes up where the previous chapter left off chronologically, with the creation and subsequent plight of the 1948 Palestinian Refugees, in an attempt to demonstrate how a lack of enforcement of the dictates of international law has led to the effective abandonment of literally millions of people in the Middle East. The indeterminate fate of Palestinian Refugees, who today number more than four million, is a result of an unwillingness of the international community to see the 'right of return' given effect, as well as its aversion to enforcing the 1951 Refugee Convention. Caught between Israel, which is unwilling to allow for return, and Arab States unwilling to allow Palestinian Refugees the possibility of local integrate, for fear of accepting the actions of 1948 as a *fait accompli*; Palestinian Refugees have witnessed the continuous violation of their rights under refugee law, human rights law, and humanitarian law. With both parties having effectively abandoned the Palestinian Refugees, the international community has been unwilling to enforce the dictates of international law, thus creating a legal vacuum wherein legal rights have become negotiable and the right to international protection under international refugee law denied. The unwillingness of the international community to enforce the dictates of international law where the Palestinian Refugees are concerned means that these people are the only group effectively excluded from the legal protection regime of the 1951 Convention. On the basis of a legal encumbrance which sees their rights to legal protection forfeited as a result of receiving material assistance from a specialized UN agency (UNRWA), Palestinian Refugees remain as vulnerable today as their fathers and forefathers did in 1948. The lack of a permanent solution to the plight of Palestinian Refugees who were forced from their homes more than fifty years ago speaks volumes of the manner in which international law is applied in the Middle East. Nowhere else can we speak of a refugee population that has been dispossessed for more than fifty years. With no solution in sight, the manifest failing of international law—in this case, its lack of enforcement—is apparent in the millions of Palestinians who remain displaced.

During the period between the start of the Iran-Iraq War and the lead-up to the UN Coalition Forces campaign against Iraq during the 1991 Gulf War, the Middle East was the locus of selective enforcement regarding acts of aggression. The differing responses of the Security Council considered in Chapter 5 demonstrate the extent to which the application of international law in this region is subservient to the geopolitical interests of States, above all, to those of the United States of America. During the Iran-Iraq War (1980–88), the Iraqi invasion of Iran was met with a muted response by the international community that was unwilling to act, for a long time, to restore international peace and security. Despite the War having started in 1980, the Security Council only acted under the rubric of the UN Charter's Chapter VII, which authorised the use of any means to restore international peace and security, by Resolution 589 passed in 1988. Though this Resolution ultimately led to the cease-fire that ended the conflict, during the interim eight years of inaction, more than a million people died and major violations of both *jus ad bellum* and *jus in bello* transpired.

In contrast to the passive neglect of the Security Council during the Iran-Iraq War, its neglect during the 1982 Israeli invasion of Lebanon was active, as the United States blocked, through recourse to its veto power, any move by the Council to seek to restore international peace. In this situation, where Israel's aggression continued, through its occupation of Southern Lebanon, until the year 2000, the region witnessed the UN Security Council being forced to forfeit its collective security mandate, by an active policy of the United States that sought to exclude Lebanon from the United Nations agenda. By contrast, Iraq's invasion of Kuwait (1990–91) marked a watershed in the ability of the Security Council to deal with issues of international peace and security. Not only did the Security Council legitimise the use of force by UN Coalition Forces to evict Iraq from Kuwait in 1991, it also imposed various measures such as an economic embargo, a disarmament regime, and established the Iraq-Kuwait border, in a bid to restore international peace and security. The irony, of course, was that throughout the 1990s, when the Security Council was asserting itself against Iraq for its occupation of Kuwait, Israel remained in occupation of Southern Lebanon. A further irony is to be found in the manner in which the UN Security Council acquiesced, after the fact, to the aggression which transpired when the United States led its 'Coalition of the Willing' against Iraq in March 2003 and subsequently occupied that country. Such selectivity reinforces the perception regarding the qualitative exceptionalism of the Middle East, whereby the dictates of the powerful override agreed norms of behaviour by States, as established by international law.

The punitive nature of international law is the focus of Chapter 6, which considers the United Nations sanctions regime imposed on Iraq as a result of its invasion of Kuwait in 1990. While law may be a coercive tool intended to modify the behaviour of States that are in violation of a norm of international law, the cumulative effects of this UN sanctions regime went beyond what could be considered as justifiable punishment, as the effects of the sanction regime transgress the *jus cogens* imperative prohibiting crimes against humanity. The comprehensive sanctions regime imposed by the UN Security Council via

Resolution 661 was maintained, originally to force Iraq out of Kuwait; when that was achieved by force of arms in 1991, the sanctions were seen as a part of the attempt by the Council to restore international peace and security in the region. By 1997, the sanctions regime had been captured by the United States which indicated that it would remain in place until the President of Iraq, Saddam Hussein, was deposed. True to its word, the sanctions were only withdrawn in 2003, after the United States took it upon itself to remove the Hussein Administration and occupy Iraq.

The sanctions imposed on Iraq in 1990 were in the guise of a comprehensive embargo that originally allowed only an exception for medical supplies. After the Gulf War, as a result of a UN Report that found that the Coalition bombing had relegated Iraq 'to a pre-industrial age', the Council modified its regime to allow for the import of food, agricultural equipment, and items related to water purification and sanitation[9]. Further, the Security Council introduced the 'oil-for-food' programme in an attempt to mitigate the effects of the sanctions on the general population. Although this programme, which allowed for the selling of oil to assist Iraq in purchasing items which were exempt from the embargo, was established in 1991, it only became operational in 1996. Despite these modifications to the sanctions regime, the UN Secretary-General noted in a March 2000 report, that even if the 'oil-for-food' programme was 'implemented perfectly, it is possible that the efforts will prove insufficient to satisfy the population's needs'[10]. The needs of the population were dire, as it was clear that hundreds of thousands if not millions of Iraqis died as a direct result of the UN sanctions regime. The modifications to the regime simply ended the free fall of the population from affluence to poverty and, to a large extent, stabilised the effect of sanctions at their 1996 level. This did not preclude what amounted to a children's holocaust where, between 1991–98 it is estimated that at least 100,000 but more likely 227,000 excess deaths of children under five took place, of which three-quarters resulted from the consequences of United Nations sanctions[11].

Though the ability to impose sanctions is well within the right of the UN Security Council as the principle agent for ensuring international peace and security, by their cumulative effect the sanctions went beyond being punitive to being criminal. This is so, as the effects of sanctions transgressed the *jus cogens* prohibition regarding the committing of crimes against humanity. It appears that the effect of the sanctions regime were of such a magnitude that they most resemble the crime against humanity known as 'extermination'. The notion of

---

[9] United Nations Security Council, *Report to the Secretary-General on humanitarian needs in Kuwait and Iraq in the immediate post-crisis environment by a mission to the area led by Mr. Martti Ahtisaari, Under-Secretary-General for Administration and Management, dated 20 March 1991*, annexed to a letter from the Secretary-General addressed to the President of the Security Council, UN Doc. S/22366, dated 20 March 1991, para. 8.

[10] As quoted in Commission on Human Rights, *The Adverse Consequences of Economic Sanctions on the Enjoyment of Human Rights: Working Paper prepared by Mr. Marc Bossuyt*, UN Doc. E/CN.4/Sub.2/2000/33, 21 June 2000, para. 62.

[11] David Cortright and George Lopez, *The Sanctions Decade: Assessing UN Strategies in the 1990s*, 2000, p. 46.

crimes against humanity are to be considered acts which are 'committed as part of a widespread or systematic attack directed against any civilian population'; while the notions of 'extermination' includes the 'intentional infliction of conditions of life [...] calculated to bring about the destruction of part of a population'. Though the Security Council attempted to mitigate the worst elements of humanitarian catastrophe the sanctions regime brought on, its own studies made clear that these modifications did not reversed the humanitarian plight that affected Iraqis for more than a decade. When the definition of extermination is considered, that is, 'intentional infliction of conditions of life [...] calculated to bring about the destruction of part of a population', it is clear that for the more than twelve years of sanctions, which killed anywhere from hundreds of thousands to nearly two million people, the United Nations regime imposed on Iraq went beyond simply being a punitive tool, to being what should be considered a crime against humanity.

Having considered the manner in which international law has been used in an instrumental manner by States outside the region, this study then turns to examine how States in the region have internalised the lessons learned regarding the balance between power and justice in the Middle East. Chapter 7 considers the human rights records of two Middle Eastern States that have maintained near-permanent states of emergency in violation of their international obligations. While perpetual states of emergency appear to have become a Middle East phenomenon, the situations in Egypt and Syria are highlighted to demonstrate the extent to which the governing elite suppresses individual human rights so as to ensure the maintenance of their rule. In the same manner in which power trumps justice on the international plane, it will become evident through this Chapter that the same lack of respect for the rule of law exists in the region at the domestic level. By considering the standards which the UN Human Rights Committee has established in its General Comment 29 regarding derogation from human rights in states of emergency, it becomes evident that both Egypt and Syria maintain states of emergency in violation of their obligations under the International Covenant on Civil and Political Rights.

Such perpetual states of emergency have allowed for the growth, in both Egypt and Syria, of an extra-constitutional security apparatus which is immune from judicial oversight. As a result, mass and systematic violations of the non-derogable rights enshrined in Article 4(2) of the International Covenant transpire with growing sophistication. In both Egypt and Syria, the imposition of states of emergency have allowed the Asad and Mubarak administrations to consolidate and maintain power by closing off peaceful means of political change. Using the threat of 'Islamists' as its basis, both Egypt and Syria have sought to criminalise dissent and to subject those that oppose the State to the worst types of human rights abuses. Consideration in this Chapter is given primarily to the issue of torture, and in the case of Syria, specifically to the extra-judicial killings that transpired in the early 1980s, which allowed President Hafez Asad to consolidate his hold on power. What this Chapter seeks to bring out is the fact that under perpetual states of emergency, there is a transformation of the institution of government whereby power is allocated disproportionately in the executive organ at the expense of the judiciary. As a result there is a diminished ability for judges to oversee the work of the 'security forces'—that arm of the executive branch meant to ensure the survival of the *status quo*. The result of this limited judicial oversight in both Egypt and Syria has led to systematic and widespread violations of non-derogable rights including the right to life and the prohibition against torture. The work of the various actors within the UN system of human rights protection, when combined with reports from non-governmental organizations, demonstrates in no uncertain terms, the manner in which Egypt and Syria have perpetuated long term states of emergency and have killed and tortured with impunity; all in violation of the most fundamental, non-derogable, human rights established by international law.

With the concluding chapter, an attempt is made to demonstrate that in the Middle East, parallel to the mainstay of lawlessness, which has been manifest with power overriding justice, has been a seldom-used stream of the peaceful settlement of disputes. Such examples as the Taba Arbitration between Israel and Egypt and the Qatar-Bahrain territorial settlement before the International Court of Justice are two clear examples of States settling their differences without recourse to force of arms. Beyond these examples, there are numerous examples of Middle Eastern States settling their differences by peaceful means with other States. Libya has established its international borders with Malta and Tunisia, Yemen has determined the sovereignty over Red Sea islands with Eritrea, and Iran is currently involved in settling on-going claims with the United States, all through international adjudication. While international adjudication and the recourse to third-party dispute settlement may not be a panacea for the Middle East, it opens the possibility of moving beyond the malaise that has power trumping justice. While the peaceful settlement of disputes has been used infrequently, the proliferation of arms in the Middle East requires that alternatives be found. Consideration is given to the level of armaments in the Middle East, to the proliferation of weapons of mass destruction, and to the deadly cocktail it creates when States have, as their first instinct, to act beyond the dictates of international law and attempt to impose their views by force of arms.

In many ways, this study speaks for itself. The violations and manipulation of international law are such that their simple exposition demonstrates the qualitatively different manner in which international law in applied in the region. Yet, simply demonstrating the manner in which international law in the Middle East has been blatantly disregarded, selectively applied and enforced, and used and abused to the advantage of powerful States fails to answer the question of how to work the region out of this predicament. In effect, what is demonstrated throughout this study is that international law has been applied and enforced in a subjective manner, in line with the interests of powerful States. To give legitimacy to international law in the Middle East would require an about-face, wherein law would have to be applied and enforced in an objective manner. By promoting the pacific settlement of disputes and demanding that third parties be able to make binding decisions regarding outstanding issues by reference to law is the best possible manner by which those within the domain of international law can hope to affect the Middle East positively.

The following chapters will demonstrate the qualitatively different manner in which international law in the Middle East has been applied. This alignment—

closer to power than justice—has left a bitter legacy in the region. The lack of legitimacy of international law in the Middle East is such that the region is a powder keg with an extremely short fuse. The fact that, on balance, international law has been outweighed by the interests of the powerful during the evolution of the modern Middle East has been translated into a legacy of war, dispossession, and bitterness. Law on the books should never be divorced from the manner in which it is actually applied. This is especially true of international law, which because of its decentralised nature, lacks a central law determination, application, and enforcement system. For any system of justice to prevail, law must show itself to be insulated as much as possible from the dictates of power politics. Where the Middle East is concerned, international law has failed to disassociate itself from those dictates of power, in effect recreating the region as an underclass of the international legal community. It should thus come as little wonder, as Thucydides wrote two thousand years ago, in his *History of the Peloponnesian War*, that: 'having destroyed a principle that is to the general good of all men' should result in repercussions that have been felt beyond the region. The legacy of the manner in which international law has been applied in the region is not a pretty one, but it is one worth recounting, as it makes clear that the issues that remain unsettled to this day—in Iraq, or with respect to the Kurds or Palestinians—did not emerge in a vacuum, but were a result of political machinations that managed to impose the realities of the current Middle East at the expense of transgressing a common standard of behaviour: international law.

Chapter 1

Beyond Positivism:
Denial of Kurdish Self-Determination

The century-long plight of the Kurdish people, denied not only the ability to establish an independent State, but to gain even a measure of autonomy over their language and culture, is a clear manifestation of the denial of self-determination justly conceived. 'Kurdistan', those areas of Armenia, Azerbaijan, Iran, Iraq, Syria, and Turkey, where Kurdish people find themselves in the minority, have had their rights, both individually and collectively, suppressed in an attempt to ensure the consolidation of those existing States. It was estimated in 1996 that there were between twenty-four and twenty-seven million Kurds living in the Middle East. This is more than the individual populations of the following States: Israel, Jordan, Kuwait, Libya, Morocco, Saudi Arabia, the United Arab Emirates, or Yemen. After Arabs and Persians, Kurds constitute the largest ethnic group in the region. Nearly half of all Kurds, thirteen million, live in Turkey, where they constitute an estimated one-fifth to one-quarter of that State's population. The same percentage of Kurds are found living in Iraq, though they amount to over four million people, while in Iran there are approximately six million Kurds, making up about ten percent of that population. Nearly a million more Kurds find themselves in Syria, with smaller populations living in both Armenia and Azerbaijan[1].

What makes the claim of the Kurdish self-determination such a strong one, is twofold: first, the pulling of the carpet from beneath the move to establish a Kurdish State in the aftermath of the First World War. Second, the repression of Kurdish identity by the newly created Middle Eastern States which, over the years, has taken various forms: from the denial of cultural rights to genocidal levels of repression. It is this mixture of past failings and present repression that demonstrates the extent to which international law, as applied in the Middle East, is qualitatively different than elsewhere. Despite the fact that the International Court of Justice noted in 1995 that self-determination is 'one of the essential principles of contemporary international law'[2], its scope—as law—is so limited as to render its applicability near to naught. In other words, when examining the content of the legal norm of self-determination it becomes evident, by its limited nature, that it reflects the will of States at the expense of the aspirations of nations, be they defined by a common culture, language, or religion. If self-determination were to

---

[1] David McDowall, *A Modern History of the Kurds*, 1996, pp. 3–4.
[2] *East Timor* case, *I.C.J. Reports, 1995*, 30 June 1995, para. 29.

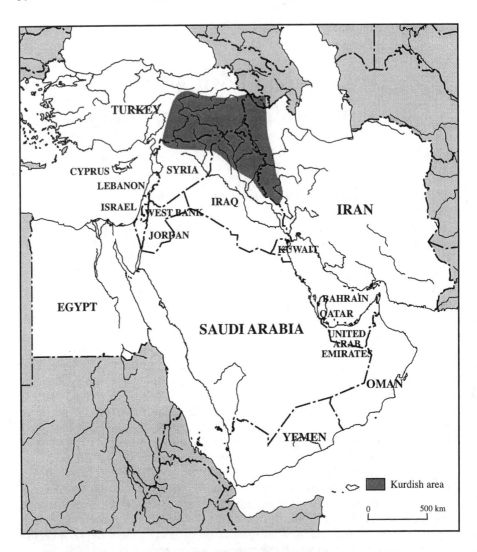

The Kurdish Area

be conceptualised in a just manner, it would surely find room to accommodate a people, which today find themselves in the neighbourhood of thirty million strong, to determine for themselves their political association. However, States have established positive international law in such a manner as to ensure that the Statist systems prevails; that self-determination takes place within the Westphalian State system which has, as of yet, been unable to accommodate aspirations of the Kurdish people.

I. Failure of a Kurdish State to Materialise

With the defeat of the Central Powers, the victors of the First World War were in agreement that the 'Sick Man of Europe' should be left to die. While it was agreed that the Middle Eastern possessions of the Ottoman Empire should be reconstituted, the Allied Powers struggled to establish a map of the region that took into consideration their varied interests and their ability to impose their conception on the people of the Middle East. The main casualty of the post-First World War settlement and, hence, the modern Middle East, was the failure of a Kurdish State to materialise. This, despite the fact that 'Kurdistan' was considered at the Paris Peace Conference as a nominally independent State that should fall under the Mandate system envisioned by the Article 22 of the Covenant of the League of Nations. That no Kurdish State would emerge was a clear indication that the notion of 'self-determination', as conceived at the end of the First World War, was little more than political rhetoric which would come a lowly second to the interests of the European Powers[3]. Yet, this was at variance with the firmly held belief of the then President of the United States, Woodrow Wilson, that the concept of self-determination should be the basis upon which a post-War order should be established. In his Fourteen Points speech, outlining the war aims of the United States, Wilson not only spoke of 'free, open-minded, and absolutely impartial adjustment of all colonial claims', but he also outlined his thoughts regarding the region of the world which encapsulated Kurdistan:

> Point XII: The Turkish portion of the present Ottoman Empire should be assured a secure sovereignty, but the other nationalities which are now under Turkish rule should be assured an undoubted security of life and an absolutely unmolested opportunity of autonomous development, [...][4].

---

[3]   In Antonio Cassese's words, 'on the whole, self–determination was deemed irrelevant where the people's will was certain to run counter to the victors' geopolitical, economic, and strategic interests'. Antonio Cassese, *Self–Determination of Peoples: A Legal Appraisal*, 1995, p. 25.
[4]   Note that when Wilson was expressing himself regarding 'other nationalities', at the forefront of the collective conscience in America was the fate of Armenians who were the victims of the first European genocide of the twentieth century committed by the Young Turks, but also with the assistance of Kurds. It is estimated that a million Armenians died in 1915–16 in an attempt by the Young Turks to cleanse the northeastern regions of the Ottoman Empire of its Christian populations that were perceived as being potential allies to

It appears that the nascent Kurdish independence movement placed its trust in the Wilsonian conception of self-determination, as was made evident in the pages of the *Jin*, the official organ of the League of Progress of Kurdistan published in Constantinople from 1918 to 1920[5]. Kamuran Bedir Khan, a leader of the Kurdish movement at the time, wrote in 1918, 'Whatever the current political changes and no matter the decisions taken, there remains the good humanitarian principles of the famous President of the United States, Mister Wilson. ... The truth and justice of these principles, of which the basis has been accepted by the European States, should be paramount over all unjust tendencies and ideas'[6]. Yet, while Germany accepted the principles expressed in the Fourteen Points speech as a basis of an armistice, as did the Allied Powers, it would come to pass that from this moment onward, the notion of self-determination as it related to Kurdistan would slowly be purged of its content. Various events—foremost amongst which was the retreat of the United States from the international system conceived by its president; the British and French in-fighting over the spoils of war, and finally, the rise of the Kemalists in Turkey—would converge to dissipate the move toward the creation of Kurdistan. Not to be left out of the equation was the lack of a nationalist movement within Kurdistan that could effectively demonstrate a unity of purpose, both in governing the Kurdish region and in articulating its claims internationally to the European Powers.

In January 1918, in the lead-up to the Paris Peace Conference, Great Britain made its war aims known, yet Prime Minister David Lloyd George failed to mention Kurdistan as one of the States that should fall under the mandate system, along with Arabia, Armenia, Mesopotamia, Palestine, and Syria. This oversight, according to Salah Jmor's doctoral study of the issue was due, in part, to the perception in Europe that Turkish Anatolia was separated on religious lines with Muslim Turks and Kurds having been associated with the genocide of the Christian Armenians. When in Paris, in 1919, the minutes of the meeting of the 'Council of Ten' of the Peace Conference, regarding the drafting of the Covenant of the League of Nations, reflect the fact that Prime Minister Lloyd George sought to amend the aims of Great Britain. The minutes read:

> He said that he was sorry that he had left out one country in Turkey which ought to have been inserted. He did not realise that it was separate. He thought Mesopotamia or Armenia would cover it, but he was informed that it did not. He referred to Kurdestan [sic], which was between Mesopotamia and Armenia. Therefore, if there was no objection, he proposed to insert the words 'and Kurdestan'[7].

---

an invading Russian Army. For their part, the Kurdish populations in this area acted as auxiliaries to Turkish troops in their 'ethnic cleansing' operations and were to benefit from the massacres by gaining '"abandoned" Armenian property'. See David McDowall, *op. cit.* n. 1, p. 104, and more generally, pp. 102–109.

[5]   See Anthony Whelan, 'Wilsonian Self–Determination and the Versailles Settlement', *International and Comparative Law Quarterly*, Vol. 43, 1994, pp. 99–115.

[6]   See Salah Jmor, *L'Origine de la question Kurde*, 1994, p. 93. Note that unless otherwise indicated, direct quotations from French sources are translated by the author.

[7]   *Id.*, p. 96, n. 123.

While no objections were heard, when the Covenant of the League of Nations was considered as a whole, the amendment regarding Kurdistan was absent from Article 22 of the French language draft. This, it has been said, was due to the unwillingness of France to allow for the introduction of Kurdistan as a mandate State which it believed would fall under the tutelage of Great Britain, and thus to French geopolitical disadvantage[8]. When Article 22 of the Covenant was finally accepted, reference to any State, that was to be placed under the League's mandate system, was omitted.

Although clearly a setback to Great Britain (not to mention the Kurds), Lloyd George persisted in seeking the establishment of a Kurdish State, not for reasons of affinity toward any Kurdish nationalist movement but for reasons of geopolitics. Great Britain saw in the creation of Kurdistan a buffer State between Turkey and Russia on the one hand and Mesopotamia on the other[9]. While the British were not willing to acknowledge that the Sykes-Picot Agreement was of relevance to the Palestinian mandate, this secret 1916 pact, setting out the spheres of influence of a dismantled Ottoman Empire between France and Great Britain, was very much the basis upon which the Kurdish region of the Middle East was partitioned. As the United States of America slowly withdrew from the post-War peace with the United States Congress unwilling to ratify the Treaty of Versailles, or accept the mandates for either Armenian or Kurdistan, Great Britain was left to fill the void. In its negotiations with France, which transpired throughout 1919–20, Great Britain, unwilling to take on the financial or military burden of acting as the mandatory power of a 'Greater' Kurdistan, slowly dismembered it with the aim of retaining its core: the oil rich vilayet (i.e. province) of Mosul. The outcome of these negotiations, which transpired both in London and San Remo, is revealed in the provisions of the 1920 Treaty of Sèvres.

The Treaty of Sèvres, meant to set the peace between the Allied Powers and Turkey, allowed for the possibility of the emergence of a Kurdish State. However, this State was to be a shadow of an ethnically based Kurdistan, as it was to encompass only twenty percent of the territory on which Kurds resided, and was less than a quarter of what had been sought by Kurdish representatives at the Paris Peace Conference[10]. As neither France nor Great Britain was willing to allow Kurdistan to be attached to the other European State's mandated territory, it was decided by the Treaty of Sèvres that the territory would be attached to Turkey, despite the supposed war aims of the Allied Forces to free such nationalities from the Ottoman Empire. By virtue of the Peace Agreement, a commission was to draft a scheme for local autonomy for these Kurdish areas; however, if within in a year of the coming into force of the Treaty of Sèvres, the Kurdish people could demonstrate to the League of Nations their wish for independence, Turkey was to oblige. The relevant provisions of the Treaty of Peace between the Allied and Associated Powers and Turkey, signed on 10 August 1920, in Sèvres, France, reads as follows:

---

[8] *Id.*, p. 99.
[9] *Id.*, p. 13.
[10] *Id.*, p. 137.

Article 62: A Commission sitting at Constantinople and composed of three members appointed by the British, French and Italian Governments respectively shall draft within six months from the coming into force of the present Treaty a scheme of local autonomy for the predominantly Kurdish areas lying east of the Euphrates, south of the southern boundary of Armenia as it may be hereafter determined, and north of the frontier of Turkey with Syria and Mesopotamia […]. If unanimity cannot be secured on any question, it will be referred by the members of the Commission to their respective Governments. The scheme shall contain full safeguards for the protection of the Assyro-Chaldeans and other racial or religious minorities within these areas, and with this object a Commission composed of British, French, Italian, Persian and Kurdish representatives shall visit the spot to examine and decide what rectifications, if any, should be made in the Turkish frontier where, under the provisions of the present Treaty, that frontier coincides with that of Persia.

Article 63: The Turkish Government hereby agrees to accept and execute the decisions of both the Commissions mentioned in Article 62 within three months from their communication to the said Government.

Article 64: If within one year from the coming into force of the present Treaty the Kurdish peoples within the areas defined in Article 62 shall address themselves to the Council of the League of Nations in such a manner as to show that a majority of the population of these areas desires independence from Turkey, and if the Council then considers that these peoples are capable of such independence and recommends that it should be granted to them, Turkey hereby agrees to execute such a recommendation, and to renounce all rights and title over these areas.

The detailed provisions for such renunciation will form the subject of a separate agreement between the Principal Allied Powers and Turkey.

If and when such renunciation takes place, no objection will be raised by the Principal Allied Powers to the voluntary adhesion to such an independent Kurdish State of the Kurds inhabiting that part of Kurdistan which has hitherto been included in the Mosul vilayet[11].

The ability of Kurds to forge their own State with the window of opportunity offered to them at Sèvres would not, however, transpire, as the Treaty of Peace was never ratified by Turkey. While Constantinople remained under Allied occupation, Mustapha Kemal (i.e. Atatürk), the Turkish General who had previously bogged down British Commonwealth forces at Gallipoli, rallied the Turkish army in central Anatolia and waited for the Allied forces to bring the war to them. By 1920, British forces in the region were in full demobilization and no European Power was willing to take on Kemal; instead it was left to Greece—which sought territorial gains—to battle Turkish forces. In September 1921, Greece was defeated and various Allied Governments broke ranks: the Treaty of Sèvres was effectively dead in the water[12]. Having deposed the Sultan and the Ottoman Government, rid Turkey of Greek forces, came face to face with occupying forces in

---

[11]   The Treaty of Peace between the Allied and Associated Powers and Turkey, 10 August 1920.
[12]   See David Fromkin, 'The Alliances Come Apart', *A Peace to End All Peace: Creating the Modern Middle East, 1914–1922*, 1989, Chapter 59, pp. 530–539.

Constantinople, and suppressed a Kurdish uprising in the southeast; Mustapha Kemal had turned the tables on the Allies and was prepared to dictate the peace. When a new agreement was signed—the Treaty of Lausanne—on 24 July 1923, Turkey had achieved all its demands except for its territorial claim over the vilayet of Mosul. Gone, therefore, were the provisions regarding Kurdish autonomy and the ability to move toward the creation of an independent Kurdish State. As for Mosul, the League of Nations was ultimately to decide whether it was to become part of Turkey or be attached to the vilayets of Basra and Baghdad to form the new Mesopotamian State of Iraq[13].

The Treaty of Lausanne stipulated that the frontier of Turkey in the southeast as between itself and Iraq would be established within nine months through negotiation with Great Britain. As no agreement could be reached, Great Britain exercised its right under that Treaty's Article 3(2) and submitted the question to the Council of the League of Nations for settlement. Article 3 of the Treaty of Lausanne reads, in part:

From the Mediterranean to the frontier of Persia, the frontier of Turkey is laid down as follows:

1) With Syria: [...]

2) With Iraq:

The frontier between Turkey and Iraq shall be laid down in friendly arrangement to be concluded between Turkey and Great Britain within nine months.

In the event of no agreement being reached between the two Governments within the time mentioned, the dispute shall be referred to the Council of the League of Nations.

The Turkish and British Governments reciprocally undertake that, pending the decision to be reached on the subject of the frontier, no military or other movement shall take place which might modify in any way the present state of the territories of which the final fate will depend upon that decision.

By allowing the Council of the League of Nations to deal with the Mosul question, Great Britain had ensured itself a privileged position as, not only did it have an occupying force in the province, it also sat on the Council, while Turkey had yet to become a member of the League of Nations. Despite assurances by both parties that no actions would be taken in an attempt to change the *status quo*, Great Britain sought to make facts on the ground, including the vilayet in the Iraq constitutional assembly elections. Kurds for their part, sought to demonstrate their displeasure with the lost of Kurdistan and the move to incorporate Mosul into either Iraq or Turkey by way of an independence movement led by Sheikh Mahmud, which ultimately was suppressed by aerial bombardment of the British Royal Air Force[14].

---

[13] McDowall, *op. cit.* n. 1, pp. 137–146.
[14] Jmor, *op. cit.* n. 6, p. 206.

While Turkey sought a determination as to the fate of the vilayet, Great Britain couched the dispute in terms of simply establishing a border frontier between Iraq and Turkey. Basing itself on the provisions of Article 3(2) of the Treaty of Lausanne, the Council of the League declined a request by Turkey to hold a plebiscite, instead opting for a Commission of Enquiry[15]. The Commission, after a fact-finding mission *in situ*, 'assigned a relative value to each of the facts which it has established, is of the opinion that important arguments, particularly of an economic and geographic nature, and the sentiments [...] of the majority of the inhabitants of the territory taken as a whole, operate in favour of the union with Iraq of the whole territory'[16]. Having decided in favour of Great Britain, the Commission considered that its decision should be subject to two conditions: First, that the territory should remain under the mandate system of the League of Nations for a twenty-five year period. Second, the Commission conditioned the attaching of the vilayet of Mosul to Iraq on the following:

> Regard must be paid to the desires expressed by the Kurds that officials of Kurdish race should be appointed for the administration of their country, the dispensation of justice and teaching in the schools, and that Kurdish should be the official language of all these services[17].

The Council, unable to reach agreement with the parties, in searching to act upon the conclusions of the Commission, sought the assistance of the Permanent Court of International Justice, by requesting an advisory opinion on the following questions:

1) What is the character of the decision to be taken by the Council in virtue of Article 3, paragraph 2, of the Treaty of Lausanne—is it an arbitral award, a recommendation or a simple mediation?

2) Must the decision be unanimous or may it be taken by a majority? May the representatives of the interested Parties take part in the vote[18]?

In formulating its opinion, the Court noted the Article 3 'is intended to *lay down* the frontier', as such 'it is clear that the object of this article is to establish a continuous and definite frontier'[19]. The Court then stated that the parties, failing agreement, had consented to a binding decision by means of dispute settlement, 'it must be concluded that the Parties, when signing that article, contemplated

---

[15]   *Id.*, pp. 214–215.

[16]   'Question of the Frontier between Turkey and Iraq: Report to the Council by the Commission instituted by the Council Resolution of September 30th, 1924', *Documents distributed to Council and State Members*, League of Nations, C. 400, M. 147, 20 August 1925, p. 88.

[17]   *Id.*, p. 89.

[18]   *Article 3, Paragraph 2, of the Treaty of Lausanne (Frontier between Turkey and Iraq)*, Advisory Opinion, *P.C.I.J. Reports*, Series B, No. 12, 21 November 1925, pp. 6–7.

[19]   *Id.*, pp. 19–20. Emphasis in the original.

intervention by a third Party—the Council—as a result of which a definitive solution would be reached'[20]. As to the question of unanimity, the Court offered the following opinion regarding the functioning of the Council, 'where the Parties have had recourse to a body already constituted and having its own rules of organization and procedure', and unless 'a contrary intention has been expressed, the interested Parties are in such cases held to have accepted such rules'[21]. Thus, the Permanent Court noted that 'unanimity, therefore, is required for the decision to be taken by the Council [...] in virtue of Article 3, paragraph 2, of the Treaty of Lausanne'[22]. Finally, the Court in an innovative manner noted that if the Council was to take into consideration the votes of the interested Parties, it would amount to a veto 'enabling them to prevent any decision from being reached. [...] The votes of the representatives of the Parties, are not, therefore, to be taken into account in ascertaining whether there is unanimity'[23].

Using the Advisory Opinion as its basis, the Council of the League decided, on 16 December 1925, to adopt 'the reasons and the proposals contained in the report' of the Committee of Enquiry, though it sought assurances from Great Britain regarding Kurdish cultural and administrative safeguards:

> The British Government, as mandatory Powers, is invited to lay before the Council the administrative measures which will be taken with a view to securing for the Kurdish populations mentioned in the report of the Commission of Enquiry the guarantees regarding local administration recommended by the Commission in its final conclusions[24].

The Turkish envoy Rouschdy Bey, upset at the Council's decision, declared that 'the sovereign rights of a State over a territory can only come to an end with its consent, and that therefore our sovereign rights over the whole of the vilayet of Mosul remain intact'[25]. Yet, it took less than a year for Turkey to accept the Council of the League of Nations' decision and to settle definitely the issue of borders. The Angora (i.e. Ankara) Treaty, between Great Britain, Iraq, and Turkey established, *inter alia*, cross-border control of Kurdish activity by stipulating the following. That the Asian States would 'refrain from all correspondence of an official or political nature with chiefs, sheikhs, or other members of tribes which are nationals of the other State and which are actually in the territory of that State. They shall not permit in the frontier zone any organisation for propaganda or

---

[20]   *Id.*, p. 20.
[21]   *Id.*, p. 31.
[22]   *Id.*, p. 31.
[23]   *Id.*, p. 32.
[24]   'Question of the Frontier between Turkey and Iraq: Decision of the Council', 16 December 1925, League of Nations, *Official Journal*, February 1926, Item 1651, pp. 191 and 192.
[25]   *Id.*, p. 187.

meeting directed against either State'[26]. The issue of the vilayet of Mosul settled between the parties, it was left to the Council of the League of Nations on 11 March 1926, having considered that Great Britain had provided the assurances required as detailed in the Commission of Enquiry report including those concerning the Kurds, to decide to incorporate the region into the State of Iraq under the British mandate[27].

The strategic objective of Great Britain in 1918, to establish a buffer State between Bolshevik Russia and both Turkey and Mesopotamia, meant that it espoused the creation of Kurdistan. Having let the genie out of the bottle by acknowledging and fostering the Kurdish nationalist movement, Great Britain would slowly abandon Kurdish aspirations in the move toward the final settlement of a dismantled Ottoman Empire. The Wilsonian conception of self-determination, as a political aspiration, was shown to be simply rhetoric where the Kurds were concerned. Having been denied a State at Paris, having been promised autonomy with the possibility of Statehood at Sèvres, Kurds would, when the smoke cleared at Lausanne, be granted limited cultural rights and administrative control in the northern Iraqi vilayet of Mosul. Yet, even these limited gains of autonomy would vanish in the wake of the termination of the Iraqi Mandate and the consolidation of that newly independent State. While the international gains of the Kurdish minority were slowly dissipating in Iraq, across the border in Turkey, where international assurances incorporated in the Treaty of Lausanne were never invoked, full-scale repression of the Kurdish population was soon underway as a means of consolidations and 'Turkification' of the remnants of the Ottoman Empire[28].

---

[26]   Article 12, Treaty between the United Kingdom and Iraq and Turkey regarding the Settlement of the Frontier between Turkey and Iraq, 5 June 1926, *British Command Papers*, Number 2679, 1926, pp. 7–8.

[27]   Council of the League of Nations, 'Decision of the Council of the League of Nations dated March 11th, 1926, relating to the application of the Principles of Article 22 of the Covenant to Iraq'; and the 'Administration of the Kurdish District of Iraq' (*Iraq*, C. 216, M. 77), 1 April 1926, VI.A.6., pp. 1–5.

[28]   While Articles 37–44 of the Treaty of Lausanne deal almost exclusively with non–Muslim minorities, a provision of Article 39 was applicable to the Kurdish minority:

> [...] No restrictions shall be imposed on the free use by any Turkish national of any language in private intercourse, in commerce, religion, in the press, or in publications of any kind or at public meetings.

> Notwithstanding the existence of the official language, adequate facilities shall be given to Turkish nationals of non–Turkish speech for the oral use of their own language before the Courts.

These provisions were to be safeguarded by Article 44 which reads, in part:

> [...] Turkey agrees that any Member of the Council of the League of Nations shall have the right to bring to the attention of the Council any infraction or danger of infraction of any of these obligations, and that the Council may thereupon take such action and give such directions as it may deem proper and effective in the circumstances.
> Turkey further agrees that any difference of opinion as to questions of law or of fact arising out of these Articles between the Turkish Government and any one of the other Signatory Powers or any other Power, a member of the Council of the League of Nations, shall be held to be a dispute of an

II. Treatment of Kurds during the Consolidation of the Modern Middle East

Kurdish history since the mid-1920s, with the creation of the modern Middle East, has been one not of advances in claims to self-determination, but quite the contrary. Fledgling Middle Eastern States, having had ethnic Kurdistan partitioned amongst themselves by European Powers sought, since their inception, to forge varying national identities at the expense of promoting things Kurdish. The legacy for Kurds, for the greater part of the twentieth century and beyond, has been the continuous suppression of their aspirations of self-determination. While the notion of 'self-determination' would not gain a foothold in international law until its inclusion as one of the purposes of the United Nations Organization in 1945, the quest for Kurdish autonomy persisted throughout the Inter-War years. The struggle for self-determination—broadly understood—has been a mainstay of Kurdish identity since the 1920s, yet even when the legal norm of 'self-determination' would emerge, it would fail to provide a basis upon which Kurds could assert a true claim on the international plane. By denying Kurdish people the possibility to assert a right to self-determination, the international community has doomed them to various levels of repression in their host States.

i. Situation of the Kurds in the State of Turkey

It was been written that from the establishment of the Turkish State until 'the early fifties, Kurdistan was held down by terror'[29]. Even nominal measures of self-determination of Kurds *within* the newly established frontiers of the Republic of Turkey were to be denied in the wake of the signing of the peace at Lausanne. In January 1923, before the signing of the Treaty of Lausanne, Mustapha Kemal announced that 'whichever provinces are predominantly Kurd will administer themselves autonomously'. However, ominously for Kurdish aspiration, the future Atatürk added:

> apart from that, we have to describe the people of Turkey together. If we do not describe them thus, we can expect problems particular to themselves ... it cannot be correct to try to draw another border [between Kurds and Turks]. We must make a new programme[30].

That new program, was to neglect Kurdish ethnicity so as to establish a secular, modern, western-oriented State based on a nationalist Turkish identity. As Turkish Prime Minister, Ismet Inönü put it, in 1925, 'we are frankly Nationalist ... and

---

international character under Article 14 of the Covenant of the League of Nations. The Turkish Government hereby consents that any such dispute shall, if the other party thereto demands, be referred to the Permanent Court of International Justice. The decision of the Permanent Court shall be final and shall have the same force and effect as an award under Article 13 of the Covenant.

[29] Kendal, 'Kurdistan in Turkey', Gerard Chaliand, (ed.), *A People without a Country: The Kurds and Kurdistan*, 1993, p. 78.

[30] McDowall, *op. cit.* n. 1, p. 190.

Nationalism is our only factor of cohesion. In the face of a Turkish majority other elements have no kind of influence. We must turkify the inhabitants of our land at any price, and we will annihilate those who oppose the Turks or *le turquisme*'[31]. The assimilationist policies seeking to consolidate the new republic on Turkish lines meant that the Kurdish identity was to be suppressed for the greater good. Emphasis on all things 'Turkish' was the basis of a State ideology which allowed the central government to consolidate its power within the 1923 borders of the newly created Republic of Turkey.

In March 1924, Turkey abolished the office of the caliphate, deporting the religious successor of the Prophet Mohammed and introduced the secular 'Law on the Unification of Education'[32]. This legislation ended religious education and demanded that Turkish be the only language taught. It was 'a fundamental step in the establishment of a unified, modern, secular, egalitarian and national education system' whereas its 'nation building role was especially vital in a country where identity was often Islamic rather than national, and which was fragmented into numerous tribal, racial, and linguistic units'[33]. Following the rationale of the forced transfer of Turkish and Greek populations as mandated by the Treaty of Lausanne, Kurds were subjected, in 1934, to the Settlement Law. This draconian measure was meant to assimilate Kurds by forcing them to move to predominately Turkish speaking areas, while making off-limits settlement to other areas of the country, and finally establishing a zone designated as being 'closed for security reasons to any form of civilian settlement'[34]. The intended purpose of the Settlement Law, as David McDowall notes in his comprehensive *A Modern History of the Kurds*, was to disperse the Kurdish population, 'to areas where it would constitute no more than 5 per cent of the population, thus extinguishing Kurdish identity'[35].

Such measures were meant to incorporate the Kurdish population into the Turkish polity at all costs, and despite its wishes. During the period 1924 to 1938, seventeen Kurdish uprisings took place in the eastern Turkey[36], of which the most noteworthy was led by Sheikh Said—noteworthy in the sense of both its failure and the measures introduced in an attempt to curb future insurrections. Robert Olson, in his monograph on the issue writes that the 'Sheikh Said rebellion was the first large-scale nationalist rebellion by the Kurds'[37]. The insurrection took place in 1925, when Kurdish troops capture large swaths of the southeast of Turkey. The Turkish response was to send more than 50,000 troops to re-conquer and pacify the area. The outcome of the suppression of the revolt was, on the one hand, to

---

[31]   See Henri Barkey and Graham Fuller, *Turkey's Kurdish Question*, 1998, p. 10.
[32]   Kemal Kirişci and Gareth Winrow, *The Kurdish Question and Turkey: An Example of Trans–state Ethnic Conflict*, 1997, p. 95.
[33]   M. Winter, 'The Modernization of Education in Kemalist Turkey' in J. Landau (ed.), *Atatürk and Modernization of Turkey*, 1984, p. 186, as quoted in Kirişci and Winrow, *id.*, p. 95.
[34]   Kirişci and Winrow, *id.*, p. 99.
[35]   McDowall, *op. cit.* n. 1, p. 207.
[36]   Kirişci and Winrow, *op. cit.* n. 32, p. 101.
[37]   Robert Olson, *The Emergence of Kurdish Nationalism and the Sheikh Said Rebellion, 1880–1925*, 1989, p. 127.

strengthen the resolve of the hard-line Kemalists in Ankara who were able to consolidate the power of a one-party State. On the other hand, the Turkish Army, 'found control of Kurdistan to be its prime function and raison d'être'[38]. Thus, the new Turkish State emerged during the inter-War years, having consolidated its ideologically based Turkish State with its manifest policy of forced assimilation or annihilation of Kurds. During the latter part of this period and for some time after the Second World War, such policies would lay dormant, having been successful in suppressing armed rebellion until the 1980s, when they would again be revived, this time in response to the Kurdistan Workers Party—the PKK.

ii. Situation of the Kurds in the State of Iraq

While the repression of Kurds in Iraq during the inter-War years was not undertaken on the same scale as in Turkey, the consolidation of the new vilayet of Mosul into Mandate Iraq, and the emergence of Iraq as an independent State in 1932 did necessitate the military suppression of Kurdish nationalism. Great Britain was active in suppressing the renewed activities of Sheikh Mahmud who, having fled to Persia (i.e. Iran) after being ousted by the Royal Air Force (RAF) in 1922, was busy fomenting insurrection during most of the British Mandate period in Iraq. Although Great Britain would report to the League of Nations in 1928 that while Kurds in Iraq 'dream of an ultimate union of all the now scattered Kurdish tribes and peoples' they 'are on the whole for the present satisfied by the special administrative treatment and privileges which they enjoy'[39]. That satisfaction, however, would be short lived as Sheikh Mahmud—that 'stormy petrel of southern Kurdistan'—would return to lead a revolt in the wake of the publication of the 1930 Anglo-Iraqi Treaty[40]. That Agreement, which provided for the end of the British Mandate and the independence of the State of Iraq in 1932, failed to include the Kurdish safeguards which had been the basis of the inclusion of the vilayet of Mosul into the Mandate for Iraq.

The RAF would again defeat Sheikh Mahmud in 1931, this time, he would be internally exiled to southern Iraq. Yet, the Kurdish revolt did manage to place Kurdish issues on the international agenda. In February 1932, Iraq passed a Local Language Law that provided that Kurdish speakers rather than ethnic Kurds would fill administrative and teaching positions in the vilayet. In such a manner, the guarantees required by the League had been rid of their content: the nominal

---

[38] McDowall, *op. cit.* n. 1, p. 199.

[39] Great Britain Colonial Office, *Report by His Majesty's Government in the United Kingdom of Great Britain and Northern Ireland to the Council of the League of Nations on the Administration of Iraq for the year 1928*, p. 26.

[40] See Great Britain Colonial Office, *Report by His Majesty's Government in the United Kingdom of Great Britain and Northern Ireland to the Council of the League of Nations on the Administration of Iraq for the Year 1927*, p. 22. To what extent Sheikh Mahmud was a thorn in the side of the British Administration was revealed in the following passage of the Report, 'Shaikh Mahmud's numerous bellicose enterprises and his persistent clinging to dreams of imperial power have, since 1922, been the worst obstacle to the orderly administration of the Sulaimaniya province', p. 23.

protection of cultural and language rights of the majority Kurdish population in the vilayet vanished. For its part, the League of Nations did not stand in the way of Iraqi independence. The Council of the League accepting the Mandates Commission's view that it was unnecessary to require from an independent Iraq the guarantees it had sought from Great Britain as Mandatory, deeming the measures of the Local Language Law adequate for the termination of the Mandate[41]. As David McDowall has noted 'it was a shady end to the high-flown promises with which British political officers had entered Kurdistan in 1918, and a betrayal of the assurances given by Arab Iraqi ministers during the formation of the Iraqi state'[42].

With the suppression of Sheikh Mahmud's nationalist ventures at the hands of the British, new leaders would emerge from a family whose name would become synonymous with Kurdish aspirations of self-determination in Iraq: Barzani. In 1932, Sheikh Ahmad Barzani's men inflicted heavy loses on Iraqi forces before surrendering to Turkish troops in June. The suppression of the Barzani rebellion was in large part due to the RAF which destroyed many villages under Barzani's control. While Sheikh Ahmad Barzani's star began to fade, his brother's, Mulla Mustafa, would rise for another twenty years. Mulla Mustafa Barzani would head a revolt that appeared to have more to do with personal animosity toward the Iraqi leadership, and was acutely related to the 1943 Kurdish famine, than to a nationalist rebellion. When his forces clashed with police in Barzan in 1943, he become the focal point of the Kurdish discontent with the Baghdad Government. The Iraqi military again took heavy casualties in attempting to suppress a Barzani, and again, this time Mulla Mustafa Barzani would flee over a border to safety. Where Mulla Mustafa Barzani would make his surname a household one would be in his new refuge—the Mahabad region of Iran.

iii. The Kurdish Republic of Mahabad

To this point, only those regions of Kurdistan which were the spoils of the First World War have been discussed, yet Kurdistan is also found on the fault line between the former Ottoman Empire and the former Persian Empire—modern day Iran. In 1941, as part of their war effort, Britain and the Soviet Union invaded Iran resulting in the abdication of the pro-German Reza Shah Pahlavi in favour of his son. While the Soviets maintained control in the northern and westerly Azerbaijani regions of Iran, Britain sought to protect Iraq by occupying areas within Iran near the common border. It was, as Archie Roosevelt, a US military attaché in Tehran at the time, would note 'in the large areas between the British and Soviet forces, in the vacuum left by the fleeing Iranians, that the Kurds were able to regain their

---

[41] See 'Mandates: Proposal of the United Kingdom Government for the Emancipation of Iraq: Report by the Committee instructed by the Council to prepare the Draft Declaration to be made by the Iraqi Government on Termination of the Mandatory Regime of Iraq, 19 May 1932, League of Nations, *Official Journal*, July 1932, Item 3081, p. 1212–1216. For the Report to the Council and the Draft Declaration by the Iraqi Government, see Annex 1373, at pp. 1342–1350.
[42] McDowall, *op. cit.* n. 1, p. 177.

autonomy'[43]. While Iranian government forces take control over much of this area during the Second World War years, the region near Lake Urmieh remained outside its sphere of control. That area, with the town of Mahabad at its center, became the focal point of a nationalist movement which would result in the establishment of the ambiguous Kurdish Republic of Mahabad which was to last less than a year.

In their attempt to attach northern Iran to the Soviet Union, nationalist ferment was actively promoted by the Soviets in both the Azerbaijani and Kurdish areas of Iran. This led to the issuing of a Kurdish manifesto that sought, above all, the following, 'The Kurdish people in Iran should have freedom and self-government in the administration of their local affairs, and obtain autonomy with in the limits of the Iranian State'[44]. While the aim of autonomy was proclaimed, the shadow of independence was never far away, and was reinforced with the arrival of Mulla Mustafa Barzani and his men. While Barzani's forces fought local Iranian forces, it was the assistance of the Soviet Red Army that allowed for the semblance of victory by blocking Iranian reinforcements from arriving in the region. With the ability to maintain control over the areas established, the local leader Qazi Mohammad declared independence on 15 December 1945. However, the Republic would have to fight for its survival almost from day one, as larger issues would come to dictate the viability of this newly created State.

As McDowall writes, 'the idea that the Republic of Mahabad was the critical moment at which the Kurds realised their freedom is arguably a rosy version of reality. [...] It never had a hope without serious Soviet support and the Republic's leaders knew in their hearts that such support was not dependable'[45]. By January 1946 the Soviets and the Iranians were in the midst of negotiating an end to Soviet occupation. By April 1946, the Soviet Union made it known to the newly established United Nations Security Council that, by way of negotiation with Iran, it intended to withdraw 'its troops as rapidly as possible'[46]. With the evacuation of Soviet forces, Iran moved to re-conquer the break-away republic. A year to the day that the independent republic had been proclaimed, Iranian troops re-entered Mahabad. In a further note of symmetry, while Mulla Mustafa Barzani was able to fight his way into exile in the Soviet Union, Qazi Mohammad was hanged, on 31 March 1947, in the same square where he had proclaimed independence less than a year and a half earlier. Thus, as in Turkey and Iraq, the fate of Iranian Kurdish nationalism was not to find expression in independence or autonomy but in repression.

---

[43]   Archie Roosevelt, 'The Kurdish Republic of Mahabad', *The Middle East Journal*, Vol. 1, 1946, p. 248.

[44]   *Id.*, p. 255.

[45]   McDowall, *op. cit.* n. 1, p. 246.

[46]   United Nations Security Council Resolution 3, 4 April 1946, S/RES/3, 1946. See also Resolutions 2 and 5 related to the Soviet troops evacuating Iran.

III. Situation of the Kurds in the Era of Self-Determination

The rise and fall of the Mahabad Republic took place in the shadow of the establishment of the United Nations Organization in San Francisco in 1945. Yet the Republic was not to benefit from the new international system. The post-Second World War order was given voice in the Charter of the United Nations, which not only set out the framework of a new international organization but also outlined the parameters of a new international order based on collective security and the peaceful settlement of disputes. The Charter further institutionalised the notion of 'self-determination', but did so not as a legal right but as a principle. Article 1 of the Charter laid out the purposes of the United Nations, which include:

> 2. To develop friendly relations among nations based on respect for the principle of equal rights and self-determination of peoples, and to take other appropriate measures to strengthen universal peace.

To give voice to the principle of 'equal rights and self-determination of peoples', the Charter sets out, at Article 55, a system of international economic and social cooperation based on this principle with an aim of ensuring the stability of the international system. Further, Article 56 calls on all States, to act either individually or collectively in assisting the United Nations in the endeavors set out in Article 55[47]. Noticeably absent from the United Nations Charter is mention of self-determination within the provisions of Chapter XI—Declaration Regarding Non-Self-Governing Territories or Chapter XII—the International Trusteeship System; those chapters relating to de-colonization. Thus, while the principle of self-determination was enshrined as a constitutional norm of the international system which emerged in 1945, its content was ill-defined and, above all would be narrowly construed[48]. However, from this principle would emerge a *right* of self-determination which would act as the 'intellectual engine of decolonization'[49].

While self-determination was lifted by the Charter of the United Nations from political rhetoric to a principle of international relations, it would finally gain true legal standing internationally through State practice as fundamental changes to the international system emerged in the 1960s and 1970s. The East-West chasm that developed in the guise of the Cold War allowed breathing space for former colonised States to agitated for independence using the notion of self-determination as found in Article 1(2) of the Charter as their guiding principle. In 1960, the United Nations General Assembly passed Resolution 1514, the Declaration on the Granting of Independence to Colonial Countries and Peoples, wherein it proclaimed that 'all peoples have the right to self-determination; by virtue of that

---

[47]   See Articles 55 and 56, Charter of the United Nations.

[48]   For the elements of the principle of self–determination as found in the Charter, see Cassese, *op. cit.* n. 3, pp. 37–42, where he concludes by noting that it 'follows that the principle enshrined in the UN Charter boils down to very little.', p. 42.

[49]   Paul Szasz, 'The Irresistible Force of Self–Determination Meets the Impregnable Fortress of Territorial Integrity: A Cautionary Fairy Tale about Clashes in Kosovo and Elsewhere', *Georgia Journal of International and Comparative Law*, Vol. 28, 1999, p. 3.

right they freely determine their political status and freely pursue their economic, social and cultural development'[50]. The affirmation of this Declaration in the General Assembly, coupled with the 1970 Declaration on Friendly Relations, amounted to *opinio juris* which, backed with the practice of States, establishes a customary *right* of self-determination. The 1970 Declaration went a step further in noting that States have a duty not to deprive people, who are subject to 'colonialism' and 'alien subjugation, domination and exploitation', of their right to self-determination[51]. Thus emerged from the United Nations, a legal right of self-determination, however, it was limited to very specific situations. The right of self-determination was to be conceived only in such situations of 'external' self-determination which allow from a people to assert their right only in the three following situations, either against: colonial regimes, racist *qua* apartheid regimes, or military occupying forces[52].

With respect to Kurdish aspirations, the right of external self-determination as developed within the United Nations is not applicable. Clearly, the external right of self-determination developed in a Statist manner was focused on ridding itself of foreign influences, but ensuring maintenance of established frontiers. Thus, while indigenous leaders in newly independent States would replace the foreign elite, the notion of *uti possidetis*, whereby colonial borders were to remain intact, became a general rule of international law. The right of self-determination was thus allowed to evolve internationally, in a quite restrictive manner, so as not to challenge the Westphalian Statist system. As for 'internal' self-determination, international law has granted such a right only in one specific situation: where racial groups are denied access to government. Antonio Cassese notes in his legal appraisal of self-determination that the United Nations, and hence States themselves, have remained 'silent in response to claims asserting the right of self-determination', be they 'on behalf of *ethnic groups*, such as the Kurds, Armenians, and Basques; *indigenous populations*, such as the native peoples of Latin America, North America,

---

[50]   Declaration on the Granting of Independence to Colonial Countries and Peoples, United Nations General Assembly Resolution 1514, 14 December 1960.
[51]   Declaration on Principles of International Law concerning Friendly Relations and Co–operation among States in Accordance with the Charter of the United Nations, United Nations General Assembly Resolution 2625, 24 October 1970.
[52]   Note that running parallel to a group right of self–determination, the 1966 human rights Covenants related to civil and political rights, and economic, social and cultural rights have a common Article 1 which reads:

1.   All peoples have the right of self–determination. By virtue of that right they freely determine their political status and freely pursue their economic, social and cultural development.

2.   All peoples may, for their own ends, freely dispose of their natural wealth and resources without prejudice to any obligations arising out of international economic co–operation, based upon the principle of mutual benefit, and international law. In no case may a people be deprived of its own means of subsistence.

3.   The States Parties to the present Covenant, including those having responsibility for the administration of Non–Self–Governing and Trust Territories, shall promote the realization of the right of self–determination, and shall respect that right, in conformity with the provisions of the Charter of the United Nations.

Australia, and New Zealand; *linguistic minorities*, such as the Québecois; and *religious groups* such as the Catholics in Northern Ireland'[53]. Instead, States, the subjects which establish the parameters of international law, have sought to close off any option that might allow for a secessionist movement that might dismantle a State. As Gérard Chaliand put it, in *Les Kurdes et le Kurdistan*, 'During international assemblies, the invocation of the "right of self-determination" is made as often as it is vague; this right is legally guaranteed, but its content is however, non-existent and it is known that it depends more often than naught to relations of power as it is measured by force of arms'[54].

Newly independent States, arguably more so than other States, were unwilling to lose their gains and to see the disintegration of their State. While emerging States took the lead in promoting decolonization, most, if not all, States were in agreement in placing far-reaching limitations on any right of self-determination. In the 1970 Declaration on Friendly Relations, States inserted a so-called 'clawback' clause that placed a definite limit on the expression of the right of self-determination:

> Nothing in the foregoing paragraphs [related to the exercising of the right of self determination] shall be construed as authorizing or encouraging any action which would dismember or impair, totally or in part, the territorial integrity or political unity of sovereign and independent States conducting themselves in compliance with the principle of equal rights and self-determination of peoples as described above and thus possessed of a government representing the whole people belonging to the territory without distinction as to race, creed or colour.

In this manner, States drew a line between the notion of self-determination and the content of the right of self-determination. While a people could aspire to self-determination, the content of the legal norms was such as to limit its exercise to a very select few. It is within this context that one can appreciate the Statist mentality from which international law gains its essence. Thus, distinct ethnic groups such as the Kurds fail to meet the criteria of a right of self-determination; instead they are doomed, in large part, to remain within a system bent on maintaining the territorial integrity of States. Throughout the Cold War era, when colonised State after colonised State gained its independence, Kurds were marginalised; repressed under an international system which designated them, by virtue of Article 2(7) of the Charter, as 'matters which are essentially within the domestic jurisdiction' of the various Middle East States.

The Cold War era was a time of nationalist awaking throughout Kurdistan. With the emergence of newly independent States in Africa and Asia, and a development of nationalist consciences amongst an ever-growing Kurdish educated class; agitation for respect of things Kurdish came to the fore. Admittedly, the States in which Kurdish minorities existed sought to stunt the growth of any movement that would challenge their territorial integrity. It thus should come as

---

[53]   Cassese, *op. cit.* n. 3, p. 103. Emphasis in the original.
[54]   Gérard Chaliand (ed.), *Les Kurdes et le Kurdistan*, 1978, p. 17.

little surprise that the fate of Kurds during the Cold War era, denied as they were the right of self-determination, should be to suffer continuous repression and further assimilation into existing Middle Eastern States. Where Kurdish areas gained some type of recognition or limited autonomy it had more to do with the geopolitics of the region than with any affinity toward their plight. During the Cold War era, it can not be said that Kurds were better off than during the inter-War period; instead, it can be said that their fate came more into focus as the discourse of human rights began to take hold internationally. While the legal right of self-determination was denied to Kurds as a people, individual human rights emerged as a means of highlighting their grievances. While collective self-determination could be denied by the various States, repressive measures meant to quell such movements came into conflict with a State's obligations under international human rights law.

i. Situation of the Kurds in the State of Turkey

The bringing of Turkey into the 'modern' world was felt quite acutely by the Kurds of Turkey. The replacement of subsistence farming by mechanised farming and the introduction of the tractors in the 1950s, meant that a large-scale migration of Kurds from rural to urban settings took place. These fundamental socio-economic changes were to play a major role in the coming years. As David McDowall explains: the Kurdish nationalist movement that would emerge later 'was born by economic deprivation, social injustice, and physical displacement as well as ideas of ethnic identity, all of which combined in the late 1970s to create the conditions for revolt'[55]. The issue of social injustice in the 1960s which was at the forefront of Kurdish disenchantment with the Turkish State included the move to replace Kurdish place names with Turkish ones, to introduce regional boarding schools in an attempt to further assimilate Kurds, and denial of the Kurdish identity by the President of the Republic[56].

While Turkey would flirt with a liberal constitutions in subsequent years, the backlash that inevitably emerged was in the form of military coups that carried with them repressive measures toward the Kurds. In 1967, not only was it illegal to use the Kurdish language in Turkey, it was decreed also 'illegal and forbidden to introduce to, or distribute, in the country, materials in the Kurdish language of foreign origin in any form published, recorded, taped, or material in similar forms'[57]. During the 1970s Kurdish nationalism found voice in leftist student organization which would mature during the 1980s. Taking a page out of the Latin-American counter-insurgency techniques, two-thirds of the Turkish army was deployed into Turkish Kurdistan in the wake of a third military *coup d'état*, which transpired in September 1980. The International League of Human Rights reported

---

[55] McDowall, *op. cit.* n. 1, p. 402.
[56] See *id.*, p. 404.
[57] *Id.*, p. 408.

that in the ensuing two years more than 81,000 Kurds had been detained in an attempt to suppress Kurdish separatism[58].

By 1984, the seed of revolt bore fruit in the guise of the Partiya Karkari Kurdistan (PKK), the radical left Kurdish Worker's Party, which declared a war of liberation against the Turkish State. During the next decade, what amounted to a civil war would claim more than twelve thousand lives, including not only Turkish forces in the southeast, but also the members of the Village Guard (Kurdish auxiliaries of the Turkish army), members of the Kurdish landlord class, but most of all, Kurdish civilians. The government response, as McDowall notes, was consistent with past actions:

> The government sought to outdo PKK intimidation, matching terror for terror, in an apparent belief that if only the Kurds were more fearful of Ankara than they were of the PKK, it would be able to stifle the insurgency. In a prosperous society that stood to lose much by civil conflict such a doctrine might have worked. But in the impoverished circumstances of Kurdistan, where the mass of population had such meager economic expectations and where traditional methods of co-operation through landlords was in advanced decay, such methods merely fuelled the conflict[59].

Laws prohibiting the spoken use of Kurdish were introduced in the 1980s, as were laws preventing the ability to give children Kurdish names, and by 1986 more than two-thirds of villages had been renamed, expunging their Kurdish identity. In 1987, a state of emergency was proclaimed in the provinces of the southeast, which allowed for the evacuation of villages; one year later provisions were enacted allowing for the deportation of the population from the region. The *modus operandi* of the military was a 'scorched-earth strategy with a vast number of human rights violations such as extrajudicial executions, burning houses, deportation, bombing of inhabited villages and provincial cities'[60]. While the level of repression in Turkey was staggering, it failed to meet the repression felt by Kurds in Iraq which would reach near genocidal proportions.

ii. Situation of the Kurds in the State of Iraq

During the Cold War era, the plight of Iraqi Kurds can be encapsulated in one word: Halabja. While Mulla Mustafa Barzani returned from Soviet exile in 1958, and although he was openly aligned with Baghdad upon his return, things soured quickly and Barzani was, by 1961, in open revolt with the Iraqi Government. That revolt would end in 1963 when Barzani agreed to a cease-fire with the Nasserist Baath Party, thus allowing it to take power in Baghdad by means of a *coup d'état*. Having assisted in the Baath march to power, Barzani received an offer of

---

[58]   *Id.*, p. 414.

[59]   *Id.*, p. 424.

[60]   See Christian Rumpf, summarizing reports of Amnesty International, Helsinki Watch and the Helsinki Federation for Human Rights in his article, 'The Protection of Human Rights in Turkey and the Significance of International Human Rights Instruments', *Human Rights Law Journal*, Vol. 14, 1993, p. 395.

'recognition on the national rights of the Kurdish people on the basis of self-administration', which he quickly discarded. Instead, Barzani sought Kurdish 'freedom over virtually all matters except foreign affairs, finances and national defense'[61], including the oil rich area around Kirkuk. Unwilling to give in, the Baathists turned from negotiation to repression and sent their troops into the northern vilayets; their fight, however, was short lived as the Baath government was overthrown in November 1963. Barzani came to terms with the new military government, but on decidedly narrower terms; gone were issues of Kurdish autonomy, replaced with the recognition of 'the nation rights of Kurds within a unified Iraqi state'[62].

When an interim constitution was brought forward, it was clear that Kurdish aspiration did not meet even those agreed to by Barzani, the result of which was again open warfare in 1965–66. A change in leadership in Baghdad coupled with the largest military defeat of Iraqi troops at the hands of Kurds led to the 1966 Bazzaz Declaration named after the new prime minister. The twelve-point program sought to include Kurds as equals with Arabs in the Iraqi Constitution, which would include provisions for a de-centralised system of government with assurances of proportional representation in, not only the Iraqi legislature, but in the 'cabinet, the government administration, the diplomatic corps and the army command'[63]. However, this Declaration failed to materialise under the leadership of Abd al Rahaman Bazzaz, who was forced to resign. With Iraqi forces caught in a military stalemate in the north, the Baath carried out a second military coup in 1968.

This time the Baath Party would consolidate its position, as Iraq would become a one-party State. The Baath aligned itself early on with Barzani's arch-rival, Jalal Talabani, in an attempt to neutralise Barzani's powerbase. However, Barzani would start to receive military assistance from both Iran and the United States which placed in jeopardy the Baathist regimes' ability to consolidate its power. Although Talabani had accepted a position within the Baath cabinet and the Bazzaz Declaration had been to a large degree implemented, Barzani held out for more. On 11 March 1970, a Peace Accord was reached by Barzani and one of the Baath's 'leading advocates of a more amenable approach to the Kurdish question': Saddam Hussein[64]. The agreement called for major autonomy for the Kurds, including a change in the Constitution to include the acknowledgment of the Kurdish nation, provided for cultural and linguistic rights; and ensured political participation of Kurds in the central government[65]. Barzani, backed more heavily by Iran and the

---

[61] McDowall, *op. cit.* n. 1, p. 314.

[62] *Id.*, p. 315.

[63] Gershon Solomon, 'The Kurdish National Struggle in Iraq', *New Outlook*, Vol. 10, 1967, p. 12–13.

[64] McDowall, *op. cit.* n. 1, p. 324.

[65] The following is what McDowall terms the essential articles of the Accord (see *id.* pp. 327–328):

United States, which sought to stem the flow of Soviet influence in the Middle East, but specifically within Iraq, was not satisfied with the 1970 Peace Accord and was unwilling to sign it. In 1974, Iraq unilaterally passed an Autonomy Law comprising the northern governorates of Ibril, Sulamaniya, and Dohuk, but excluding oil-rich Kirkuk, thus constituting a *casus belli* for Barzani. When the Iraqi army demonstrated that it could hold its own against the Kurds, Iran pulled its support of Barzani in exchange for an agreement in its favour regarding the territorial dispute surrounding their common access to Persian Gulf: the Shatt al Arab. With the signing of the 1975 Algiers Accord between Iraq and Iran, the high stakes poker match was at an end for Barzani.

With the military defeat of Barzani, Iraq undertook to secure the region and to put an end to any notions of Kurdish autonomy. It created a *cordon sanitaire* to a width of thirty kilometres along the Iranian and Turkish borders razing more than a thousand villages by 1978 and displacing more than half a million Kurds to 'resettlement camps'[66]. Playing on the turmoil in Iran, which saw the deposing of the Shah and the establishment of a revolutionary theocracy in 1980, Iraq sought to regain what it had lost through the Algiers Accord by way of a military invasion. It was only in 1982 that Iran was able to repulse Iraqi forces enough to open a second, northern front, in its war against Iraq. This meant calling on Kurds to once more destabilise Baghdad, thus forcing Iraq to divert troops from their main theatre of war in the south. When it became clear in 1984, that neither Washington nor Moscow was willing to allow Iraq to lose the War, 'Saddam [Hussein] no longer needed to make concessions to the Kurds'[67]. As atrocities mounted at the hands of Iraqi troops, Masud Barzani, the son of Mulla Mustafa, and Jalal Talabani met in

---

1. The Kurdish language shall be, alongside the Arabic language, the official language in areas with a Kurdish majority; and will be the language of instruction in those area and taught throughout Iraq as a second language.
2. Kurds will participate fully in government, including senior and sensitive posts in the cabinet and the army.
3. Kurdish education and culture will be reinforced.
4. All officials in Kurdish majority areas shall be Kurds or at least Kurdish–speaking.
5. Kurds shall be free to establish student, youth, womens' and teachers' organizations of their own.
6. Funds will be set aside for the development of Kurdistan.
7. Pensions and assistance will be provided for the families of martyrs and other stricken by poverty, unemployment or homelessness.
8. Kurds and Arabs will be restored to their former place of habitation.
9. Agrarian Reform will be implemented.
10. The Constitution will be amended to read 'the Iraqi people is made up of two nationalities, the Arab nationality and the Kurdish nationality'.
11. The broadcasting station and heavy weapons will be returned to the Government.
12. A Kurd shall be one of the vice–presidents.
13. The Governorates (Provincial) Law shall be amended in a manner conforming with the substance of this declaration.
14. Unification of areas with a Kurdish majority as a self–governing unit.
15. The Kurdish people shall share in the legislative power in a manner proportionate to its population in Iraq.

[66]   *Id.,* p. 339.
[67]   *Id.,* p. 350.

Tehran in November 1986 to form a united front against the Iraqi government. This Kurdish unity was to grow with the establishment of the Kurdish Front in May 1987 comprising the five leading Kurdish groups and the Assyrian Democratic Movement. Baghdad saw in Kurdistan a 'Trojan horse for an Iranian victory, as enemy troops flooded into the area'[68]. The response of the Iraqi Government was to make large areas of Kurdistan free-fire zones. In March 1987, Saddam Hussein appointed his cousin General Ali Hasan al-Majid as Governor of the Northern Bureau granting him *carte blanche* to deal with Kurdish 'traitors'.

What ensued was a scorched earth policy not unlike that occurring in Turkey. But where al-Majid would out do his northern neighbour was both in the intensity of the campaign and his methods, which Human Rights Watch would consider as 'intent to destroy, in whole or in part, a national, ethnical, racial or religious group'. In other words, meeting the threshold of genocidal behaviour as expressed in Article 2 of the Convention on the Prevention and Punishment of the Crime of Genocide[69]. During the final phase of the Iran-Iraq War, when it was evident that Iran could no longer sustain a southern flank offensive, Iraq turned to the north, both to attempt to repel Iranian incursions, but also to seek what amounted to a 'final solution' *vis-à-vis* the Kurdish population[70]. Human Rights Watch, which had reported on al-Majid's *Anfal* Campaign as it transpired from February to September 1988, confirmed its finding when it was able to retrieve the Iraqi archives in the Kurdish areas protected by the Western imposed 'no-fly zones' after the 1991 Gulf War. The campaign undertaken by al-Majid's forces in Iraqi Kurdistan included 'prohibited areas' where shoot-to-kill orders were instituted that also called for 'random bombardments, using artillery, helicopters and aircraft, at all times of the day or night, in order to kill the largest number of persons present in ... prohibited zones'[71]. Further, the Hussein Administration, 'became the first in history to attack its own civilian population with chemical weapons'[72], culminating in more than five thousand people being gassed to death in Halabja in March 1988.

Halabja, a town that had recently been occupied by Kurdish guerrillas—the *peshmerga*—with the assistance of the Iranian Revolutionary Guard was but one of thirty-nine known gas attacks against Kurds that had commenced as early as April 1987[73]. The international response to this use of chemical weapons was negligible. The fact that both the United States and Moscow were allied with Iraq in its war

---

[68]   *Id.*, p. 352.

[69]   For the Genocide Convention see Eric Suy, *Corpus Iuris Gentium: A Collection of Basic Texts on Modern Interstate Relations*, 1992, pp. 426–428.

[70]   Ali Hassan al–Majid spoke in these terms, 'to solve the Kurdish problem and slaughter the saboteurs'. See Human Rights Watch/ Middle East, *Iraq's Crime of Genocide: The Anfal Campaign against the Kurds*, 1995, p. 1.

[71]   Clause 5 directed that 'all persons captured in those villages shall be detained and interrogated by the security services and those between the ages of 15 and 70 shall be executed after any useful information has been obtained from them, of which we should be duly notified'. Clause 4, Directive SF/4008, 20 June 1987, *id.*, p. 5.

[72]   *Id.*, p. 6.

[73]   See Appendix C, *id.*, pp. 263–264.

against Revolutionary Iran, meant that the issue of crimes against humanity and violations of the Genocide Convention would be treaded upon lightly. Thus the UN Security Council failed to mention chemical attacks against the Kurdish populations or to identify Iraq when it twice resolved to condemn 'the use of chemical weapons in the conflict between the Islamic Republic of Iran and Iraq, in violation of the obligations under the Protocol for the Prohibition of the Use in War of Asphyxiating, Poisonous or Other Gases, and of Bacteriological Methods of Warfare, signed at Geneva on 17 June 1925'[74]. The fate of Kurds in Iraq during the Cold War era—and more precisely during the era of self-determination—is well symbolised by Halabja. The *Anfal* Campaign claimed the lives of tens of thousands of Kurdish civilians who were either summarily executed or disappeared, the wholesale destruction of more than two thousand villages, and the forced displacement of hundreds of thousands of Kurds[75]. With the end of the Cold War, the fate of Iraqi Kurds would be radically altered, as the State of Iraq would become the testing ground of the 'New World Order'.

IV. Situation of the Kurds in the 'New World Order'

The 'New World Order' proclaimed by United States President George Bush in response to Iraqi aggression against Kuwait in 1990 had diametrically opposite effects on the Kurds of Iraq as compared to those of Turkey. Where Iraqi Kurds gained a semblance of autonomy under an international umbrella, Turkish Kurds found the screws of repression tightened. While the treatment of Kurdish minorities was radically different in Iraq and Turkey, the legal dimensions of the right of self-determination were placed in flux. Events of the post-Cold War era, it transpired, placed in question the content of the right of self-determination. With the break-up of the former Soviet Union, most notably in the case of the dissolution of Czechoslovakia into its component parts, and more importantly the fragmentation of the former Yugoslavia, the ability to claim a right of self-determination beyond limits set during the Cold War era seemed possible. Yet, even within this expanding notion of the right of self-determination, the fate of Kurds appears to be driven more by geopolitics than by legal norms. Thus, while the evolution of the right of self-determination may come to encompass some type of recognition for Kurds; that recognition will inevitably fall within the framework of the modern Middle East as established after the First World War. Thus issues Kurdish will be dealt with, subject to the greater concerns of the six States which include parts of ethnic Kurdistan.

The content of the right of self-determination has been placed into question as a result of the response of the international community to the dismemberment of the Federal Republic of Yugoslavia. When Yugoslavia was threatened with

---

[74]   United Nations Security Council Resolution 620, 26 August 1988, S/RES/620, 1988; para. 1; see also United Nations Security Council Resolution 612, 9 May 1988, S/RES/612, 1988; para. 1.

[75]   Human Rights Watch, *op. cit.* n. 70, pp. 1–2.

atomization in the early 1990s, Europe took the lead in attempting to reach a peaceful solution amongst the various members of the Federation. The European Community (the precursor to the European Union) sought to base its decisions regarding Yugoslavia on international law, and to that end established an Arbitration Commission consisting of members of European Constitutional Courts. The Badinter Commission, named after its chairman, the President of the French *Conseil Constitutionnel*, rendered fifteen opinions between January 1992 and 13 August 1993[76]. It its Opinion Number 2, the Commission considered 'that international law as it currently stands does not spell out all the implications of the right of self-determination'[77]. It then went on to consider, in its Opinion Number 3, the internal borders of the Yugoslav Republic, i.e. those separating Bosnia-Herzegovina, Croatia, and Serbia, and, in fact, it did spell out some further implications of the right of self-determination. The Commission determined that while external borders were to be considered inviolable, what amounted to succession could take place within a State as long as those internal borders were 'not altered except by agreement freely arrived at'[78].

The Commission based its determination that self-determination could take place in such a manner as to allow a State to disintegrate into its component parts by basing itself on the innovative interpretation of the doctrine of *uti possidetis* which, until that point had applied *only* to external borders[79]. The Commission stated that the former internal boundaries of Yugoslavia, upon desolation would 'become frontiers protected by international law'. The Commission based this decision by taking out of context a *dictum* of the International Court of Justice's *Frontier Dispute* case, The Commission stated that:

> *Uti possidetis*, though initially applied in settling decolonization issues in America and Africa, is today recognised as a general principle, as stated by the International Court of Justice [...], 'Nevertheless the principle is not a special rule which pertains solely to one specific system of international law. It is a general principle, which is logically connected with the phenomenon of the obtaining of independence, wherever it occurs. Its obvious purpose is to prevent the independence and stability of new States being endangered by fratricidal struggles[80].

As Hurst Hannum points out, the opinion is of dubious legal value, as the Commission truncated the final sentence which goes on to read 'provoked by the challenging of frontiers following the withdrawal of the administering powers'[81].

---

[76] The first ten Advisory Opinions of the Badinter Commission are found at *International Legal Materials*, Vol. 31, 1992, pp. 1488–1526; the last five at *International Legal Materials*, Vol. 32, 1993, pp. 1586–1583.

[77] See p. 1498.

[78] See p. 1500.

[79] See Malcolm Shaw 'The Heritage of States: The Principle of *Uti Possidetis Juris* Today', *British Yearbook of International Law*, Vol. 67, 1996, pp. 75–154.

[80] Opinion Number 3, *op. cit.* n. 71, p. 1500.

[81] Hurst Hannum, 'Self–Determination, Yugoslavia, and Europe: Old Wine in New Bottles?' *Transnational Law and Contemporary Problems*, Vol. 3, 1993, p. 66. See also

In other words, the *dictum* was to be understood as applying only in the colonial context; it did not purport to give credence to any other forms of self-determination. In fact, the International Court of Justice drove that point home in the next paragraph of its Judgment:

> The fact that the new African States have respected the administrative boundaries and frontiers established by the colonial powers must be seen not as a mere practice contributing to the gradual emergence of a principle of customary international law, limited in its impact to the African continent as it had previously been to Spanish America, but as the application in Africa of a rule of general scope[82].

The willingness of the international community to use the Opinions as a legal basis to justify its policy toward the break-up of the former Yugoslavia in large part validates the Badinter Commission's reasoning[83]. Thus, it opens a new avenue of the right of self-determination, whereby (if one bases oneself on the precedent of Yugoslavia) units within a State may dissolve along internal *qua* administrative borders. In subsequent years, no sub-unit within a State has exploited this avenue of self-determination. However, in the case of the Kurds of Iraq, where a *de facto* State existed in the north, the fact that the right of self-determination was expanded can assist in ensuring some type of formal, permanent autonomy for Kurds in the Middle East. Whether this autonomy would take the form of an independent Kurdistan ceded from Iraq or an imposed decentralised Iraqi system of government allowing for a large measure of Kurdish local autonomy will come as a result of a final settlement of the 1991 Gulf War. What appears to be clear, as reflected by the actions of the Turkish Government *vis-à-vis* its Kurdish population, is that the denial of Kurdish self-determination will persist unless there is geo-political advantage in promoting such a Kurdish right. The diverging treatment of Kurds in Turkey and Iraq during the post-Cold War era demonstrates to what extent the right of self-determination is a concept of international law which is so vague as to be malleable to geopolitical demands.

Michla Pomerance, 'The Badinter Commission: The Use and Misuse of the International Court of Justice's Jurisprudence', *Michigan Journal of International Law*, Vol. 20, 1998, pp. 31–58; and Benedict Kingsbury, 'Claims by Non–State Groups in International Law', *Cornell International Law Journal*, Vol. 25, 1992, pp. 481–513 at p. 506 where he states the opinions of the Commission are 'an interesting blend of traditional and innovative international law. They are propositions that would not be generally accepted by international lawyers but clearly appealed to constitutional law judges seeking to address unusual and difficult situations'.

[82]   *Case concerning the Frontier Dispute* (Burkina Faso/Mali), Judgement, *I.C.J. Reports 1986*, 22 December 1986, para. 21.

[83]   Consider the analysis of the Badinter Commission, as well as the Pellet Report regarding the issue of Quebec in the chapter entitled 'Revisiting the Right of Self–Determination' in Richard Falk, *Human Rights Horizons: The Pursuit of Justice in a Globalizing World*, 2000, pp. 98–125.

i. Situation of the Kurds in the State of Turkey

For the Kurdish people in Turkey, the post-Cold War era has brought no improvement to their lot. In fact, it may be said that as a result of the 1991 Gulf War and the establishment of the Kurdish Autonomous Area in the north of Iraq, Turkish Kurds witnessed an increase in their suppression. This was a result of the ability of the PKK to use Northern Iraq as a launching ground for its attacks within Turkey. Human Rights Watch reported that the war entered an increasingly brutal stage only in 1992, following the Gulf War when 'the Turkish military reorganised in the southeast and launched an urban offensive against the PKK'[84]. With this new strategy, 'security forces adopted a policy of overwhelming and disproportionate response to PKK actions'[85], including 'no-go zones' much like the 'prohibited areas' utilised during the Iraqi *Anfal* Campaign and the use of village eradication and punitive destruction. While fighting the PKK insurrection, Turkish forces sought to suppress any manifestation of Kurdish nationalism. Amnesty International reported that at a 1993 Kurdish New Year celebration, twenty-two civilians were killed when police opened fire on protestors who refused to allow male police officers to search female demonstrators[86].

In 1994, the Human Rights Foundation of Turkey reported that the 'dimension of the violence' in the Kurdish areas of the southeast 'grew bigger day by day'[87]. Its 1994 report states that the most pressing issue in Turkey remains the 'Kurdish problem' which is predominantly dealt with by military means:

> Systematic and widespread torture, extra-judicial executions, murders by unknown assailants, disappearances, prosecution of person for their writings and speeches especially under Article 8 of the 'Law to Fight Terrorism', in which freedom of expression is equated with terrorism, abuses of civilian's rights—by security forces or armed groups—in the Emergency State Region [re: Kurdish region], village burning/evacuations, forced migrations, destruction of villager's belongings, defilement of food, prevention of agriculture and stock-breeding, the killing of animals and burning of forests, aerial and surface bombardment of villages and hamlets during operations continued[88].

Mining the same vein, in 1996 the European Court of Human Rights found, for the first time in its history, a State Party guilty of 'torture'. It held that Turkey was in violation of Article 3 of the European Convention; and that its police used 'Palestinian hanging' against Zeki Aksoy, a suspected PKK sympathiser who

---

[84] See Introduction to Human Rights Watch, *Weapons Transfers and Violations of the Laws of War in Turkey*, 1995.

[85] *Id.*

[86] Amnesty International, *Report 1993*, 1993, pp. 291–292.

[87] Human Rights Foundation of Turkey, *1994 Turkey Human Rights Report*, 1995, p. 35.

[88] *Id.*, p. 9.

raised it to the level of torture as opposed to simply inhuman treatment[89]. It has been estimated that by 1999 in the civil war which resulted from the insurrection of the PKK and the Turkish Government's counter-insurgency war, there have been 'more than 31,000 deaths, as many as 3000 villages destroyed, and some 3,000,000 people internally displaced'[90].

In February of 1999, the PKK leader Abdullah Öcalan was captured by Turkish authorities, kidnapped from Kenya where he had been seeking refuge, and placed on trial. On 29 June 1999, Öcalan was found guilty by Ankara National Security Court of 'carrying out acts designed to bring about the secession of part of Turkey's territory and of training and leading a gang of armed terrorists for that purpose', and was sentenced to death[91]. As a result of Öcalan's call in 1999 for a cease-fire, the PKK insurrection has ended. Amnesty International reported in 2001 that 'the armed conflict between government forces and the Kurdish Workers' Party (PKK) effectively came to an end in 1999'. Despite this, it went on to say that nevertheless, 'repression of political parties and organizations in south-eastern Turkey, continues unabated'[92].

ii. Situation of the Kurds in the State of Iraq

In contrast to the continued suppression of Kurds in Turkey, Iraqi Kurds have been able to gain a semblance of autonomy. Despite the fact that the international law of self-determination appears to be in flux, the ability of Iraqi Kurds to gain a measure of autonomy has been based primarily on geopolitics, but also at variance with international law. The willingness of the United States and the United Kingdom to maintain, during the 1990s, their illegal 'no-fly zone' over northern Iraqi has meant that a *de facto* Kurdish State has been able to mature under the umbrella of Western sponsorship[93]. Further, the willingness of Iraq Kurds to support the United States in the lead-up to its invasion of Iraq in 2003 meant that the breathing space established during the 1990s has been consolidated to their advantage.

The invasion of Kuwait by Iraq in August 1990 marked a far greater turning point for Iraqi Kurds. As a result of the US President George Bush's vision of a 'New World Order', the United States gained United Nations' approval by virtue of UN Security Council Resolution 678 of 29 November 1990 to 'use all necessary means'[94] to rid Kuwait of Iraqi forces. On 16 January 1991, an alliance led by the

---

[89]   See P. van Dijk and G.J.H. van Hoof, *Theory and Practice of the European Convention on Human Rights*, 1998, p. 310. *Aksoy* case, Judgement, 18 December 1996, *Reports of Judgements and Decisions*, 1996–VI.

[90]   Michael Gunter, 'The Continuing Kurdish Problem in Turkey after Öcalan's Capture', *Third World Quarterly*, Vol. 21, 2000, p. 849.

[91]   See *Öcalan v. Turkey*, European Court of Justice, Decision as to the Admissibility of Application no. 46221/99, 14 January, 2000.

[92]   Amnesty International, *Report 2001*, 2001, pp. 291–292.

[93]   See Michael Gunter, 'A *de facto* Kurdish State in Northern Iraq', *Third World Quarterly*, Vol. 14, 1993, pp. 295–319.

[94]   United Nations Security Council Resolution 678, 29 November 1990, S/RES/678, 1990. See Appendix 12.

United States, which included most Western States as well as Egypt, Jordan, Saudi Arabia, and Syria, 'subjected Iraq to the devastating experience of modern aerial bombardment for six weeks before ground troops became seriously engaged'[95]. The allied coalition forced Iraq out of Kuwait and, on 28 February, a cease-fire agreement was signed. An uprising in the *Shi'i* south against the weakened regime in Baghdad was followed by a rebellion in the north by the Kurds. When the Iraqi Government's elite Republican Guard ended the *Shi'i* revolt, it turned to the north and quickly recaptured Kirkuk. Aware of the methods of suppression used by the Iraqi Government, most notably at Halabja, Kurdish civilians, fearful of the coming onslaught, took flight. This mass exodus of upwards of two million people headed toward the borders of Iran and Turkey led to the establishment of a United Nations 'safe-haven'.

With Turkey moving to close its border, unwilling to allow more Kurds to arrive in its southeastern provinces, the international community was forced to respond 'to provide aid and sanctuary for the one million starving and freezing refugees' along Turkey's border[96]. The United Nations Security Council passed Resolution 688 of 5 April 1991 which condemned Iraq for its repression of 'civilian population in many parts of Iraq, including most recently in Kurdish populated areas' and insisted that Iraq 'allow immediate access by international humanitarian organizations to all those in need of assistance'[97]. Five days later the United States announced that it, France, and the United Kingdom would join to establish a 'no-fly zone' north of the thirty-sixth parallel over Iraqi airspace[98]. The no-fly zone lacked a legal foundation, as the UN Security Council had never authorised its establishment. These military actions, taken outside the framework of UN collective security system—and hence illegal under international law—were maintained from 1996 to 2003 by the United States and the United Kingdom. In December of 1996 France decided to withdraw its support for the no-fly zone citing that it 'no longer involved a humanitarian relief element'[99]. Despite its illegality, the no-fly zone provided Kurds with political breathing space. Although first conceived to provide safety to international humanitarian agencies assisting internally displaced Kurds, the no-fly zone was transformed into a protective shield allowing for an autonomous, *de facto*, Kurdish State to develop, as it did, for more than a ten years.

Under this shield, Kurds were able to develop the three northern vilayets of Ibril, Sulamaniya, and Dohuk, in a manner autonomous from Baghdad, yet they were hesitant in their call for the establishment of an independent Kurdistan. In

---

[95]   Charles Tripp. *A History of Iraq*, 2000, p. 254.
[96]   Fernando R. Teson, 'Collective Humanitarian Intervention', *Michigan Journal of International Law*, Vol. 17, p. 344.
[97]   United Nations Security Council Resolution 688, 5 April 1991, S/RES/688, 1991; para. 1. See Appendix 14.
[98]   See Timothy McIlmail, 'No–Fly Zones: The Imposition and Enforcement of Air Exclusion Regimes over Bosnia and Iraq', *Loyola of Los Angeles International and Comparative Law Journal*, Vol. 17, 1994, p. 48.
[99]   See Christopher Lockwood and Julian Nunday, 'France pulls aircraft from Iraq no–Fly zone', *The Daily Telegraph* (London), 28 December 1996, p. 19.

1992, the Kurdish Front held parliamentary elections that led to Masud Barzani and Jalal Talabani gaining an almost identical percentage of the votes and decided to split power equally in a coalition government[100]. However, this arrangement proved unworkable and civil war between Barzani's Kurdistan Democratic Party (KDP) and Talabani's Patriotic Union of Kurdistan (PUK) persisted from 1993 until the Barzani-Talabani Accord of 17 September 1998 was concluded through the mediation of the United States. In that Accord, the Kurdish parties endeavored 'to create a united, pluralistic, and democratic Iraq [...] on a federative basis that would maintain the nation's unity and territorial integrity'[101]. Yet, this agreement did not mask the fact that Iraqi Kurds had lost their chance to create a unitary Kurdish government in northern Iraq. As a result of the infighting between the KDP and the PUK, the establishment of an overall *de facto* Kurdish autonomous zone had been replaced by a 'two separate rump governments in Iraqi Kurdistan: the KDP's in Ibril, and the PUK's in Sulamaniya'[102].

The establishment of this KDP-PUK Kurdish federation within what amounts to a larger Iraqi-Kurdish federation, meant that the northern vilayets, since 1991, developed politically, culturally, and economically, at arms-length from Baghdad. This autonomy from the central government allowed Kurds to develop various items, including their own currency; teaching, publishing, and broadcasting in Kurdish; and the establishment of Kurdish police and border patrol[103]. Further, as a result of the United Nations Security Council 'oil-for-food' programme established as part of its sanctions regime against Baghdad, the three northern vilayets received billions of dollars which assisted in rebuilding the areas devastated by the *Anfal* Campaign, thus providing for the 'greatest economic boom in 20 years'[104]. Despite the clear autonomy in Ibril, Sulamaniya, and Dohuk, Kurdish leaders were unwilling to move from their *de facto* State status to a *de jure* one, fearful as they were of the reaction of neighbouring States.

This fear was well placed. As early as November 1992, Turkey, Iran, and Syria warned that any change to the *status quo* in the region would have to transpire only through consultation between the States in the region. The Syrian foreign minister noted that there 'is currently a de facto situation in the form of a Kurdish federal state. This must be prevented'[105]. Nearly ten years on, this still proved to be true as the Turkish *Daily News* reported in May 2001 that its foreign ministry was rattling sabres by emphasizing that 'no possibility is seen for the establishment of a Kurdish state in northern Iraq' while a prime minister's office circulars 'were talking about military actions against northern Iraq'[106]. As a result, Kurdish

---

[100]   Michael Gunter, *The Kurdish Predicament in Iraq: A Political Analysis*, 1999, p. 68.
[101]   *Id.*, p. 102.
[102]   *Id.*, p. 111.
[103]   See David Aquila, 'Iraqi Kurds Enjoy a *de facto* State', *Christian Science Monitor*, 5 March 2000, p. 6.
[104]   *Id.*
[105]   Quoted in Gunter, *op. cit.* n. 93, p. 312.
[106]   Saadet Ocruc, 'Ecevit Worried about the Current Situation in Northern Iraq', *Turkish Daily News*, 18 May 2001, at www.turkishdailynews.com. The Washington Kurdish Institute carried an *Agence France Press* report dated 16 May 2001 which stated that a

representatives were unwilling to moot the possibility of establishing a State in northern Iraq. Instead, they found themselves content within the current framework of continuing to solidify the transformation of northern Iraq into an autonomous Kurdish area.

The position of Iraqi Kurds fundamentally shifted with the United States-led attack and occupation of Iraq in March 2003. Though, in the lead-up to the war, their fate was precarious at best. As originally conceived, the United States was meant to attack Iraq not only from Kuwait, but by opening a northern front by way of Turkey. In exchange for allowing the United States to use its military bases, Turkey was not only to receive 31 billion dollars in aid, but its military was to be allowed to follow the United States military into Iraq and establish control over the rearguard positions[107]. This in effect would have allowed Turkey to occupy large swaths of the Kurdish areas of northern Iraq. This, however, did not transpire as a newly elected legislature established in the wake of a victorious 'Islamic democratic' party heeded the call of the vast majority of Turks and refused to allow United States troops to launch their attack from the north.

Despite the unwillingness to participate in the original invasion of Iraq, Turkey did make plain that it would not allow Iraqi Kurds to gain the means to establish a State (i.e. control over oil fields). When, on 10 April 2003, Kurdish *peshmerga* overran the city of Kirkuk and seised the nearby oil installations, Turkey declared publicly that this was a *causa belli* and that if action was not taken to reverse the situation it would take it upon itself to force the Kurds out[108]. For its part, the United States intervened almost immediately and forced the Iraqi Kurds to vacate the city, taking control over the oil fields. Beyond these minor hiccups, Kurds faired well during the original attack. In the lead-up to the bombing of Baghdad, Masud Barzani and Jalal Talabani put their differences aside as a result of US mediation and presented a united front when it became evident that the United States was, in fact, going to invade Iraq[109]. Shortly after the occupation of Iraq by the United States and its allies, both Barzani and Talabani were appointed to the twenty-five seat Iraqi Governing Council meant to provide indigenous leadership in the wake of the demise of the Hussein Administration. Having played their geopolitical cards in a sound manner, Iraqi Kurds appeared well placed to ensure that their interests would be accommodated in a future Iraq void of not only Saddam Hussein but of foreign occupation.

---

secret report by Turkish foreign ministry established that 'the scenario which is impossible for us to accept is the declaration of an independent Kurdish state in northern Iraq. Such a declaration must be regarded as a reason for intervention'.

[107] Suna Erdem, 'Last–Ditch Talks over Row with Iraqi Kurds', *The Times* (London), 17 March 2003, p. 14; and Bronwen Maddox, 'Turkish Compromise is a Recipe for More Conflict', *The Times* (London), 20 March 2003, p. 8.

[108] Suna Erdem, 'US Assures Turks that Kurds will Withdraw', *The Times* (London), 11 April 2003, p. 7.

[109] Michael Howard, 'Threat of War: Kurd Leader says Saddam will Comply Despite Loss of Face: Opposition: US Sees Forces Already in Iraq as Crucial Allies', *The Guardian* (London), 11 November 2002, p. 5.

V. Conclusion

Richard Falk, Albert G. Milbank Professor of International Law and Practice at the Princeton University wrote in an essay regarding the Kurds that 'the right of self-determination to be realised in practice does not have a definitive content or status but reflects both a contest of political wills and the play of forces'[110]. The near century-long plight of Kurds clearly demonstrates the manner in which international law has been aligned with the powers of geopolitics at the expense of repressing millions of people. While provisions were made for the establishment of an independent Kurdistan as a result of the dismemberment of the Ottoman Empire, the ability of Turkey to fight on meant that the Wilsonian conception of self-determination was to be irrelevant to the determination of the fate of Kurds. As a result of the creation of the modern Middle East, Kurds have been dispersed as minorities throughout Armenia, Azerbaijan, Iran, Iraq, Syria, and Turkey. The legacy of such a scattering has been primarily that of the suppressing of the Kurdish identity. Such measures, from the suppression of the Kurdish language in Turkey to the *Anfal* Campaign in Iraq have been taken against attempts by Kurds to manifest elements of self-determination.

The concept of self-determination, first conceived as a political aspiration, but later as a principle and legal right, has failed to provide for any semblance of autonomy for Kurds. Without the backing of Western States and the alignment of law with geopolitics, Kurds have had to face persistent and gross abuses of their human rights. While it may be that the status of the right of self-determination appears to have been expanded by the willingness of the international community to accept the reasoning of the Badinter Commission which allowed for the dismemberment of the Yugoslav Federation along its administrative borders, such a legal basis, however, as a means of asserting a Kurdish right of self-determination seems impractical when placed against the interests of States such as Turkey and Iraq to maintain their territorial integrity. Further, in both situations where Kurds have managed to gain a measured level of autonomy—during the era of the Mahabad Republic in Iran and since 1991 in Iraq—it has been as a result of foreign interventions and not the dictates of international law. It appears today that of any group of Kurds, those of northern Iraq have positioned themselves best to gain some type of autonomy. If this transpires, it will have been as a result of the alignment of international law with geopolitics and not the other way around. The establishment of a *de facto* State in northern Iraq has been, after all, a reality because of the willingness of the United States and the United Kingdom to impose it. Though it remains to be seen, the manner in which this *de facto* State will be transformed into an autonomous region of Iraq, as a result of the removal, in 2003, of the Hussein Administration, it will clearly indicate the extent to which Iraqi Kurds are able to gain a measure of self-determination within a State-centric international system.

---

[110] Richard Falk, 'Problems and Prospects for the Kurdish Struggle for Self–Determination after the End of the Gulf and Cold Wars', *Michigan Journal of International Law*, Vol. 15, 1994, p. 595.

The denial of self-determination to Kurds, who today constitute around thirty million people, if not more, demonstrates that positive international law has a blind spot with respect to providing a semblance of justice to a large swath of people living in the Middle East. The failure of positive international law to accommodate Kurdish self-determination has meant that the fate of the Kurds has been one of continuous State repression, manifesting itself in systematic and gross violations of human rights. As a result, questions of legitimacy must be raised when one considers international law from the perspective of the Middle East. If a system of international law fails to find room for the aspirations of the third-largest ethnic group in the region and, as a result, subjects those people to perpetual repression and attempts at cultural obliteration, it should not come as a surprise that the people in the region do not consider the regime of international law as a fully-encompassing, benign, and neutral order. Yet, to a large extent, the lack of legitimacy of international law in the Middle East does not emerge as a result of the failure of positive international law to accommodate the needs of the region. As the following chapters indicate, the issue is not so much the system of international law but the qualitatively different manner in which the law on the books is interpreted and applied in the Middle East. Attention now turns to the precarious nature of the evolution of the legal regime that has governed the Suez Canal. By demonstrating the British imperialist attitude toward 'its' Canal, the following chapter draws out the exceptionalism which has seen international law applied in a qualitatively different manner in the Middle East.

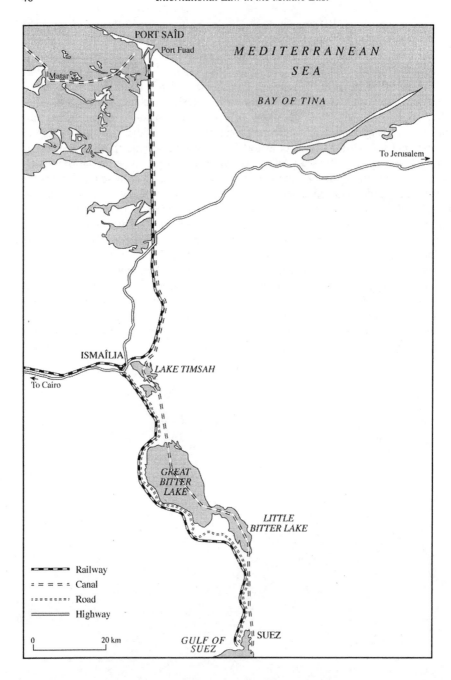

The Suez Canal Region

Chapter 2

Imperial Attitude toward the Suez Canal

The precarious nature of the legal regime that has governed the Suez Canal during most of its existence has been as a result of an imperial attitude emanating from Europe. Although the regime governing the Suez Canal, manifest in the 1888 Constantinople Convention, appears to be on a solid legal footing today, this has not always been the case, as France and Great Britain vied for control of this waterway which separates the Mediterranean from the Red Sea. The building of the Suez Canal, though originally mooted by Napoleon was the life work of Ferdinand de Lesseps, who saw his goal accomplished in 1869. The process of building the Canal, however, bankrupted Egypt which was thereafter placed under an Anglo-French condominium, which would last until Britain sought to occupy Egypt in 1882. Having effectively suppressed an Egyptian rebellion by 1888, the British would go on to occupy the north-eastern African State until 1956. With the British occupation of Egypt came a call by the Maritime Powers of the day to ensure that the Suez Canal would remain open to commercial and military shipping despite the privileged position of Great Britain.

The 1888 Constantinople Convention was meant to achieve that aim, though it would take some time, as the treaty failed to come into force due to a British reservation that made the Convention technically inoperative until the limitation was lifted in the wake of the Anglo-French 1904 *Entente Cordiale*. Though the Canal was meant to be 'always free and open, in time of war as in time of peace', in fact, Great Britain was to open the Canal to the imperial adventure of Italy in Abyssinia despite the actions of Mussolini having been considered by the Council of the League of Nations as aggression, while closing the waterway to its enemies during the two World Wars. In the aftermath of the Second World War, Britain was forced to leave Egypt in a piecemeal manner as a growing Egyptian nationalist movement and the break-up of the British Empire called for a reassessment of its presence in Egypt. With the nationalization of the Suez Canal Company in 1956, the Empire's last gasp of breath was heard with 'the catastrophe of the Suez débâcle'. When Britain and France colluded with Israel to attack Egypt, its failure marked a changing of the guard in the Middle East. No longer would Britain hold sway in the region, the mantle having effectively been passed to the United States of America, which would thereafter impose its geopolitical framework on the region. In effect, it was not until the United States brokered peace between Israel and Egypt in 1979, that the regime governing the Suez Canal settled on sound legal footing.

The precarious nature of the legal regime that has governed the Suez Canal is reflective of the qualitatively different manner in which international law has been applied in the Middle East. Despite having established an international convention regulating the Canal, Britain sought and was able to modify the provisions of the Constantinople Convention so as to conform to its imperialist interests and as against its obligations under international law. Its final act regarding the Canal was to mastermind a tripartite aggression, which sought not only to re-establish control over the Suez Canal, but also to eliminate Egyptian President Nasser. This final salvo by Great Britain marked a fitting end to the regime which had governed the Suez Canal since its inception—a regime governed by imperial interests at the expense of international law. Though it would take another twenty years for the Canal to settle on a solid legal base, the legacy of the regime of the Suez Canal is one which adds credence to the assertion that international law in the Middle East is applied in a qualitatively different manner, weighing in more on the side of power than of justice.

I. The Establishment of the Suez Canal

A canal linking the Mediterranean to the Red Sea through the Isthmus of Suez has, since time immemorial, been a scheme which set statesmen dreaming. Although a canal was built linking the Gulf of Suez to the River Nile during the time of the Pharaoh Ptolemy II (285–246 B.C.), it fell into disuse. It was later restored by the invading Romans, in 98 A.D., but shortly thereafter, lapsed into neglect; only to once again be reopened for a limited period by Caliph Omar in 641. This canal, however, was meant primarily for regional use, to the benefit of the rulers of Egypt and was used sparingly as a transit point between the seas. The potential of a waterway through the Isthmus of Suez lay dormant for more than a thousand years, in part, because of limitations to maritime transport that meant that commerce and travel remained perilous over long distances. However, with advances in maritime technology from the twelfth century onward, which allowed for the Republics of Genoa, Pisa, and Venice to prosper, the viability of a maritime route to the East was mooted. Yet, the animosity and mistrust between Europe and the Islamic world resulting from the expansion of Islam into Europe and the Christian 'Crusades' to the Holy places stunted the practicality of any such venture.

With the opening of the sea route to the East via the Cape of Good Hope by Vasco da Gama in the late fifteenth century, the need to pierce the Isthmus no longer reigned paramount for the European mercantile class. Instead of commerce, it was political machinations that saw Napoleon's Army of the East conquering Egypt and, as a by-product, consider the building of a Canal to give France geopolitical advantage over Great Britain. If France could build a canal, it would mean that troops, leaving its Mediterranean ports, could be ushered through Suez to India and other Far East British colonies in advance of a British reaction. Yet this French venture was not to be, as Napoleon's engineers who surveyed the

Isthmus erroneously found the Red Sea to be some ten meters above the level of the Mediterranean[1]. With the viability of establishing a direct link between the two seas placed into question, consideration of digging a canal would not emerge again until it was proposed fifty years later by Ferdinand de Lesseps. Lesseps, acting as the French Vice-Consul in Alexandria in the 1830s, had befriended a young Mohammed Said who, although fifth in line to become the hereditary leader of Egypt, would, by 1854, at age thirty-two, inherit the mantel of the Viceroy of Egypt and agree to Lesseps' enterprise.

Ferdinand de Lesseps' zealousness in seeking to establish the Suez Canal was the primary factor in its establishment in 1869[2]. Had it not been for his ability to threaten, prod, and play Cairo, Constantinople, London, and Paris off against one another, ultimately providing the interested States with a *fait accompli*, the Canal might well have never been built. In so many ways Lesseps was the perfect man for the job: his skills as a diplomat, as a propagandist, as a financier; his perseverance against great odds; and his vision of the project allowed him to move ahead where others would have retreated or simply given up. Above all else, however, Lesseps was a product of an imperialist attitude that sought to promote the interests of Europe at the expense of Egypt. Nearly bankrupting Egypt along the way, Lesseps had no cares about using forced labour or turning to France to ensure that disputes regarding money, land, or labour were settled in his favour.

Mohammed Said made the building of the Canal possible by the granting of concessions personally to Lesseps in 1854 and 1856; of which the former provided, by virtue of Article 1, that:

> Mr. Ferdinand de Lesseps shall establish a company, the management of which we shall entrust to him, to be known as the *Compagnie Universelle du Canal Maritime de Suez*, to cut through the Isthmus of Suez, to operate a passage suitable for large vessels, to establish or adapt two adequate entrances, one on the Mediterranean, the other on the Red Sea, and to establish one or two ports[3].

This first Concession, to last ninety-nine years from the date of opening of the Canal, established the Suez Canal Company whose managers were to be appointed by the Egyptian Government and whose work was to be carried out at its own expense. The Company was granted 'all the necessary land not belonging to private individuals' without charge and could, with the granting of permission to build a sweet-water feeder canal from the Nile, use those lands as it sought fit for a period of ten years, tax-free. In exchange, the Company would receive fifteen percent of

[1] John Marlowe, *The Making of the Suez Canal*, 1964, p. 35.

[2] For works related to Ferdinand de Lessep see: Charles Beatty, *Ferdinand de Lessep*, 1956; Ferdinand de Lessep, *Lettres, Journal et Documents pour servir à l'histoire du canal de Suez*, 5 Volumes, 1875–81; and Marlowe, *op. cit.* n. 1, Chapter 3.

[3] 'Act of Concession of the Viceroy of Egypt for the Construction and Operation of the Suez Maritime Canal and Appurtenances Between the Mediterranean and the Red Sea', 20 November 1854, United States Department of State, *The Suez Canal Problem: A Documentary Publication*, 1956, p. 1. See also Boutros Boutros-Ghali and Youssef Chlala, *Le Canal de Suez: 1854–1957*, 1958, p. 1.

the net profits from the enterprise. Yet, to this Concession was attached a proviso —that it 'must be ratified by His Imperial Majesty the Sultan' of the Ottoman Empire before 'work relating to the digging of the Suez Canal' could commence. In the second Concession, that of 1856, it was deemed 'desirable to stipulate in advance, in a more detailed and more complete act, on the one hand, the responsibilities, obligations and charges to which [the Suez Canal Company] will be subject and, on the other hand, the concessions, immunities, and advantages to which it shall be entitled'[4]. The Company was charged with building the Canal within a six-year period from the time the Sublime Porte (the government of the Ottoman Empire) gave its consent to build a canal, barring *force majeure*. The Company was incorporated as an Egyptian company and Lesseps was made its president for the first ten-year period after the Canal came into use. In exchange the Company was exempt from 'all customs, entry and other duties' of material of any kind needed in the construction and operation of the Canal. Further, as a means of recuperating its losses, the government allowed the Company to 'establish and collect, for passage in the canals and the ports belonging thereto, navigation, pilotage, towage, and anchorage fees'.

On the basis of the ratification by the Sublime Porte of the Concession of 1856, which attached certain conditions, a Convention was signed in 1866 between the new viceroy of Egypt, Mohammed Ismail, and the Universal Suez Maritime Canal Company. The Convention, which took into account the award delivered by the Empire of France in 1864 arbitration, abrogated a number of concessions which had previously been granted in exchange for payment of nearly a hundred million French Francs by the Egyptian Government to the Company. The Canal Zone was placed under the jurisdiction of Egyptian police and the Company was to be 'governed by the laws and customs of the country'. By the time the Convention was signed it was clear that a canal would become operational. Lesseps had made sure of this as, from 1854 onward, as preliminary work on the canal, he actually started to make facts on the ground, using up to 25,000 forced labourers to build the ports and dig large segments of the canal. On 17 November 1869, led by the ship of the French Empress Eugénie, a procession of ships entered the canal at Port Said, on the Mediterranean coast, and travelled through the 'long corridor' to Lake Timsah, the midway point of the canal. Spending the night in Ismailia, the procession continued the next day through the Great Bitter Lakes to reach the Port of Suez and thus successfully found themselves moored in the Red Sea.

II. 1888 Constantinople Convention

From the 1850s onward, Egypt was on a slippery slope of indebtedness. Nominally independent from the Ottoman Empire, both khedives (or hereditary leaders of Egypt), Said and Ismail, were extravagant in their spending and, with the

---

[4]   'Act of Concession of the Viceroy of Egypt, and Terms and Conditions for the Construction and Operation of the Suez Maritime Canal and Appurtenances', 5 January 1856. See United States Department of State, *id.*, p. 4.

willingness of European States to curry favour by providing loans, it meant that Egypt was doomed to financial crisis. In 1875, the Egyptian Government sold what amounted to nearly half the Suez Canal Company shares to the United Kingdom for a hundred million French Francs. With this transaction, the Canal, conceived by a Frenchman and built primarily with French diplomatic support and capital, became of vital British interest. The selling of the shares, however, did little to settle the looming financial crisis, as, in April 1876, Egypt defaulted on loans and was thus technically bankrupt[5]. As a result, Egypt, although a part of the Ottoman Empire, was placed under an Anglo-French condominium whereby its finances were controlled by the European powers in the interest of their bond-holding citizens. The European Powers compelled Constantinople to depose the uncooperative Ismail in 1879 in favour of his son Tewfiq. A resulting uprising by the Egyptian army led to the destabilization of the new khedive, the targeting of Europeans and their interests, and placed in question, for the European States, the security of the Canal. When in June 1882 anti-foreign riots broke out in Alexandria, foreigners scrambled to make their way to safety either in the Canal Zone or to the British and French warships lying off the Mediterranean city. In July, when the British notified the French that they would be opening fire on gun batteries near Alexandria, the French 'weighed anchor and sailed from Alexandria' effectively ending the condominium and paving the way for a solely British occupation of Egypt[6].

Although the Suez Canal zone had been declared neutral in the 1856 Concession[7], this bilateral agreement between Egypt and the Ottoman Empire meant little to Britain, which used the Canal as the basis of its attack against the nationalist Ahmed Arabi, who was in effective control of Egypt at the time. The defeat of the Egyptian forces at Tel el-Kebir in 1888 would ultimately result in British occupation of Egypt for more than sixty-five years. For their part, the European Powers, led by France, sought assurances from Great Britain that its occupation would not affect their ability to utilise the Canal for either commercial or military transit. In 1883, Britain suggested a number of basic principles that should be incorporated into an international agreement that would 'put upon a clearer footing the position of the Canal for the future, and provide against possible dangers'[8]. In 1885, a Commission of the European Powers was established to draft a Convention that was eventually signed by the representatives of Austria, France, Germany, Great Britain, Italy, The Netherlands, Russia, Spain, and Turkey, in Constantinople, on 29 October 1888. Although ratifications were deposited later that year, they were not exchanged as Great Britain attached to its instrument, a

[5] Marlowe, *op. cit.* n. 1, p. 312.
[6] *Id.*, p. 317.
[7] Act of Concession, *op. cit.* n. 4, Article 14.
[8] H. S. Knapp, 'The Real Status of the Panama Canal as Regards Neutralization', *American Journal of International Law*, Vol. 4, 1910, p. 343.

reservation which sought to suspend the provisions of the Convention that were not compatible with its occupation—which it termed 'transitory and exceptional'[9].

More than anything, the 1888 Convention Respecting the Free Navigation of the Suez Maritime Canal infringed 'on Egyptian rights to control transit through its own territory and territorial waters'[10]. Whereas international law governs natural straits, canals, which are constructed through a State's territory, should clearly fall under its sovereign prerogative. The Egyptian jurist Moustapha El-Hefnaoui has written that because a canal 'constitutes an integral part of the territory of a State which has established it [... this] State has not renounced nor can it renounce its propriety over this part of its territory'[11]. However, the fact that Britain was occupying Egypt at the time and that it undertook to internationalise its interests by imposing a Convention on the Isthmus meant that its status was to be different. Because of its strategic and economic importance, the fact that the Suez Canal was built by foreign capital, and traversed a weak State, meant that the status of its 'internationalization' could be imposed with little resistance[12]. The limitation exacted on Egyptian sovereign ability to act has been described as such: 'It forbade Egypt to fortify the Canal, to fight in its own waters, to exercise the right of blockade or to prohibit the passage of foreign warships through the Canal'[13].

What the Constantinople Convention provided for, was to establish 'a definite system destined to guarantee at all items, and to all the Powers, the free use of the Suez Maritime Canal, and thus to complete the system under which navigation of this Canal has been placed' by virtue of the 1866 Convention[14]. The Constantinople Convention stipulates, at Article 1, that:

> The Suez Maritime Canal shall always be free and open, in time of war as in time of peace, to every vessel of commerce or of war, without distinction of flag. Consequently, the High Contracting Parties agree not in any way to interfere with the free use of the Canal, in time of war as in time of peace. The Canal shall never be subjected to the exercise of the right of blockade.

The Convention seeks to ensure that the Canal remains open to 'innocent passage' in times of war, even to belligerents, while limiting their ability to take on supplies, to embark or disembark troops, and to stay in the Canal zone for more than twenty-four hours. Egyptian agents were mandated with ensuring respect for, and execution of, the Convention. However, Egypt, like the Ottoman Empire, did not

---

[9]   *Id.*, p. 344; see also George W. Davis, 'Fortification of Panama', *American Journal of International Law*, Vol. 3, 1909, p. 897.

[10]   D. A. Farnie, *East and West of Suez: The Suez Canal in History, 1854–1956*, 1969, p. 339.

[11]   Moustapha El-Hefnaoui, *Les problèmes contemporains posés par le canal de Suez*, 1951, p. 144.

[12]   Mohamed Olwan, 'International Canals', M. Bedjaoui (ed.), *International Law: Achievements and Prospects*, 1991, pp. 999–1000.

[13]   Farnie, *op. cit.* n. 10, p. 339.

[14]   Preamble of the Convention Respecting the Free Navigation of the Suez Maritime Canal, Constantinople, 29 October 1888. See Appendix 1.

have to apply provisions regarding belligerents where they 'might find it necessary to take [action] to assure by their own forces the defense of Egypt and the maintenance of public order'[15]. Yet this provision was also limited, as Article 11 noted that the exclusion of warships was 'not to interfere with the free use of the Canal'.

i. The British Reservation

Under the traditional regime of reservations to treaties, all States had to be in agreement with the reservation of Great Britain to the Constantinople Convention[16]. The British reservation reads in full:

> The delegates of Great Britain, in offering this text as the definite rule to secure the free use of the Suez Canal believe it is their duty to announce a general reservation as to the applicability of its provisions in so far as they are incompatible with the transitory and exceptional state in which Egypt is actually found and so far as they might fetter the liberty of action of the government during the occupation of Egypt by the British forces[17].

Though France accepted the reservation, it noted that, by virtue of the principle of reciprocity, all Powers could invoke the British limitation. In effect, France made it plain that the Convention was 'reduced to an academic declaration' which remained 'technically inoperative'[18]. It was not until the 1904 *Entente Cordiale* between France and Great Britain that the reservation was lifted and the Convention came into force. However, this was at a cost of bringing the regime of the Suez Canal in line with Britain's occupation of Egypt. Article 6 of the *Entente Cordiale*—which sought to settle British claims in Egypt in exchange for French claims in Morocco—reads as follows:

> In order to ensure the free passage of the Suez Canal, His Britannic Majesty's Government declare that they adhere to the treaty of the 29th October, 1888, and that they agree to their being put in force. The free passage of the Canal being thus

---

[15] *Id.*, Article 10. For the obligations of Egypt during times of war see Josph Obieta, *The International Status of the Suez Canal*, 1960, pp. 87–89.

[16] The traditional regime of reservation was based on the integrity of the treaty which allowed for reservations only if all parties agreed. This regime was effectively replaced as a result of the 1951 *Reservation to the Convention on the Prevention and Punishment of the Crime of Genocide* Advisory Opinion by the International Court of Justice which allowed for the 'Latin American' approach of a constellation of relations to emerge as between States making reservations and States bilaterally either accepting or rejecting those reservations. This decentralised regime was codified in Articles 19–23 of the 1969 Vienna Convention on the Law of Treaties.

[17] Knapp, *op. cit.* n. 8, p. 344.

[18] See Halford Hoskins, 'The Suez Canal as an International Waterway', *American Journal of International Law*, Vol. 37, 1943, pp. 373–385.

guaranteed, the execution of the last sentence of paragraph 1 as well as of paragraph 2 of Article of that treaty will remain in abeyance.

The provisions of the Constaninople Convention which were thus to 'remain in abeyance' were the elements of Article 8, regarding the summoning of Powers by the Egyptian Government when it deemed the security or free passage of the Canal to be threatened[19]. And in abeyance it would remain, as Halford Hoskins, Dean of the Fletcher School of Law and Diplomacy, was to write during the Second World War. It appears that British actions up until the 1940s were driven more by the spirit of its reservation than by the obligation of the 1888 Convention.

While Egypt declared 'on 5 August 1914 that navigation through the canal was free to all ships regardless of flag'[20] the British, at war with Turkey, had other ideas and transformed its occupation, making Egypt a British Protectorate. As Hoskins noted, the British thus occupied strategic points along the Canal, limited merchant traffic to daylight hours, and closed the Canal to enemy States; all in breach of the Convention[21]. D.A. Farnie, in his seminal study on the history of the Canal, was willing to go further, stating that 'Britain infringed almost every article of the Convention, systematically restricting the rights thereunder of neutrals and even signatory powers'[22]. At the close of hostilities, Great Britain sought to retroactively justify its actions through imposing on the vanquished, provisions of the Treaty of Versailles whereby Germany recognised the British Protectorate over Egypt and agreed that it was to take over the powers conferred to the Ottoman Empire in relation to the Constantinople Convention[23]. With the dismemberment of the Ottoman Empire, Egypt became nominally independent, yet Great Britain which

---

[19] Knapp, *op. cit.* n. 8, p. 349. Knapp cites Oppenheim as saying, ' By Article 6 of the Declaration respecting Egypt and Morocco signed at London on April 8, 1904. Great Britain and France has done away with this reservation', p. 350. Likewise, while Nicolas Politis was to acknowledge that in fact 'the freedom of the Canal continues to remain at the mercy of Great Britain' however, noted that, 'Mais on peut dire qu'en droit, le régime du canal se trouve fortifié et mis hors de doute par la cessation de tout malentendu au sujet du caractère obligatoire de la convention de Constantinople', *Id.,* p. 351. See Appendix 2.

[20] Olwan, *op. cit.* n. 12, p. 1003.

[21] As Hoskins put it, these steps 'could find legal warrant only under the reservation attached to the 1888 Convention' which of course had been renounced in 1904'. Hoskins, *op. cit.* n. 18, p. 378.

[22] Farnie, *op. cit.* n. 10, p. 549.

[23] Article 147 of the Treaty of Versailles Treaty reads:

Germany declares that she recognises the Protectorate proclaimed over Egypt by Great Britain on December 18, 1914, and that she renounces the regime of the Capitulations in Egypt.

While Article 152 states:

Germany consents, in so far as she is concerned, to the transfer to His Britannic Majesty's Government of the powers conferred on His Imperial Majesty the Sultan by the Convention signed at Constantinople on October 29, 1888, relating to the free navigation of the Suez Canal.

remained in occupation, was unwilling to surrender its prerogatives regarding the Suez Canal.

On 28 February 1922, the United Kingdom made a unilateral declaration which 'absolutely reserved to discretion of His Majesty's Government, among other matters,

a) the security of the communication of the British Government in Egypt [i.e. the Canal]; and
b) the defense of Egypt against all foreign aggression or interference'[24].

Hoskins notes that this declaration appeared to be based on 'the assumption that, since the special position occupied by the United Kingdom relative to the Canal since 1888 had existed prior to the Protectorate, it would be unaffected by the establishment of Egyptian independence'[25]. In its actions thereafter, the United Kingdom sought to maintain its privileged position regarding the Suez Canal, ensuring through declarations that, for instance, the Briand-Kellogg Pact could not be invoked by Egypt as against it, or that the 1924 Geneva Protocol for the Pacific Settlement of International Disputes would not allow the League of Nations to deal with issues regarding Suez. With every such declaration by the United Kingdom, Egypt made a point of refusing 'to recognize extraordinary British rights with regard to communications or other special interests' as part of its sovereign prerogative[26].

In the mid-1930s, the rise of fascism in Europe and the gaze of Benito Mussolini's Italy toward Abyssinia meant that the United Kingdom's self-styled prerogative over the Suez Canal came into conflict with its obligations under the Covenant of the League of Nations. Central to undertaking the 'total solution' in Ethiopia was Italy's ability to transit through the Suez Canal. Access to the Canal, however, was placed into question as the Council of the League of Nations, in 1935, invoked the League's collective security regime and 'adjudged Italy an aggressor in contravention of the terms of the Covenant and officially applied sanctions'[27]. If the Canal was to be closed to Italian forces the war in Abyssinia would effectively cease and the League system of security shown to be effective. As the United Kingdom was under an obligation, by virtue of Article 20, to abrogate 'all obligations or understandings *inter se* which are inconsistent with the terms' of the Covenant, the legal status of the 1888 Convention was placed in question[28]. Did the obligations of the League of Nations Covenant override the Constantinople Convention's obligation to ensure that a Canal 'shall always be free and open, in time of war as in time of peace'? The verdict in Hoskins' 1943 piece is a reflection of the times, 'The Council of the League, on the one hand, and the British Government, on the other, found their respective positions too delicate to

---

24 See Hoskins, *op. cit.* n. 18, p. 380.
25 *Id.*
26 *Id.*, p. 381.
27 *Id.*
28 Note specifically Articles 16 and 20, Covenant of the League of Nations.

admit of adventure in *the twilight zone of international law*'[29]! The delicate position in which the United Kingdom found itself was that its passage to India was at the mercy of Italian gunboats in the Mediterranean and the closing of the Canal would, as Mussolini made clear, constitute a *casus belli*[30].

A year after making it plain to Italy that the Canal was open to its war venture, Egyptian nationalists pressed the United Kingdom into moving to end its military occupation of Egypt by signing a Treaty of Alliance. The 1936 Alliance recognised Egyptian sovereign independence, but allowed British troops to retreat to the Canal zone where they were to be stationed for a twenty-year period, until 'the Egyptian Army is in a position to ensure [...] the security of navigation of the Canal'[31]. As European States rushed toward the Second World War, the United Kingdom and Italy signed an agreement in 1938 thereby confirming Italy's 'ill-gotten gains in East Africa' and reaffirming British commitment to free access to the Suez Canal[32]. However, this agreement meant little when Italy entered the war against the British in June 1940. Italian ships, like those of Germany before it, and Japanese ships after it, were excluded from using the Canal in breach of the 1888 Convention. While Hoskins likened the actions of the United Kingdom to those it undertook during the First World War[33], the difference came as a result of the fact that the Canal did come under attack by Axis Powers during the early 1940s. It is clear that these attacks were a result of the unwillingness of the United Kingdom to allow transit of Axis shipping through the Canal despite the obligations of the Constantinople Convention. Central to Italian attempts to break free of the Mediterranean, the Canal was the target of nearly fifty air raids during 1941 alone, and was often closed to traffic as a result of Italian aerial mining. So precarious was the Allied position in the summer of 1941, that as a contingency plan 'Churchill and Roosevelt decided, like Arabi in 1882, to destroy the Canal rather than allow it to pass under enemy control'[34]. This was not to be, however, as the victory at el-Alamein, in northwest Egypt in 1942, shifted the tide of the Second World War in favour of the Allied Forces and thus ensured British control of the Canal zone for the immediate future.

---

[29] Hoskins, *op. cit.* n. 18, p. 383. Emphasis added.

[30] Farnie, *op. cit.* n. 10, p. 598. Farine's assessment of British policy was the following, 'In the last resort England had no wish to create a binding precedent whereby the Canal might be closed to an aggressor and valued the free use of the Canal more than the continued existence of Ethiopia as an independent state'. *Id.*

[31] Article 8, Treaty of Alliance between His Majesty, in Respect of the United Kingdom, and His Majesty the King of Egypt, ratified 22 December 1936. See *American Journal of International Law*, Vol. 31, 1937 (Supplement Official Documents), pp. 77–90.

[32] Hoskins, *op. cit.* n. 18, p. 384. The agreement is the Anglo-Italian Agreement of 16 April 1938.

[33] *Id.*, p. 385.

[34] Farnie, *op. cit.* n. 10, p. 628.

III. Egyptian Nationalisation of the Suez Canal Company

In the aftermath of the Second World War, Egyptian nationalists, strengthened in their resolve by independence movements throughout the world, agitated for the end of the 1936 Treaty of Alliance with Britain. Frustration was accompanied by shock in 1948, in the crushing defeat of Arab forces in their war against the newly declared State of Israel. With the return to Egypt of a military in disgrace, having shown itself ill-trained and poorly equipped on the battlefield, the seeds of discontent were sown. When Britain rejected the unilateral abrogation of the Treaty of Alliance in 1951, Egyptians rebelled: riots broke out in the Canal cities, local Canal Company employees went on strike, boycotts of British goods and citizens were undertaken, and a full-fledged guerrilla war ensued. When British forces attacked a police station in Ismailia in January 1952 killing forty-one people, mass riots broke out targeting western interests in the capital, Cairo. The response of the Egyptian monarchy in the aftermath of this agitation was lost in its inability to form a government to the satisfaction of the country. In July 1952, the 'Free Officers' staged a bloodless *coup d'état*, bringing to an end the Ottoman dynasty established by Mohamed Ali in 1805. Colonel Gamal Abdel Nasser, who was to emerge as the leader of the Free Officers, negotiated the Suez Canal Base Agreement of 1954[35] ending the Treaty of Alliance, and mandating the evacuation of British Forces by mid-June 1956. The Agreement was meant to last for seven years, a period in which Egypt agreed, under Article 4, to maintain the Suez Canal base allowing the British to access it 'in the event of an armed attack' as against a Member of the Arab League or Turkey.

A month after the evacuation of British Forces from Egypt, Nasser declared, on the basis of a decision of his Revolutionary Council, the nationalization of the Suez Canal Company. The circumventious route by which the Egyptian leader came to make this decision was based on the inability of the Egyptian military to protect the Gaza Strip from 'retaliatory' raids by Israeli forces. As a result of the 1948 War, Egypt held the Gaza Strip as a benevolent occupying force; Israeli policy at the time was to shoot-on-sight anybody crossing the Armistice line. Such 'infiltrators' were 'by and large [Palestinian] refugees seeking to go back to their homes and fields'[36]. As a means of dealing with the unwillingness of Egyptian forces to stop such passage back into Palestine, the Israeli Defence Forces undertook, from 1955 onward, retaliatory raids against military targets which, although at their inception were small affairs, evolved to include 'battalions and even brigades'[37]. The inability to stop such Israeli incursions due to the moratorium on weapons sales instituted by France, the United Kingdom and the United States

---

[35]   For the 1954 Agreement, see Anthony Gorst and Lewis Johman, *The Suez Crisis*, 1997, pp. 32–33.
[36]   Benny Morris, *Righteous Victims: A History of the Zionist-Arab Conflict, 1881–1999*, 1999, p. 272–281, at p. 274.
[37]   *Id.*, p. 276.

of America[38], meant that Egypt looked to the Socialist Eastern Block to acquire arms. On 27 September 1955, Nasser's announcement of a large-scale weapons deal with Czechoslovakia sent shockwaves around the world. Western States saw such an initiative as the opening of a new Cold War front by the Soviet Union. When it appeared that Egypt would not return to their fold, Western States took action. On 19 July 1956, US Secretary of State, John Foster Dulles, informed Egypt that the United States was withdrawing its support for World Bank financing of the High Aswan Dam project[39].

The building of the High Aswan Dam was meant to regulate the flow of the Nile River, to expand Egypt's 'cultivated area by 30 per cent [...] and supply power for the manufacture of high-grade steel'[40]. Thus the project was seen by Egypt as being vital, not only to the country's development, but as a means of assisting in its quest for true independence from foreign interference. It is this route which led to Nasser's declaration, on 26 July 1956—the fourth anniversary of King Farouk's send-off from Alexandria—that 'we shall build the High Dam as we want it'[41]. By Presidential Decree of the same day, Nasser nationalised the Suez Canal Company; its Article 1 reads:

> The Universal Company of the Suez Maritime Canal (Egyptian joint-stock company) is hereby nationalized. All its assets, rights and obligations are transferred to the Nation and all the organizations and committees that now operate its management are hereby dissolved.
>
> Stockholders and holder of the founders shares shall be compensated for the ordinary or founders shares they own in accordance with the value of the shares shown in the closing quotations of the Paris Stock Exchange on the day preceding the effective date of the present law.
>
> The payment of said indemnity shall be effected after the Nation has taken delivery of all the assets and properties of the nationalized company[42].

With the trigger of the use of the code-word 'de Lesseps' in Nasser's speech, the Egyptian military surrounded the buildings of the Company and took over its management and administration[43]. In the ensuing days and months, Egypt was to demonstrate that it could effectively and efficiently administer the Canal, much to the chagrin of the United Kingdom, which had sent a large number of ships to the

---

[38]   The Tripartite Declaration of May 1950 was meant to ration the sale of arms to Arab States and Israel to those required solely for internal security and self–defence reasons. See Mohamed Heikal, *Cutting the Lion's Tail: Suez*, 1986, p. 52.

[39]   Gorst and Johman, *op. cit.* n. 35, p. 53.

[40]   Farnie, *op. cit.* n. 10, p. 719.

[41]   United State Department of State, 'Speech by President Nasser, Alexandria, July 26', *The Suez Canal Problem (A Documentary Publication)*, 1956, p. 28.

[42]   'Presidential Decree on the Nationalization of the Suez Canal Company, July 26', *id.*, p. 31.

[43]   For the occupation of the Company's buildings in Egypt see Heikal, *op. cit.* n. 38, pp. 127–128.

Isthmus in a failed attempt to demonstrate Egypt's ineptitude in managing the Canal[44].

The nationalization of the Suez Canal Company was well within Egypt's rights under international law. Such a right can be seen as being a corollary of sovereignty whereby a State has the ability to exercise control over its own territory. Further, it has been made clear, in cases such as the nationalization of property in Russia after the 1917 Revolution and in Mexico in the 1920s and 1930s, that the issue was not whether or not a State has the right to nationalise, but the modality of compensation[45]. In 1940, the lines were drawn; on one side, the United States put forward, *vis-à-vis* Mexico's agrarian and petroleum nationalization, that 'the right to expropriate property is coupled with and conditioned on the obligation to make adequate, effective and prompt compensation'. On the other side, Mexico responded that 'there is in international law no rule universally accepted in theory nor carried out in practice which makes obligatory the payment of immediate compensation nor even of deferred compensation'[46]. In Oppenheim's *International Law* of 1955, Lauterpacht sets out a middle ground regarding a State's capacity to pay as a determinant of compensation. In effect, this seems to have been borne out in practice, as Robert Delson points out, in a *Columbia Law Review* article, that 'in general, postwar compensation agreements provide neither for full compensation, nor for immediate payment'[47]. With regard to the nationalization of the Suez Canal Company, compensation was paid to the shareholders in a mediated settlement brokered by the World Bank in 1958[48].

---

[44]   See Farnie, *op. cit.* n. 10, pp. 719 and 743; as well as Gorst and Johman, *op. cit.* n. 35, p. 84.

[45]   See Phillipe Cahier, 'Cour général', *Collected Courses of The Hague Academy of International Law*, Vol. 195, 1985, p. 53. For a consideration of the evolution of the regime dealing with compensation due in situations of nationalization since 1956, see Georges Abi-Saab, 'Permanent Sovereignty over Natural Resources and Economic Activities', Bedjaoui (ed.), *op. cit.* n. 12, pp. 597–617.

[46]   See Robert Delson, 'Nationalization of the Suez Canal Company: Issues of Public and Private International Law', *Columbia Law Review*, Vol. 57, 1957, p. 763. Delson notes that Charles de Visscher, amongst others, was of the view that nationalization was not conditional on providing compensation, see p. 764. For other views regarding the legality of nationalization see Thomas Huang, 'Some International and Legal Aspects of the Suez Canal Question', *American Journal of International Law*, Vol. 51, 1957, pp. 277–307; and Georges Scelle, 'La nationalisation du canal de Suez et le droit international', *Annuaire français de droit international*, 1956, pp. 3–19.

[47]   *Id.*, p. 766.

[48]   See *infra.*, n. 86.

IV. Seeking a Peaceful Settlement of the Suez Dispute

While it was within Egypt's legal right to nationalise the Suez Canal Company, the United Kingdom sought, nevertheless to challenge its action. The morning after Egypt announced the nationalization of the Canal Company, the minutes of the British Cabinet meeting reflect the opposition within British Government and the options it contemplated taking in attempting to reverse the situation:

> The Cabinet next considered the legal position and the basis on which we could sustain and justify to international opinion, a refusal to accept the decision of the Egyptian Minister, Colonel Nasser, to nationalise the Canal.
>
> The Cabinet agreed that we should be on weak ground in basing our resistance on the narrow argument that Colonel Nasser had acted illegally. The Suez Canal Company was registered as an Egyptian Company under Egyptian Law; and Colonel Nasser had indicated that he intended to compensate the shareholders at ruling market prices. From a narrow legal point of view his action amounted to no more than a decision to buy out the shareholders. Our case must be presented on wider international grounds: our argument must be that the canal was an important international asset and facility and that Egypt had not the technical ability to manage it effectively; and their recent behaviour gave no confidence that they would recognise their international obligations in respect of it. [...] The Canal was the vital link between the East and the West and its importance as an international waterway, recognized in the Convention signed in 1888, had increased with the development of the oil industry and the dependence of the world on oil supplies. It was not a piece of Egyptian property but an international asset of the highest importance and its should be managed as an international trust.
>
> The Cabinet agreed that for these reasons every effort must be made to restore effective international control over the Canal. It was evident that the Egyptians would not yield to economic pressures alone. They must be subject to the maximum political pressure which could be exerted by the maritime and trading nations whose interests were most directly affected. And, in the last resort, this political pressure must be backed by the threat—and, if need by, the use—of force[49].

While the British Prime Minister Anthony Eden made United States President Dwight Eisenhower aware of his Cabinet's resolve, the President made it plain that the United States was against the use of force. Eisenhower wrote to Eden, 'I have given you my personal conviction, as well as that of my associates, as to the unwisdom even of contemplating the use of military force at this moment'[50]. Despite this, and the fact that no military campaign could be launched for a month and a half, Eden's preferred option remained military intervention. As Anthony Grost and Lewis Johman have noted, however, this left the Prime Minister with two problems, 'First, what if a diplomatic solution were achieved, and, second, what was the *casus belli* for military action to be months after the nationalization of the Canal'[51]? To these questions, we shall return shortly; first, the use of force

---

[49] 'Document 3.1, Cabinet Discussion of Initial Reactions to the Nationalisation of the Suez Canal, 27 July 1956', in Gorst and Johman, *op. cit.* n. 35, p. 58.
[50] 'Document 3.5, Eisenhower Warns Eden against Use of Force, 31 July 1956', *id.*, p. 66.
[51] Gorst and Johman, *op. cit.* n. 35, p. 64.

and its alternatives under the United Nations Charter will be considered so as to draw out the legal parameters of the actions which were to follow.

With the Allied victory in the Second World War came a fundamental change in the international system. The move from the Allied 'United Nations' coalition toward the establishment of the post-War United Nations Organization ushered in radical changes regarding war and the use of force. While the Covenant of the League of Nations did not exclude war, but simply delayed it, and the 'Briand-Kellogg Pact' sought to outlaw war as a instrument of national policy; neither succeeded in stalling the advent of the Second World War[52]. Seeking to rectify the failures of the past, the Charter of the United Nations determined that not only war but, in fact, any use of force, was no longer to be the purview of States[53]. Instead, the legitimate use force was to be internationalised, to be handed over to the United Nations Security Council which was to act on behalf of the international community. While States did not disavow their 'inherent right' of self-defence, such use of force was to be contemplated only 'until the Security Council has taken measure necessary to maintain international peace and security'[54]. Beyond acting in self-defence, States forfeited any unilateral determination to use force. Where the use of force was to be projected beyond one's border, it was to be undertaken in line with the collective security arrangements found in Chapter VII of the Charter. Within the dictates of Chapter VII, where the Security Council determined that, by virtue of Article 39, there existed a threat or a breach of the peace or an act of aggression, it is empowered to take measures including 'such action by air, sea, or land forces as my be necessary to maintain or restore international peace and security'[55].

Thus, from the perspective of international law, the United Kingdom, short of seeking a mandate from the United Nations Security Council to act on its behalf, was contemplating an illegal act of aggression against Egypt[56]. The avenues of legal recourse, which were open to the United Kingdom, were to either do nothing or seek settlement with Egypt by pacific means. As the UN Charter moved to outlaw unilateral recourse to the use of force, it also mandated that States 'shall settle their international disputes by peaceful means' and set out the modalities by which States are to do so in its Chapter VI[57]. As the United Kingdom did not have a military option in the early aftermath of the nationalization of the Canal Company, Eden advanced on the diplomatic track, not so much in an attempt to reach a settlement, but to provide enough time for his forces to prepare for an invasion. On 2 August 1956, France, with its historic interest in the Canal, the

---

[52] See Article 12, Covenant of the League of Nations; and Article 1, 1928 Pact of Paris.
[53] See Article 2(4), Charter of the United Nations.
[54] See Article 51, *id.*
[55] See Article 42, *id.*
[56] Such an act, would not only entail the responsibility of the State but would also, by the dictates of the Nuremberg Principles which had been affirmed by the United Nations General Assembly in 1946, entail individual criminal responsibility. See United Nations General Assembly Resolution 95(I) of 11 December 1946 as noted in Adam Roberts and Richard Guelff, *Documents on the Laws of War*, 2000, p. 176.
[57] See Article 2(3), Charter of the United Nations.

United Kingdom, and the United States, issued a Tripartite Statement, acknowledging:

> the right of Egypt to enjoy and exercise all powers of a fully sovereign and independent nation, including the generally recognized right, under appropriate condition, to nationalize assets, not impressed with an international interest [...]. But the present action involves more than a simple act of nationalisation. It involves the arbitrary and unilateral seizure by one nation of an international agency which has the responsibility to maintain and to operate the Suez Canal so that all the signatories, and beneficiaries of, the Treaty of 1888 can effectively enjoy the use of an international waterway upon which the economy, commerce, and security of much of the worlds depends[58].

Within that Statement, the States proposed that a conference be held in London of the States party to the Constantinople Convention and 'other nations largely concerned with the use of the Canal' with an aim to establishing 'operating arrangements under an international system designed to assure that the parties of the continuity of the operation of the Canal as guaranteed by the Convention'.

On the basis of their Statement, it is clear that these States were shifting the goal posts. The issue was not the nationalization of the Suez Canal Company *per se*, it was the need to have an international regime established to ensure the 'free and open' use of the Canal. Yet, in law there was little basis for such a demand. The only provision of an international nature found in the 1888 Convention is Article 8. This article relates to the formation of a Commission of three signatories to inform the Egyptian government of danger perceived to the Canal so that it might take actions to 'assure the protection and free use of the Canal'[59]. To extrapolate from that, an obligation to establish an international regime over the administration of the Canal stretches treaty interpretation beyond its limits[60]. Egypt refused to attend the London Conference of 16 to 23 August, seeing the Tripartite Statement as an attempt 'to invest the Suez Canal Company with a symbolic significance in order to provide an excuse for foreign interference with Egyptian sovereignty'[61]. The outcome of the London Conference was a proposal which

---

[58]   United States Department of State, 'Three-Power London Talks: Tripartite Statement, August 2', *op. cit.* n. 41, p. 35.

[59]   Article VIII, Constantinople Convention. See Appendix 1.

[60]   The position of the United Kingdom and France can be considered to be further weakened by the fact that in 1904 they had agreed that Article 8 was 'to remain in abeyance'. See n. 19.

[61]   The *Aide-Mémoire* attributed to Nasser, goes on to state:

> Although the Egyptian government is prepared to endorse its adherence to the 1888 Convention, it cannot accept the implication that freedom of navigation in the canal can only be ensured by its internationalization. The 1888 Convention remains valid whether the canal is under the control of the Egyptian government or any other management. The Suez Canal Company has never at any time been responsible for maintaining freedom of navigation in the canal, which remains the concern of the 1888 Convention. By representing the Suez Canal Company as an international authority with power to guarantee freedom of navigation, the three-power declaration represents a threat to Egyptian sovereignty and to the control by the government of Egypt over a part of its

sought to establish an international board responsible for the operations of the Canal. That plan, like the one formulated at the second London Conference of 19 to 21 September 1956 calling for the establishment of Suez Canal Users Associations, was rejected by Egypt as infringing its sovereignty[62].

Throughout this period, it was clear that both the United Kingdom and now France—which saw Egypt as the main supplier of arms to the independence movement in Algeria—were preparing for a military expedition, wherein their military objective was not only to ensure safe passage through Suez, but the removal of Nasser[63]. Yet the United States remained firm in its wish to find a peaceful resolution to the dispute. Eisenhower, in the lead-up to the second London Conference, confided in Eden that there 'are many areas of endeavours which are not yet fully explored because exploration takes time [...]. But to resort to military action when the world believes there are other means available for resolving the dispute would set in motion forces that can lead, in the years to come, to the most distressing results'[64]. With this clear difference of opinion emerging after the second London Conference, the United Kingdom and France decided to bring matters to the United Nations for face-to-face negotiations with Egypt. With the mediation of the UN Secretary-General, Dag Hammarskjöld, the following UN Security Council Resolution 118 was passed:

The Security Council,

Noting the declaration made before it and the accounts of the development of the exploratory conversations on the Suez question given by the Secretary General of the United Nations and the Foreign Ministers of Egypt, France and the United Kingdom.

---

territory. The Egyptian government considers the proposal to internationalize control over the canal as being the equivalent of introducing international colonialism.

Heikal, *op. cit.* n. 38, p. 145.

[62] The Suez Canal Users Associations was a proposal put forward by the American Secretary of State Dulles, who sought to establish a regime whereby Egypt would not benefit financially from the canal, as it would fall to the user to provide pilots, and collect fees, and thus leave it simply to Egypt to ensure that the Canal remained open and free. See 'Document 3.14, Dulles and the Genesis of SCUA, 5 September 1956', Gorst and Johman, *op. cit.* n. 35, p. 77.

[63] Gorst and Johman write that the French were 'adamant about the necessity to bring down Nasser by force as soon as possible. This was entirely consistent with French Policy throughout the crisis', *op. cit.* n. 35, p. 85; see also Lloyd Free (ed.), *French Motivations in the Suez Crisis*, 1956; and Paul Gaujac, France and the Crisis of Suez: An Appraisal, Forty Years On', David Tal (ed.), *The 1956 War: Collusion and Rivalry in the Middle East*, 2001, pp. 47–63. For the British, minutes of its Cabinet meeting revealed that it, 'recognised that our objectives would not be fully attained if we accepted a settlement of the Suez Canal dispute which left Colonel Nasser's influence undiminished throughout the Middle East'. 'Document 3.21, Eden Reaffirms Necessity of Removing Nasser, 3 October 1956', see Gorst and Johman, *id.*, p. 86.

[64] 'Document 3.16, Eisenhower Informs Eden of the Need for a Peaceful Resolution, 8 September 1956', *id.*, p. 80.

Agree that any settlement of the Suez question should meet the following requirements:

1) There should be free and open transit through the Canal without discrimination, overt or covert—this covers both political and technical aspects;
2) The sovereignty of Egypt should be respected;
3) The operation of the Canal should be isolated from the politics of any country;
4) The manner of fixing tolls and charges should be decided by agreement between Egypt and the users;
5) A fair proportion of the dues should be allotted to development;
6) In case of disputes, unresolved affairs between the Suez Canal Company and the Egyptian Government should be settled by arbitration with suitable terms of reference and suitable provisions for the payment of sums found to be due[65].

These Six Principles, set down on 13 October 1956, would ultimately prove to be the basis of the settlement regarding the Suez dispute; however, in the interim, Egypt was to fall victim to a tripartite aggression led by France and the United Kingdom in collusion with Israel.

V. The Tripartite Aggression against Egypt

The day following the setting down of the Six Principles, British Prime Minister Antony Eden and his Minister of State at the Foreign Office, Anthony Nutting, lunched with the acting French Foreign Minister, Albert Gazier, and General Maurice Challe. The *casus belli* which Eden had sought was placed on his plate: What if, Challe posited, Israel was to attack Egypt across the Sinai. Would not France and the United Kingdom be justified in a military intervention to separate the forces and protect the Canal[66]? From this thunderbolt suggestion onward, the diplomatic track was sidelined by the European States in favour of a planned invasion of Egypt. Discussions between high-ranking members of the Britsh, French, and Israeli (including its Prime Minister David Ben-Gurion) governments led to the signing of the Sèvres Protocol of 24 October 1956. Although Eden attempted to cover up the collusion by seeking to destroy copies of the Protocol, a copy did survive which stated that Israel was required to launch an attack on 29 October 'with the aim of reaching the Canal zone'[67], to which the British and the French would 'respectively and simultaneously make appeals' for both parties to end their military activities and withdraw their troops 'ten miles from the Canal'[68].

---

[65] United Nations Security Council Resolution 118, 3 October 1956, S/RES/118, 1956.
[66] Gorst and Johman, *op. cit.* n. 35, p. 90.
[67] For the Sèvres Protocol, see Keith Kyle, *Suez: Britain's End of Empire in the Middle East*, 2003, pp. 587–589. See Appendix 3.
[68] *Id.*, pp. 93–103. The Israeli author Mordechai Bar-On, who acted as the private secretary of the Israel Defence Minister, Moshe Dayan, during this period, notes that from the Israel perspective their had been no collusion, 'Most wartime alliances involve secret agreements, disinformation, and even deception of a common enemy. Not in every case are such plots and stratagems deemed to be 'collusion'—certainly not when the deception is aim against a common enemy as part of the war effort itself, with the ultimate goal a defeating

Further, the European States were to demand that Egypt allow Anglo-French forces to occupy key areas along the Canal to ensure freedom of navigation. If, within twelve hours, either State refused the ultimatum, the European forces would attack. For its efforts, Israel would be allowed to occupy strategic positions at the mouth of the Gulf of Aqaba, the gateway to the Israeli port of Eilat[69]. Further, during the period of intervention, the United Kingdom was to unilaterally suspend the Anglo-Jordanian mutual assistance Treaty of 1948 without the consent or knowledge of the Hashemite Kingdom. As Avi Shlaim of Oxford University writes, 'In effect, it meant that Britain and Israel were guilty of collusion against Jordan as well as against Egypt'[70].

Renewed talks between Egypt, France, and the United Kingdom on the basis of the Six Principles were meant to start at the United Nations in Geneva, on 29 October 1956, however, events on the ground quickly overtook them. At this point, as Robert Bowie was to write in a piece commissioned by the American Society of International Law, the 'efforts for a peaceful solution, whether serious or a pretence, were at an end'[71]. With the Gaza Raid of 1955, in which Israel had undertaken a retaliatory strike that had left fifty-eight dead, the tension between the neighbours had been in a heightened state. In response to the Raid, Egypt's President Nasser unleashed the *fedayeen*—irregular guerrillas—across the Armistice lines in a clear escalation of cross-border fighting despite the cease-fire agreement. The breakdown of the Armistice agreement, the *de facto* blockade of the Suez Canal and the Strait of Tiran to ships heading to Israeli ports, and the Egypt-Czech arms deal all played a part in Israel's willingness to assist the European States, by initiating the war against Egypt[72]. On the afternoon of 29

---

that enemy'. Bar-On then goes on to say 'Egypt had given Israel no end of *casus belli* over the past years, insisting as it did on maintaining a state of belligerency despite the Armistice Agreement'. Mordechai Bar-On, *The Gates of Gaza: Israel's Road to Suez and Back, 1955–1957*, 1994, p. 246.

[69] Beyond the wish to ensure that the Gulf of Aqaba would be secure for Israeli shipping, Leo Gross notes that the Egyptian closure of the Canal to Israeli shipping, 'played a significant rôle' in the 'military action of Israel' of 29 October 1956. See Leo Gross, 'Passage Through the Suez Canal of Israel-Bound Cargo and Israel Ships', *American Journal of International Law*, Vol. 51, 1957, pp. 530–568. It should be mentioned that Egypt was in violation of Security Council Resolution 95 which '*Calls upon* Egypt to terminate the restrictions on the passage of international commercial shipping and goods through the Suez Canal wherever bound and to cease all interference ...'. Note: The Council had made clear in the paragraph preceding this statement that it was speaking about 'restriction on the passage of goods through the Suez Canal to Israeli ports'. See United Nations Security Council Resolution 95, 1 September 1951, S/2322, 1951.

[70] Avi Shlaim, 'The Protocol of Sèvres, 1956: Anatomy of a War Plot', David Tal (ed.), *op. cit.* n. 63, pp. 135–136.

[71] Robert Bowie, *International Crises and the Role of Law: Suez 1956*, p. 1974, p. 52.

[72] Bar-On, *op. cit.* n. 68, pp. 315–316. As to the exclusion of Israeli shipping through the Suez Canal by Egypt, Quincy Wright points out, that until 1954, 'British troops were in occupation of the Canal area and the Canal was operated by the Universal Suez Canal Company. It therefore appears that the British Government and the Company acquiesced in the Egyptian policy of discrimination, although it was apparently in violation of the

October 1956, Israeli forces crossed into the Sinai; their deepest incursion being a paratrooper drop at the Mitla Pass fifty kilometres (twenty-five miles) from the southern Canal city of Suez. The next day the United States called an emergency meeting of the UN Security Council in which it sought to have Israel end its attack and retreat back behind the Armistice lines. 'While this resolution was under debate the Security Council was informed that France and the United Kingdom had sent a twelve-hour ultimatum to Egypt and Israel demanding that they stop all warlike actions, withdraw forces ten miles from the Suez Canal, and accept Anglo-French occupation of key positions at Port Said, Ismailia, and Suez'[73].

Despite the ultimatum, the following United States-sponsored draft resolution was put to the Security Council on 30 October, but was vetoed by both France and the United Kingdom (having both used their Security Council veto prerogative for the first time):

The Security Council,

Noting that the armed forces of Israel have penetrated deeply into Egyptian territory in violation of the armistice agreement between Egypt and Israel;

Expressing its grave concern at this violation of the armistice agreement;

1.   Calls upon Israel and Egypt immediately to cease fire;

2.   Calls upon Israel immediately to withdraw its armed forces behind the established armistice lines;

3.   Call upon all members

   a)   to refrain from the use of force or threat of force in the area in any manner inconsistent with the Purposes of the United Nations;
   b)   to assist the United Nations in ensuring the integrity of the armistice agreements;
   c)   to refrain from giving military, economic or financial assistance to Israel so long as it has not complied with the resolution;
4.   Requests the Secretary-General to keep the Security Council informed of compliance with this resolution and to make whatever recommendation he deems appropriate for the maintenance of international peace and security in the area by the implementation of this and prior resolutions[74].

Convention of 1888 and in defiance of the Security Council's resolution'. Quincy Wright, 'Intervention, 1956', *American Journal of International Law*, Vol. 51, 1957, p. 272. For more on the issues of the closing of Egyptian waters see the three articles in the section entitled 'Freedom of Navigation Through the Strait of Tiran, the Gulf of Aqaba, and the Suez Canal', in John Norton Moore (ed.), *The Arab-Israeli Conflict: Readings and Documents*, 1977, pp. 185–220.

[73]   Wright, *id.*, pp. 257–258.

[74]   'Document 3.35, United States Resolution in the Security Council (UN Doc. S/3710) on Middle East Aggression, 30 October 1956', Gorst and Johman, *op. cit.* n. 35, p. 106.

As the European States' ultimatum did not affect Israel's position in the Sinai—its troops were not within twenty-two kilometres (ten miles) of the Canal—the ultimatum was meant to make a *fait accompli* of Israel's occupation of the Sinai. Not surprisingly, Egypt rejected the ultimatum, and, on 31 October, joint Anglo-French forces began bombing Egyptian airbases, followed thereafter by paratrooper and land forces invading Port Said. Thus, despite the provisions of the Constantinople Convention, the Suez Canal Zone became the locus of a direct military attack by the Europe States. With this tripartite aggression against Egypt in full swing, the United States sought a solution through the United Nations. Blocked as it was in the Security Council, the American delegation turned to the General Assembly[75].

While the UN Security Council is vested with 'primary responsibility for the maintenance of international peace and security', that responsibility is not exclusive[76]. The Secretary-General, for instance, has the option to 'bring to the attention of the Security Council any matter which in his opinion may threaten the maintenance of international peace and security'[77]. Likewise, the General Assembly has power 'to discuss any questions relating to maintenance of international peace and security' and 'to make recommendations', but only in situations where the Security Council is not exercising its primary responsibility[78]. When the General Assembly invoked, on 2 November 1956, the 'Uniting for Peace' Resolution of 1950, it was asserting its power to make recommendations where there was a 'failure of the Security Council to discharge its responsibility' due to the veto power of its permanent members[79]. UN General Assembly Resolution 997, which was introduced by the United States of America, urged 'all parties now involved in hostilities in the area to agree to an immediate cease-fire', that Egypt and Israel 'withdraw all forces behind the armistice lines [...] and to observe scrupulously the provisions of the armistice agreements'[80]. The Resolution recommended that UN Members refrain from supplying arms to the parties and urged that after the cease-fire,' effective steps be taken to re-open the Suez Canal',

---

[75] Paraphrasing Eisenhower and Dulles comments on 31 October and 1 November, Bowie writes 'More should be done soon to deal with the many injustices in the Middle East situation. But to accept that whenever a nation felt itself subject to injustice it had a right to resort to force would destroy the U.N. and create anarchy. Great efforts had been made to resolve the Suez Canal dispute by peaceful means , and the October negotiations opened the prospect that a just and acceptable solution could be found soon. Certainly, peaceful processes had not been exhausted. The armed attack by the three members was a grave error, contrary to the U.N. principles and purposes'. Bowie, *op. cit.* n. 71, p. 70.
[76] See Article 24, Charter of the United Nations.
[77] See Article 99, *id.*
[78] See Articles 11 and 12, *id..*
[79] See United Nations General Assembly Resolution 377(v), 3 November 1950. For discussion of the legality of the Uniting for Peace Resolution see Bruno Simma (ed.), *The Charter of the United Nations: A Commentary*, 1995, pp. 234–236.
[80] 'Document 4.2, General Assembly Resolution 997(ES-1), Adopted 2 November 1956', Gorst and Johman, *op. cit.* n. 35, p. 115.

which had been closed to traffic by the scuttling of ships and destruction of bridges by Egyptian forces.

Resolution 997 also requested that Hammarskjöld report back to the General Assembly and the Security Council with a plan for further action which they might 'deem appropriate in accordance with the Charter'. Taking the led on an initiative proposed by the Canadian Minister of Foreign Affairs, Lester Pearson, the General Assembly, on 4 November, requested the Secretary-General submit 'within 48 hours, a plan for the setting up, with the consent of the nations concerned, of an emergency international UN Force to secure and supervise the cessation of hostilities in accordance with all the terms of the aforementioned (November 2) resolution'[81]. By virtue of its Resolution 1000 of 5 November 1956, the General Assembly gave the green light to the formation of the first ever UN Peacekeeping forces: United Nations Emergency Force (UNEF). UNEF was to be the prototype of subsequent peacekeeping efforts, as it excluded the personnel of the permanent members of the Security Council; it was mandated to secure the cease-fire as outlined in Resolution 997, thus acting to ensure the peace and not as an occupying force; and it acted on the basis of consent of the parties[82]. With international pressure mounting against the aggressors, the United Kingdom was first to capitulate. Its economy pushed into financial crisis by oil shortages brought on by the hostilities and the unwillingness of the United States to step in to shore up the Pound, the British Cabinet agreed, on 6 November 1956, to a cease-fire. With the French following suit, the tripartite aggression dissipated on 6 November, having failed in its military objectives (securing less than a quarter of the Canal) and its political objectives (President Nasser remained—and would prosper—in power).

VI. The Aftermath of the Tripartite Aggression

With all parties accepting the cease-fire as outlined in Resolution 997, which came into effect on 7 November, the United Nations moved to institute it by forming UNEF and establishing an international consortium to assist, under its auspices, the clearing of the Suez Canal. While the British were involved in salvage operations at Port Said, the move to play any part in clearing the whole Canal was thwarted by the General Assembly: crews employed by the United Nations in their stead cleared the Canal by April 1957[83]. The deployment of UNEF, by mid-December was considered strong enough by Anglo-French forces, to allow them to withdraw, and under continuous pressure to do so by the international community, they quit Port Said on 22 December. As has been noted in the United Nations' review of peacekeeping the 'negotiations undertaken by Hammarskjöld to achieve the

---

[81]   See Joseph Lash, *Dag Hammarskjöld*, 1961, p. 86. The request was made by virtue of UN General Assembly Resolution 998(ES-1), 4 November 1956.

[82]   See the Chapter III, 'First United Nations Emergency Force', in United Nations, *The Blue Helmets: A Review of United Nations Peace-keeping*, 1990, pp. 43–78.

[83]   For UN salvage operations see Bowie, *op. cit.* n. 71, pp. 83–85 and Lash, *op. cit.* n. 81, pp. 95–98.

withdrawal of the Anglo-French forces required nearly two months; those regarding the withdrawal of Israeli forces took much longer'[84]. Israeli resistance to vacating the Sinai was withdrawn with the realization that UNEF forces would be placed at the Sharm el-Sheikh—the strategic southern point of the Sinai Peninsula—and thus freedom of navigation through the Strait of Tiran would be assured[85]. On 8 March 1957, Israeli troops completed their withdrawal of both the Sinai Peninsula and the Gaza Strip; the tripartite aggression had thus ended in all its forms.

On 24 April 1957 Egypt made a unilateral Declaration regarding the Suez Canal, wherein it reaffirmed its commitment to the Constantinople Convention and outlined the basis upon which it would henceforth operate the Canal. While France and the United Kingdom argued that the Declaration did not go far enough in addressing the Six Principles enunciated in Resolution 118, the United States was willing to accept the Declaration *de facto*, while reserving the right (which it never exercised) to revisit its juridical nature in the future. The Soviet Union, for its part, considered the issue closed, thus further debate became moot; 'in practice, Egypt was given the opportunity to prove that it was up to the challenge to operate the Canal in a normal fashion'[86]. The substance of the Egypt Declaration was meant to ease the fears of maritime powers, by attempting to ensure that the nationalization of the Canal Company would not have an effect on transit through the Canal[87]. But more important to States was the willingness of Egypt to place the Constantinople Convention under the supervision of an international entity. While the Canal Company was not to be administered by an international regime as the Americans, French, and British had sought in making their Tripartite Declaration on May 1950, Egypt was, on the basis of paragraph 9(b) of its Declaration, willing to have disputes regarding the Convention settled by the International Court of Justice[88]. On 18 July 1957, Egypt joined the optional clause system of the International Court of Justice. On the basis of Article 36(2) of the Statute of the Court, the Egyptian Government undertook to accept the compulsory jurisdiction of the Court, but limited its acceptance to the narrowest of terms, solely to the interpretation or application of the provisions of the Constantinople Convention. Egypt's Declaration reads:

I, Mamound Fawzi, Minister of Foreign Affairs of the Republic of Egypt, declare on behalf of the Government of the Republic of Egypt, that, in accordance with Article 36(2) of the Statute of the International Court of Justice and in pursuance and for the purposes of paragraph 9(b) of the Declaration of the Government of the Republic of Egypt dated April 24, 1957, on 'the Suez Canal and the arrangements for its operation', the Government of the Republic of Egypt accepts as compulsory *ipso facto*, on

---

[84] United Nations, *op. cit.* n. 82, p. 61.

[85] For Israel's withdrawal from the Sinai, see Bar-On, *op. cit.* n. 68, pp. 271–314.

[86] Yves van de Mesbrugghe, *Les garanties de la liberté de navigation dans le canal de Suez*, 1964, p. 101.

[87] See 'Declaration on the Suez Canal and the Arrangements for its Operation, April 24, 1957', in Elihu Lauterpacht (ed.), *The Suez Canal Settlement*, 1960, pp. 35–38.

[88] Article 9(a), *id*. For the Tripartite Declaration see *supra.* n. 38.

condition of reciprocity and without special agreement, the jurisdiction of the International Court of Justice in all legal disputes that may arise under the said paragraph 9(b) of the above Declaration dated April 24, 1957, with effect from that date.

Facilitated by the mediation of the World Bank, Egypt signed an agreement with the representatives of the stockholders of the Suez Canal Company on 29 April 1958[89]. The various agreements amounted to a final settlement whereby the 'Company abandoned its claim to compensation for the loss of twelve years' future revenue [based on the 100 year concession of the 1866 Convention] and accepted £28,300,000 in settlement of its original claim of £204,000,000. Egypt abandoned its claim to the assets of the Company outside Egypt and recognised the survival of the Company outside Egypt after 26 July 1956'[90]. With the paying of compensation to stockholders for the nationalization of the Suez Canal Company, the way was cleared for the settlement of all outstanding claims as a result of the rupture of the peace during the fall of 1956. In August 1958 and February 1959, France and the United Kingdom respectively, signed agreements with Egypt regarding claims by the European States of measures taken against property of their nationals and by Egypt with respect to the freezing of its assets abroad and the actions of the Anglo-French forces in 1956[91]. These agreements brought to end what recent British historians have termed 'the catastrophe of the Suez débâcle'[92]. The manifest political defeat at Suez made it clear that the French and British Middle Eastern colonial empires were quickly receding from the horizons of history; and that, by virtue of the Eisenhower Doctrine of January 1957, the United States was stepping into the breach[93].

VII. Conclusion

The manifest disregard for the fundamental underpinnings of the international system that were in evidence in the aftermath of the nationalization of the Suez Canal Company, demonstrates to what length France and the United Kingdom were willing to transgress international law to achieve their aims in the Middle East. The history of the Suez Canal, from its establishment through the British occupation of Egypt and the Constantinople Convention, to the tripartite aggression of 1956, is littered with examples of actions taken in violation of the prescriptions of international law. From the time that Ferdinand de Lesseps first proposed the building of a canal through the Isthmus of Suez, Egypt was treated as the object of

---

[89]   See 'The Agreements Relating to Compensation for the Nationalization of the Suez Canal Company', Lauterpacht, *op. cit.* n. 86, pp. 3–33; also, Lazar Focsaneanu, 'L'accord ayant pour object l'indemnisation de la Compagnie de suez nationalisée par l'Égypte', *Annuaire Français de droit international*, Vol. 5, 1959, pp. 161–204.

[90]   Farnie, *op. cit.* n. 10, p. 742.

[91]   Lauterpacht, *op. cit.* n. 87, pp. 47–80.

[92]   Gorst and Johman, *op. cit.* n. 35, p. 151.

[93]   See 'Document 5.2.5, The Eisenhower Doctrine, 5 January 1957', *id.*, pp. 157–158.

European geopolitics. The Suez Canal was deemed too important by France, and especially by Britain, to be left either to the vagaries of local control or to the solid foundation of international law. Instead, first through the Anglo-French condominium, and later by British occupation, the fate of Egypt for nearly one hundred years as the object of European imperialism was a result of the piercing of the land bridge between the Mediterranean and the Red Sea.

The Constantinople Convention of 1888, although it appears today to be on a solid foundation, has truly only found its footing in the last twenty years. The Convention itself did not come into force until 1904, when the *Entente Cordiale* allowed Britain to removed its reservation, which sought to place the elements of the Convention which were incompatible with its occupation of Egypt in abeyance. However, that agreement recognised *de facto* British occupation and allowed Great Britain to substitute its general reservation for a limited one, thus precluding Egypt from acting, in concert with other State Parties, to declare the British occupation as a threat to legal regime of the Suez Canal. As its actions in the future would demonstrate, the British occupation was indeed a threat to ensuring that the Canal will 'always be free and open, in time of war as in time of peace' to all ships without distinction of flag. Instead of relying on legal dictates, as outlined in the 1888 Convention, Great Britain was quick to forgo those obligations in exchange for gaining the political advantages of acting *hors de la loi*. Thus, Britain closed the Canal to the Central Powers during the First World War, but was willing to allow Italy to undertake its war against Ethiopia despite Mussolini having been branded the aggressor by the League of Nations. However, when Italy sought to ally itself with Germany in 1940 and declared war on Great Britain, the Canal was closed to it, as an Axis Power. Great Britain, having breached the neutrality of the 1888 Convention and made the Suez Canal an Allied asset, also made it the target of attack.

Thus the juridical footing of the Constantinople Convention during the British occupation of Egypt leaves much to be desired. In 1951, well before the Free Officers *coup d'état*, and the subsequent nationalization of the Suez Canal Company, an Egyptian jurist Moustapha El-Hefnaoui undertook a study of the Suez Canal. In his study, El-Hefnaoui clearly demonstrates the nationalist sentiments which gripped Egypt at the time; however, his analysis of the evolution of the legal regime of the Suez Canal from 1888 until 1950 clearly resonates. El-Hefnaoui writes:

> Since its opening the Canal has had an obscure and unstable position, a position that neither the Concessions, nor the opinions of international jurists, nor precedence has been able to establish. England retracted one day what it had declared the previous, as per its designs and interests.

Amplifying his views, El-Hefnaoui went on to state that:

> It can be said, first and foremost, that free passage through the Canal, in times of peace and war, and on the basis of strict equality of States—principles invoked since the opening of the Canal—is not yet on a sound juridical base. It could not be otherwise as

long as the English maintain their troops in the Canal zone, and as long as they benefit from this privileged position they will not be willing to renounce it. Before establishing the true legal status of the Canal, the Powers must seek an end of this occupation which, in a flagrant manner, harms the legal position of the Canal[94].

The status of the Suez Canal since 1956 appears to bear out El-Hefnaoui's analysis. With the major hiccup of the tripartite aggression and despite the fact that the Canal was closed as a result of the 1967 War between Egypt and Israel, the regime of the Suez Canal has slowly settled onto a sound juridical base. The major hindrance to full implementation of the 1888 Convention was access of Israeli ships to the Canal, this however was settled by the Peace Agreement signed by Egypt and Israel in 1979 which established that:

> Ships of Israel, and cargoes destined for or coming from Israel, shall enjoy the right of free passage through the Suez Canal and its approaches through the Gulf of Suez and the Mediterranean Sea on the basis of the Constantinople Convention of 1888, applying to all nations, Israeli nationals, vessels and cargoes, as well as persons, vessels and cargoes destined for or coming from Israel, shall be accorded non-discriminatory treatment in all matters connected with usage of the canal[95].

With this major hurdle overcome, the Canal has been open without discrimination for more than twenty years. Despite the two Gulf Wars, and Israel's war against Lebanon, the operation of the Canal has remained constant. Yet, despite war in the region, Egypt has not been threatened by attack since the signing of the Peace Treaty which emerged from the Camp David agreements. Thus, whether the Canal will 'always be free and open, in time of war as in time of peace', remains to be seen. The fact that the Canal is no longer under the occupation of a colonial power which considered it the 'jugular vein' of its empire lends credence to the provisions of the Constantinople Convention being interpreted in line with the dictates of international law and not those of political expediency[96].

---

[94]   El-Hefnaoui, *op. cit.* n. 11, p. 153.
[95]   Article 5(1), Treaty of Peace between the Arab Republic of Egypt and the State of Israel, March 26, 1979.
[96]   See Anthony Gorst and Lewis Johman, *op. cit.* n. 35, p. 1, quoting Lord Hankey.

Chapter 3

Disregard for International Law in the Evolution toward the Formation of the State of Israel

The case of the imposition of the State of Israel on the Middle East is the most obvious example of the qualitatively different manner in which international law is applied in the region. In the move toward the establishment of the State of Israel, Western States, with Britain at the forefront, paid little heed to the dictates of international law, preferring instead to impose an imperial policy, which included Zionism, through political expediency. This expediency, however, was in glaring variance with the fundamental underpinnings of the international system as established at the end of the First World War. Although the Wilsonian conception of self-determination was at the heart of the new international order created in Paris in 1919, Palestine was to prove the exception. The Allied Powers agreed that where Palestine was concerned, the interests of the local inhabitants would have to take second place to their wish to settle the 'Jewish Question' in their own countries. Thus, by supporting Zionist aspirations, the Allied Powers forewent obligations of international law, and instead imposed what amounted to the last European colonial venture, by allowing for the mass emigration of European Jewry to Palestine.

While the aspirations of Zionism found voice in the British 'Balfour Declaration', it failed to gain a legal foothold until the Declaration was inserted into the British Mandate for Palestine authorised by the League of Nations. That the Mandate failed to take into consideration the wishes of the vast majority of the local inhabitants meant that it was serving the interests of the Allied Powers and not those who lived in Palestine. The incompatibility of the Mandate for Palestine with the Covenant of the League of Nations did not lead to its invalidation; instead, Allied support meant that international law would have to be side-stepped in the 'special' case of Palestine. Although attempts were made to have the Mandate rescinded, it was all for naught, as the United Kingdom would support, as part of its larger imperial aims, Zionist policies in Palestine from 1920 to 1923 in violation of the laws of occupation, and thereafter *only* in violation of the dictates of the Covenant. From 1920 to 1948, the British Mandate for Palestine was imposed by force of arms on an indigenous population bent on ridding itself of foreign domination.

At the end of the Second World War, with 100,000 troops in Palestine and the Arab, and now Jewish, populations turning on Britain, the United Kingdom washed its hands of Palestine and turned the matter over to the United Nations. The United Kingdom, unwilling to maintain the Mandate had, by virtue of the establishment of the United Nations Organization and the impending end of the League of Nations, two options: to grant Palestine independence or pass the Mandate over to the United Nations Trusteeship system. Yet it chose neither, instead it placed the future of Palestine into the hands of the UN General Assembly. Despite the fact that the General Assembly lacks the power to make binding decisions, Resolution 181 was passed, calling for the partition of Palestine into Arab and Jewish States with an international *corpus separatum* to govern Jerusalem. In the wake of this Resolution, Palestine plunged into civil war and, on the eve of the termination of Palestine, David Ben-Gurion, basing himself on Resolution 181, proclaimed the establishment of the State of Israel. Despite the dubious legal value of the Mandate for Palestine which allowed for the Jewish population to increase ten-fold during the Mandate period, and the lack of binding force of Resolution 181, States—led by the United States of America—were quick to grant recognition to the State of Israel. With a critical mass of Jewish people in Palestine, and a determination to establish a State which they saw as being biblically ordained, Israelis were able to consolidate effective control over large swaths of Palestine. This ability to establish a presence on the ground coupled with recognition by key members of the international community meant that Israel, as a State, had managed to impose itself on the Middle East despite its dubious legal foundations and against the will of the majority in Palestine.

I. Support for Zionism

Zionism, as a State policy, found voice in November 1917, with the declaration by the British War Cabinet of its government's sympathy toward 'Jewish Zionist aspirations' and thus calling for the 'establishment in Palestine of a national homeland for Jewish people'. Leading up to this—the Balfour Declaration—was a movement spearheaded in the latter part of the nineteenth century by a number of Eastern European and Russian Jewish people who, in the face of pogroms and discriminatory practices, sought refuge in the creation of a Jewish State. Finding voice in Theodor Herzl's *Der Judenstaat*, 'political Zionism'[1] was given form with the declaration of the First Zionist Congress in Basle, Switzerland, in 1897:

> The aim of Zionism is to create for the Jewish people a home in Palestine secured by public law. The Congress contemplates that following means to the attainment of this end:

---

[1]   John McTague, *British Policy in Palestine, 1917–1922*, p. 5.

1.   The promotion, on suitable lines, of colonization of Palestine by Jewish agricultural and industrial workers.

2.   The organization and binding together of the whole of Jewry by means of appropriate institutions, local and international, in accordance with the laws of each country.

3.   The strengthening and fostering of Jewish national sentiment and consciousness.

4.   Preparatory steps towards obtaining of government consent, where necessary, to the attainment of the aim of Zionism[2].

Despite the Basle Declaration, early manifestations of Zionism did not necessarily seek a homeland within the shadow of biblical Mount Zion. Beyond Palestine, Theodor Herzl had also proposed Argentina[3] as a possible location for a Jewish State, and the British Government had offered Herzl 'an autonomous territory in Uganda', which was accepted by the Sixth Zionist Congress in 1903[4].

Such pragmatism was at the heart of Herzl's Zionist thinking, which sought to acknowledge that the 'Jewish question still exists' and to remedy the plight of those that suffered from anti-Semitism. As Herzl explained:

> I believe that I understand Anti-Semitism, which is really a highly complex movement. [...] I believe that I can see what elements there are in it of vulgar sport, of common trade jealousy, of inherited prejudice, of religious intolerance, and also of pretended self-defence. I think the Jewish question is no more a social than a religious one, notwithstanding that it sometimes takes these and other forms. It is a national question, which can only be solved by making it a political worked question to be discussed and settled by the civilised nations of the world in council[5].

---

[2]   Walter Laqueur, (ed.), 'The Basle Declaration', *The Israel-Arab Reader: A Documentary History of the Middle East Conflict*, 1969, p. 6.

[3]   Theodor Herzl, 'The Jewish State', in Laqueur, *id.*, p. 11.

[4]   Chaim Weizmann, the future first President of Israel (1948–52), explained Herzl's pragmatic politics in the following manner:

> How was it that Herzl could contemplate such a shift of objective? It was the logical consequence of his conception of Zionism and the role which the movement had to play in the life of the Jews. To him, and to many with him—perhaps the majority of the representatives of the Jews assembled in Basle [in 1903]—Zionism meant an *immediate* solution of the problems besetting their sorely tried people. If it was not that, it was nothing at all. [...] If Palestine was not, at the moment, feasible, he could not wait for the flood of anti-Semitism was rising minute by minute—to use his own words—'the lower strata of the Jewish edifice were already inundated.' If anything were to happen, then there might not be enough Jews left to build Palestine; hence the offer of the British Government was providential; it had come just in the nick of time—a very present help in time of trouble. It would be cruel, heartless, un-Jewish and un-Zionistic to throw away a chance which might never again occur in the history of the Jewish people.

Chaim Weizmann, *Trial and Error: The Autobiography of Chaim Weizmann*, 1949, pp. 84–85. With respect to Uganda, see *id.*, pp. 83–89.

[5]   Theodor Herzl, 'The Jewish State', in Laqueur, *op. cit.* n. 2, p. 6.

Herzl believed that the means of dealing with anti-Semitism was to provide the Jewish people with a sanctuary from persecution, understanding full well that this would be in line with States seeking to deal with their own so-called 'Jewish Question'. As Herzl noted, 'The Governments of all countries scourged by Anti-Semitism will be keenly interested in assisting us in obtaining the sovereignty we want'[6]. Although it is clear that various British politicians such as Prime Minister David Lloyd George, Arthur Balfour, and Winston Churchill were ideologically of a Zionist bent, they ultimately lent their support to Zionism not of its own accord but with the recognition that it 'served as a tool with which to both cloak and to further imperial ambitions'[7].

While the Uganda proposal was to be voted down by a Zionist Congress—which had accepted it only two years previously—the link between the support of Western States toward Zionism and solving their own so-called 'Jewish Question' would continue to be an underlying factor in supporting Jewish claims to Palestine. This was most obviously expressed in a discussion between United States Supreme Court Justice Louis Brandeis, the main proponent of Zionism in the United States of America, and Arthur Balfour in 1919. The minutes of their meeting reflect Brandeis' thinking, 'as an American he was confronted with the disposition of the vast number of Jews, particularly Russian Jews that were pouring into the United States year by year. It was then that by chance a pamphlet on Zionism came his way and led him to the study of the Jewish problem and to the conviction that Zionism was the answer'. Balfour agreed with this statement, adding, 'Of course, these are the reasons that make you and me such ardent Zionists'[8].

Beyond supporting Zionism as an attempt to limit Jewish immigration from Eastern Europe, Western States found in Zionism greater political advantages. When the British Secretary of State for Colonies, the Duke of Devonshire, undertook a study of British policy regarding Palestine five years after the pronouncement of the 1917 Balfour Declaration he stated, 'it must always be remembered that the Declaration was made at a time of extreme peril to the cause of the Allies … . The Balfour Declaration was a war measure … designed to secure tangible benefits which it was hoped could contribute to the ultimate victory of the Allies'[9]. The benefits to the war effort of getting international Jewry on-side included securing the United States of America's entry into the war[10] and seeking

[6]   *Id.*, p. 9.
[7]   Benny Morris, *Righteous Victims: A History of the Zionist-Arab Conflict, 1881–1999*, 1999, p. 71.
[8]   Felix Frankfurter, 'An Interview in Mr. Balfour's Apartment', Walid Khalidi (ed.), *From Haven to Conquest: Readings in Zionism and the Palestine Problem Until 1948*, 1987, p. 196.
[9]   See Doreen Ingrams, *Palestine Papers, 1917–1922: Seeds of Conflict*, 1972, p. 173.
[10] *Id.*, p. 173: 'It is arguable that the negotiations with the Zionist, which had been in progress for many months before the Declaration was acutely published, did, in fact, have considerable effect in advancing the date at which the United States Government intervened in the war'.

to circumvent German espousal of the Zionist cause[11]. But the support by Britain of Zionist aspirations was also meant to stem Bolshevism in Western Europe[12], and to justify gaining Palestine for itself as the strategic northern flank of the Suez Canal—the gateway to India[13].

II. The Balfour Declaration

The Balfour Declaration was approved by the British War Cabinet on 2 November 1917. Addressed to Lord Rothschild and signed by Arthur Balfour, it reads:

> I have much pleasure in conveying to you, on behalf of His Majesty's Government, the following declaration of sympathy with Jewish Zionist aspirations which has been submitted to, and approved by, the Cabinet.
>
> 'His Majesty's Government views with favour the establishment in Palestine of a national home for the Jewish people, and will use their best endeavours to facilitate the achievement of this object, it being clearly understood that nothing shall be done which may prejudice the civil and religious rights of existing non-Jewish communities in Palestine, or the rights and political status enjoyed by Jews in any other country'.
>
> I should be grateful if you would bring this declaration to the knowledge of the Zionist Federation.

The nature of the Balfour Declaration as a 'war measure' becomes plain when it is realised that in 1917, Palestine was not under the control of Great Britain but was an integrated part of the Ottoman Empire. It was the pledge to a people, of a

---

[11]　Leonard Stein, 'Contact between German Zionist Leaders and the German Government during World War I', Khalidi, *op. cit.* n. 8, pp. 153–161.

[12]　Note the interjection of General MacDonough, British Director of Military Intelligence, at a meeting of the Eastern Committee of the War Cabinet in 1918:

> I suggest the most important thing in the consideration of the position of Palestine is not its topographical relations to Syria or anything else, but its being, as Mr. Balfour says, the home of the Jewish people, and therefore interesting the whole of the Jews all over the world. I see a good many of the Zionists, and one suggested to me the day before yesterday that if the Jewish people did not get what they were asking for in Palestine we should have the whole of Jewry turning Bolshevik and supporting Bolshevism in all the other countries as they have done in Russia.

Minutes of the Eastern Committee, 5 December 1918, as noted in Ingrams, *op. cit.* n. 9, p. 50.

[13]　See the discussion between the British Prime Minister Lloyd George and his generals during the Paris Peace Conference of 1919 where General Shea said 'that from the point of view of the air he thought it was essential to have Palestine. The necessity for this was to enable us to break up an air attack on the Suez Canal'. See Ingrams, *id.*, p. 77. Note also, more generally, Isaiah Friedman, *The Question of Palestine, 1914–1918: British-Jewish-Arab Relations*, 1973, pp. 274–277; and Herbert Sidebotham, 'British Interests in Palestine', 1917, in Khalidi, *op. cit.* n. 8, pp. 125–142.

country of which the British Empire lacked not only title, but to which it had no claim. Thus, this pledge, like the overlapping one made to Sharif Hussein of Mecca over areas of the Middle East in 1915, was void of legal obligation *vis-à-vis* the local inhabitants. Both the Balfour Declaration and the British commitments to Arab nationalism as found in the 'McMahon-Hussein Correspondence'[14] while being contradictory were political commitments that could only be honoured through imperial dictates after a British victory over the Ottomans. Although, as Lord Curzon, the British Foreign Secretary, was to point out in 1918, these were overlapping pledges, they were the engagements which Great Britain had taken as being politically expedient in the Allies' attempt to weaken the Central Powers through its southern flank:

> Lord Curzon: The Palestine position is this. If we deal with our commitments, there is first the general pledge to Hussein in October 1915, under which Palestine was included in the areas as to which Great Britain pledged itself that they should be Arab and independent in the future … . Great Britain and France—Italy subsequently agreeing— committed themselves to an international administration of Palestine in consultation with Russia, who was an ally at the time … . A new feature was brought into the case in November 1917, when Mr. Balfour, with the authority of the War Cabinet, issued his famous declaration to the Zionists that Palestine should be the national home of the Jewish people, but that nothing should be done—and this, of course, was a most important proviso—to prejudice the civil and religious rights of the existing non-Jewish communities in Palestine. Those, as far as I know, are the only actual engagements into which we entered with regard to Palestine[15].

Where the Balfour Declaration moves from being a political pledge lacking legal validity to a legally binding obligation is through its inclusion in the League of Nations Mandate over Palestine in 1922. Thus, at the date of issue, the juridical value of the Balfour Declaration was nil. A simple reading of the Declaration makes it evident that, as a policy announcement, it was ambiguous in its generalities[16]. The Government declaring that it would use 'its best endeavours to

---

[14]   'The McMahon Letter', in Laqueur, *op. cit.* n. 2, pp. 15–17. Note that Laqueur writes that Palestine was not included in the pledge.
[15]   Minutes of the Eastern Committee, 5 December 1918, see Ingrams, *op. cit.* n. 9, p. 48. Note that no mention is made by the Curzon of the 1916 Sykes-Picot Agreement delineating spheres of influence between itself and the French if the Ottoman Empire was to be dismantled. Note also the overall assessment of pledges made by Avi Shlaim: 'Britain's public promise to the Jews could not be reconciled either with its earlier promise to Hussein the Sharif of Mecca to support the establishment of an independent Arab kingdom after the war in return for an Arab revolt against the Ottoman Empire or the secret Sykes-Picot agreement of 1916 to divide the Middle East into British and French spheres of influence in the event of an Allied victory'. Avi Shlaim, *The Iron Wall*, 2000, p. 7.
[16]   For writings regarding the Balfour Declaration see: Leonard Stein, *The Balfour Declaration*, 1961, Ronald Sanders, *The High Walls of Jerusalem: A History of the Balfour Declaration and the Birth of the British Mandate for Palestine*, 1983; 'International Law Appraisal of the Balfour Declaration', W.T. Mallison and Sally V. Mallison, *The Palestine*

facilitate the achievement' of 'a national home for the Jewish people' in Palestine hardly makes plain the obligation it was undertaking. At the time of the Declaration in 1917, it is not surprising that the British Government could not commit to more, lacking, as it did, any claim to Palestine. The torturous nature of the phrasing of the Declaration belies the fact that it went through a number of revisions, having originally been prepared by British Zionists. While early drafts of the Declaration stated that 'Palestine should be *reconstituted* as *the* national home of the Jewish People', what was finally agreed to was a watered down version which reads in part, 'the *establishment* in Palestine of *a* national home for the Jewish people' [17]. While it is clear that Britain was not promising formally a Jewish State in Palestine, it is not clear what was being pledged through the establishment of 'a national home', as this notion held no currency in legal or diplomatic language at the time.

Further absent from early drafts, were safeguards that found their way into the Declaration at the insistence of the assimilationist Edwin Montagu, the only Jewish Cabinet Minister at the time of the Balfour Declaration [18]. Those safeguards where meant to first, protect the civil and religious rights of Palestinians, and second, protect assimilationist Jewish persons in their native countries. It should be noted at this point that the wording of the Declaration's first safeguard, using the term 'protect the civil and religious rights of *non-Jewish communities* in Palestine' was at once, an acknowledgement of a significant Christian minority which was nearly the size of its Jewish counterpart. But it also masked the reality that, conservatively, the population in Palestine was, by 1918, more than seventy-five percent Arab [19]. Regardless of its content, where the Balfour Declaration gained international standing, first and foremost, was through the Allied victory in the Great War and the British occupation of much of the Middle East. That, and the willingness of the Allied Powers to include the Declaration in the British mandate for Palestine, was to raise this pronouncement from a political pledge to a legal obligation.

Problem in International Law and World Order, 1986, pp. 18–78; and N. Jefferies, 'Analysis of the Balfour Declaration', in Khalidi, *op. cit.* n. 8, Document 16, pp. 173–188.

[17] Mallison and Mallison, *id.*, p. 33. Emphasis added. Chaim Weizmann wrote that a comparison of early drafts with the Declaration 'shows a painful recession' and that the revisions to the drafts 'can be interpreted to mean such limitations on our work as completely to cripple it'. See Weizmann, *op. cit.* n. 4, p. 207. When Mark Sykes stated 'Dr. Weizmann, it's a boy', upon handing him the original Balfour Declaration. Weizmann writes: 'Well—I did not like the boy at first. He was not the one I had expected. But I knew that this was a great departure', *id.*, p. 208.

[18] Montagu's response to early drafts of the Balfour Declaration where made known to his Cabinet colleagues through a memorandum entitled: 'Anti-Semitism of the Present Government'. See 'Edwin Montagu and Zionism', in Khalidi, *op. cit.* n. 8, pp. 143–147.

[19] General Clayton of the British expeditionary force in Egypt noted, in 1918, that 'according to the latest reports by Administrators, the present population of Palestine consists of approximately of: Moslems 512,000, Christians 61,000, Jews 66,000'. See General Gilbert Clayton, British Chief Political Officer, Egyptian Expeditionary Force, Report to the Foreign Office, 6 December 1918, in Ingrams, *op. cit.* n. 9, p. 44.

III. The British Mandate for Palestine

The ability of Britain to gain the League of Nations' Mandate for Palestine which it accepted in 1920, stems from its military successes in the Middle East and the commitment by Allied States to the Balfour Declaration. In July 1917, the war effort of Britain in the Middle East changed from having gained little headway in the region to a string of successes which would ultimately led to the expulsion of Ottoman Turks from the region. The successful campaign started with a change of command which saw Edmund Allenby taking charge of the Egyptian Expeditionary Force that summer. By the end of 1917, Allenby's forces had captured Palestine, entering Jerusalem on 10 December. By the time a general armistice was declared in November 1918, British forces had expelled the Ottoman Turks from Lebanon, Palestine, Syria, and the Trans-Jordan. Palestine, like all territories in the region under the command of Allenby, was placed under the Occupied Enemy Territory Administration.

Great Britain, being party to the 1907 Convention regarding the Laws and Customs of War[20], was bound as the belligerent occupier to maintain, as far as possible, the *status quo* in Palestine until a permanent settlement with the Ottoman Empire was concluded. However, this was not to be, as Turkey proved recalcitrant in making peace, only ratifying an armistice treaty in 1923; while Britain came under increased pressure to make good on the Balfour Declaration. Britain maintained a regime of belligerent occupation over Palestine in line with the dictates of international law, but did so only from December 1917 until July 1920. Between 1920 and the 1923 Treaty of Lausanne, which officially ended hostilities with Turkey, Britain undertook to consolidate its control over the occupied territory by implementing Zionist policies in Palestine despite the provisions of the 1907 Convention. From 1 July 1920 onward, Britain no longer felt compelled to act in conformity with international law it having been decided, amongst the Allied Powers in San Remo, that Great Britain would receive the League of Nations'

---

[20] Great Britain becomes party to the 1907 Convention on November 27, 1909. See Clive Parry and Charity Hopkins, *An Index to British Treaties*, 1970, Vol. 2, p. 536. Its obligations as a belligerent occupier included:

> Article 43: The authority of the legitimate power having in fact passed into the hands of the occupant, the latter shall take all the measures in his power to restore, and ensure, as far as possible, public order and safety, while respecting, unless absolutely prevented, the laws in force in the country.

> Article 55: The occupying State shall be regarded only as administrator and usufructuary of public buildings, real estate, forests, and agricultural estates belonging to the hostile State, and situated in the occupied country. It must safeguard the capital of these properties, and administer them in accordance with the rules of usufruct.

Convention (IV) respecting the Laws and Customs of War on Land and its annex: Regulations concerning the Laws and Customs of War on Land, 18 October 1907. Usufruct: 'The right to use and enjoyment of property belonging to another without waste or destruction of its substance', *The Cassell Concise Dictionary*, 1997, 1615.

Mandate for Palestine. As such, the British 'decided to scrap the old system'—the Occupied Enemy Territory Administration—'and treat Palestine as a territory under their possession'[21].

At the Peace Conference of Versailles in 1919, the Allied Powers set the peace based on United States President Woodrow Wilson's 'Fourteen Points'[22]. Among the Fourteen Points that President Wilson put forward in January 1918, as the United States' vision of a post-War settlement, was a notion of self-determination:

> Point V: A free, open-minded, and absolutely impartial adjustment of all colonial claims, based upon a strict observance of the principle that in determining all such questions of sovereignty the interests of the populations concerned must have equal weight with the equitable claims of the government whose title is to be determined.

Thus Wilson saw in the notion of self-determination an end to European colonialism, and sought to ensure that the local inhabitants would have as much of a say as their governments in determining the boundaries of newly independent States. Wilson explained, in his address, that the underlying principle by which the United States sought to establish the post-War peace was 'justice to all peoples and nationalities, and their right to live on equal terms of liberty and safety with one another, whether they be strong or weak'. Wilson concluded by stating 'unless this principle be made its foundation no part of the structure of international justice can stand'[23].

Out of the Peace Conference emerged, a year later, the 1920 Covenant of the League of Nations which institutionalised Wilson's vision of an internationalist *qua* liberal post-War system. The Covenant did not, however, do away with colonialism, instead it established the halfway house of the mandate system. Under this system, the League of Nations was to assist 'peoples not yet able to stand by themselves under the strenuous conditions of the modern world' by assigning them tutors—Mandatories—from the 'advanced nations'. The relationship was no longer to be formally one of colonised/coloniser, instead 'the well-being and development' of the people under the mandate was to be considered a 'sacred trust of civilization'[24]. The Mandate system was a tiered system whereby those under former Ottoman occupation were considered the most advanced and thus worthy of moving toward independence on the fastest track. Article 22 of the Covenant reads, in part:

> Certain communities formerly belonging to the Turkish Empire have reached a stage of development where their existence as independent nations can be provisionally recognized subject to the rendering of administrative advice and assistance by a

---

[21] McTague, *op. cit.* n. 1, p. 110. McTague continues: 'Technically, this decision was illegal, since Turkey had not yet ratified the peace treaty, but [His Majesty's Government] felt after San Remo that ratification would be only a formality'.

[22] See Rohan Butler, 'The Peace Settlement of Versailles, 1918–1933', *The New Cambridge Modern History*, 1979, pp. 209–210.

[23] See United States President Woodrow Wilson's Fourteen Points Speech.

[24] Article 22, Covenant of the League of Nations.

Mandatory until such time as they are able to stand alone. *The wishes of these communities must be a principal consideration in the selection of the Mandatory*[25].

While Britain was pursuing the Mandate for Palestine, it was understood that it would not implement its mandate in favour of the majority of the population. In correspondence in February 1919 with Prime Minister Lloyd George, Arthur Balfour noted:

> The weak point of our position of course is that in the case of Palestine we deliberately and rightly decline to accept the principle of self-determination. If the present inhabitants were consulted they would unquestionably give an anti-Jewish verdict. Our justification for our policy is that we regard Palestine as being absolutely exceptional; that we consider the question of the Jews outside Palestine as one of world importance and that we conceive Jews to have a historic claim to a home in their ancient land; provided that home can be given them without either dispossessing or oppressing the present inhabitants[26].

Yet, it was not clear at the Peace Conference whether Great Britain would, in fact, receive the mandate, as it and France could not agree on the spoils of the Allied victory over the Ottomans. President Wilson thus suggested that an inter-Allied commission be sent to the region to ascertain the views of the inhabitants as to which State they would prefer as their Mandatory. With the British and French unable to agree on sending their delegates, the King-Crane Commission was ultimately an American fact-finding mission. It found that 'the non-Jewish population of Palestine—nearly nine-tenths of the whole—are emphatically against the entire Zionist program' and recommended a 'serious modification of the extreme Zionist Program for Palestine of unlimited immigration of Jews, looking finally to make Palestine distinctly a Jewish State'[27]. The recommendations of the Commission were suppressed, as the British and French were unwilling to accept them *in toto* and the United States was unwilling to force the issue.

Unable to come to an understanding, the Allied States convened later in San Remo to discuss a settlement with Turkey, but also to settle on the mandates for Iraq, Palestine, and Syria. United States President Wilson would later describe the Conference as a 'whole disgusting scramble' whereby the 'decisions accorded neither with the wishes of the inhabitants nor with the unqualified end-of-war undertakings about freedom of choice. They were pieces of unabashed self-interest, suggesting to many onlookers that all talk of liberating small nations from oppression was so much cant'[28]. The outcome, in April 1920, of the San Remo Conference was the Allied Powers' decision to designate to Great Britain the Mandate for Palestine. As the British Foreign Minister related to Allenby in the field, the British mandate was 'defined by a verbatim repetition of Mr. Balfour's

---

[25] *Id*. Emphasis added.
[26] See Ingrams, *op. cit.* n. 9, p. 61.
[27] See Sanders, *op. cit.* n. 16, p. 649.
[28] See Ingrams, *op. cit.* n. 9, p. 91, where she quotes Elizabeth Monroe, *Britain's Moment in the Middle East, 1914–1956*, 1963, p. 66.

declaration of November 1917'[29]. The legality of this decision, it bears repeating, only gained validity with the peace treaty between the Allied Powers and Turkey three years later.

The League of Nations confirmed the Mandate for Palestine on 24 July 1922. The two-year gap between the designation at the San Remo Conference and the League's confirmation can be attributed to the disagreement which existed within the British establishment as to the manner in which the Balfour Declaration should be given effect. The Mandate for Palestine, as approved by the Council of the League of Nations in 1922, provides in its preamble that:

> Whereas the Principal Allied Powers have also agreed that the Mandatory should be responsible for putting into effect the declaration originally made on November 2nd, 1917, by the Government of His Britannic Majesty, and adopted by the said Powers, in favour of the establishment in Palestine of a national home for the Jewish people, it being clearly understood that nothing should be done which might prejudice the civil and religious rights of existing non-Jewish communities in Palestine, or the rights and political status enjoyed by Jews in any other country [...][30].

The Mandate, as a result, moved closer to Zionist wishes than the Balfour Declaration by providing for the '*re*constitution' not of '*a* homeland', but the '*re*constitution' of '*their* homeland'. The provision reads in full:

> Whereas recognition has thereby been given to the historical connection of the Jewish people with Palestine and to the grounds for reconstituting their national home in that country [...].

To give substance to these aims, the Mandate for Palestine, in Article 2, provided that, 'The Mandatory shall be responsible for placing the country under such political, administrative and economic conditions as will secure the establishment of the Jewish national home [...]'. The Mandate established a Jewish agency to advise and co-operate with the Administration of Palestine to ensure that those aims were fulfilled. Beyond its general administrative mandate to enact laws, establish a judiciary, control foreign relations, preserve law and order, and manage the Holy Places and archaeological sites, the Mandate sought to give further voice to the Balfour Declaration. While making Hebrew an official language in Palestine, the Mandate also provided preferential treatment for Jewish people in the area of immigration. Article 6 reads:

> The Administration of Palestine, while ensuring that the rights and position of other sections of the population are not prejudiced, shall facilitate Jewish immigration under suitable conditions and shall encourage, in co-operation with the Jewish agency referred to in Article 4, close settlement by Jews on the land, including State lands and waste lands not required for public purposes.

---

[29] Telegraph from George Curzon to Allenby, *id.*, pp. 91–92.
[30] League of Nations, Mandate for Palestine, 1922.

i. Incompatibility of the Mandate with the Covenant

The issue of whether the Mandate for Palestine was compatible with the legal obligations which States accepted under the Covenant of the League of Nations is fundamental to understanding the extent to which Western States were willing to impose their will on the Middle East despite its variance with the dictates of international law. By integrating the Balfour Declaration into the various provisions of the Mandate for Palestine, the Allied Powers were demonstrating that, where Palestine was concerned, the Covenant had no independent legal value beyond what they were willing to attribute to it. Consider a decidedly frank Memorandum from Arthur Balfour to his Foreign Secretary George Curzon of 11 August 1919:

> The contradiction between the letters of the Covenant and the policy of the Allies is even more flagrant in the case of the 'independent nation' of Palestine than in that of the 'independent nation' of Syria. For in Palestine we do not propose even to go through the form of consulting the wishes of the present inhabitants of the country, though the American [King-Crane] Commission has been going through the form of asking what they are.
>
> The Four Great Powers are committed to Zionism, and Zionism, be it right or wrong, good or bad, is rooted in age-long traditions, in present needs, in future hopes, of far profounder import than the desire and prejudices of 700,000 Arabs who now inhabit that ancient land.
>
> In my opinion that is right. What I have never been able to understand is how it can be harmonized with the declaration[31], the Covenant, or the instruction to the [King-Crane] Commission of Enquiry.
>
> I do not think that Zionism will hurt the Arabs, but they will never say they want it. Whatever the future of Palestine it is not now an 'independent nation', nor is it yet on the way to become one. Whatever deference should be paid to the views of those living there, the Powers in their selection of a mandatory do not propose, as I understand the matter, to consult them. In short, so far as Palestine is concerned, the Powers have made no statement of fact which is not admittedly wrong, and no declaration of policy which, at least in the letter, they have not always intended to violate[32].

While the candour of the final statement may leave one dumb-struck, the proposition that Balfour puts forward regarding the harmonization of Zionism and the Covenant is worthy of consideration.

That the Zionism plan was integrated, three years after Balfour's Memorandum to Curzon, into the Mandate for Palestine accepted by the League of Nations raises issues from that of simple British imperial policy to international legal validity. The willingness of the Council of the League of Nations to accept the British Mandate for Palestine belies the manifest violations of its own

---

[31]   Reference here is to the 1918 Anglo-French Declaration related to the establishment of Arab national governments that would derive their authority from the free choice of the indigenous population.

[32]   See Ingrams, *op. cit.* n. 9, p. 73.

Covenant. In what Hersch Lauterpacht termed 'the leading monograph on the subject', J. Stoyanovsky's *The Mandate for Palestine*, the author attempts to demonstrate the compatibility of the Mandate with the Covenant[33]. In his work, Stoyanovsky asks rhetorically, 'Is the Palestine Mandate inconsistent with Article XXII of the Covenant?'[34]. He acknowledges that:

> it has been said that the mandate for Palestine, in its present form, is incompatible with Article XXII of the Covenant, because the mandates system as contemplated in that Article is instituted in the interests of the actual inhabitants of the mandated territories, while the Palestine mandate contemplates the interests of a people actually outside the territory. The criticism is thus concerned with the underlying principles of the mandates system as applied to Palestine[35].

But Stoyanovsky insists that the 'object of the system is to guide towards independence and self-government those *races, peoples or communities* who for various reasons are not yet able to stand alone. This is the very object of the national home policy, which aims at giving the Jewish people the necessary assistance to form in Palestine an independent and self-governing community'[36]. He goes on to state that the 'underlying principles, not only of the mandates system but of the Covenant as a whole, are thus given effect to in the national policy. There seems to be no valid reason for doubting that this policy in itself follows directly from the principles of nationality and self-determination upon which the Covenant of the League of Nations largely rests'[37]. Stoyanovsky further buttress his argument by noting that the addition of the elements of the Balfour Declaration regarding a national home to the 'Palestine mandate merely widens the scope of the latter and does not affect the fundamental principles of the system as a whole; it simply gives a wider meaning to the term 'community' used in Article XXII with regard to certain ex-Turkish provinces, of which Palestine is one'[38].

Yet, the notion of 'community' mentioned in the third paragraph of Article 22 is clearly defined in the opening paragraph of that provision which reads:

> To those colonies and territories which as a consequence of the late war have ceased to be under the sovereignty of the States which formerly governed them and which are inhabited by peoples not yet able to stand by themselves under the strenuous conditions of the modern world, there should be applied the principle that the well-being and development of such peoples form a sacred trust of civilisation and that securities for the performance of this trust should be embodied in this Covenant.

---

[33]   See Hersch Lauterpacht (ed.), *Oppenheim's International Law: A Treaties*, 1937, p. 191, n. 1.

[34]   J. Stoyanovsky's *The Mandate for Palestine: A Contribution to the Theory and Practice of International Mandates*, 1928, p. 42. For studies dealing with legal issues regarding the Mandate for Palestine generally, see Abraham Baumkoller, *Le Mandate sur la Palestine*, 1931 and Paltiel Novik, *La situation de la Palestine en droit international*, 1927.

[35]   *Id.*, pp. 42–43.

[36]   *Id.*, p. 42. Emphasis added.

[37]   *Id.*, p. 43.

[38]   *Id.*, pp. 43–44.

Thus the mandate system is clear in its application to the local inhabitants, to the 'colonies and territories [...] which are inhabited by peoples not yet able to stand by themselves'. As such, there is little validity in Stoyanovsky's assertion that the mandate system left room for European Jewry by allowing for the 'self-government [of] those races, peoples or communities who for various reasons are not yet able to stand alone'. It follows from this that the Council of the League of Nations, in agreeing to the Mandate, in no way sought to protect 'the well-being and development' of the local inhabitants; nor took into consideration 'the wishes of these communities' despite it being 'a principal consideration in the selection of the Mandatory'. As Berriedale Keith, Regius Professor at Edinburgh University, noted, 'it is impossible not to recognize the gravity of the difficulty created for the mandatory by the fact that the adoption of the principle of the Jewish national home runs directly counter to the doctrine of the right of each people to self-determination'[39].

The Council violated the sacred trust despite the safeguards mentioned in the final phrase of the first paragraph of Article 22 which pointed to the 'securities [...] embodied in this Covenant'. Those securities, found at Article 20 of the Covenant, sought to ensure that all future agreements conformed to the dictates of the Covenant. Article 20 of the Covenant of the League of Nations, although awkward in its formulation, appears to be the forerunner of Article 103 of the United Nations Charter. The Article sought to make a clean break from the past international system (the European-based Balance of Power system), and to endow a constitutional nature upon the Covenant of the League of Nations. Article 20 reads:

> The Members of the League severally agree that this Covenant is accepted as abrogating all obligations or understandings *inter se* which are inconsistent with the terms thereof, and solemnly undertake that they will not hereafter enter into any engagements inconsistent with the terms thereof.

By virtue of this provision, States could not enter into agreements, which were inconsistent with the terms of the Covenant, including those related to the establishment of mandates. When the Palestine Arab Congress challenged the incompatibility of the Mandate for Palestine with the Covenant before the League of Nations, it found the League unwilling to act. The contentions came to light when Great Britain produced its first annual report on its administration of Palestine in 1924. The body delegated to consider the report, the Permanent Mandates Commission took note of a petition from the Executive Committee of the Palestine Arab Congress which challenged the terms of the Mandate for Palestine, more specifically seeking 'the establishment in Palestine of a fundamentally different régime from that of the mandate'. The Permanent Mandates Commission found that such a task was *ultra vires* its competence, 'the Commission,

---

[39]   Berriedale Keith, 'Mandate', *Journal of Comparative Legislation and International Law*, Vol. 4, 1922, p. 78. See also, generally, W. F. Boustani, *Palestine Mandate, Invalid and Impracticable*, 1936 and Saadi Bississo, *La politique anglo-sioniste en Palestine: Etude juridique, politique et critique du sionisme et du mandat anglais*, 1937.

considering that its task is confined to supervising the execution of the mandate in the terms prescribed by the Council, is of the opinion that it is not competent to discuss the matter'[40]. It then fell to the Council of the League of Nations, as the League's executive organ to pass judgement on the nature of the Mandate for Palestine as being in conformity with the sacred trust envisioned in Article 22 of the Covenant. The Council, on 10 December 1924, passed a resolution expressing its satisfaction that Palestine is 'in general administered in accordance with the spirit and letter of Article 22 of the Covenant and the terms of the mandates'[41].

The Council of the League of Nations having passed judgement meant that the manifest incompatibility of the Mandate for Palestine with the Covenant was to remain. Despite its incompatibility with the Covenant, the Council of the League was willing to accept the regime of the Mandate for Palestine granted to Britain. Against this backdrop, no challenge could be made to the Zionist-orientated mandate already introduced in Palestine. It was, instead, left to the likes of Pitman Potter, the sitting American judge on the International Court of Justice, to point out the obvious in a 1948 edition of the *American Journal of International Law*. Judge Potter wrote that the 'Arabs deny the binding force of the Mandate, now or ever, as they deny the validity of the Balfour Declaration on which it was based, and again they are probably quite correct juridically'[42].

ii. Palestine under the Mandate

Although Britain sought to implement Zionist policies in Palestine from the 1920 San Remo Conference onwards, it did so until 1923, as has been mentioned, in violation of the laws of war. In August 1920, Turkey signed the Treaty of Sèvres, in which it agreed to the British implementation of the Balfour Declaration, however, the Treaty was never ratified[43]. Instead, Turkish nationalists, led by Mustapha Kemal Atatürk, concluded the First World War by ratifying the 1923 Treaty of Lausanne in September of that year. Through its willingness to fight on, Turkey forced the Allied Powers to not only drop demands regarding the move toward an independent Kurdistan and cessation of territory to Armenia, but also

---

[40]   Fannine Fern, *The Holy Land under Mandate*, Vol. 2, 1931, pp. 152–153.

[41]   *Id.*, p. 153.

[42]   Pitman Potter, 'The Palestine Problem Before the United Nations', *American Journal of Internationals Law*, Vol. 42, 1948, p. 860.

[43]   Article 95, The Treaty of Peace between the Allied and Associated Powers and Turkey, 10 August 1920, reads:

> The High Contracting Parties agree to entrust, by application of the provisions of Article 22, the administration of Palestine, within such boundaries as may be determined by the Principal Allied Powers, to a Mandatory to be selected by the said Powers. The Mandatory will be responsible for putting into effect the declaration originally made on November 2, 1917, by the British Government, and adopted by the other Allied Powers, in favour of the establishment in Palestine of a national home for the Jewish people, it being clearly understood that nothing shall be done which may prejudice the civil and religious rights of existing non-Jewish communities in Palestine, or the rights and political status enjoyed by Jews in any other country. [...]

toward recognizing the Balfour Declaration[44]. Yet, this was of no consequence to Palestine, as from 1920 onward, Britain ruled in line with the Balfour Declaration. At San Remo, British Prime Minister Lloyd George offered to Herbert Samuel the position of first High Commissioner of the civil administration which Britain instituted in Palestine shortly thereafter effectively ending their regime of belligerent occupation.

Thus began the last traditional colonial venture of the modern era, whereby a European State sought to institute its control on a foreign land by supporting European colonial *qua* settler immigration. The Civil Administration sought to implement numerous Zionist policies, though many British in Palestine could see that the task was going to be neither easy nor peaceful. Even during the period 1920–1923 when the mandate had not yet become binding, the British moved to change the character of Palestine in line with its imperial aims which entailed reconstituting the Jewish 'national home in that country'. From 1920 onward, the Administration increased the immigration quota of Jewish people; it agreed, in 1921, to the establishment of Tel Aviv as autonomous from Jaffa, and it showed favour with Jewish business dealings. Well known in the annals of public international law are the Rutenberg concessions which led to the *Mavrommatis* cases before the Permanent Court of International Justice[45]. Pinhas Rutenberg had been granted, in 1921, a monopoly to establish and deliver electric energy throughout Palestine by virtue of an agreement, which stipulated that he could demand, at any time, that the Civil Administration annul previous concessions.

Greece, invoking diplomatic protection on behalf of its national, Euripide Mavrommatis, brought a claim against Great Britain to the Permanent Court by virtue of a compromissory clause related to Mandatory Powers found in the Covenant of the League of Nations[46]. The Hellenic State pointed to the fact that the Rutenberg concession overlapped with the rights which its nation possessed regarding the supply of electrical light and power to Jerusalem gained in 1914. In its 1925 Judgement, the Court held that 'so long as M. Rutenberg possessed the right to require the expropriation of the Mavrommatis concessions, the clause in question was contrary to the obligations contracted by the Mandatory [...]'[47]. While the Court found that Great Britain had violated its international obligations

---

[44]   Article 16, Treaty of Peace between the Allied and Associated Powers and Turkey, 24 July 1923, states:

> Turkey hereby renounces all rights and title whatsoever over or respecting the territories situated outside the frontiers laid down in the present Treaty and the islands other than those over which her sovereignty is recognised by the said Treaty, the future of these territories and islands being settled or to be settled by the parties concerned. [...]

[45]   Three cases regarding this matter were dealt with by the Permanent Court: *Mavrommatis Palestine Concessions* case, *P.C.I.J. Reports*, Series A, No. 2, 30 August 1924; *Mavrommatis Jerusalem Concessions* case, *P.C.I.J. Reports*, Series A, No. 5, 26 March 1925; and, *Case of the Readaption of the Mavrommatis Jerusalem Concessions*, *P.C.I.J. Reports*, Series A, No. 10, 10 October 1927.

[46]   See Article 26, Covenant of the League of Nations.

[47]   *Mavrommatis Jerusalem Concessions* case, *op. cit.* n. 36, p. 40.

while acting as the Mandatory Power, it also pointed out that the Rutenberg concession had not, in fact, led to the annulment of the Mavrommatis concessions and, as such, no reparations were due to the Greek State in compensation for losses to Mavrommatis[48].

British policy favouring Zionist ventures in the early 1920s, such as those put forward by Rutenberg were such that when the Treaty of Lausanne came into force in 1923 and the Mandate for Palestine was accepted by the League of Nations in 1924, they had no noticeable effect in Palestine. While the local Arab and Christian populations sought to have the Mandate rescinded, Zionists were critical of the British for not moving quickly enough in its implementation. Though Britain wavered in its commitment to Zionism, most notably in the White Papers of 1930 and 1939, its policies in Palestine remained pro-Zionist throughout the twenty-eight years of the Mandate[49]. Tom Segev, a columnist for the leading Israeli newspaper *Ha'aretz* and member of the Israeli 'new historiography' stream[50], put forward the following assessment of the British during the Mandate:

> The British kept their promise to the Zionists. They opened up the country to mass Jewish immigration; by 1948, the Jewish population had increased by more than tenfold. The Jews were permitted to purchase land, develop agriculture, and establish industries and banks. The British allowed them to set up hundreds of new settlements, including several towns. They created a school system and an army; they had a political leadership and elected institutions; and with the help of all these they in the end defeated the Arabs, all under British sponsorship, all in the wake of the promise of 1917. Contrary to the widely held belief of Britain's pro-Arabism, British actions considerably favored the Zionist enterprise[51].

During the 1920s the Jewish population in Palestine doubled. Although more than 100,000 immigrated, 'one out of every four newcomers did not remain in the country'. As Segev notes, 'most of those who settled in the country during the 1920s came in search of a better life chose Palestine only after the United States shut its door to mass immigration in 1924'[52]. However, 'during the second decade of British rule, more than a quarter of a million Jews settled in Palestine, twice as many as in the previous ten years. In 1936 [alone] the number of immigrants exceeded sixty thousand'[53]. Whereas the economic conditions spoke against Jewish

---

[48] *Id.*, p. 45.
[49] Tom Segev, *One Palestine, Complete: Jews and Arabs Under the British Mandate*, 2000. For the 1930 White Paper see pp. 335–341; for the 1939 White Paper see pp. 440–443 and 449.
[50] For an exposition of this stream consider: Benny Morris, 'The New Historiography; Israel and its Past', *1948 and After: Israel and the Palestinians*, 1994, pp. 1–48.
[51] Segev, *op. cit.* n. 49 at p. 5.
[52] *Id.*, p. 225. Implicit in this quotation is that immigrants where not Zionist in their outlook. Later, Segev, speaking of Jewish immigrants, noted: 'Many left. In 1926, the number of emigrants was close to half the total of immigrants; in 1927 emigration exceed immigration, and in 1928 the two figures were equal'. See p. 261.
[53] *Id.*, p. 377. Segev adds: 'At the beginning of the 1930s the Jews were about 17 percent of the total population; by the mid-1940s they were 30 percent—almost half a million'. See

immigration to Palestine during the 1920s, the rise of the National Socialist Party in Germany left little choice for many Jewish people in Europe but to seek refuge in Palestine. By the mid-1930s, a critical mass of Jewish people started to emerge in Palestine and with it, a fundamental shift in Zionist thinking: no longer was the sole focus of Zionism in Palestine on saving European Jewry; instead, a 'new Zionist rationale coincided with the growing awareness that war with the Arabs was inevitable'[54].

From the very beginning of the British occupation, its policies being in line with the Balfour Declaration was not well received by the near totality of the local inhabitants. In Jerusalem in 1920, in Jaffa in 1921, and in Hebron in 1929, Jewish people were targeted in violent mob attacks. From the Hebron attacks onward, violence would plague the British Mandate—it became persistent, amounting to an Arab rebellion. Although the Mandate specified that the 'Administration of Palestine may organise on a voluntary basis the forces necessary for the preservation of peace and order', it did not provide for British occupying forces[55]. In 1937, however, there were 25,000 British soldiers and police on Palestinian soil; by 1946 that number had increased to more than 100,000[56]. The British used the imperial tactic honed in India and especially in Ireland to quell subversive activities amongst the Arab population. As Segev writes, 'the laws and regulations under which the authorities conducted their counter-terrorism operations placed responsibility for crimes on the entire community—whole villages, neighborhoods, sometimes even cities. The guiding principle was that everyone is guilty until proven otherwise and everyone was to be punished'[57]. Curfews, collective fines, and home demolition were the order of the day[58]. During the 1930s, the Jewish Agency, the entity mandated to represent Jewish interests in Palestine 'joined forces to suppress the uprising'[59].

The rebels undertook guerrilla tactics, cutting telephone lines, attacking bridges, police stations, and other public targets. The insurgency against the

---

p. 378. Benny Morris places the figures in 1939 at: '1,070,000 Arabs (950,000 Muslims) and 460,000 Jews', *op. cit.* n. 7, p. 122.

[54]   Segev, *id.*, p. 393.

[55]   Article 17, Mandate for Palestine. A reading of Article 17, in conjunction with Article 1 of the Mandate for Palestine, would seem to preclude the mobilization of a foreign professional army or police force: 'The Mandatory shall have full powers of legislation and of administration, save as they may be limited by the terms of this mandate'.

[56]   Segev, *op. cit.* n. 49, pp. 415 and 475.

[57]   *Id.*, p. 420.

[58]   See Segev's Chapter entitled 'Ireland in Palestine', pp. 415–443; as for the destruction of several hundred houses in the Old City of Jaffa in 1936, see pp. 399–400. Such collective punishment was, of course, *later* outlawed by the 1949 Geneva Convention (IV), Article 33 reads: 'No protected person may be punished for an offence he or she has not personally committed. Collective penalties and likewise all measures of intimidation or of terrorism are prohibited'.

[59]   *Id.*, p. 382. Segev writes: 'Jewish and British officials coordinated manhunts and collective actions against villages and discussed the imposition of penalties and sentences', p. 428.

Mandate and the general strike of 1936, which lasted six months, led the British to create the Peel Commission meant to examine the disturbances in Palestine and to make recommendations with an aim to removing the grievances. The Royal Commission determined that the Mandate was unworkable and called for a two-State solution with the partition of Palestine and the transfer of populations[60]. David Ben-Gurion, later Israel's first Prime Minister, saw this as the Israeli 'Declaration of Independence' as, for the first time, the British were calling for the creation of a solely Jewish State. The lull of the Arab revolt, caused by the Peel Commission's visit to Palestine in late 1936, did not last, as the recommendations of the Commission were rejected by the British Government, violence resumed. However, after the prospect of an independent Jewish State—free of the Arab population—was mooted, the British had to contend with the growing agitation of the Jewish population.

In Palestine, Jewish underground organizations were formed and took it upon themselves to initiate 'counter-terrorist' activities. In retribution for attacks against the ever growing number of Jewish colonies and settlements, these clandestine organizations introduced, in the late 1930s, 'a new dimension into the conflict'— 'bombing against Arab crowds and buses' which 'soon found Arab imitators and became something of a "tradition" during the coming decades'[61]. When the British determined in 1938, that the Peel Commission's partition plan was, itself, unworkable, it followed with the 1939 White Paper that sought to place limits on Jewish immigration over a five-year period, to be followed by an Arab agreement over all future immigration to Palestine[62]. Further, restrictions were proposed on Jewish land purchases and the Paper called for an end to British involvement and an 'independent Palestine with majority rule within ten years'[63]. With what was seen as a reversal of policy in Palestine, the Zionist leadership turned on its British patrons. Ben-Gurion, despite being the leader of the Jewish Agency, stepped up illegal immigration and ordered the establishment of underground 'special operations' squads meant to undertake 'retaliatory strikes against Arab terrorist' but also aiming 'attacks on British installations and the elimination of informers'[64].

These attacks against the British Administration were suspended for a short period in the early 1940s as a larger issue came to dominate Zionist considerations: the beginning of the Second World War. With the clearly anti-Semitic National Socialist Party leading Germany's territorial expansion, the Jewish Agency delivered an 'unequivocal declaration of allegiance to the United Kingdom'[65]. However, illegal immigration continued to take place as European Jews sought refuge from—in what must be considered one of the darkest chapters of history—

---

[60] Morris, *op. cit.* n. 7, pp. 138–144.
[61] *Id.*, p. 147.
[62] See Nevill Barbour, 'The White Paper of 1939', in Khalidi, *op. cit.* n. 8, pp. 461–475.
[63] Morris, *op. cit.* n. 7, p. 158.
[64] *Id.*, p. 148. Segev puts it this way: 'According to Nachum Shadmi, the unit commander, the Special Operations Units were established to strike at Arabs who killed Jews, but also the British administration, and at Jewish informers and traitors', *op. cit.* n. 49, p. 386.
[65] Morris, *op. cit.* n. 7, p. 161.

persecution, later to be revealed as the Nazi Holocaust. Policy decisions during this era hardly reflect well on the United Kingdom. British reaction to continued illegal immigration was to suspend all immigration to Palestine. The British 'adopted a policy of capturing' ships carrying Jewish refugees destined for Palestine 'and deporting the immigrants en masse to special islands camps', must notably in Cyprus[66]. The very existence of the Zionist venture was under pressure during the War years as Italy and Germany opened a North African front and moved halfway across Egypt's Mediterranean coast until they were defeated at the hands of Allied forces at el-Alamein. When it became clear that the Allied Powers would emerge from the Second World War victorious, the tide of Zionist support shifted against the British. Zionists sought a new patron in the United States of America, while Menachem Begin, later Prime Minister of Israel, issued, on behalf of the extremist underground group *Etzel*, a 'declaration of war' against the British in February 1944[67].

IV. Toward the State of Israel

After the Second World War, the British found little gratification in the Mandate. The United Kingdom, exhausted by the war effort, found it difficult to justify maintaining 100,000 men in Palestine in a situation where both the Arab and Jewish populations were targeting them for attack. At a loss to further justify maintaining the Mandate was the fact that the independence of India was looming. The strategic rationale for having supported Zionist policies in Palestine, the protection of the northern flank of the Suez Canal as the 'jugular vein'[68] of the British Empire no longer held. To add insult to injury, the United States subverted British policy by openly supporting increased immigration to Palestine despite the moratorium imposed by the British White Paper of 1939[69]. Exasperated, the United Kingdom sought to exit Palestine and as a result, in February 1946, the Foreign Secretary, Ernest Bevin declared in the House of Commons:

> His Majesty's Government have of themselves no power, under the terms of the Mandate, to award the country either to the Arabs or to the Jews, or even to partition it between them. [...] We have therefore, reached the conclusion that the only course now

---

[66] *Id.*, p. 163. Morris goes on to note: 'but British policy was highlighted as inhumane, and the need for a sanctuary for the world's oppressed Jews was made clear to the community of nations, especially the United States. The Royal [British] Navy and the security forces in Palestine had managed to keep Jewish immigration down and the Arabs quiescent, but the persistent, cumulative embarrassment that the policy engendered was among the factors that led to Britain's eventual withdrawal from Palestine after the war', p. 164.

[67] See David Ben-Gurion, 'We Look Towards America, 1939', in Khalidi, *op. cit.* n. 8, pp. 481–488. With respect to *Etzel* see Segev, *op. cit.* n. 49, p. 456.

[68] Anthony Gorst and Lewis Johman, *The Suez Crisis*, 1997, p. 1; quoting Lord Hankey.

[69] For the role played by the United States in Palestine during the 1945–1948 period, see Dan Tschirgi, *The Politics of Indecision: Origins and Implications of American Involvement with the Palestine Problem*, 1983.

open to us is to submit the problem to the judgment of the United Nations. We intend to place before them an historical account of the way in which H. M. Government have discharged their trust in Palestine over the last 25 years. We shall explain that the Mandate has proved to be unworkable in practice, and that the obligations undertaken to the two communities in Palestine have been shown to be irreconcilable. [...] We shall then ask the United Nations to consider our report, and to *recommend* a settlement of the problem. We do not intend ourselves to recommend any particular solution[70].

i. *United Nations' Action Regarding Palestine*

Although the League of Nations was superseded with the creation of the United Nations Organization after the Second World War, the mandate system envisioned by Article 22 of the Covenant was not automatically transferred to the new International Trusteeship System incorporated into the UN Charter[71]. Instead, the transfer of mandates to the new system was to be achieved by virtue of an agreement as between the United Nations and the Mandatory State[72]. By agreeing to shift a Mandate to the International Trusteeship System, a State was undertaking the:

> responsibilities for the administration of territories whose peoples have not yet attained a full measure of self-government, recognize the principle that the interests of the inhabitants of these territories are paramount, and accept as a sacred trust the obligation to promote to the utmost, within the system of international peace and security established by the present Charter, the well-being of the inhabitants of these territories[73].

While the United Kingdom indicated that it was prepared to place Palestine under the Trusteeship System, it would do so only if the United Nations was in agreement on this point[74]. Despite an American proposal to establish such a trusteeship for

---

[70] Jacob Robinson, *Palestine and the United Nations*, 1971, pp. 34–35. Emphasis added.

[71] The Assembly of the League of Nations terminated the League of Nations on 18 April 1946. See Bruno Simma (ed.), *The Charter of the United Nations: A Commentary*, 1995, p. 995.

[72] See Articles 75 and 80, Charter of the United Nations. The Trusteeship System went beyond simply applying to former mandates, it also was meant to apply to all territories that were not self-governed including: territories lost to the Axis Powers, defeated during the Second World War, and those territories that were to be voluntarily placed under the System. See Article 77.

[73] *Id.*, Article 73.

[74] Note that this was in line with the obligations under Chapter XII of the Charter: To simply work toward gaining a trustee agreement (the other alternative was to grant full independence), Although Hersch Lauterpacht noted that the obligations came close to being legal ones:

> Although, according to its wording, the Charter imposes no clear obligation upon states which were mandatories by virtue of Article 22 of the Covenant to place the territories in question under the system of trusteeship, it is clear that an obligation to this effect closely approaching a legal duty follows from the principles of the Charter.

Palestine in March 1948, it came to naught[75]. Instead, the avenue by which the United Kingdom sought the assistance of the United Nations was through the UN General Assembly.

Between the voluntary nature of turning mandates to trusts under the United Nations and the termination of the Covenant of the League of Nations with its supervisory mechanism for mandates, the Mandate for Palestine was to be dealt with by the United Nations within a legal vacuum. There were only two legal options available to the United Kingdom: it could grant independence or hand the Mandate over to the United Nations via the International Trusteeship System. However, neither option bode well for the Jewish population in Palestine. A fundamental principle of the United Nations Charter, found at Article 2(2), is that of 'self-determination of peoples'. Under such a regime, autonomy might well be offered to the minority Jewish population but the likelihood of Arab agreement to autonomy was remote; statehood non-existent. The second option was no better, as the International Trusteeship System was established, in part, to amplify on the dictates of Article 2(2). In this vein, Article 73 calls for the development of self-government whereby the interests of the inhabitants is to be paramount. With the shift in the balance of power from Europe to America, it was clear that the Trusteeship System was not going to be the half-way house for colonialism that the mandate system had been. As such, the United Kingdom sought to avoid a solution which would be detrimental to its previous policies but at the same time to avoid the wrath of Arab States, and thus turned, in 1947, to the UN General Assembly.

A Special Session of the UN General Assembly convened in May 1947 and agreed to the establishment of an eleven-State Special Committee on Palestine (UNSCOP) which considered the issue and return to the General Assembly with two proposed solutions. UNSCOP was unanimous in calling for the end of the Mandate for Palestine, however, the Committee could not agree on what would come in its stead. The report delivered at the end of August 1947 consisted of a minority report—calling for a federal State which ended up being still-born—and a majority report which called for the partition of Palestine. The majority report proposed the creation of an Arab and Jewish State with an economic union, while Jerusalem was to be governed by an international regime[76]. In the lead-up to the November vote before the General Assembly on the proposals being put forward by UNSCOP, the British Cabinet decided that it would evacuate Palestine[77]. Irrespective of the outcome of UN deliberations, the United Kingdom's public posture would forthwith be to abstain from taking any active part in seeking a solution to the Palestine issue. Fearful of aggravating its position *vis-à-vis* Arab

---

See Hersch Lauterpacht (ed.), *Oppenheim's International Law: A Treaties*, 1947, p. 208.

[75]   See Michael Cohen, *Palestine and the Great Powers: 1945–1948*, 1982, pp. 354–366.

[76]   For a discussion of the work of UNSCOP and its aftermath see Martin Jones, *Failure in Palestine: British and United States Policy after the Second World War*, pp. 249–307.

[77]   See Morris, *op. cit.* n. 7, pp. 183–184.

States and their Jewish constituency, the United Kingdom simply sought, publicly at least, to wash its hands of the whole affair[78].

ii. United Nations General Assembly Resolution 181

On 29 November 1947, amidst much arm-twisting, the majority proposal for partition was passed by the UN General Assembly as Resolution 181[79] by a vote of thirty-three to thirteen with ten abstentions[80]. Resolution 181 called on the Security Council to take the necessary measures to ensure the Resolution's implementation. However this was not to be, as Warren Austin, United States Ambassador to the United Nations, at the time, correctly pointed out:

> The Security Council is authorized to take forceful measures with respect to Palestine to remove a threat to international peace. The Charter of the United Nations does not empower the Security Council to enforce a political settlement whether it is pursuant to a recommendation of the General Assembly or of the Security Council itself ... the Security Council's action, in other words, is directed to keeping the peace and not to enforce partition[81].

Thus, without the willingness of the Security Council to act in implementing Resolution 181, it was left, as was noted in its preamble to 'the United Kingdom, as the mandatory Power for Palestine, and to all other Members of the United Nations' to adopt and implement the Resolution. Resolution 181 called for the termination of the Mandate for Palestine with the evacuation of British forces by August 1948, with the establishment of a UN Commission to assist in the transition from British tutelage to self-rule. The Resolution sets out the basis upon which both an Arab and Jewish State were to declare their independence, with a view to protecting the Holy Places, and the rights of minority groups. UN General Assembly Resolution 181 then called for the establishment of an economic union with a customs union, joint currency, and the establishment of a mechanism for joint operation of common interests including 'railways, postal, telephone and telegraphic services'. Further, the Union sought to establish joint economic development in the guise of 'irrigation, land reclamation and soil conservation'; and to provide for each State and Jerusalem to have access on a 'non-discriminatory basis' to water and power facilities.

---

[78] For the British role in subverting the UN Partition Plan and supporting King Abdullah's wish to annex the West Bank to Jordan see the section entitled 'Abul Huda and Bevin: the collusion' in Alvi Shlaim, *Collusion across the Jordan: King Abdullah, the Zionist Movement, and the Partition of Palestine*, 1988, pp. 132–140.
[79] United Nations General Assembly Resolution 181, 29 November 1947.
[80] See Cohen, *op. cit.* n. 75, pp. 292–300; but also Sir Muhammad Khan, 'Thanksgiving Day at Lake Success, November 27, 1947, General Carlos Romulo, 'The Philippines Changes its Vote', and Kermit Roosevelt, 'The Partition of Palestine: A Lesson in Pressure Politics', in Khalidi, *op. cit.* n. 8, pp. 709–730.
[81] Cohen, *op. cit.* n. 75, pp. 351–352.

The borders of the Arab State were spelled out in great detail in Resolution 181 while the Jewish State, which was to consist of fifty-five percent of Palestine[82], was outlined by reference to international borders and juxtaposed to the borders of the Arab State. The borders of the city of Jerusalem were not only to include the municipality of Jerusalem, but were to include surrounding villages including Bethlehem. The regime governing Jerusalem was to be a *corpus separatum* administered by the United Nations, with the Trusteeship Council being charged with the responsibility for administrating the trust. In effect a city-state, Jerusalem was to be a demilitarised, neutral, enclave which allowed for local autonomy, but was to be headed by a United Nations governor. The Trusteeship Council was obliged to prepare a detailed Statute of the City in which it would ensure the protection of the Holy Places with an aim of ensuring that 'order and peace, and especially religious peace, reign in Jerusalem'. Further the Statute was to foster cooperation amongst the inhabitants with the aim of developing 'the mutual relations between the two Palestinian peoples throughout the Holy Land'. The Statute was to last for a ten-year period after which a referendum was to take place as to the future governing of the city.

The British for their part, abstained from voting on Resolution 181; in line with the British Cabinet decision that it would not endorse any recommendations emanating from the United Nations. As noted by Israeli historian Benny Morris, the British Cabinet had decided shortly after UNSCOP's findings that 'either the UN would set up the machinery for an orderly transfer of power or else the Arabs and the Jews would settle the problem on their own, by force of arms. In either case, it was no longer Britain's responsibility'[83]. The United Kingdom had announced in December that it was pulling out of Palestine on 15 May 1948, and that henceforth its policy would be 'one of "manful abstention" in order to preserve her "neutrality" and her relations with Arab States'[84]. Despite the United Kingdom having been responsible for changing the character of Palestine which led to a spiral of violence, it was unwilling to formally accept the recommendations of Resolution 181. Instead, it 'stuck doggedly to its opposition to the arrival of the UN Commission' which was meant to fill the gap after the termination of the Mandate[85].

While British support for Resolution 181 might well have lent political legitimacy to the partition plan, its attitude toward the General Assembly's recommendation is irrelevant when considering the legal value of the United Nations' proposal regarding the future of Palestine. This is so, because, by its very nature, resolutions of the United Nations General Assembly lack the binding authority of law[86]. With respect to the powers of the General Assembly there are no parallel provisions within the Charter to that of Article 25 which provides that the

---

[82] Morris, *op. cit.* n. 7, p. 184.

[83] *Id.*, pp. 183–184.

[84] Jones, *op. cit.* n. 76, p. 309.

[85] *Id.*

[86] See Ian Brownlie, *Principles of Public International Law*, 1995, p. 14 and footnote citations.

Members 'agree to accept and carry out the decisions of the Security Council in accordance with the present Charter'. The powers of the UN General Assembly are outlined in Article 10, but the Charter limits the General Assembly's functions to that of making recommendations regarding any 'question or matters within the scope' of the Charter. When the United Nations first considered the issue of Palestine, it was clear that the Member States recognised the lack of authority of the General Assembly. As Jacob Robinson, Head of the World Jewish Congress, wrote the Members:

> wanted to be satisfied that the results of their labors would not be in vain, and they wanted to have a clear-cut answer from Great Britain as to how far Great Britain would be committed to a recommendation made of the General Assembly. It was fully realized that a recommendation of the General Assembly had, in the legal sense, no binding force[87].

Where resolutions of the UN General Assembly might act as a source of law is in the ability of the Assembly to act as the locus of the expression of *opinio juris* of the community of States. However, such an expression is part of a process which, if accompanied by State practice, may lead to the formation of a customary norm of international law. As a one-off resolution, Resolution 181 could not, in and of itself, constitute a binding obligation on States. Further, the fact that the vote of the General Assembly was not unanimous and lacked the support of neighboring States meant that the value of Resolution 181, even from the perspective of an expression of *opinio juris* was of little juridical value[88]. In sum, General Assembly Resolution 181, like the Balfour Declaration before it, lacked legal obligation. The United Nations did not possess sovereignty over Palestine and thus could not partition it; likewise United Nations General Assembly Resolution 181 did not bind the UN Members to any course of action, it being a recommendation. As Ian Brownlie has noted in his *Principles of International Law*:

> It is doubtful if the United Nations 'has a capacity to convey title' in part because the Organization cannot assume the role of territorial sovereign [...] the Organization is not a state and the General Assembly only has the power of recommendation. Thus the resolution of 1947 containing a partition plan for Palestine was probably *ultra vires*, and, if it was not, was not binding on member states in any case[89].

---

[87]   Jacob Robinson, *Palestine and the United Nations*, 1971, p. 57.

[88]   The States that voted against Resolution 181 were Afghanistan, Cuba, Egypt, Greece, India, Iran, Iraq, Lebanon, Pakistan, Saudi Arabia, Syria, Turkey, and Yemen.

[89]   See Ian Brownlie, *op. cit.* n. 86, pp. 172–173. Brownlie goes on to say: 'However, this may be, the fact is that states may agree to delegate a power of disposition to a political organ of the United Nations, at least where the previous sovereign has relinquished title and there is no transfer of sovereignty and no disposition of a title inhering in the Organization. The latter acts primarily as a referee'. Note also the appraisal of Quincy Wright in John Halderman (ed.), *The Middle East Crisis: Test of International Law*, 1969, at p. 12 where he states: 'The legality of the General Assembly's recommendation for partition of Palestine was doubtful'.

Thus, excluding the United Nations from the equation, upon the termination of the mandate, Palestine should have been granted independence. Article 22 of the Covenant made it plain that the former Ottoman possession, having 'reached a stage of development where their existence as independent nations' was provisionally recognised but for 'the rendering of administrative advice and assistance by a Mandatory'[90]. As such, and in light of the United Nations Charter's institutionalization of the notion of self-determination, Palestine should have been granted independence.

iii. Proclamation of the State of Israel

Between the passing of UN General Assembly Resolution 181 on 29 November 1947 and the termination of the British Mandate scheduled for 15 May 1948, Palestine plunged into civil war. The events in Palestine were quickly outstripping efforts to find a peaceful solution within the United Nations Organization, where support for the partition plan was wavering in light of the reception which Resolution 181 was receiving in Palestine and the obstinacy of the United Kingdom in sticking to its date of departure. In Tel Aviv, on 14 May 1948, the first Prime Minister of Israel, David Ben-Gurion, made the following Proclamation:

> [...] Accordingly we, the members of the National Council, representing the Jewish people in Palestine and the World Zionist Movement, are met together in solemn assembly today, the day of termination of the British Mandate for Palestine; and by virtue of the natural and historical rights of the Jewish people and of the Resolution of the General Assembly of the United Nations,
>
> We hereby proclaim the establishment of the Jewish State in Palestine, to be called Medinath Yisrael (The State of Israel)[91].

A few hours after this proclamation, the United States of America was the first to recognise the Provisional Government as the *de facto* authority of the State of Israel, followed, two days later, by *de jure* recognition of the State of Israel by the Soviet Union, and thereafter recognition by a majority of Member States of the United Nations.

The Proclamation of the State of Israel, in and of itself, carries no juridical weight internationally. However, the ability to sustain the existence of a State in the face of attacks of neighbouring Arab States, and the willingness of other States to give recognition to Israel as being a member of the community of States meant that its existence as a State gained juridical validation. It is clear that had Israel not been able to repel the intervention of 1948, its status as a State would have receded, becoming little more than an historical footnote. Yet Israel was able to establish its control over substantial parts of Palestine. The ability to hold this territory does

---

[90]   Where the Mandate for Palestine mentions termination, it did so only in relations to protecting the Holy Places. See Article 28, Mandate for Palestine.

[91]   See Henry Cattan, *Palestine and International Law: The Legal Aspects of the Arab-Israeli Conflict*, 1973, p. 87.

not, in and of itself, however amount to statehood. As early as 1933, the norms that underlie the constitutive elements of a State were expressed in the Montevideo Convention on Rights and Duties of States. The Treaty provides that a State 'as a person of international law should possess the following qualifications: a) a permanent population; b) a defined territory; c) government; and d) capacity to enter into relations with other States'[92]. Thus the establishment of a State is posited on meeting what amounts to two objective criteria: a defined population and territory; and two subject elements: the effective control of a government and recognition by other States.

At the end of the day, the ability of the State of Israel to demonstrate that it had effective control over a certain territory and population—in other words that it could maintain sovereignty over a portion of territory to the exclusion of others, meant that it was demonstrating traits of independence. However, the willingness of States to recognise Israel before it had established itself was clearly a leap of faith that had little to do with the legal validity of the claim. Regarding the recognition of newly established States, Hersch Lauterpacht wrote in 1947, 'there is probably no other subject in the field of international relations in which law and politics appear to be more closely interwoven'[93]. Yet, while recognition leads to the granting of legal personality on the international plane, the determination of whether a State will be recognised is, in the words of Malcolm Shaw, Sir Robert Jennings Professor of International Law at the University of Leicester, 'highly political and is given in a number of cases for purely political reasons'[94]. It is for each State to make a determination as to whether a would-be-State fulfills the criteria of statehood; that its decision may be based on criteria beyond those generally understood to be the basis of a State is left to the sovereign prerogative of the determining State[95]. Thus, the establishment of the State of Israel ultimately came about as a result of the ability of Zionists to establish and maintain effective control over areas of Palestine and the recognition by members of the international community that Israel indeed constituted a sovereign State.

V. Conclusion

There is no question as to the legal validity of the creation of the State of Israel. The establishment of States in international law is predicated on the ability to demonstrate control over a certain population and a specific territory coupled with

---

[92]   See Brownlie, *op. cit.* n. 86, p. 72.
[93]   Hersch Lauterpacht, *Recognition in International Law*, 1947, p. v.
[94]   Malcolm Shaw, *International Law*, 1997, p. 297.
[95]   See Ian Brownlie, 'Recognition in Theory and Practice', *British Yearbook of International Law*, Vol. 53, 1982, pp. 197–211. For a general examination of the topic of the evolution toward the creation of the State of Israel see James Crawford, 'Israel (1948–1949) and Palestine (1998–1999); Two Studies in the Creation of States', Guy Goodwin-Gill and Stefen Talmon, (eds.), *The Reality of International Law: Essays in Honour of Ian Brownlie*, 1999, pp. 95–124.

recognition of the status of a sovereign State by other members of the league of States. The issue raised here concerns the qualitatively different manner in which international law is applied and interpreted in the Middle East. The process that allowed a critical mass of European Jewish immigrants to be in a position to fight for, and establish, the State of Israel came about as a result of a manifest disregard for the international legal obligation by Britain toward the 1907 Convention related to the laws of war, and in violation of the Covenant of the League of Nations through the incorporation of the Balfour Declaration into the Mandate for Palestine. The historical irony is that it is Lord Balfour himself who makes this plain in his personal correspondence with Lloyd George, noting that in the 'case of Palestine' Great Britain, 'deliberately and rightly decline to accept the principle of self-determination'[96]; and with Lord Curzon, where he acknowledges that the 'contradiction between the letters of the Covenant and the policy of the Allies is flagrant in the case of the "independent nation" of Palestine'. Where Balfour noted that 'the Powers have made no statement of fact which is not admittedly wrong, and no declaration of policy which, at least in the letter, they have not always intended to violate'[97].

The case of the evolution toward the creation of the State of Israel demonstrates the willingness of Great Britain, but also other European Powers and the United States, to impose their will on the region at the expense of the dictates of international law. In the next chapter, consideration is given to an effect of the creation of the State of Israel which persists to this day in the guise of the nearly one million Palestinian Refugees and their offspring who not only fled their homes but have been effectively abandoned by the State of Israel, that has been unwilling to allow them to return to their homes; by neighbouring Arab States, which have been unwilling to allow for integration into the local communities; and by the international community, which has been unwilling to ensure that the rights of Palestinian Refugees are respected or upheld. With these three failings in mind, this study now turns to the case of the abandonment of Palestinian Refugees.

---

[96] See *supra.*, n. 26.
[97] See *supra.*, n. 32.

Chapter 4

Lack of Enforcement of International Law and the Abandonment of Palestinian Refugees

The abandonment of the Palestinian Refugees has transpired through parallel abandonment of international law. An unwillingness by the international community to see its legal pronouncements upheld has meant that where the Palestinian Refugees are concerned, few laws hold, be they refugee law, human rights law, or humanitarian law. This legal vacuum, which has enveloped Palestinian Refugees, has meant that their ultimate fate is to be decided through a political outcome in which their *rights* are negotiable, their wishes inconsequential, and their physical well-being negligible. Forced to flee their homes more than fifty years ago, in the period surrounding the creation of the State of Israel in 1948, Palestinian Refugees found themselves abandoned, by Israel which rejected their return, and surrounding Arab States which were unwilling to integrate them for want of recognizing *un fait accompli*. Beyond this abandonment, Palestinian Refugees have seen their rights as refugees abandoned by the international community that has been unwilling to apply or enforce international legal obligations on their behalf.

Although international law provides for the right of return and the protection of refugees, the failings of international law are manifest in the inability to provide a solution to the nearly four million Palestinian Refugees who, by the start of the twenty–first century, remain in exile. The effective abandonment of the Palestinian Refugees is today reflected in the fact that they are the only refugee population excluded from the international protection of UNHCR. While the Palestinian Refugees in Jordan, Lebanon, and Syria receive material assistance from the international community through UNRWA, their level of integration into host States has been hampered by the unwillingness of these States to allow Palestinians to settle permanently. As a result, hardship has endured and little more than sustenance has been a way of life for these stateless persons existing in perpetual limbo. In the territories occupied by Israel in 1967, large numbers of Palestinians became refugees for a second time, while the 1948 Refugees who decided to stay have seen their human rights and international humanitarian law systematically violated through the Israeli occupation. In this case, through omission—through an inability or unwillingness to act—the Middle East bears witness to the failing of

States to respect the dictates of international law leading to a manifest qualitative difference in the manner in which international law is applied is the region.

I. Creating Palestinian Refugees

As issues surrounding Palestinian Refugees directly impact on a final settlement in Palestine, it is little wonder that this area has been politicised to the extent that many myths and fabrications find their way in to the public discourse. Yet, for the specialists many of these misconceptions have fallen to the wayside as declassified material from both the Israeli and British archives has emerged regarding the War of 1948. The ability of historians and researchers to examine this material has allowed them to move away—at least where Israel is concerned—from 'official' State history, spawning a movement of 'new historiography'. Primary amongst the 'New Historians' is Benny Morris, Professor of History at Ben-Gurion University, who has used this archival material as a basis of a fundamental re-evaluation of events that led to the exodus of Palestinians in the late 1940s. Thus, while events surrounding the creation of the 1948 Palestinian Refugees remain controversial at the political level, at the level of scholarship, while debate remains, a general understanding has emerged.

i. Palestinian Flight

The first wave of Palestinian exodus resulted from the passing of the United Nations' Partition Plan—General Assembly Resolution 181—of 29 November 1947. With the termination of the British Mandate for Palestine looming and the will of the international community to allow for a bi-State solution, many well-off Palestinians in the areas earmarked to become part of a Jewish State began to take refuge in neighbouring States[1]. As hostilities increased, approaching open warfare, between Palestinian Arabs and Jews, its causal effect on Palestinian flight was not lost on Zionist leaders, such as David Ben-Gurion. In December 1947, he related to his political party that fighting had depopulated large segments of Jerusalem:

> what has happened in Jerusalem ... could well happen in great parts of the country—if we [the Jewish community] hold on ... And if we hold on, it is very possible that in the coming six or eight or ten months of the war there will take place great changes ... and not all of them to our detriment. Certainly there will be great changes in the composition of the population of the country[2].

---

[1]   The flight of many of the elite in Palestine has been attributed to the fact that, during the Mandate, Britain excluded the formation of Palestinian institutions which would have allowed for the galvanization of institutions thus building a sense of community. Without this sense of community, those that were well off were more concerned with their own well-being than that of the community at large. See Rashid Khalidi, 'The Palestinians and 1948: the underlying causes of failure', Eugene Rogan and Avi Shlaim (eds.), *The War for Palestine: Rewriting the History of 1948*, 2001, pp. 12–36.
[2]   Benny Morris, *The Birth of the Palestinian Refugee Problem, 1947–1949*, 1987, p. 52.

While no premeditated political plan existed to rid a newly created State of Israel of its Arab population, the Jewish military was given the green light, in March 1948, under 'Plan D' 'for the conquest and permanent occupation, or leveling, of Arab villages and towns', that interfered with the securing of the interior of Israel[3]. This was considered vital from a military perspective as Jewish forces expected an imminent attack by Arab States, and thus would have to concentrate on attempting to defend their external frontiers. As the State of Israel moved to consolidate itself, the expulsion of Palestinians became acute. Where previously a 'psychosis of flight'[4] had been enough to frighten off large numbers of Palestinians, with the defeat of invading Arab forces, came a push by the Israeli Defence Force (IDF) to clear newly gained territories.

It may be said that in the period leading up to the declaration of the creation of the State of Israel on 14 May 1948, Palestinian flight was caused by a number of factors, the greatest being 'direct Jewish operations against Arab settlements'[5]. Included in these military actions was Operation Nahshon, which sought to establish Jewish control over the Tel Aviv-Jerusalem corridor, and did so by clearing 'whole areas, permanently, of Arab villages and hostile or potentially hostile villagers'[6]. A report prepared by the Intelligence Services of the IDF relates that 'it is possible to say that at least fifty-five percent of the total of the exodus was caused by our [regular and irregular Jewish forces] operations and by their influence'[7]. By comparison, both orders by Arab leaders to evacuate villages, and orders of expulsion by Jewish forces, amount to less than five percent of between 300,000 and 400,000 Palestinians who fled before the end of the British Mandate and the creation of the State of Israel[8]. Benny Morris states that Operation Nahshon was a watershed for the Zionists of Palestine:

> If at the start of the war the Yishuv [Jewish community] had been reluctantly willing to countenance a Jewish State with a large, peaceful Arab minority, by April the military commanders' thinking had radically changed: the toll on Jewish life and security in the battle of the roads and the dire prospects of the invasion of Palestine by Arab armies had left the Haganah [Jewish military] with very narrow margins of safety. [...] This was certainly true with the regard to strategically vital roads, and areas such as the Jerusalem corridor.
>
> No comprehensive expulsion directive—beyond the preamble of Plan D—was ever issued; no hard and fast orders went out to front, [sic] brigade and battalion commanders to expel Arab villages *en masse* or to level villages. But the doctrinal underpinning of Plan D was taken for granted by the majority of the Haganah commanders at this crucial

---

[3]   *Id.*, p. 63.

[4]   *Id.*, p. 287, quoting the Israel Defence Forces Intelligence Service Analysis mentioned at n. 7.

[5]   See Benny Morris, 'The Cause and Character of the Arab Exodus from Palestine: The Israel Defence Forces Intelligence Service Analysis of June 1948', *1948 and After: Israel and the Palestinians*, 1994, p. 88.

[6]   Morris (*The Birth of the Palestinian Refugee Problem*), *op. cit.* n. 2, p. 112.

[7]   Morris (*1948 and After*), *op. cit.* n. 5, p. 89.

[8]   *Id.*, pp. 90–91 and 102.

juncture of the war, when the Yishuv faced, and knew it faced, a life and death struggle. The gloves had to be, and were, taken off[9].

The most pertinent example of this 'gloves off' approach was the 'qualified consent of the Haganah commander in Jerusalem' to allow the paramilitary *qua* terrorist Irgun and Stern gangs to undertake an operation in April 1948 against the village of Deir Yassin which resulted in the massacre of at least two hundred and fifty Arab civilians[10]. This attack, the United Nations Conciliation Commission for Palestine would report, 'added further impetus to the flight of the Arab refugees by providing all too tangible grounds for previously ill-defined fears'[11]. The alarm manifested by the events at Deir Yassin precipitated a new wave of Palestinian flight which resulted from the collapse of Arab forces after their ill-fated invasion of the newly proclaimed State of Israel. With the defeat of Arab forces during the summer of 1948, the Jewish community in Palestine turned from the defensive to consolidate the State of Israel beyond the borders of the UN Partition Plan. In the aftermath of the war, the Israeli Defence Force placed various levels of physical pressure on Palestinians, using 'black propaganda', intimidation, threats of eviction, and, finally, expulsion to clear areas meant to be incorporated into the new State. IDF 'clearing operations', which were undertaken in growing numbers during the latter half of 1948, were meant to remove rural Arabs from the interior of the burgeoning State of Israel. As a result of these clearing operations more than 100,000 Palestinians fled[12].

In October and November 1948, Israeli forces undertook offensive operations, which greatly expanded the land mass of the new State; this included the conquering of the Negev Desert in the south to the Gulf of Aqaba and in the north, of Galilee. By this time, IDF commanders were inclined to force out Arab civilian populations, while these civilians lived in fear of the manner in which they would be treated by Israeli forces. 'Hence when the offensives were unleashed, there was a "coalescence" of Jewish and Arab expectations, which led, especially in the south, to spontaneous flight by the locals and "nudging" if not direct expulsion orders by the advancing IDF columns'[13]. These operations resulted in the exodus of another 100,000 to 150,000 Palestinians. Benny Morris has summarised his research in the following manner, 'The Palestinian refugee problem was born of war, not by design, Jewish or Arab'[14]. However, a more accurate assessment, having considered

---

[9]   Morris (*The Birth of the Palestinian Refugee Problem*), *op. cit.* n. 2, p. 113. Emphasis in the original.

[10]   *Id.*

[11]   United Nations Conciliation Commission for Palestine, *Historical Survey of the Question of Compensation*, A/AC.25/W.81, 6 April, 1955, para. 11.

[12]   Morris (*The Birth of the Palestinian Refugee Problem*), *op. cit.* n. 2, p. 216. See also Morris' reevaluation of this book in Benny Morris, 'Revisiting the Palestinian exodus of 1948', Rogan and Shlaim, *op. cit.* n. 1, pp. 37–59.

[13]   *Id.*, p. 235.

[14]   *Id.*, p. 286. Morris lays waste to both the myth that there was a grand design by Zionists to rid Palestine of its non-Jewish population and to the myth that Palestinians were asked to leave their homes by Arab leaders. For the latter consider Morris' statement, 'at no point

Morris' work and its critiques, appears to be that the flight of Palestinian refugee was caused in large measure by a victorious army seeking to conquer and consolidate its gains at the expense of the local inhabitants[15]. While having been born of war, the IDF understood, as did the civilian leadership, that a State of Israel divested of a large Arab population would ensure its continued existence. As such, where flight did not take place spontaneously, Israeli forces, in fact, 'nudged', through various means of psychological and physical intimidation, the Palestinians on their way. Physical expulsion was the last means on a continuum of intimidation meant to achieve 'Arab-clean' areas[16].

ii. Barring Return

The outcome of these various waves of exodus was that nearly half of all Palestinians, between 600,000 and 760,000 were made refugees by the UN Partition Plan and the ensuing 1948 War[17]. What makes the issue of Palestinian Refugees unique is not the number of refugees—ten million refugees resulted from Bangladesh's cessation from Pakistan in the early 1970s—but their inability to

---

during the war did the Arab leaders issue a blanket call to Palestine's Arabs to leave their homes and villages and wander into exile. Nor was there an Arab radio and press campaign urging or ordering the Palestinians to flee. Indeed, I have found no trace of such a campaign and had it taken place, had there been such broadcasts, they would have been quoted or at least left traces in the documentation'. See Benny Morris, 'The New Historiography; Israel and its Past', (*1948 and After*), *op. cit.* n. 5, pp. 17–18.

[15] The conclusions that Morris draws from his analysis in *The Birth of the Palestinian Refugee Problem* was criticised early on by Norman Finkelstein and Nur Masalha in their separate articles in the *Journal of Palestine Studies*, Vol. 21, 1991, pp. 68–97. Morris responds to the issues raised in his 'Revisiting the Palestinian exodus of 1948', in Rogan and Shlaim, *op. cit.* n. 1. Note, however, Laila Parsons, 'The Druze and the birth of Israel', *id.*, pp. 60–78, at pp. 69–70, where she states, 'With regard to the question of a master plan to expel Palestinians during the war as a whole, however, Morris sticks to the original position articulated in *The Birth*: given the absence in the Israeli archives of any evidence of such a master plan, we must concluded that no such plan existed. But such a preoccupation with the existence or non–existence of an ultimate 'smoking gun' document begs the following question: given Morris' significant changes of view over the past ten years on the question of proportion of Palestinians who were forcibly expelled for those who left on their own accord; given the newly declassified evidence he presents of a clearly articulated policy of expulsion during Operation Hiram; and given the evidence I have just presented of preferential treatment towards Druze during the war, which buttresses the arguments for design and against randomness in the process of expulsion; is it not possible that the debate has now reached the stage where the protagonist are no longer taking about substance but about labels [i.e. whether it was a 'policy' or not]?'

[16] Morris quoting General Yigal Allon, commander of Operation Yoav meant to capture the Negev in October – November 1948, in Morris (*The Birth of the Palestinian Refugee Problem*), *op. cit.* n. 2, p. 235.

[17] See Appendix I, 'The number of Palestinian refugees' in *Id.*, pp. 297–298. Further consider the section entitled, 'Magic Numbers': Dispersal of 1948 and 1949, in Donna Arzt, *Refugees into Citizens: Palestinians and the End of the Arab–Israeli Conflict*, 1996, pp. 13–17.

return. The overriding factor in establishing the fate of Palestinian Refugees *as living in perpetual exile* has been not only the fact that more than half a million Palestinians were forced to leave their homes, but that they were barred from returning—effectively expelled. While attempts to return took place even before the establishment of the State of Israel, joint Arab-British efforts, such as those regarding Jaffa, were thwarted by the forerunner of the IDF, the Haganah[18]. Such actions became policy on 16 June 1948 as the Cabinet of Israeli Prime Minister Ben–Gurion decided that Palestinians were not to be allowed to return. Despite pressure by the international community, Israel stymied attempts at the political level, while on the ground making it impossible for refugees to actually return. The IDF argued that such returnees would have a destabilizing effect on the newly born State and would place its very existence in jeopardy. Ben-Gurion had consented to a plan in June that would prevent Arabs from returning by way of 'destruction of villages as much as possible during military operations' as well as the 'prevention of any cultivation of land by them, including reaping, collection, picking and so on, also during times of ceasefire', and the 'settlement of Jews in a number of villages and towns so that no 'vacuum' is created'[19].

Benny Morris has written that, in the aftermath of the Arab-Israeli War of 1948, a number of processes took place which 'changed the physical and demographic face of Palestine' ensuring that return would become impossible:

> These processes were the gradual destruction of the abandoned Arab villages, the cultivation and/or destruction of Arab fields and the share-out of the Arab lands to Jewish settlements, the establishment of new settlements on abandoned lands and sites and the settlement of Jewish immigrants in empty Arab housing in the country side and in urban neighborhoods. Taken together, they assured that the refugees would have nowhere, and nothing, to return to[20].

Morris details a further method by which the newly created State of Israel curtailed the return of Palestinians in his book *Israel's Border Wars: 1949–1956*. Here Morris uses the IDF terminology to label refugees seeking to return to their homes as 'infiltrators' and considers the response which the IDF took to stem the flow of such individuals. It is considered that less than ten percent of all Palestinians who 'infiltrated' Israel were 'politically motivated or undertaken for terrorist purposes', instead the vast majority of returnees were the result of 'dearth, a separation from source of income or from family members, and of the reality of the refugee camps near the border'[21]. Israeli Intelligence, for their part, considered that the return of

---

[18] Morris (*The Birth of the Palestinian Refugee Problem*), *op. cit.* n. 2, p. 134.

[19] Morris, 'Yosef Weitz and the Transfer Committees', (*1948 and After*), *op. cit.* n. 5, 119.

[20] Morris (*The Birth of the Palestinian Refugee Problem*), *op. cit.* n. 2, p. 155. For more detail see Morris (*1948 and After*), *op. cit.* n. 5, especially the following chapters, 'Yosef Weitz and the Transfer Committees', pp. 103–158; and 'The Harvest of 1948 and the Creation of the Palestinian Refugee Problem', pp. 239–256.

[21] Benny Morris, *Israel's Border Wars: 1949–1956: Arab Infiltration, Israeli Retaliation, and Countdown to the Suez War*, 1993, p. 46. The quote is attributed to an official of the Research Department of the Israel Foreign Ministry.

refugees would be a threat to the new State, 'The infiltration of individual Arabs, ostensibly for reaping and threshing, alone could in time bring with it the re-establishment in villages, something which could seriously endanger many of our achievements during the six months of war'[22]. As such, the Israeli leadership undertook a number of initiatives from 1948 onward, in an attempt to stem the flow of returnees. This included shoot-to-kill orders along the Armistice lines, the use of land mines and booby-traps, and impunity for those within the armed forces who killed, tortured, or raped Palestinian returnees. After 1949, these measures were backed by armed reprisals in the neighbouring Arab States or in the West Bank and Gaza, as against whole villages or areas. These retaliatory assaults were meant to collectively punish regions from which 'infiltrators' emerged. The aim of this Israeli policy was 'of both frightening the locals into reining in the infiltrators and forcing the relevant Arab governments to curb infiltration'[23]. By precipitating the flight of Palestinian Refugees and by barring their return, Israel, in effect, created the plight of the Palestinian Refugees. The unwillingness of Arab States along with Israel to provide a permanent solution to this plight would effectively abandon the Palestinian Refugees to their indeterminate fate.

II. Conditions of Palestinian Refugees in Exile

The first waves of Palestinian Refugees to arrive in neighbouring States were taken in and hosted by the Arab States and their citizens:

> Some of these Palestinians brought with them enough to live on, or to establish themselves in the host countries, but over 800,000 were virtually destitute. At the beginning they were assisted by both public and private generosity; but, in an area where there is little margin between subsistence and starvation, and no store of wealth to fall back upon if things go wrong, a million extra mouths is too big a burden to be borne for very long[24].

As a response to the growing emergency, the United Nations Mediator for Palestine established, in June 1948, a disaster relief project in an attempt to coordinate aid efforts amongst local governments and relief organizations. In November 1948, the General Assembly institutionalised this process by establishing the United Nations Relief for Palestine Refugees organization which, with the assistance of the International Committee of the Red Cross, the League of Red Cross Societies, and the American Friends (Quakers) Service Committee, undertook relief activities[25]. Within a year's time, it having become evident that Palestinian Refugees would not

---

[22] *Id.*, p. 116.
[23] *Id.*, p. 419.
[24] UNRWA, *Assistance to Palestine Refugees: Report of the Director of the United Nations Work and Relief Agency for Palestine Refugees in the Near East*, 1951, UN Doc. A/6/1905, Foreword.
[25] *Assistance to Palestine refugees*, United Nations General Assembly Resolution 212 (III), 19 November 1948.

be returning to their homes in the near future, the United Nations dispatched an Economic Survey Mission to consider what future activities the UN should undertake. The Mission recommended 'the creation of a new agency, which would not only carry out relief on a diminishing scale, but would inaugurate a work programme in which able-bodied refugees could become self-supporting [...]'[26].

This recommendation was acted upon by the General Assembly when, by virtue of its Resolution 302(IV) of December 1949, it created the United Nations Relief and Works Agency for Palestine Refugees in the Near East (UNRWA)[27]. The Resolution recognised that 'continued assistance for the relief of the Palestine refugees is necessary to prevent conditions of starvation and distress [...] and that constructive measures should be undertaken at an early date with a view to the termination of international assistance for relief'. On this basis, the General Assembly created UNRWA with a two-fold mandate:

> a) To carry out in collaboration with local governments the direct relief and works programmes as recommended by the Economic Survey Mission;
>
> b) To consult with the interested Near Eastern Governments concerning measures to be taken by them preparatory to the time when international assistance for relief and works projects is no longer available.

UNRWA took up its responsibilities in May 1950 and has been, since that time, in constant operation; it being the only United Nations agency established to provide assistance to a specific group of refugees.

With initial attempts at 'work' schemes failing, UNRWA settled into providing education as its largest program, taking up more than half its annual budget, followed by its health program, which constitutes 17.6 percent of its budget. The relief and social services program is the last substantive aid, making up an additional ten percent of the UNRWA budget, which amounted to just over 300 million US dollars for the year 2000[28]. UNRWA's original estimate of refugees in May 1950 was over 950,000; however, it noted that that 'an accurate statement of the number of genuine refugees resulting from the war in Palestine is unlikely to be provided now or in the future'[29]. Pressure from donor States caused that number to be lowered to 850,000 during a census conducted during 1950–1951. As Lex Takkenberg writes, in his *The Status of Palestinian Refugees in International Law*, 'pressure to reduce the number of relief recipients, demanded year after year by

---

[26]   UNRWA, *Assistance to Palestine Refugees: Interim Report of the Director of the United Nations Work and Relief Agency for Palestine Refugees in the Near East*, October 1950, UN Doc. A/5/1451, p. 6, para. 5.

[27]   *Establishing the United Nations Relief and Works Agency for Palestine Refugees in the Near East*, United Nations General Assembly Resolution 302 (IV), 8 December 1948. See Appendix 4.

[28]   UNRWA, *Report of the Commissioner–General of the United Nations Relief and Works Agency for Palestine Refugees in the Near East*, 30 June 2000, UN. Doc. A/55/13, paras. 35, 50, and 64.

[29]   UNRWA, *(Interim Report of the Director, 1950)*, op. cit. n. 24, p. 6, para. 7.

UNRWA's major donors, thus dictated the primary approach to eligibility and registration matters for a very substantial period'[30]. This attempt to reduce numbers however, has gone against the tide of Malthusian logic, which means that by the year 2001, the original UNRWA registered refugees and their descendents constituted more than 3.7 million[31].

UNRWA maintains a working definition of those under its mandate as follows:

> [Palestine refugee] shall mean any person whose normal place of residence was Palestine during the period 1 June 1946 to 15 May 1948 and who lost both home and means of livelihood as a result of the 1948 conflict[32].

However, the 3.7 million also includes Palestinians made refugees as a result of the 1967 War, and the subsequent Israeli occupation of the Gaza Strip and the West Bank of the Jordan River. Of the more than 400,000 Palestinians who were forced to flee in 1967, more than 175,000 became refugees for a second time, having originally fled to Arab controlled areas in the late 1940s[33]. While these second-time refugees were already covered by the UNRWA definition of refugees, the ordinary residents of Gaza and the West Bank fleeing did not automatically fall under the Agency's mandate. Despite this, UNRWA did provide emergency assistance, establishing 'new tented 'emergency camps', ration distributions and provisional health care'[34]. The General Assembly would later endorse this move by calling on UNRWA to maintain its efforts to:

> [...] provide humanitarian assistance, as far as practicable, on an emergency and as a temporary basis and as a temporary measure, to other persons in the area who are at present displaced and are in serious need of immediate assistance as a result of the recent hostilities[35].

The General Assembly has, in subsequent years, reiterated this pronouncement in its resolutions and thus has endorsed the *de facto* inclusion of the 1967 Palestinian Refugees into UNRWA's mandate[36].

i. Situation in Arab States

In his 1950 Interim Report on Assistance to Palestinian Refugees, the first Director of UNRWA, Howard Kennedy, explained the conditions in which the Refugees found themselves:

---

[30] Lex Takkenberg, *The Status of Palestinian Refugees in International Law*, 1998, p. 70.
[31] See UNRWA, (*Report of the Commissioner–General—2000*), *op. cit.* n. 28, para. 1; see also Table 1: Number of Registered Persons, for a breakdown of population by decade.
[32] See Takkenberg, (*The Status of Palestinian Refugees*), *op. cit.* n. 30, p. 77.
[33] See *id.*, pp. 81–82.
[34] See *id.*, p. 82.
[35] See United Nations General Assembly Resolution 2252(ES–V), 4 July 1967.
[36] See Takkenberg, (*The Status of Palestinian Refugees*), *op. cit.* n. 30, p. 82.

It would be necessary to visit refugee encampments or improvised quarters, [...] really to appreciate the desperate situation in which these poor unfortunates find themselves. Generally speaking, their clothing and the few household articles they were able to bring with them have reached or are beyond the end of their normal life and usage. A condition which was expected to last a few months is now into its third year.

[...] Most people have the idea that a majority of the refugees are located in tented camps. This is an erroneous belief, as two-thirds of the total are housed in improvised quarters, many of which were, and are unsuited for anything except temporary emergency use.

[...] Some of the buildings have neither sufficient light nor ventilation for the number using them. It speaks volumes for the hardihood of the Palestinian and the efficiency of the medical services that no epidemics have as yet reached more than incipient stages.

[...] Clothing carried with the refugees in their original flight and subsequent issues of clothing by voluntary agencies is now generally in rags and tatters, and, because of the living conditions, in a filthy state.

Under such conditions, Kennedy noted that 'strangely enough the general morale of the refugees is higher than might be expected after spending more than two years in exile under the most trying conditions'. By way of conclusion as to the refugees' living conditions the Director of UNRWA writes:

It is, however, a fact that the refugee, individually and collectively, is tired of his present condition. Above all, he wishes to return to his former home and means of livelihood. He has been repeatedly told, and generally believes, that his present condition is due to the interference of the Western world in his affairs.

He is resentful of the fact that he is forced to live away from his former home and that he has received no compensation for his losses. He is also resentful of the fact that his money in banks in Israel is withheld from him.

He considers the United Nations mainly responsible for his plight. He expresses little, if any, gratitude for the efforts of [UNRWA] to maintain or improve his condition. He persistently demands increased medical and educational services and improved rations both in quantity and quality.

After more than two years of enforced idleness living under uncertain and trying conditions, more than 800,000 of these refugees constitute a serious threat to the peace and stability of the Near East countries[37].

Fifty years into UNRWA's mandate, the conditions which Palestinian Refugees find themselves in, while in exile, is most often a result of the direction in which they or their kin took flight and thus the State in which they find themselves exiled. Nearly half of the Palestinian Refugees under UNRWA's mandate, more than 1.5 million, live in Jordan. By a 1954 law, Palestinian Refugees on the East Bank of the Jordan and those living under the annexed West Bank acquired Jordanian citizenship. When Israel occupied the West Bank in 1967, the status of all

---

[37]   UNRWA, (*Interim Report of the Director, 1950*), *op. cit.* n. 26, pp. 11–15, at paras. 20–23, 26, and 28.

Palestinians, including refugees remained unchanged. However, in 1988, Jordan renounced its claim to the West Bank with a look to the creation of a Palestinian State; with the result that West Bank Jordanians have formally lost their citizenship. By contrast, Palestinians on the East Bank remain nationals of Jordan with full access to government services. Despite being the most integrated of the Palestinian Refugees, after fifty years in exile, 40,000 Palestinians living in Jordan are still considered by UNRWA to be hardship cases and therefore in need of receiving food rations[38].

In comparison with Palestinian Refugees in Jordan, those that sought refuge in Lebanon have fared much worse. Although 1948 Palestinian Refugees are considered legal residents in Lebanon they have effectively been prevented from being absorbed into Lebanese society. The 2000 Annual Report by UNRWA notes that the Palestinian refugee community in Lebanon 'was among the most disadvantaged of any field, suffered from poor living and housing conditions, restrictions on mobility and high rates of unemployment'. The Report goes on to state that:

> The difficult socio-economic conditions were reflected in the high proportion of special hardship cases registered with the Agency [ten percent of the more than 375,000 refugees]. UNRWA remained the main provider of basic education, health and relief and social services to Palestine refugees, who had limited access to governmental services and whose access to expensive private services was restricted by limited financial resources. The Lebanese authorities continued to prohibit construction in certain refugee camps, and in other camps entry of construction materials and construction was subject to military approval, which was not always granted[39].

The precarious nature of Palestinian Refugees in Lebanon relates to the nature of the Lebanese polity, which has consistently attempted to strike a balance between its Christian and Muslim populations. The influx of Palestinian Refugees was seen as a destabilizing influence and thus, the response was to seek to isolate the Refugees as much as possible from the Lebanese mainstream[40]. In fact, such concerns were justified as Palestinians indeed proved to be a destabilizing element in Lebanon. As a result of their forced exile from Jordan during the 1970 *Black September* operations undertaken to expel the Palestinian Liberation Organization (PLO) from Jordan, most fighters settled in Lebanon where they continued commando raids against Israel. In response, the IDF undertook retaliatory raids against Palestinian Refugee Camps. In 1982, Israel invaded Lebanon, moving as far north as Beirut where, notably, Israeli troops—having forced the majority of the PLO into exile—facilitated access of the Christian Phalange to the Palestinian

---

[38]   See UNRWA, (*Report of the Commissioner–General—2000*), *op. cit.* n. 28, Table 3 —
Number and Distribution of Special Hardship Cases.
[39]   *Id.*, para. 15.
[40]   With respect to the plight of Palestinian Refugees in Lebanon see Walid Said, 'The Obligations of Host Countries to Refugees under International Law: the Case of Lebanon', and Nahla Ghandour 'Meeting the Needs of Palestinian Refugees in Lebanon' in Naseer Aruri (ed.), *Palestinian Refugees: The Right of Return*, 2001, pp. 123–161.

refugee camps of Sabra and Shatila which precipitated a massacre of the civilian population[41]. In contrast to Lebanon, Syria has sought to integrate Palestinians as much as possible into the fabric of Syrian society. The 100,000 original Palestinian Refugees (now nearly 400,000) have 'never constituted more than 2 to 3 per cent of the population', thus facilitating their absorption in Syrian society[42]. While remaining Palestinians—and thus refugees—they 'benefited from a policy permitting full access to governmental services'[43]. Despite this, fifty years after their flight, more than 100,000 Palestinians still live in approximately a dozen camps, where fifteen percent of the shelters lack access to safe water or adequate sewage facilities[44].

Beyond these host States where there is UNRWA assistance, mention should also be made to Palestinian Refugees who have taken up residency in other Arab States including Egypt, Iraq, Kuwait, Libya, and the United Arab Emirates where UNRWA does not provide assistance[45]. In these States, the fate of Palestinian Refugees has been precarious. Although originally welcomed as refugees, or as migrant workers in certain instances, their situation has deteriorated. For instance, while Palestinians were considered as being equal under the law to Egyptians during the Nasser era, from the 1980s onward their various privileges have dissipated. However, this loss of privileges cannot compare to the fortune of Palestinian Refugees who had migrated to work in Kuwait. During the 1991 Gulf War when the PLO sided with Iraq which had invaded Kuwait, Palestinian Refugees were accused of collaborating with the Iraqi occupying forces. As such, the Palestinians, who numbered nearly half a million, were forced to flee in large numbers having been declared by the Emirate's Government to be '"undesirable" aliens'. By 1992, less than 25,000 Palestinians remained in Kuwait. In Libya, Palestinians who, for a long time, benefited from one of the most liberal policies of any Arab States *vis-à-vis* their presence in the territory, in 1995, learnt a harsh lesson as to the precariousness of their status. As a result of the stalled nature of the Israeli–Palestinian 'Peace Process', and the acceptance by the PLO of the Oslo Interim Accords, the Libyan leader, Muammar el-Qaddafi decreed, in September of that year, that as Palestinians now had their own State, they could thus go home. Calling the PLO Chairman Yasser Arafat's bluff, the Libyan Government expelled more than 30,000 Palestinians who were forced to return, not to a Palestinian State,

---

[41]   Consider the Final Report of the (Kahane) Commission of Inquiry in the Events at the Refugee Camps in Beirut, *International Legal Materials*, Vol. 22, 1983, pp. 473–520. For an eyewitness account see Robert Fisk, *Pity the Nation: Lebanon at War*, 2001, pp. 359–400. Further, consider that the UN General Assembly resolved that the 'massacre was an act of genocide', see UN General Assembly Resolution 37/123, A/RES/37/123(A–F), 16 December 1982.

[42]   See Takkenberg, (*The Status of Palestinian Refugees*), *op. cit.* n. 30, p. 167.

[43]   See UNRWA, (*Report of the Commissioner–General—2000*), *op. cit.* n. 28, para.16.

[44]   *Id.*, see Table 7 — Selected Health Status Indicators for Palestine Refugees.

[45]   Note that conditions of Palestinian Refugees in the Occupied Territories controlled by Israel and provided assistance by UNRWA is considered separately at *infra.*, Section IV.

but to their original host States[46]. In their conclusions regarding the lack of protection afforded to Palestinian Refugees in neighbouring Arab States, Susan Akram and Guy Goodwin-Gill have submitted the following assessment of the Palestinian Refugees in the Arab Middle East which is:

> underscored by the lack of permanent status and lack of protection by third states in which they have found temporary refuge These states themselves have, at various times, either engaged directly in persecuting the Palestinian Refugees, or failed to provide them with appropriate protection either from Israeli persecution or persecution by other groups within those states. As far as states persecution, Lebanon, Syria, Jordan, Egypt and various states in the Arabian Gulf have killed, imprisoned, tortured, expelled and denied basic human and economic rights to Palestinians residing in their territories[47].

ii. Situation in Israel

By comparison, Palestinians in Arab States have faired much better then those under Israeli occupation. Most of the daily human rights violations which have transpired in Arab States, are a result of inaction by Arab Governments and fit into the general manner in which Arab States treat their own citizenry[48]. By contrast, the violation of the human rights of Palestinians living in the Occupied Territories has been a result of active policies by the State of Israel. As a result of the 1967 Arab–Israeli War, Israel occupied the Gaza Strip, the Golan Heights, the Sinai Peninsula, and the West Bank (including East Jerusalem). While the Golan and East Jerusalem have been illegally annexed to Israel and the Sinai returned to Egypt under the 1979 Peace Treaty, Gaza and the West Bank remain under Israeli occupation. The legal regime of such occupied territories is governed by the dictates of the Fourth Geneva Convention relative to the Protection of Civilian Persons in Time of War of 1949. Thus, in these areas of occupied Palestine, not only should international refugee law hold (Israel is party to the 1951 Convention), and international human rights law be applied (to the extent that Israel has undertaken obligations under human rights conventions), but so too should international humanitarian law.

The record of Israeli violations of the rights of Palestinian Refugees, both of their human rights and of their rights under humanitarian law, is well documented. However, reference should be made to a number of sources that not only outline

---

[46] For the treatment of Palestinians in Egypt, Kuwait, and Libya see Takkenberg, (*The Status of Palestinian Refugees*), *op. cit.* n. 30, pp. 150–154; 158–162; and 166–167, respectively.

[47] Susan Akram and Guy Goodwin–Gill, *Brief Amicus Curiae*, to the United States Department of Justice, Executive Office for Immigration Review, United States Board of Immigration Appeals, 2000. p. 28. [Original footnotes omitted.] See http://www.badil.org/Publications/Other/O_Pubs.htm.

[48] For the general human rights situation in the Arab States mentioned, consider Amnesty International, *Amnesty International Report 2001*, 2001; and Human Rights Watch, *World Report 2001*, 2001.

various Israeli violations, but cite substantial sources of credible documentation. Consider, for instance the work of Akram and Goodwin-Gill, where they note:

> Israel has systematically engaged in such widespread abuses of the human and humanitarian rights of Palestinians over the past fifty-plus years that it is impossible to adequately recount in this brief the categories and numbers of such violations. They included widespread and systematic torture, sanction by the Israeli Supreme Court; extra-judicial killing; expulsion of the civilian population from the occupied and disputed territories; prolonged detention with charge or fair trial; use of excessive force, including deliberately breaking the bones of children and youths for stone-throwing; and collective punishment, such as demolishing Palestinian homes, military closures of entire civilian areas, and expropriation of Palestinian land for the sole benefit of the Jewish state and Jewish settlers, without notice or compensation[49].

Likewise, in their 1992 article, Richard Falk and Burns Weston consider, having thoroughly cited documented violations of human rights and humanitarian law during the Israeli occupation, that 'Israeli policies and practices over the last twenty-one years cannot reasonably be reconciled with these [i.e. human rights and humanitarian law] rules and standards of international law. Indeed, by its severity and cumulative impact the pattern of Israeli transgression appears to violate with historic irony, even the principles laid down at Nuremberg [...]'[50]. While it may be said that the Israeli occupation was somewhat benign during the period of the Oslo Accords as a result of the role played by the Palestinian Authority in the Occupied Territories, it is clear that during both *intifadas*, Palestinians generally, and Palestinian Refugees in particular, lacked even a modicum of protection against systematic violation of their rights[51].

III. International Refugee Law and Palestinian Refugees

The conditions of Palestinian Refugees in exile remain overall insecure, in part due to their lack of standing as subjects of international law. Where they have been given standing in international law, in areas such as international human rights law or international humanitarian law, there has been a lack of willingness by host

---

[49]   See Akram and Goodwin–Gill, *op. cit.* n. 47, pp. 29–30. [Footnotes in the original omitted.]

[50]   Richard Falk and Burns H. Weston, 'The Relevance of International Law to Palestinian Rights in the West Bank and Gaza: In Legal Defense of the Intifada', *Harvard International Law Journal*, Vol. 32, 1991, p. 129. Consider the polemic which was created by the publishing of this piece: see Michael Curtis, 'International Law and the Territories', *Harvard International Law Journal*, Vol. 32, 1991, pp. 457–495 and the rebuttal which appeared as Richard Falk and Burns H. Weston, 'The Israeli–Occupied Territories, International Law, and the Boundaries of Scholarly Discourse: A Reply to Michael Curtis', *Harvard International Law Journal*, Vol. 33, 1992, pp. 190–204.

[51]   See *infra*, n. 69, where the 2001 UN Human Rights Inquiry Commission stated that the Palestinian Refugees were 'enduring hardships that exceeded those being experienced by the general Palestinian population'.

States to respect these norms, and the international community to ensure observance of those obligations. Yet, in the areas of law which should be directly relevant—international refugee law—Palestinian Refugees find themselves excluded from the international protection afforded all other refugees. Without access to the rights incorporated in the 1951 Refugee Convention or to the protection provided by the United Nations High Commissioner for Refugees (UNHCR), Palestinian Refugees appear to have been completely abandoned to their fate. Yet, as will be demonstrated shortly, Palestinian Refugees do, in law, fall under the protection of the 1951 Convention. To date, this has not been the case, in large part, because the international community has been unwilling to provide UNHCR with the mandate to offer international protection to Palestinians, effectively excluding them from the regime of international refugee law.

i. Palestinian Rights as Refugees

The international response to the exodus of Palestinian Refugees was first addressed by the United Nations Mediator for Palestine. The Mediator, Count Folke Bernadotte, reported in September 1948, that beyond his overall role of seeking to mediate a settlement regarding Palestine, 'a new and difficult element has entered into the Palestine problem as a result of the exodus of more than 300,000 Arabs from their former homes in Palestine'[52]. Bernadotte was the source of the call for the establishment of the return of Palestinians *as a right*, 'From the start, I held the firm view that, taking into consideration all the circumstances, the right of these refugees to return to their homes at the earliest practical date should be established'[53]. Bernadotte, outlined his rationale in the following manner:

> The exodus of Palestinian Arabs resulted from panic created by fighting in their communities, by rumours, concerning real and alleged acts of terrorism, or expulsion. It would be an offence against the principles of elemental justice if these innocent victims of the conflict were denied the right to return to their homes while Jewish immigrants flow into Palestine, and, indeed, at least offer the threat of permanent replacement of the Arab refugees who have been rooted in the land for centuries[54].

---

[52] United Nations Mediator of Palestine, *Progress Report*, General Assembly Official Record, 3rd Session, supplement 11, 16 September 1948, UN Doc. A/648, p. 7, para. 14.
Note that Count Bernadotte was assassinated the following day in Palestine. His murderers were never brought to justice, though the State of Israel acknowledged its responsibility by providing compensation in line with the *Reparations for Injuries Suffered in the Service of the United Nations* Advisory Opinion requested by the UN General Assembly as a direct result of Bernadotte's murder. See *Reparations for Injuries case, I.C.J. Reports, 1949*, 11 April 1949, pp. 174–189. For more details regarding the assassination of Bernadotte by the Stern gang, see Kati Marton, *A Death in Jerusalem*, 1996.
[53] UN Mediator, *op. cit.* n. 52, p. 13, para. 3.
[54] *Id.*, p. 14, para. 6.

He then concluded by calling upon the General Assembly to affirm the right of return and to establish a conciliation commission to supervise a final settlement of the claims of Palestinian Refugees.

Taking up the recommendation of the Mediator, the UN General Assembly, on 11 December 1948, established the United Nations Conciliation Commission for Palestine, to 'assist the Governments and authorities concerned to achieve a final settlement of all questions outstanding between them'[55]. The Commission, in replacing the Mediator, took on his previous functions but was also given additional tasks[56]. In Paragraph 11 of Resolution 194 (III), the General Assembly spelled out one such responsibility specific to Palestinian Refugees:

> *Resolves* that the refugees wishing to return to their homes and live in peace with their neighbors should be permitted to do so at the earliest practicable date, and that compensation should be paid for the property of those choosing not to return and for loss of or damage to property which, under principles of international law or in equity, should be made good by the Governments or authorities responsible.

> *Instructs* the Conciliation Commission to facilitate the reparations, resettlement and economic and social rehabilitation of the refugees and the payment of compensation [...][57].

Beyond its role in attempting to gain an overall solution to the plight of the Palestinian Refugees, the Conciliation Commission also dealt in a limited manner with issues of protection *vis-à-vis* the Refugees. In 1950, the General Assembly specifically directed the Commission to, 'Continue consultations with the parties concerned regarding measures for the protection of the rights, property, and interests of the refugees'[58]. Yet, such consultations were not successful. In fact, by 1951, the Commission considered that it was no longer possible to carry out its mandate.

The Commission considered the calling of the 1951 Paris Conference as its last attempt to give the parties an opportunity to achieve an overall peace agreement regarding Palestine. It noted in its report to the General Assembly:

> 84. In particular, the Government of Israel is not prepared to implement the part of paragraph 11 of the General Assembly resolution of 11 December 1948 which resolves that the refugees wishing to return to their homes and live at peace with their neighbours should be permitted to do so at the earliest practicable date.

---

[55]   *Palestine – Progress Report of the United Nations Mediator*, United Nations General Assembly Resolution 194 (III), 11 December 1948, para. 6, pp. 22–23.

[56]   The role of the Mediator for Palestine were spelled out in *Appointment and Terms of Reference of a United Nations Mediator for Palestine*, United Nations General Assembly Resolution 186 (S–2), 14 May 1948, para. 1(a)(i). The Mediator's functions were handed to the Conciliation Commission by virtue of UNGA Resolution 194(III), para. 2(a).

[57]   *Palestine – Progress Report of the United Nations Mediator, op. cit.* n. 64, p. 24.

[58]   *Palestine: Progress Report of the United Nations Commission for Palestine; Reparation or resettlement of Palestine refugees and payment of compensation due to them*, United Nations General Assembly Resolution 394(V), 14 December 1950, para. 2(c).

85. The Arab Governments, on the other hand, are not prepared fully to implement paragraph 5 of the said resolution, which calls for the final settlement of all questions outstanding between them and Israel. The Arab Governments in their contacts with the Commission have evinced no readiness to arrive at such a peace settlement with the Government of Israel.

87. The Commission is of the opinion [...] that the present unwillingness of the parties fully to implement the General Assembly resolutions under which the Commission is operating, as well as the changes which have occurred in Palestine during the past three years, have made it impossible for the Commission to carry out its mandate, and this fact should be taken into consideration in any further approach to the Palestine problem[59].

Thus the fate of Palestinian Refugees would be abandoned, falling victim to the irreconcilable positions of the Israeli and Arab States. Future events would confirm the Commission's assessment of its inability to carry out its mandate. Despite calls by the General Assembly in the 1960s to 'intensify its efforts', the Commission was compelled to acknowledge, in its 1972 Report, 'that it had not been in a position to carry forward its work'[60]. Thus, while the Commission had a nominal protection function regarding 'rights, property and interests of the refugees' it became evident, even as early as 1951, that it could not carry out this role.

Despite the growth in the juridical weight of Paragraph 11 of Resolution 194, having been reasserted almost every year by the General Assembly, its nature as customary international law while being established, is awkward. While paragraph 11 of General Assembly Resolution 194 may lack the *opinio juris* required to lift State practice to the level of international law, the norms which underlie this provision are to be considered customary international law[61]. In other words, there exists beyond the provisions Resolution 194—*vis-à-vis* a refugee—a right of return and/or a right to compensation in general international law and thus, while the General Assembly Resolution 194 may not be legally binding *per se*, the elements

---

[59] United Nations Conciliation Commission for Palestine, *Progress Report*, UN. Doc. A/6/1985, 20 November 1951.

[60] United Nations Conciliation Commission for Palestine, *Report*, UN. Doc. A/27/8830, 28 September 1972, para. 3. The General Assembly pronouncement of the 1960s include Resolutions 2052(XX) of 15 December 1965 and 2154 (XXI) of 17 November 1966. Note that the last substantive report of the UN Conciliation Commission was in 1961 which provides an overall picture of its work to that point, see United Nations Conciliation Commission for Palestine, *Historical Survey of Efforts of the United Nations Commission for Palestine to Secure the Implementation of Paragraph 11 of General Assembly Resolution 194 (III)*, UN. Doc. A/AC.25/W.81/Rev.2, 2 October 1961.

[61] The question of whether paragraph 11 meets the threshold of *opinio juris* should be considered in the following manner: despite the fact that States have reiterated their support for Resolution 194(III) annually, it cannot be said that this has raised the legal norms found therein to the level of customary international law. Paragraph 11, itself does not speak of a 'right', nor does is the paragraph couched in juridically obligatory terms. As such, the reiteration of support is a political act, lacking the expressed intention that support is being given to Resolution 194(III) because there is a legal obligation to do so.

expressed therein are binding. As to the issue of the right of compensation, the United Nations Conciliation Commission for Palestine prepared a working paper in 1950 demonstrating the historical precedents regarding compensation to refugees[62]. Regarding the issue of the 'right of return', the issue is more complicated. Lacking in historical precedent, the issue of the 'right of return' runs up against the notion of *post facto* laws as expressed in the Latin idiom: *nullum crimen sine lege*. While it cannot be asserted that the 'right of return' existed in the late 1940s, it has been consolidated in subsequent years[63]. The issue is not date of flight (i.e. during the 1948 War), but the exercise of the right of individuals who find themselves in exile after the norm of the 'right of return' has crossed the threshold of customary law. As such, Palestinians today who find themselves in exile as refugees, have appropriated a legal 'right of return'. However, as has been pointed out, the crux of the matter is that 'although some Palestinians may successfully claim a right of return [...] the successful *implementation* of the right is another matter'[64]. Despite the call by the General Assembly to allow for the repatriation of Palestinians, the barring of the return of refugees by Israel has persisted, finding justification in being tied to the larger issue of recognition and establishing a comprehensive peace in the Middle East.

As early as July 1948, it appears that Israel and neighbouring Arab States had fallen into entrenched positions, which were both mutually exclusive and ensured the abandonment of the Palestinian Refugees. Bernadotte had noted that Arab States, 'had become greatly concerned and incensed about the mounting distress among the huge number of Arab refugees' and as such rejected 'any suggestion of acceptance or recognition of the Jewish State, and would not meet with Jewish representatives'[65]. For its part, the Provisional Government of Israel was unwilling to allow for the readmission of refugees, considering them a threat to its security and war-readiness and would come to regard their fate as linked to an overall peace settlement[66]. Thus, the issue of settling the Palestinian refugee question became for

---

[62]   United Nations Conciliation Commission for Palestine, *Historical Survey of the Question of Compensation*, Annex I, 'Historical Precedents for Restitution of Property or Payment of Compensation to Refugees, 6 April 1955, UN. Doc. A/AC.25/W, p. 81.
[63]   See Kathleen Lawland, 'The Right of Return of Palestinians in International Law, *International Journal of Refugee Law*, Vol. 8, 1996, pp. 532–568, where she asserts at p. 544:

> The fact that the right to return is expressly recognized in most international human rights instruments and draft declarations, that the constitutions, laws and jurisprudence of many States formally recognize it, that it is expressly protected in international humanitarian law instruments, and that it is consistently referred to in resolution of the UN organs dealing with the rights of refugees generally, supports the argument that the right exists in customary international law, although its precise content is difficult to define. [Footnotes in the original omitted.]

See also Takkenberg, (*The Status of Palestinian Refugees*), *op. cit.* n. 30, pp. 230–250.
[64]   *Id.*, p. 568. Emphasis in the original.
[65]   United Nations Mediator, *op. cit.* n. 52, p. 10, para. 14.
[66]   See United Nations Conciliation Commission for Palestine, *op. cit.* n. 58, p. 19, paras. 41, which reads in part; 'The Government of Israel, on the other hand, was not prepared to

one, a pre-requisite for moving toward an overall peace; for the other, a part of an overall negotiated peace. Unable to implement the provisions of paragraph 11, the United Nations Conciliation Commission for Palestine slowly saw its work dwindle, and since 1964, has effectively fallen into abeyance[67]. Faced early on with intransigent States—Israel unwilling to allow for return, Arab States averse to allow for absorption—the United Nations stepped into the breach to provide assistance to the Palestinian Refugees who had been abandoned to their fate.

ii. False Denial of International Protection

In the language of international refugee law, the Palestinian Refugees slowly lost their 'international protection', which had nominally been mandated to the Conciliation Commission[68]. Instead, the focus of the international community, which persists to this day, remains 'assistance' in the guise of the functions undertaken by the UNRWA. This early loss of international protection, as the United Nations Human Rights Inquiry Commission pointed out in its report to the Commission on Human Rights in March 2001, 'is not trivial'[69]. International protection is meant to emerge in substitution of municipal protection where the former is unavailable. Going beyond the traditional notion of protection, usually associated with diplomatic protection, the international protection functions attached to refugee populations can be manifold. Guy Goodwin-Gill has pointed out, in his leading treatise *The Refugee in International Law*, that the 'day-to-day protection activities are necessarily dictated by the needs of refugees'[70]. Such international protection functions may include physical protection in the sense of protection of basic human rights, with the cornerstone of refugee law being protection against *refoulement*[71]. Beyond physical protection, international

---

accept as a principle the injunction contained in paragraph 11, and further, was not prepared to negotiate on any point separately and outside the framework of a general settlement'.

[67] See United Nations General Assembly, *Report of the United Nations Conciliation Commission for Palestine*, 31 August 2000, UN. Doc. A/55/329, which consists of two paragraphs.

[68] See *supra.*, n. 58.

[69] See United Nations Commission on Human Rights, *Question of the Violation of Human Rights in the Occupied Arab Territories, including Palestine*, (Report of the Human Rights Inquiry Commission established pursuant to Commission resolution S–5/1 of 19 October 2000), 16 March 2001, E/CN.4/2001/121, para. 100, in Jean Allain (ed.), *Unlocking the Middle East: the Writings of Richard Falk*, 2003.

[70] Guy Goodwin–Gill, *The Refugee in International Law*, 1996, p. 230.

[71] Article 33(1) of the 1951 Convention relating to the Status of Refugees reads:

No Contracting State shall expel or return ('refouler') a refugee in any manner whatsoever to the frontiers of territories where his life or freedom would be threatened on account of his race, religion, nationality, membership of a particular social group or political opinion.

The right of *non–refoulement*, however is not at issue with the Palestinian Refugees as they are effectively barred from access to Israel or the Occupied Territories. For the relationship

protection may include traditional surrogate legal protection such as representation in legal matters, in issues of detention, or refugee and asylum determination, as well as the providing of definite solutions to flight including resettlement and repatriation[72].

The UN Inquiry Commission, which included the noted international jurists John Dugard and Richard Falk, was mandated by the UN Commission on Human Rights to 'investigate violations of human rights and humanitarian law in the occupied Palestinian territories' in the wake of the start of the *Al-Aqsa Intifada*[73]. The Commission of Inquiry, noted that the Palestinian Refugees remain the only refugee group which is excluded from the mandate of UNHCR and hence from international protection. As such, the Commission noted that the failure of the international community to provide such international protection to Palestinian Refugees living in the Occupied Territories was directly responsible for their 'enduring hardships that exceeded those being experienced by the general Palestinian population'[74]. While the Palestinian Refugees can be considered as falling within the purview of the 1951 Convention (although to date, they have not been), they remain outside the mandate assigned to the United Nations High Commissioner for Refugees by the General Assembly. As Professor James Hathaway has noted, regarding Palestinian Refugees, 'their wholesale exclusion is inconsistent with the commitment to a truly universal protection system'[75]. Yet that exclusion persists to this day.

The fact that Palestinian Refugees are effectively excluded from the international protection of UNHCR is a result of the mandate given to it by the General Assembly. The Office of the High Commissioner for Refugees was established to deal with the overall issues of refugees in the wake of the end of the Second World War, and was established before the 1951 Geneva Convention relating to the Status of Refugees. As such, its mandate was not originally conceived simply to supervise the 1951 Convention, *per se*; its mandate, as outlined

---

between *jus cogens* and *non–refoulement* see Jean Allain, 'The *Jus Cogens* Nature of *Non–Refoulement*', *International Journal of Refugee Law*, Vol. 13, 2001, pp. 533–558.

[72]   Goodwin–Gill, *op. cit.* n. 70, p. 230.

[73]   United Nations Commission on Human Rights, *op. cit.* n. 69.

[74]   *Id.*, para. 100. The Commission goes on to state:

> These protective concerns are directly associated with the distinctive pressures exerted by Israeli responses to the second intifada. The refugee camps are often prominent flashpoints in relations with the IDF and the settlements, prompting retaliatory 'security' measures, especially prolonged closures, including blockages of access roads. Refugees are trapped in these overcrowded camps, prevented from going to places of employment and often denied access to educational and medical facilities. The incidence of destitution resulting from the impact of the second intifada is significantly higher for refugees than for non–refugees, and is felt more keenly, as refugees lack land for subsistence agriculture or within which to move about. Our visits to several Palestinian refugee camps revealed to us the special sense of material and psychological hardship associated with the confinement and curfews of this period of intifada. Under such conditions, it is hardly surprising that much of the support for Palestinian militancy and armed struggle is generated within the refugee camps.

[75]   James Hathaway, *The Law of Refugee Status*, 1991, p. 209.

in its 1950 Statute, is to provide international protection to refugees who had received such protection during the inter-War years, and those that emerged from Europe as 'a result of events occurring before 1 January 1951'[76]. While the Statute incorporates, in Article 1, the well-known legal definition of who is to be considered a refugee, 'any person who [...] owing to well-founded fear of being persecuted for reasons of race, religion, nationality or political opinion', the Statute also includes a number exceptions that would deny an individual such status. These clauses are meant to remove from the competence of UNHCR individuals who either no longer require international protection or are deemed unworthy of it, for reasons such as their involvement in war crimes or crimes against humanity[77]. Beyond these, there is an exception clause that is directly relevant to Palestinian Refugees.

Article 7 of the Statute of UNHCR excludes an individual:

(c) Who continues to receive from other organs or agencies of the United Nations protection or assistance.

When the Statute was being drafted, there existed two such groups that were receiving protection or assistance from the United Nations: Koreans and Palestinians[78]. However, Article 7(c) was included in the Statute at the behest of Arab States that were concerned 'lest the refugee definition then being debated in the United Nations lose sight of groups which were the particular concern of the General Assembly, and whose right to repatriate had been recognised in various resolutions'[79]. As Palestinian Refugees were, by 1950, receiving assistance from UNRWA and the Conciliation Commission had undertaken a limited protection function, they were excluded from the protection function of UNHCR. It should be emphasised at this juncture that these two functions—protection and assistance— were provided to the Palestinian Refugees via two separate United Nations agencies: UNRWA and the UN Conciliation Commission.

While the prominence of UNHCR today is found in its ability to provide assistance to refugees, its mandate as outlined in its Statute is principally international protection[80]. Where UNHCR has gained in stature, it has done so as a result of the willingness of the General Assembly to expand its mandate from one originally envisioned as being effectively 'international protection' to one focused, in large part, on 'assistance'. This 'mission-creep' finds an outlet in Article 9 of the Statute which reads, 'The High Commissioner shall engage in such additional activities, including repatriation and resettlement, as the General Assembly may determine, within the limits of the resources placed at his disposal'. While UNHCR

---

[76] *Statute of the Office of the United Nations High Commissioner for Refugees*, United Nations General Assembly Resolution 428(V), 14 December 1950, see Articles 1 and 6(A).
[77] The cessations clause is found at Article 1(C), while the exclusion clause is located at Article 1(F).
[78] Hathaway, *op. cit.* n. 75, pp. 205–206.
[79] Goodwin–Gill, *op. cit.* n. 70, p. 91.
[80] See Article 8, Statute of the Office of the United Nations High Commissioner for Refugees, in *id.*, pp. 385–389.

remains, at least on paper, the agency endowed with a universal mandate of international protection, its inability to bestow protection on Palestinian Refugees is a result of the exclusive 'assistance' mandate of UNRWA. Yet, as the subsequent negotiations of the 1951 Convention were to show, this was neither the wish of Arabs States nor that of the greater international community.

During the fall 1951 Conference of Plenipotentiaries, which gathered to negotiate a refugee convention, Arab States emphasised the fact that the United Nations was responsible, in large part, for the plight of Palestinian Refugees, the General Assembly having approved the Partition Plan. As such, Arab representatives sought to have the Palestinian Refugees remain a *sui generis* regime where they could 'receive the special attention due to them'[81]. Using Article 7(c) of the UNHCR Statute as a basis, Article 1(D) of the 1951 Refugee Convention emerged with the objective 'to free the Arab host countries from direct responsibility for these refugees under the Convention'[82]. Article 1(D) of the 1951 Convention reads in part:

> This convention shall not apply to persons who are at present receiving from organs or agencies of the United Nations other than the United Nations High Commissioner for Refugees protection or assistance.

Yet, beyond this simple transferring of Article 7(c) of the UNHCR Statute to the 1951 Convention, the Egyptian Delegation introduced an amendment which was later accepted without modification[83]. That provision was incorporated into the 1951 Convention as the second paragraph of Article 1(D), which reads:

> When such protection or assistance has ceased for any reason, without the persons being definitively settled in accordance with the relevant resolutions adopted by the General Assembly of the United Nations, these persons shall *ipso facto* be entitled to the benefits of this Convention.

This amendment radically alters the character of Article 1(D) taken as a whole. No longer is it an exclusionary clause (as is the nature of Article 7(c) of the UNHCR Statute), but Article 1(D), read in its entirety, takes on the character of a delayed inclusion clause[84]. The amendment was presented with this objective: to ensure that if protection ceased, the Palestinians would be included in the 1951 Convention:

> Introducing his [Mostafa Bey (Egypt)] amendment (A.CONF.2/13), he said that the aim of his delegation at the present juncture was to grant to all refugees the status for which the Convention provided. To withhold the benefits of the Convention from certain

---

[81]   Lex Takkenberg, 'The Protection of Palestine Refugees in the Territories occupied by Israel', *International Journal of Refugee Law*, Vol. 3, 1991, p. 419.

[82]   Takkenberg, (*The Status of Palestinian Refugees*), *op. cit.* n. 30, p. 90.

[83]   See Lex Takkenberg and Christopher Tahbaz, *The Collected Travaux Préparatoires of the 1951 Convention relating to the Status of Refugees*, Vol. II, p. 20.

[84]   Note that Atle Grahl–Madsen considered Article 1(D) a 'suspensive clause'. See Takkenberg, (*The Status of Palestinian Refugees*), *op. cit.* n. 30, pp. 86–122, at p. 92.

categories of refugees would be to create a class of human beings who would enjoy no protection at all. In that connection, it should be noted that article 6 of Chapter II of the Statute of the High Commissioner's Office for Refugees contained a comprehensive definition covering all categories of refugees. The limiting clause contained in paragraph [D] of article 1 of the Convention at present covered Arab refugees from Palestine. From the Egyptian Government's point of view it was clear that so long as United Nations institutions and organs cared for such refugees their protection would be a matter for the United Nations alone. *However, when that aid came to an end the question would arise of how their continued protection was to be ensured. It would only be natural to extend the benefits of the Convention to them; hence the introduction of the Egyptian amendment*[85].

The Egyptian Representative thus made a clear distinction between protection and assistance. In introducing the second paragraph of Article 1(D), Mostafa Bey sought to deal with protection *only*, as being separate from assistance. However, In *The Status of Palestinian Refugees in International Law*, Takkenberg argues that 'the words protection or assistance in the first [paragraph] do not refer to the actual receipt of protection or assistance, but rather to falling under the mandate of a specialised UN agency, UNRWA'[86]. For Takkenberg there is no distinction to be made between 'protection' on the one hand, and 'assistance' on the other. Yet, as has already been noted, UNRWA was never mandated with a protection function, its mandate is humanitarian: to provide assistance in the form of relief and work[87]. With respect to the issue of Palestinian Refugees, the United Nations General Assembly established two entities, directing UNRWA to consult with the other, the UN Conciliation Commission, 'in the best interests of *their respective tasks*, with particular reference to paragraph 11 of General Assembly Resolution 194(III) of 11 December 1948'[88]. It was for the UN Conciliation Commission for Palestine— though its mandate was limited ('protection of the rights, property and interests of the refugees') and unsuccessful in its implementation (it ceased to be effective by 1951)—to ensure protection. Takkenberg's line of argument challenges the fundamental *raison d'être* for the introduction of Egyptian amendment: that the 1951 Convention would kick in if protection ceased. It is clear that Palestinian

---

[85]   Conference of Plenipotentiaries on the Status of Refugees and Stateless Persons, *Summary Record of the Twenty-Ninth Meeting*, UN. Doc. A/CONF. 2/SR.29, 28 November 1951, pp. 16–17; as found in Lex Takkenberg and Christopher Tahbaz, *The Collected Travaux Préparatoires of the 1951 Convention relating to the Status of Refugees*, Vol. II, pp. 378–379. Emphasis added.

[86]   Takkenberg, (*The Status of Palestinian Refugees*), *op. cit.* n. 30, p. 104.

[87]   Consider, however, the creation of UNRWA's 'programme of general assistance and protection' which was introduced during the first *intifada*, for which Takkenberg considers that 'UNRWA is currently sufficiently mandated to carry out'. Note that a scaled down version of programme had been reintroduced as a result of the *al-Aqsa Intifada*, but the level of conflict did not allow for the programme to expand without placing UNRWA's refugee affairs officers in harm's way. See Takkenberg, (The Protection of Palestine Refugees), *op. cit.* n. 81.

[88]   *Assistance to Palestine refugees*, United Nations General Assembly Resolution 302 (IV), 11 December 1946, para. 20. Emphasis added.

Refugees, having ceased to receive protection from the Conciliation Commission are thus entitled, by that fact alone, to the benefits of the 1951 Convention[89].

Flowing from this analysis is the fact that while all Palestinian Refugees should receive the benefits of the 1951 Convention, their ability to receive international protection from UNHCR remains unattainable due to Article 7(c) of the Statute of the Office of the High Commissioner. The ability to vest UNHCR with an international protection function is—legally—an easy operation. The United Nations General Assembly could revisit the Statute of UNHCR and make the changes required to remove the effects of Article 7(c) by either deleting it or adding a second paragraph like the one found in Article 1(D) of the 1951 Convention. Although the PLO Representative attempted this in 1984, it was considered that the time was not right, and his effort came to naught[90]. Alternatively the UN General Assembly could designate Palestinian Refugees as 'persons of concern', thus transforming them into so-called 'mandate refugees' falling under the protection of UNHCR. Granting UNHCR the mandate to deal with Palestinian Refugees, in much the same way as it has gained this role with respect to internally displaced persons, would allow it to provide international protection to refugees both in Arab States and in the areas under the jurisdiction of the State of Israel. In this vein the 2001 UN Human Rights Inquiry Commission investigating human rights abuses in the Occupied Territories, in its conclusions, called on the United Nations to act to ensure that Palestinians are no longer excluded from the 1951 Convention and 'to ensure that a regime of protection under the authority of the United Nations High Commissioner for Refugees is extended to Palestinian Refugees, especially those currently residing in West Bank and Gaza camps[91].

IV. Conclusion

The unwillingness of the UN General Assembly to vest UNHCR with a mandate to protect Palestinian Refugees is not based on legal encumbrances; such limitations could be swept aside quite easily. Instead, while the international community may base its inertia by pointing to the lack of legal mandate afforded to protect Palestinian Refugees as a result of their exclusion from the Statute of the High Commissioner for Refugees, it is clear that the abandonment of Palestinian

---

[89] See Akram and Goodwin-Gill, *op. cit.* n. 46. Note that the authors draw different conclusions in their assessment of Article 1(D):

> Article 1(D) acts as a contingent inclusion clause for Palestinians who are at present receiving aid from UNRWA. Once the aid [from UNRWA] ceases 'for any reason', they should be *ipso facto* included in the protective regime established by the 1951 Refugee Convention. Thus, Palestinians who do not already have full and unconditional citizenship in a state in which their lives and rights are protected, who are either living outside of UNRWA's area of operation or alternatively within the area but not registered with UNRWA, should be *ipso facto* entitled to refugee status in any nation that is signatory to the 1951 Refugee Convention or subsequent 1967 Protocol. [p. 52.]

[90] Takkenberg, (The Protection of Palestine Refugees), *op. cit.* n. 81, pp. 416–417, n. 10.
[91] United Nations Commission on Human Rights, *op. cit.* n. 69, para. 129.

Refugees by the international community is based on a lack of political will to see international law enforced. If Palestinian Refugees were to fall under the mandate of UNHCR, then issues of resettlement and local integration as a means of finding a permanent solution to their future would become an issue—this at the expense of the wishes of Arab States that Palestinian Refugees not escape the responsibility of the State of Israel. Likewise, Israel is unwilling to allow UNHCR into the Occupied Territories to provide Palestinian Refugees with international protection—above all, physical protection.

In this manner, where the Palestinian Refugees are concerned, there has been a twin abandonment. In the first measure, they have seen their fate abandoned as falling between Israel, which rejects their return, and surrounding Arab States, which are unwilling to allow them to integrate or resettle for fear of losing a bargaining chip when the final status of Palestine is decided. In the second measure, the international community *has been willing* to allow millions of Palestinians to live in perpetual exile, abandoning the dictates of international refugee law, by effectively denying them the international protection afforded to all other refugees. This abandonment is manifest in the fact that the 1951 Convention is applicable to Palestinians, and has been from the Convention's inception, as the UN Conciliation Commission effectively ceased to provide protection from the 1951 Paris Peace Conference onward. Yet for the international community to hide behind the fig-leaf of a legal distinction between 'assistance or protection' clearly demonstrates the lack of political resolve needed to settle the fate of Palestinian Refugees.

It is not surprising that in a region of the world where the fate of millions of Palestinians remains indeterminate, denied their fundamental rights for more than fifty years, this has engendered a healthy disrespect for the legitimacy of international law. The legal vacuum which envelopes Palestinian Refugees, means that their fate is to be decided not by the dictates of international law but through a political process that denies them their fundamental *rights* as refugees and allows such rights to become mere pawns in political negotiations. With an international community unwilling to see its own pronouncements of international law upheld, it is not surprising that on balance, where law is weighed between a tool of the powerful against a system providing for justice, the abandonment of Palestinian Refugees adds further weight to the side of the scale where power if found at the expense justice.

Chapter 5

Selective Enforcement of International Law: The Security Council and its Varied Responses to a Decade of Aggression (1980–90)

The ten-year period that commenced with the Iraqi offensive against Iran in September 1980, followed by Israel's invasion of Lebanon in 1982, and ended with Iraq's attack against Kuwait in August 1990, is instructive as to the manner in which the international community has responded to acts of aggression in the Middle East. The international community has delegated that power, through the United Nations Charter, to the Security Council so that it might take the primary responsibility to ensure international peace and security. However, the Security Council is not an obligatory collective security arrangement which must act whenever international peace is contravened; it is a political body which decides, in each situation, whether a given act constitutes a threat to or breach of the peace or an act of aggression and whether and how it will respond. The three cases noted above are instructive as they demonstrate the selective manner of enforcement by the UN Security Council, which has acted in three distinct ways in attempting to deal with aggression and restore international peace and security in the region. Throughout the Iran-Iraq War, the Security Council failed to act through passive neglect, only invoking Chapter VII of the UN Charter seven years after the start of the conflict. In the case of the Israeli invasion and occupation of Lebanon, the neglect was, by comparison, active; as the United States blocked, through recourse to its veto power, any move by the Council to seek to restore international peace. Finally, the Iraqi annexation of Kuwait witnessed a Security Council which invoked Chapter VII within hours of the Iraqi invasion of Kuwait and used its powers in a far-reaching manner as it sought to restore the peace.

These three cases demonstrate that when States move from law in the books to law in fact, political considerations allow for the selective application of international law. This selectivity of application has resonance in the region, where the perception is that the Security Council is carrying out its function in an instrumental manner, not in the interests of international peace and security, but in the interests of the United States of America. Granted, much changed in the international system during the decade under review, most importantly the demise of the Soviet Union. As a result of the end of the Cold War, the Security Council emerged from its hibernation to introduce a 'New World Order' that manifested itself against Iraq during the 1990s but went little further. The irony, of course, was that throughout that decade, when the Security Council was asserting itself against Iraq for its taking of Kuwait, Israel remained in occupation of southern Lebanon. Thus, the selective manner in which international law has been enforced in the region says much about the qualitative exceptionalism of the Middle East, whereby power trumps justice and expediency overrides law.

I. Aggression in International Law

The notion of 'aggression' only truly gains standing in international relations after the First World War. Article 10 of the Covenant of the League of Nations, which in many ways mirrors the modern manifestation of the prohibition against the use of force, sought to protect States from aggression:

> The Members of the League undertake to respect and preserve as against external aggression the territorial integrity and existing political independence of all Members of the League. In case of any such aggression or in case of any threat or danger of such aggression the Council shall advise upon the means by which this obligation shall be fulfilled.

Ian Brownlie writes that its 'basic meaning', at the turn of the twentieth century, was a 'military attack by the forces of a state against the territory or vessels of another state'[1]. During the 1930s, a number of non-aggression pacts were signed by the Soviet Union and its allies which defined aggression, establishing that a 'State which is the first to commit' a number of acts, such as declaring war, invading the territory of another State or attacking its military forces, establishing a naval blockade, or assisting or failing to prevent the invasion of 'armed bands' emanating from another State's territory, committed aggression[2]. With the breakout of the Second World War, the notion of aggression would gain prominence both as an act imputable to States and, through the Moscow Declaration of 1943, to individuals.

The Charter of the Tribunal that would try German leaders at Nuremberg provided that the judges would 'have the power to try and punish persons who [...]

---

[1]   Ian Brownlie, *International Law and the Use of Force by States*, 1991, p. 352.

[2]   See Article 2, Convention for the Definition of Aggression between Roumania (*sic*), the Union of Soviet Socialist Republics, Czechoslovakia, Turkey and Yugoslavia, 4 July 1933; Convention between Lithuania and the Union of Soviet Socialist Republics for the Definition of Aggression, 5 July 1933; and Treaty of Non-Aggression between the Kingdom of Afghanistan, the Kingdom of Iraq, the Empire of Iran and the Republic of Turkey, 8 July 1937 as found in: Benjamin Ferencz, *Defining International Aggression: The Search for World Peace—A Documentary History and Analysis*, 1975, Vol. 1, pp. 255–269.

committed any of the following crimes': war crimes, crimes against humanity; but also of relevance for this study:

> Crimes against peace. Namely, planning, preparation, initiation, or waging of a war of aggression or a war in violation of international treaties, agreements [...][3].

Beyond trying individuals and holding them criminally responsible for acts of aggression after the Second World War, the United Nations—or rather those victorious Powers allied during the War against the Axis States—established the United Nations Organization which was meant as a collective security system which allowed for an international response to acts of aggression. The collective security system found in the Charter of the Organization internationalises control of the use of force. Thus, from 1945 onward, not only are wars of aggression outlawed, but all means of offensive use of military force are deemed to be in violation of the new international legal order given voice in the Charter of the United Nations. The Member States of the United Nations, in ratifying the Charter, in effect, agreed to limit the use of force to two specific situations, and took the ultimate control of force out of their own hands, that is, out of the hands of individual States, and internationalised that control.

The fundamental purpose of the United Nations Organization, expressed in Article 1(1) of the Charter is to 'maintain international peace and security, and to that end: to take effective collective measures for the prevention and removal of threats to the peace, and for the suppression of acts of aggression or other breaches of the peace [...]'. With this in mind, the Members of the United Nations agreed that they will act in accordance with a number of principles, one of which is expressed at Article 2(4), stating that they shall refrain 'in their international relations from the threat or use of force against the territorial integrity or political independence of any state, or in any other manner inconsistent with the Purposes of the United Nations'. Putting aside the dead-letter provisions of the Charter, which allowed for the ability to use force to suppress the Second World War 'enemy states', the post-1945 order allows States to use force only in two situations: in self-defence and through the collective security arrangement found at Chapter VII of the UN Charter[4]. While Article 51 of the Charter provides that States may use force as part of their 'inherent right of individual or collective self-defence', they may only do so 'until the Security Council has taken measures necessary to maintain international peace and security'. Thus, even in situations where States are acting in self-defence, they must yield to an international order manifest in provisions of Chapter VII.

In becoming party to the Charter of the United Nations, States have foregone their traditional right to use force against one and another and have, instead, established a collective security system which, in essence, recognises that an attack

---

[3]   Brownlie, *op. cit.* n. 1, p. 164.

[4]   The provisions regarding enemy states are found at Articles 53 and 107 of the Charter. As to the non-applicability of these provisions, see Bruno Simma (ed.), *The Charter of the United Nations: A Commentary*, 1995, pp. 727–729 and 738–743.

against one of its Members is to be considered an attack against all. To put this
theory into practice, the Member States, in 1945, agreed that they would renounce
their individual right to use force beyond self-defence; and instead, place that right
in the hands of the United Nations Security Council. Within the provisions of
Chapter VII of the United Nations Charter, States have agreed that it is for the
Security Council Members—the five permanent members (China, France, the
Soviet Union (now Russia), the United Kingdom, and the United States) and ten
other members who rotate on two-year terms—to make a determination and to act,
using force if necessary, to maintain or restore international peace and security.
The Security Council is thus endowed with the only legal means to project force
internationally: all other manifestation of the use of force by a State beyond its
borders that is not in collective self-defence, or sanctioned by the Council, is *prima
facie* illegal under international law. For its part, it should be understood that the
Security Council may use force, not in an active manner, but as a means of
reacting to a 'threat to the peace, breach of the peace, or [an] act of aggression'[5].

Chapter VII of the Charter, entitled *Action with Respect to Threats to the
Peace, Breaches of the Peace, and acts of Aggression*, deems that if the Security
Council makes a determination that there does, in fact, exist a threat to the peace,
breach of the peace, or act of aggression, it can, under Article 39, 'make
recommendations, or decide what measures shall be taken in accordance with
Articles 41 and 42, to maintain or restore international peace and security'. Thus,
once having made a determination regarding a breach or threat to the peace or an
act of aggression, the Council can make recommendations, but can also, by virtue
of Article 41, take any measure short of the use of force to attempt to maintain or
restore the peace. Independent of its powers under Article 41, the Council can
invoke Article 42, which reads:

> Should the Security Council consider that measures provided for in Article 41 would be
> inadequate or have proved to be inadequate, it may take such action by air, sea, or land
> forces as may be necessary to maintain or restore international peace and security. Such
> action may include demonstrations, blockade, and other operations by air, sea, or land
> forces of Members of the United Nations.

It is through the provisions of Chapter VII, and specifically those of Articles 41
and 42, that the international community had decided that it would deal with acts of
aggression. Yet, it should be understood that the system established by the United
Nations Charter is not a 'pure' collective security system, as not all threats or
breaches of the peace or acts of aggression necessarily activate the provisions of
Chapter VII. The Charter's collective security system is restricted by the fact that
the Council must first make a determination that situations which affect
international peace and security do, in fact, exist; and that the Council considers it
so by majority vote. Making such a determination, however, is qualified to the
extent that it must not only be by a majority vote but must also receive the

---

[5]   See Article 39, Charter of the United Nations.

concurring votes of the permanent members, thus effectively providing those five members with the ability to veto the passage of any Security Council resolution[6].

Despite the fact that the Security Council may act under Chapter VII when it considers that an act of aggression has transpired, it has never chosen to do so. Two reasons come to mind as to why this is: one, that by such a determination the Council would be taking sides in the dispute and would thus be unable to assist in re-establishing the peace by diplomatic means, thus committing itself to acting by force against one party[7]. Second, that the notion of 'aggression' entails such grave consequences and has been so stigmatised that the Council has deemed it prudent to, typically, describe events as either a threat to or a breach of the peace. While the parameters of the terms 'threat to the peace' and 'breach of the peace', are quite fluid, thus giving the Security Council leeway in using them, the notion of 'aggression' has been narrowed in law, through the acceptance, by consensus, in 1974, of UN General Assembly Resolution 3314, which had attached as an annex a 'Definition of Aggression'[8]. The Assembly considered that 'since aggression is the most serious and dangerous form of the illegal use of force [... it] should be defined at the present stage'; as it might well 'have the effect of deterring a potential aggressor, [... and protect] the rights and lawful interests of, and the rendering of assistance to, the victim'[9]. The Definition repeats, *mutatis mutandis*, Article 2(4) of the Charter stating that:

Aggression is the use of armed force by a State against the sovereignty, territorial integrity or political independence of another State, or in any other manner inconsistent with the Charter of the United Nations, as set out in this Definition.

The Definition of Aggression then goes on to state in Article 2, that the 'first use of armed force by a State in contravention of the Charter shall constitute *prima facie* evidence of an act of aggression'. Beyond providing this general understanding, the Definition also enumerates a number of acts that qualify as aggression, if they transpire as a first use of armed force. Such acts include bombardment or the use of any weapons by a State against another, blockade of ports or the coast of another State, or an armed attack against a State's armed forces. Beyond these enumerated examples of acts of aggression, Article 3 notes, as its first provision that, primarily, aggression is to be understood as:

The invasion or attack by the armed forces of a State on the territory of another State, or any military occupation, however temporary, resulting from such invasion or attack, or any annexation by the use of force of the territory of another State or part thereof.

---

[6]   See Article 27(3), *id.*
[7]   See Patrick Dailler and Alain Pellet, *Droit International Public*, 1994, p. 929.
[8]   For a documentary evolution of the definition of aggression see Ferencz, *op. cit.* n. 2. For a scathing critique of Resolution 3314 see Julius Stone, 'Hopes and Loopholes in the 1974 Definition of Aggression', *American Journal of International Law*, Vol. 71, 1977, pp. 224–246.
[9]   Preamble to the annexed 'Definition of Aggression', United Nations General Assembly Resolution 3314 (XXIX), 14 December 1974. See Appendix 5.

The Definition then points to fact that, ultimately, it is the Security Council, which is to make a determination as to whether an act of aggression has transpired. Article 4 states that the 'acts enumerated above are not exhaustive and the Security Council may determine that other acts constitute aggression under the provisions of the Charter'. In fact, Resolution 3314 makes this plain when it recommends to the Security Council that 'it should, as appropriate, take account of the Definition as guidance in determination, in accordance with the Charter, the existence of an act of aggression'. To that end, Article 2, although it notes that the first use of armed force constitutes a *prima facie* act of aggression, goes on to state that it is for the Security Council to 'conclude that a determination that an act of aggression has been committed would not be justified in the light of other relevant circumstances, including the fact that the acts concerned or their consequences are not of sufficient gravity'.

Aggression, having been considered by the General Assembly as the 'most serious and dangerous form of the illegal use of force' has, through its evolution over the last century, developed an aura of stigmatization which, in part has been brought on by the eventual elimination of the use of force by States acting independently from the United Nations collective security system; but also because the consequences of a third-party finding regarding acts of aggression not only entail State responsibility, but individual criminal responsibility. That aura was in evidence in Rome in 1998 when diplomats gathered to draft the Statute of the International Criminal Court which is meant to try individuals for the crimes of genocide, crimes against humanity, war crimes, and the crime of aggression[10]. While the plenipotentiaries could agree to the inclusion of the crime of aggression into the Statue they could not agree on a definition of aggression to which they would be held. As William Schabas writes in his *Introduction to the International Criminal Court*, when 'States realise they are setting a standard by which they themselves, or their leaders and military personnel, may be judged, they seem to take greater care and insist upon many safeguards'[11]. In the case of the crime of aggression, the safeguard established was to include the crime as part of the subject matter jurisdiction, but to put off its applicability until States agreed to a definition and the 'conditions under which the Court shall exercise jurisdiction over this crime'[12]. The notion of aggression within the context of the Statute of the International Criminal Court is of interest as it must 'be consistent with the relevant provisions of the Charter'; in other words, it must pay heed to the discretion given to the Security Council to make a determination that an act of aggression has transpired.

If the past is any indication, the Security Council has been quite hesitant to make such a determination. Where it has constituted an act as 'aggression', it has done so outside its powers under Chapter VII. Thus, in 1976, the Council, for the first time, used the term 'aggression' as it condemned 'South Africa's aggression

---

[10] See Article 5, Statute of the International Criminal Court, 17 July 1998, as found in William Schabas, *An Introduction to the International Criminal Court*, 2001, p. 169.
[11] *Id.*, p. 22.
[12] See Article 5, *id.*, p. 169.

against the People's Republic of Angola' and demanded that it "scrupulously respect the independence, sovereignty and territorial integrity" of Angola'[13]. Though the Council would speak of an 'act of armed aggression perpetrated against the People's Republic of Benin' in 1977, this would be at the hands of mercenaries and would not be imputed to any State[14]. One would have to wait until 1985 for the Council to again use the term 'aggression', this time as it relates to events in the Middle East. On 4 October 1985, the Council once again acting outside of Chapter VII condemned 'vigorously the act of armed aggression perpetrated by Israel against Tunisian territory in flagrant violation of the Charter of the United Nations, international law and norms of conduct' and, as a result, demanded 'that Israel refrain from perpetrating such acts of aggression or from the threat to do so'[15]. The issuing of this, the last Security Council resolution to mention the term aggression, was as a result of an Israeli air raid in Tunisia against the headquarters of the Palestinian Liberation Organization which left seventy-one people dead[16].

The unwillingness of the Security Council to deem a situation as constituting an act of aggression has, however, not impaired it from acting under Chapter VII. As we shall now see the Security Council has been willing to function as a collective security arrangement by making determination that threats the peace and breaches of the peace have transpired and thus allowed it to act in seeking to re-establish or maintain international peace and security. Yet, as the following three cases demonstrate, the Security Council has acted selectively to enforce violations of the prohibition against the use of force, which is at the heart of its collective security mandate. In the case of the Iran-Iraq War, the invasion and occupation of Lebanon, and the 1991 Gulf War, which transpired between September 1980 and August 1990, a State invaded another in clear violation of the prohibition against aggression, yet the Security Council responded in three, fundamentally, different ways: with indifference, with forfeiture, and with vigour. While the Security Council considered both the Iraq-Iran and Gulf War as breaches of the peace, it failed to invoke Chapter VII in the case of the Israeli invasion of Lebanon and its subsequent nineteen-year occupation of the south of the country. Further, while it took the Council seven years to constitute the Iran-Iraq conflict as a breach of the peace, it took less than twelve hours for it to determine that Iraq's invasion of Kuwait represents such a fact.

---

[13] See United Nations Security Council Resolution 387, 31 March 1976, S/RES/387, 1976.
[14] See United Nations Security Council Resolutions 405 and 406, 14 April 1977 and 24 November 1977, S/RES/405 and 406, 1977.
[15] See United Nations Security Council Resolution 573, 4 October 1985, S/RES/573, 1985.
[16] See a short description in Avi Shlaim, *The Iron Wall: Israel and the Arab World*, 2000, p. 434.

II. Response to the Iran-Iraq War

In essence, the Iraqi invasion of Iran on 22 September 1980, was a case of opportunism disguised as aggression. Iraq had, five days earlier, declared the 1975 Baghdad Treaty on International Borders and Good Neighbourly Relations null and void, and sought by force of arms to regain rights in the *Shatt al-Arab* waterway which it had ceded five years previously[17]. The opportunism was to be found in the fact that Iraq sought to take advantage of the political instability which had been brought on by a revolution which witnessed the ousting of the Shah of Iran, Muhammad Reza Pahlavi, and the installation of an Islamic theocracy under the spiritual leadership of Ayatollah Ruhollah Khomeini[18]. In attacking Iran, Iraq sought to redress the balance which it felt its larger and more powerful Persian neighbour had skewed through the 1975 Algiers Accord, which led to the Baghdad Treaty. In 1975, Iran under the Shah had used its withdrawal of support of an Iraqi Kurd insurrection as a means of extracting concessions from the Hussein Administration regarding the *Shatt al-Arab*. As Charles Tripp of the University of London notes, regarding the calculus to go to war in 1980, in his *A History of Iraq*: 'from the perspective of Baghdad, the regime in Tehran looked weak, disorganised and isolated—in some respects a mirror image of the conditions of the Iraqi regime [...] which had so encouraged the shah to press for the concessions which he had eventually won in 1975'[19]. Opportunism, however, failed to materialise as Iranians saw the invasion as a challenge not only to their country but also to the Revolution itself, and were thus able to turn the engagement into a long, drawn-out war of attrition as opposed to the short decisive conflict that Iraq had envisioned.

Although Iraq did not let up with its invasion of Iran and increasingly occupied Iranian territory following 22 September, the United Nations Security Council only decided to act a week later. On 28 September 1980, the Security Council passed Resolution 479, which not only did not identify Iraq as the aggressor, but failed to even invoke Chapter VII of the Charter, unwilling as it was to characterise the situation as one which threatened or breached international peace and security. Despite the fact that the 'Iraqis penetrated as deep as 50 miles [90 km]', and had, within weeks 'occupied 5,400 square miles [10,000 square km] of Iranian territory, including the country's most important port, Khorranshahr on the *Shatt al-Arab* waterway', the Security Council was unwilling to impute Iraq with the title of

---

[17]   For a discussion of the abrogation of the 1975 Treaty see Harry Post, 'Border Conflicts between Iran and Iraq: Review and Legal Reflections', Ige Dekker and Harry Post (eds.), *The Gulf War of 1980–1988: The Iran-Iraq War in International Legal Perspective*, pp. 7–36. Post notes that on 'the basis of the available documents, the unilateral denunciation by Iraq at the time of the outbreak of hostilities in September 1980 of the Treaty of Baghdad of 13 June 1975, cannot be seen as valid.'; see p. 32.

[18]   For an interesting account of the Iranian Revolution see Suroosh Irfani, *Iran's Islamic Revolution: Popular Liberation or Religious Dictatorship?*, 1983. Consider also John Esposito, 'The Iranian Revolution: A Ten Year Perspective', John Esposito (ed.), *The Iranian Revolution: Its Global Impact*, 1990, pp. 17–39.

[19]   Charles Tripp. *A History of Iraq*, 2000, p. 232.

aggressor[20]. Instead, Resolution 479 turned to Chapter VI of the Charter and called on 'Iran and Iraq to refrain immediately from any further use of force and to settle their dispute by peaceful means and in conformity with principles of justice and international law'[21]. Further, the resolving of the dispute was handed over to the UN Secretary-General, as the Council endorsed the 'efforts of the Secretary-General and the offer of his good offices for the resolution of the situation'. Anthony Clark Arend of Georgetown University notes that these 'initial U.N. actions are quite revealing. They demonstrate a clear reluctance on the part of the organization to serve as a collective security body'[22].

From the present perspective, at the start of the twenty-first century, Arend's comment seems hard to digest and, yet, for much of its first 45 years, the UN Security Council was frozen by the inaction brought on by the Cold War dynamics of a zero-sum game between the Soviet Union and the United States whereby any advantage gained by one side was seen as a loss by the other. With this type of logic, the lack of effectiveness of the Security Council to carry out its primary responsibility regarding the maintenance of international peace and security was the most visible instance of the stalemate brought on by the ideological battle between the socialist and capitalist camps. As Cameron Hume notes in his *The United Nations, Iran and Iraq: How Peacemaking Changed*, by the time the Gulf War started, the Council appeared to be little more than a paper tiger:

> Despite much huffing and puffing by council members over the violations of international legal norms and charter obligations, the mandatory provisions of chapter VII, including sanctions, had so far proved to be a dead letter. Both governments had grounds to conclude that the Security Council was unlikely ever to take decisive action[23].

Thus, in this climate, the actions of the Security Council appeared to be well in line with the manner in which it had acted in the past, despite the fact that the Iran-Iraq War would prove over the next eight years to be the most destructive confrontation since the Second World War[24].

---

[20] Eric Hooglund, 'Strategic and Political Objectives in the Gulf War: Iran's View', Christopher Joyner (ed.) *The Persian Gulf War: Lessons for Strategy, Law, and Diplomacy*, 1990, pp. 40–41.
[21] United Nations Security Council Resolution 479, 28 September 1980, S/RES/479, 1980; para. 1. See Appendix 7.
[22] Anthony Clark Arend, 'The Role of the United Nations in the Iran-Iraq War', in Joyner, *op. cit.* n. 20, p. 192.
[23] Cameron Hume, *The United Nations, Iran and Iraq: How Peacemaking Changed*, 1994, p. 34.
[24] See the Introduction to Dekker and Post, *op. cit.* n. 17, where the editors state: 'due to its length and the way it was conducted this war shall probably be counted among the most vicious of modern times. Both in terms of the number of victims among solders and civilians—estimated at over a million—and in view of the virtually immeasurable material damage caused [...].', p. 1.

With regards to the Iran-Iraq War, the Council passed a mere eight resolutions during the conflict and only sought to invoke Chapter VII in 1987, in a resolution that ultimately proved to be the basis for a cease-fire and the end of the conflict. Beyond the original Resolution 479, it would take nearly two years before the Council would pass its second resolution regarding the conflict. Resolution 514 reiterated the call, in Resolution 479 to settle the dispute by peaceful means, but went some way in balancing the requirements sought by Iran to start to negotiate the end of the conflict. In its earlier Resolution 479, the Council had called on both parties to 'refrain immediately from any further use of force' and to settle their dispute. Yet Iran rejected this resolution noting that the Security Council 'should condemn the premeditated act of aggression that has taken place, call for the immediate withdrawal of Iraqi forces from Iranian territory and call upon Iraq to compensate Iran for damages'[25]. By calling for an immediate cessation of the use of force in 1980, the Council was allowing Iraq to hold the territory it had acquired through its act of aggression. During the intervening year and a half between resolutions, however, Iran had stemmed and reversed the tide of aggression to the extent that it appeared to be taking the fight to Iraqi territory. As a result, the Security Council was willing, not only to call for a cease-fire, but was now calling for 'a withdrawal of forces to internationally recognized boundaries'[26].

At the start of the war it was clear that Iran, under its new leadership, had become, in the eyes of the United States, a pariah. The storming of the United States Embassy by Iranian students, in 1979, in the aftermath of the fall of the Shah, and the endorsement, by the Ayatollah Khomeini, of both the seizure of the Embassy and the detention of diplomats meant that the United States sought to isolate Iran internationally[27]. That isolation went so far as to seek to invoke Chapter VII and impose UN Security Council sanctions on Iran in January 1980; a move vetoed by the Soviet Union[28]. Yet Iran did much to indicate that it was not simply switching Super Power allegiance, as it sought to export its Islamic Revolution to Soviet Central Asia and backed the Afghan *Mujahidin* in their attempt to reverse the 1979 Soviet invasion of Afghanistan[29]. The 1982 UN Security Council Resolution 514 was thus in no way a reflection of a new-found amity for Iran by the Super Powers, but was due to an Iranian counter-attack during that year which saw Iraqi forces 'driven out of most of the territory they had occupied in 1980,

---

[25]   Security Council Official Records, 35th Year, 2252nd Meeting, as quoted in Marc Weller, 'Comments: The Use of Force and Collective Security', Dekker and Post, *op. cit.* n. 17, p. 74.

[26]   United Nations Security Council Resolution 514, 12 July 1982, S/RES/514, 1982; paras. 1 and 2.

[27]   See *Case concerning United States Diplomatic and Consular Staff in Tehran*, 24 May 1980, *I.C.J. Reports 1981*.

[28]   See Anjali Patil, *The UN Veto in World Affairs, 1946–1990: A Complete Record and Case Histories of the Security Council's Veto*, 1992, pp. 348–354.

[29]   See Oliver Roy 'The Mujahidin and the Future of Afganistan' and Martha Brill Olcott, 'Soviet Central Asia: Does Moscow Fear Iranian Influence', in Esposito, *op. cit.* n. 18, pp. 179–230.

suffering heavy casualties, with an estimated 40,000 Iraqi troops taken prisoner'[30].
By October 1982, Iraq indicated that it was willing to accept a cease-fire on the
basis of Resolution 514, but Iran, for its part, was not so inclined; instead, it sought
to press its advantage[31].

The nature of the Iran-Iraq War started to change in 1982, as Iran appeared to
be gaining the upper hand. Fearful that it would be defeated, Iraq started to target
civilian populations and oil tankers in the Persian Gulf. The Security Council for
its part, passed Resolution 540 in October 1983, condemning 'all violations of
international humanitarian law' and calling for 'the immediate cessation of all
military operations against civilian targets, including city and residential areas'[32].
In February 1984, Iraq not only failed to heed the Security Council obligations
regarding humanitarian law, but went one better. In attempting to forestall a
planned Iranian offensive, Iraq announced that it would target eleven Iranian cities,
'giving the civilian population a week to evacuate; Iran threatened reprisal'[33].
When Iran followed through with its offensive, the parties followed suit and
initiated what would come to be known as the 'war of the cities'. While Resolution
540 only touched in part on attacks in the Persian Gulf, Resolution 552 of June
1984 dealt specifically with the issue, as the Council considered that 'these attacks
constitute a threat to the safety and stability of the area and have serious
implications for international peace and security'[34]. Iraq's rationale for expanding
the war to the Gulf was to weaken Iran's economy by affecting its oil-exports, but
primarily to internationalise the conflict so as to gain assistance from third parties.
The 'Tanker War' turned the Iran-Iraq War—for many Permanent Members of the
Security Council and Gulf States—from being an Iraqi war of aggression to a war
to attempt to stem the export of the Iranian Revolution[35].

---

[30]   Tripp, *op. cit.* n. 19, p. 235.
[31]   See United Nations Security Council Resolution 522, 4 October 1982, S/RES/522,
1982; para. 3, where the Security Council welcomed 'the fact that one of the parties has
already expressed it readiness to co-operate in the implementation of resolution 514 (1982)
and calls upon the other to do likewise'. Note that Marc Weller concludes that Resolutions
514 and 522 ended Iran's right to self-defence. He writes: 'Once the implementation of this
acceptance [Iraq's acceptance of the cease-fire as noted in Resolution 522] was assured,
Iran's right of self-defence lapsed. The continuance of hostilities by the government of Iran
amounted to a breach of the obligations to refrain from the use of force and to settle disputes
peacefully'. Weller, in Dekker and Post, *op. cit.* n. 17, p. 90.
[32]   United Nations Security Council Resolution 540, 31 October 1983, S/RES/540, 1983;
para. 2.
[33]   Hume, *op. cit.* n. 23, p. 48.
[34]   United Nations Security Council Resolution 552, 1 June 1984, S/RES/552, 1984;
preambular para. 6.
[35]   Nadia El-Sayed El-Shazly, *The Gulf Tanker War: Iran and Iraq's Maritime Swordplay*,
1998, p. 1 and 195 where the author notes that beyond US support, 'Saudi Arabia and
Kuwait underwrote the Iraqi war effort to the tune of $100 million a day'. For
documentation as to the reaction of selected States see: Andrea de Gutty and Natalino
Ronzitti, *The Iran-Iraq War (1980–1988) and the Law of Naval Warfare*, 1993.

138   *International Law in the Middle East*

The nature of the War was also to change due to the Iraqi introduction of the use of chemical weapons. In 1986, in its Resolution 582, the Security Council deplored:

> the escalation of the conflict, especially territorial incursions, the bombing of purely civilian population centers, attacks on neutral shipping or civilian aircraft, the violation of international humanitarian law and other laws of armed conflict and, in particular, the use of chemical weapons contrary to obligations under the 1925 Geneva Protocol[36].

While the Security Council was unwilling to point the finger at Iraq for its use of chemical weapons in its resolutions, on the basis of a unanimous report of specialists who had been sent to the region to investigate allegations of chemical weapons, the Council did identify Iraq through a Statement of the President of the Security Council in March 1986. The Statement read in part, that 'chemical weapons on many occasions have been used by Iraqi forces against Iranian forces, most recently in the course of the present Iranian offensive into Iraqi territory'. The statement went on to say that 'the Members of the Council strongly condemn this continued use of chemical weapons in clear violation of the Geneva Protocol of 1925 which prohibits the use in war of chemical weapons'[37]. This Statement was followed up by another in May 1987, in which the Council expressed that it was deeply 'dismayed by the unanimous conclusions of the specialists that there has been repeated use of chemical weapons against Iranian forces by Iraqi forces, that civilians in Iran also have been injured by chemical weapons, and that Iraqi military personnel have sustained injuries from chemical warfare agents'[38].

Resolutions 514, 540, and 582 are instructive as they demonstrate a pattern of concession by the Security Council to move closer to the demands of Iran for ending the hostilities. As noted earlier, Resolution 514 (1982) called for withdrawal 'to internationally recognized boundaries', and thus relieved Iran of having to acquiesce to allowing Iraq to hold territory it had gained by force of arms[39]. The Council moved closer to the Iranian position when, in a preambular paragraph of Resolution 540 (1983), it affirmed 'the desirability of an objective examination of the causes of the war', and hence was paying attention to Iran's call for determining the aggressor[40]. In 1986, the Security Council followed this trend by stating, this time in an operative paragraph of the Resolution 582, that it 'Deplores the initial acts which gave rise to the conflict between the Islamic

---

[36] United Nations Security Council Resolution 582, 24 February 1986, S/RES/582, 1986; para. 2.
[37] Statement of the President of the United Nations Security Council, 21 March 1986, S/17932.
[38] Statement of the President of the United Nations Security Council, 14 May 1987, S/18863. As no indication has been made that Iran used chemical weapons, the reference to Iraqi military personnel must relate to either prisoners of war in Iran, or Iraqi forces, caught by the effects of their own attack.
[39] See Resolution 514, *op. cit.* n. 26.
[40] See Resolution 540, *op. cit.* n. 32.

Republic of Iran and Iraq and deplores the continuation of the conflict'[41]. In January 1987, the UN Secretary-General Javier Pérez de Cuéllar, 'called for a new approach to ending the Iran-Iraq War' which bore fruit in the framework Resolution 598[42]. Resolution 598 adopted on 20 July 1987 would provide a further concession to Iran in an attempt to have it accept a cease-fire that Iraq had been willing to contemplate since 1982[43]. As noted earlier, the three demands which Iran had in rejecting the original Security Council Resolution were to determine Iraq as the aggressor, to have it withdraw its troops, and to provide reparations[44]. While the Council called on Iran and Iraq to withdraw to their international borders as early as Resolution 1982, and was prepared to consider the causes of the war in Resolution 540; in resolution 598 the Security Council requested:

> the Secretary-General to explore in consultation with Iran and Iraq, the question of entrusting an impartial body with inquiring in to responsibility for the conflict and to report to the Council as soon as possible[45].

As it is axiomatic in international relations that a corollary of responsibility is the obligation to make full reparations for injuries caused, the Council apparently had met the three Iranian demands for a cease-fire. The way, thus, appeared clear for a settlement.

Through Resolution 598, the UN Security Council expressed its determination 'to bring to an end all military actions between Iran and Iraq', as it was worried that a 'further escalation and widening of the conflict may take place'. As such, the Council sought to act, for the first time during the Iran-Iraq War as a collective security body and determined 'that there exists a breach of the peace as regards the conflict between Iran and Iraq'[46]. On that basis, The Security Council *demanded* that,

> as a first step towards a negotiated settlement, the Islamic Republic of Iran and Iraq observe an immediate cease-fire, discontinue all military actions on land, at sea and in the air, and withdraw all forces to the internationally recognized boundaries without delay[47].

The Resolution called on the Secretary-General to mediate the cease-fire, to send observers to oversee it, and to send a team to consider the issue of reconstructing the war-torn societies. As for the parties, the Resolution called on Iran and Iraq to cooperate with the Secretary-General in implementing the Resolution with a look

---

[41] See Resolution 582, *op. cit.* n. 36.

[42] Arend, *op. cit.* n. 22. For the actions of the Secretary-General see Chapter 7 entitled 'Pérez de Cuéllar's Move' in Hume, *op. cit.* n. 23, p. 88–102.

[43] See Resolution 522, *op. cit.* n. 31.

[44] See *supra.*, text associated with n. 25.

[45] United Nations Security Council Resolution 598, 20 July 1987, S/RES/598, 1987; para. 6. See Appendix 9.

[46] *Id.*, see various paragraphs in the preamble.

[47] *Id.*, para. 1.

to a 'comprehensive, just and honourable settlement' of all issues, and further called on the parties to release and repatriate prisoners of war. While Iraq indicated that it was prepared to use Resolution 598 as a basis for ending the war, Iran rejected it, claiming that the Resolution had 'been formulated by the United States with the explicit intention of intervention in the Persian Gulf region, that Iran had not been consulted, and that it would, in effect, terminate the war in favour of an aggressor state'[48].

During the following year, factors on the ground would, however, change the Iranian stance, making it amenable to agreeing to Resolution 598 as a basis for ending the conflict. While some have argued that by April 1988, Iran was a 'defeated nation', as it could no longer respond to Iraq's renewed 'war of the cities' and it had met a reversal of fortunes on the battle field, it appears, however, that the main determinant for Iran in seeking an end to the Iran-Iraq War was an incident that took place on 3 July 1988[49]. On that date, a United States warship—the *USS Vincennes*—downed an Iranian civilian aircraft killing 290 people[50]. Two weeks later, the UN Secretary-General received a letter from the Iranian President, Ali Khamenei, which noted that the war had 'now gained unprecedented dimensions, bringing other countries into the war and even engulfing innocent civilians'; as such 'the Islamic Republic of Iran—because of the importance it attaches to saving the lives of human beings and the establishment of justice and regional and international peace and security—accepts Security Council Resolution 598'[51]. The UN Secretary-General followed this up with discussion with both parties and, on 8 August 1988, called:

> upon the Islamic Republic of Iran and Iraq to observe a cease-fire and to discontinue all military action on land, at sea and in the air as of 0300 (GMT) on 20 August 1988. I have been assured by the two parties to the conflict that they will observe this cease-fire in the context of the full implementation of resolution 598 (1987)[52].

Thus ended the hostilities of the Iran-Iraq War, 'the longest war in modern history since the Battle of Waterloo, [which] raged from September 22, 1980, when Iraqi forces invaded Iranian territory, until August 20, 1988, when a formal cease-fire between Iran and Iraq took effect'[53]. The wording of Resolution 598 was such that

---

48   Weller, in Dekker and Post, *op. cit.* n. 17, p. 76.
49   See Charles MacDonald, 'Iran, Iraq, and the Cease-Fire Negotiations—Contemporary Legal Issues', in Joyner, *op. cit.* n. 20, p. 211.
50   See United Nations Security Council Resolution 616, 20 July 1988, S/RES/616, 1988, which was passed one year, to the day, after Resolution 598, which expressed the Security Council's 'deep distress at the downing of an Iranian civil aircraft by a missile fired from a United States warship and profound regret over the tragic loss of innocent lives'. The Council went on to stress 'the need for a full and rapid implementation of its resolution 598', paras. 1 and 5.
51   As quoted in Hume, *op. cit.* n. 23, p. 167.
52   Statement by the Secretary-General to the United Nations Security Council Resolution, 8 August 1988, S/20095.
53   MacDonald, *op. cit.* n. 49, p. 210.

the Security Council did not impose a settlement on the parties, but saw the cease-fire as the first step toward a final settlement. While the Security Council would establish the UN Iran-Iraq Military Observer Group to monitor the cease-fire, the final withdrawal would not take place until 1990, when Iraq, in the midst of its invasion of Kuwait, sought to secure its eastern flank[54]. In an exchange of letters during July and August 1990, Iraq first sought to terminate the war on the basis of Resolution 598, however, it would later concede to Iranian demands that the 1975 Baghdad Treaty would hold sway, and thus the parties agreed to a termination of the War on that basis[55].

Writing in 1990, Anthony Clark Arend concludes his consideration of the UN role in the Iran-Iraq War in the following terms:

> the United Nations continued to be largely ineffective as a collective security organization. The framers of the U.N. Charter intended the organization to respond quickly to aggression. When one state used force against another, the United Nations was to take necessary action to determine the aggressor state and then stop it. The United Nations was quite reluctant to assume that role in the Iran-Iraq War. [...]
> The reasons for this unwillingness to be a collective security body are well known. Since the adoption of the Charter in 1945, states have generally been reluctant to brand another state as an aggressor, let alone take action against it. This judgment reflects a political choice that most states do not wish to make. In the Iran-Iraq War there was a clear desire to avoid such a determination, at least initially. [...] Finally, the organization's inaction must be linked to a general unwillingness by states to become involved in using force. Unless there exists a direct threat to national security or the force in question is at a fairly low level, states tend to refrain from becoming involved in international conflicts[56].

While Arend's evaluation seems to hit all the salient points of the manner in which the Security Council acted during its first 45 years, it is interesting to note that between the Council and the Secretary-General, the United Nations managed to graft a settlement which held. While Security Council Resolution 598 brought to an end the hostilities of the Iran-Iraq War, the fact that it took seven years for the Security Council to invoke Chapter VII says much about that organisation during the Cold War period. Unwilling to take on its primary responsibility regarding international peace and security during this conflict, it was sending a message to States regarding acts of aggression, that the Council was unlikely to act to deter. While the Security Council acted with indifference during much of the Iran-Iraq War, unwilling to invoke Chapter VII; the Council would forfeit it obligations, where the Israeli invasion of Lebanon was concerned, by the use of the veto powers exercised primarily by the United States of America.

---

[54] See United Nations Security Council Resolution 619, 9 August 1988, S/RES/619, 1988.
[55] See 'Exchange of Letters between Iran and Iraq establishing the basis of a Peace Agreement, July and August 1990', Elihu Lauterpact et al. (eds.), *The Kuwait Crisis: Basic Documents*, 1991, pp. 63–69.
[56] Arend, *op. cit.* n. 22, p. 204.

III. Response to the Israeli Invasion and Occupation of Lebanon

Few commentators accept Israel's pretext for its 6 July 1982 invasion of Lebanon as being the true motivation behind its undertaking of an act of aggression against its northern neighbour[57]. Though the attempted assassination of the Israeli ambassador in London was the event that sparked the advance on Beirut, the motivation for Israel's invasion was linked to its attempt to destroy the Palestinian Liberation Organization (PLO) which had established its headquarters in Lebanon after having been forced out of Jordan in 1970, during *Black September*[58]. Israel sought to justify its use of force as being an act of self-defence. Shabtai Rosenne, the legal advisor to the Israeli Foreign Office would say that:

> It is not a matter of dispute that PLO units, operating from Lebanese territory, have attacked Israeli towns and villages along the whole of the northern frontier. Israeli actions in self-defence against those terrorist concentrations are designed to repel those recurrent attacks and end the constant, grave threat to the safety and welfare of Israel's civilian population in Galilee[59].

The problem with Rosenne's justification for Israel's 'Peace in Galilee' military operation was that the PLO had scrupulously maintained a cease-fire along the border for the previous year[60]. The UN Security Council, for its part, passed a resolution one day before the Israeli invasion, calling for a cease-fire, as Israel had undertaken a handful of air raids on 5 July, to which the PLO responded with artillery gunfire on northern Israeli villages[61]. United Nations Security Council Resolution 508 of 5 June 1982 reiterated a number of previous resolutions, it expressed the Council's deep concern 'at the deterioration of the present situation in Lebanon and in the Lebanese-Israeli border area' as well as 'violations of the territorial integrity, independence and sovereignty of Lebanon', and called on the

---

[57]   See Shlaim, *op. cit.* n. 16, pp. 400–407; Benny Morris, *Righteous Victims*, 1999, pp. 508–514.

[58]   Morris notes that Israel could feel confident that its invasion would not lead to a general war with Arab States primarily because of the Egyptian-Israeli Peace Treaty of 1979 which had in effect 'safeguarded its southern flank' thus 'Israel felt free [...] in 1982 to invade Lebanon'. *Id.*, p. 493.

[59]   See Istvan Pogany, *The Security Council and the Arab-Israeli Conflict*, 1984, p. 156. In the Security Council the Delegate of the United Kingdom noted that the attempted assassination 'does not in any way justify the massive attacks', and later that 'Israel has invaded Lebanon in flagrant violation of international law and of paragraph 4 of Article 2 of the Charter, as well as in complete disregard of the demands of the Security Council. My government regards the invasion and occupation as a violation of Lebanon's sovereignty, and we cannot accept that the Israeli action amounted to self-defence'. See p. 155.

[60]   Morris writes: '[...] the PLO took great pains not to violate the agreement of July 1981 [the US brokered cease-fire]. Indeed, subsequent Israeli propaganda notwithstanding, the border between July 1981 and June 1982 enjoyed a state of calm unprecedented since 1968'. Morris, *op. cit.* n. 57, p. 509.

[61]   See Shlaim, *op. cit.* n. 16, p. 404; Morris, *op. cit.* n. 57, p. 515.

'parties to the conflict to cease immediately and simultaneously all military activities [...] no later than 0600 hours, local time, on Sunday, 6 June 1982'[62].

The reiteration of previous resolutions by the Security Council was an indication that the border had been the locus of hostilities prior to June 1982. In fact, since the mid-1970s, Lebanon had been in the throws of a civil war, in large part because of the influx of Palestinians which had disturbed the Christian-Muslim balance incorporated in the 1943 National Pact. That Pact, which established the representation in government of the various ethnic and religious groups that make up the Lebanese mosaic, unravelled as a major demographic shift took place in the intervening thirty years[63]. Though originally placed, in 1920, under the French Mandate for Lebanon and Syria, the French would constitute Lebanon as a Christian enclave, separating it from Syria in 1926. Lebanon would gain its independence in 1944, using the National Pact as the basis of governance; however, by the mid-1970s it became clear that the Pact was no longer workable. When an attempt was made on the life of the founder of the Christian Phalange Party in April 1975, its militia responded by ambushing a bus from the Shatila Palestinian refugee camp killing twenty-seven people: it was the opening salvo of a sixteen-year civil war. By June 1976, Syria sent troops to Lebanon in an attempt to end the fighting. Syria's unilateral intervention was replaced in October by a League of Arab States' sponsored Arab Deterrent Force, though eighty percent of that force would be Syrian. By November 1976, the Arab Deterrent Force managed to stop the fighting.

The precarious peace would hold until March 1977 when the leader of the Druze was assassinated. Lebanon was once again plunged into war, however, the divide between Christians and Muslims was growing as 'Syria seemed to be consolidating its dominant position in Lebanon, much to the chagrin of the Maronite [Christian Phalange] leaders and their foreign backers, Israel'[64]. On 14 March 1978 Israel invaded Lebanon, the 'campaign, code-named Operation Litani, was mounted with the aim of creating a 10 km-wide buffer zone along the 100 km-long [Israeli-Lebanese] border'[65]. On 19 March, the UN Security Council called on Israel to immediately 'cease its military action against Lebanese territorial integrity and withdraw forthwith its forces from all Lebanese territory'. Resolution 425 also established the United Nations Interim Force for Southern Lebanon (UNIFL)

---

[62] United Nations Security Council Resolution 508, 5 July 1982, S/RES/508, 1982. See Appendix 8.
[63] A 1932 census showed that 54 percent of Lebanese were Christian; while a 1973 population estimate found that the Muslim-Christian balance had reversed whereby Muslims constituted 54 percent of the population. See Dilip Hiro, *Lebanon: Fire and Embers—a History of the Lebanese Civil* War, 1992, pp. 5 and 8–9. The various groupings in Lebanon include Armenian Catholic, Assyrian and Chaldenan Catholic, Greek Catholic, Maronite Catholic, Roman Catholic, Syrian Catholic, Armenian Orthodox, Greek Orthodox, Syrian Orthodox, Protestant, Bahai, Jew, Alawi, Druze, Shia, and Sunni.
[64] Hiro, *id.*, p. 51.
[65] *Id.*, p. 52.

meant to confirm 'the withdrawal of Israeli forces'[66]. While the Council would take note of the withdrawal of some Israeli forces in a resolution in May 1978, the Israeli Defence Force (IDF) would carry out its major withdrawal in June, leaving behind a proxy Lebanese militia—the South Lebanon Army[67]. Thus created a 10 km buffer 'Security Zone' on the Lebanese side of its southern border, followed by a demilitarised zone north of that controlled by UNIFIL which separated Israel from PLO fighters. 'Nevertheless', as Benny Morris writes, 'Palestinians and Israelis were still able to get to each other'[68].

By June 1982, when Israel was to invade Lebanon for a second time, UNIFIL had been unable to confirm whether Israel had, in fact, withdrawn from Southern Lebanon, as neither Israel nor the South Lebanon Army was willing to cooperate with UNIFIL. As early as January 1979, the Security Council was starting to show its displeasure with Israel's intransigence in not maintaining a cease-fire or completely pulling out of Southern Lebanon. In Resolution 444, the Council expressed its concern regarding the 'grave situation in Southern Lebanon resulting from obstacles placed in the way of the full implementation of resolution 425' while '[r]eiterating its conviction that the continuation of the situation constitutes a challenge to its authority and defiance of its resolutions'. It then went on to deplore 'the lack of co-operation, particularly on the part of Israel, with the efforts of the [UNIFIL] fully to implement its mandate, including assistance lent by Israel to irregular armed groups in Southern Lebanon'[69]. In June 1979, the Council considered that the 'present situation has serious consequences for peace and security in the Middle East and impedes the achievement of a just, comprehensive and durable peace in the area'. As a result, it called on 'Israel to cease forthwith its acts against the territorial integrity, unity, sovereignty and political independence of Lebanon, in particular its incursions into Lebanon and the assistance it continues to lend to irresponsible armed groups'[70]. By February 1982, the Council made plain that no progress had been made, calling on 'Israel immediately to cease its military action against Lebanese territorial integrity and withdraw forthwith its forces from all Lebanese territory'[71].

Israel failed to heed the call found in UN Security Council Resolution 508 to cease-fire by 6 a.m. on 6 June 1982; instead it commenced an invasion which would include '76,000 troops, 1,250 tanks, and 1,500 armoured personnel carriers, [as well as] naval and air support'[72]. The response of the Security Council came the same day as Resolution 509, demanding respect for the cease-fire called for in Resolution 508, but also demanding, 'that Israel withdraw all its military forces forthwith and unconditionally to the internationally recognized boundaries of

---

[66]   UN Security Council Resolution 425, 19 March 1978, S/RES/425, 1978, paras. 2 and 3. See Appendix 6.
[67]   See UN Security Council Resolution 427, 3 May 1978, S/RES/427, 1978, para. 2.
[68]   Morris, *op. cit.* n. 57, p. 502.
[69]   UN Security Council Resolution 444, 19 January 1979, S/RES/444, 1979, para. 1.
[70]   UN Security Council Resolution 450, 14 June 1979, S/RES/450, 1979, para. 2.
[71]   UN Security Council Resolution 501, 25 February 1982, S/RES/501, 1982, para. 2.
[72]   Hiro, *op. cit.* n. 63, p. 82.

Lebanon'[73]. The language of the Security Council is instructive: in February, its resolution 'calls on' Israel to withdraw; while in June, Resolution 508, 'demands' Israeli withdrawal. The Council was moving toward imposing a cease-fire by indicating that it was heading toward acting under Chapter VII; however, that momentum was halted by the failure to pass a draft resolution considered on 8 June 1982. On that day, the Security Council was prepared to turn up the heat on Israel by condemning 'the non-compliance with resolution 508 (1982) and 509 (1982) by Israel' while reiterating 'its demand that Israel withdraw all its military forces forthwith and unconditionally to the internationally recognized boundaries of Lebanon'[74]. However, the United States of America vetoed that resolution, its representative explaining that she considered that it 'was not sufficiently balanced to accomplish the objectives of ending the cycle of violence and establishing the conditions for a just and lasting peace in Lebanon'[75].

Yet such a justification seems little more than diplomatic cover for an operation which the United States was made party to, in May, when the Israeli Defence Minister Ariel Sharon met with the US Secretary of State, Alexander Haig. In that meeting, Sharon obtained a limited go-ahead—it was not a green light, more like 'a dim yellow light'—but the Defence Minister was told that the invasion could transpire only if it was provoked[76]. The attempted assassination in London was thus the pretext which turned the light from amber to green and precipitated the wholesale invasion of Lebanon. The use of the veto by the United States effectively sidelined the Security Council during both the invasions of Lebanon by Israel, which would last until 1985, as well as throughout its occupation of Southern Lebanon which would only end during the year 2000. The first of nine vetos cast by the United States regarding the Israeli aggression in Lebanon, the veto of 8 June 1982 was the most significant as it sent a message that the United States was unwilling to allow the UN Security Council to have a hand in attempting to restore peace in Lebanon, by its halting of any momentum toward invoking Chapter VII. While the invading Israeli forces would make their way to the outskirts of the Lebanese capital, Beirut, on 11 July, the Council would not convene again in formal session until 18 June, a move which 'reflected the lack of consensus amongst Council members rather than the cessation of hostilities'[77].

This change in nature of the next Security Council resolutions which were issued, on 18 and 19 June, is almost palatable. Gone were Security Council 'demands', and mention of Israel by name; instead the focus was not on seeking to end the Israeli invasion, but to mitigate its effects by invoking the need to respect humanitarian law. While Resolution 511 simply extended the mandate of UNIFIL, Resolution 512 called on the parties 'to respect the rights of civilian populations, and to refrain from all acts of violence against those populations and take all

---

[73] UN Security Council Resolution 509, 6 June 1982, S/RES/509, 1982, paras. 1 and 2.
[74] See Patil, *op. cit.* n. 28, pp. 298–299.
[75] *Id.*, p. 299.
[76] Morris, *op. cit.* n. 57, p. 515.
[77] Pogany, *op. cit.* n. 59, p. 154.

appropriate measures to alleviate the suffering caused by the conflict'[78]. By this
time, Israel had encircled Beirut and started to lay siege to it with the aim of
forcing the PLO fighters out of Lebanon. On 26 June, the United States again
vetoed a draft resolution, whereby the Security Council expressed its concern about
the 'constant deterioration of the situation in Lebanon, resulting from the violation
of the sovereignty, integrity, independence and unity of that country' and
demanded the 'immediate withdrawal of the Israeli forces engaged around Beirut
to a distance of 10 kilometres from the periphery of that city, as the first step
towards the complete withdrawal of Israeli forces from Lebanon'[79]. Israel, for its
part, tightened its blockade, slowly squeezing the PLO into smaller areas of West
Beirut, seeking to have it capitulate through 'bombardment from air, land and sea',
by cutting off water and electricity, and by refusing to allow food or medicine to
this sector of the city[80].

By late July, the IDF had intensified its campaign against West Beirut, on 1
August 'it carried out fourteen hours of non-stop air, naval and artillery pounding
of West Beirut'[81] while on 4 August it started to indiscriminately bomb residential
sectors of West Beirut which held no Palestinians[82]. The UN Security Council,
which had demanded a cease-fire on 1 August, stated, three days later in
Resolution 517, that it was:

Deeply shocked and alarmed by the deplorable consequences of the Israeli invasion of
Beirut on 3 August 1982,

1. *Reconfirms* its resolutions 508 (1982), 509 (1982), 512 (1982), 513 (1982),
515 (1982) and 516 (1982);

2. *Confirms* once again its demand for an immediate cease-fire and withdrawal
of Israeli forces from Lebanon;

3. *Censures* Israel for its failure to comply with the above resolutions;

4. *Calls* for the prompt return of Israeli troops which have moved forward
subsequent to 1325 hours EDT on 1 August 1982;

5. *Takes note* of the decision of the Palestinian Liberation Organization to move
the Palestinian armed forces from Beirut; [...][83]

---

[78] United Nations Security Council Resolution 512, 19 June 1982, S/RES/512, 1982, para. 1.
[79] Patil, *op. cit.* n. 28, pp. 299–300. The Resolution goes on to say: 'as well as the
simultaneous withdrawal of the Palestinian armed forces from Beirut which shall retire to the
existing camps'.
[80] Hiro, *op. cit.* n. 63, p. 87. See also United Nations Security Council Resolution 513,
4 July 1982, S/RES/513, 1982, para. 2, which called 'for the restoration of the normal supply
of vital facilities such as water, electricity, food, and medical provisions'.
[81] Hiro, *id.*, p. 87.
[82] *Id.*, p. 87.
[83] United Nations Security Council Resolution 517, 4 August 1982, S/RES/517, 1982.

The Security Council, however, would be unable to follow-up this strongly worded resolution, as the United States would, less than a week later, once again, veto a resolution. On 6 August 1982, the Soviet Union submitted a draft resolution which sought to express that the Council was '[d]eeply indignant at the refusal of Israel to comply with the decisions of the Security Council aimed at terminating the bloodshed in Beirut' and, as such, sought to impose what amounted to an arms embargo. The relevant paragraph reads:

> 2. *Decides* that, in order to carry out the above-mentioned decision of the Security Council, all the States Members of the United Nations shall refrain from supplying Israel with any weapons and from providing it with any military aid until the full withdrawal of Israeli forces from all Lebanese territory[84].

Beyond vetoing this move, the United States would not issue another veto regarding the war in Lebanon until 1984; instead, it by-passed the Council by getting directly involved in the conflict through its contribution of the largest contingency to the Multi-National Force (MNF) meant to escort the PLO fighters out of Beirut and protect the other Palestinian refugees in Beirut.

Though the MNF ensured that the PLO fighters, including Yasser Arafat, left Beirut—having completed their evacuation to a ship destined for their new refuge in Tunisia on 31 August 1982 —the Force would not remain to finish its mandate, pulling out of Lebanon on 13 September. This action would have tragic consequences as the next day, the Israeli backed President-elect of Lebanon, the Phalangist leader, Bashir Gemayel, was assassinated. As Avi Shlaim notes, the 'assassination knocked out the central prop from underneath Israel's entire policy in Lebanon', which was to establish a Christian dominated vassal State on its northern border[85]. The murder was used as a pretext by the IDF to occupy all of West Beirut, thus filling the vacuum left by the departure of both the PLO and the Multi-National Force; a move which the Security Council condemned, calling for the immediate 'return to the positions occupied by Israel before 15 September 1982'[86]. Shlaim, Professor of International Relations at Oxford University, explains what happened next:

> [Israeli Defense Minister Ariel] Sharon ordered the IDF commanders to allow the Phalangists to enter the Palestinian refugee camps of Sabra and Shatila, on the south side of Beirut, in order to 'clean out' the terrorists who, he claimed, were lurking there. Inside the camps the revenge-thirsty Christian militiamen perpetrated a terrible massacre, killing hundreds of men, women and children, Israel estimated the number of dead at seven to eight hundred, while the Palestinian Red Crescent put the number at over two thousand[87].

---

[84] Patil, *op. cit.* n. 28, p. 301.
[85] See Shlaim, *op. cit.* n. 16, p. 415.
[86] United Nations Security Council Resolution 520, 17 September 1982, S/RES/520, 1982, para. 3.
[87] See Shlaim, *op. cit.* n. 16, p. 416.

While the United Nations General Assembly would consider that the 'massacre was an act of genocide', the Security Council condemned 'the criminal massacre of Palestinians civilians in Beirut'[88]. As a result of the massacre, the MNF returned, though not before 'intense American pressure' forced the IDF out of Beirut[89].

Though Israel still occupied a third of Lebanon, its Government was facing growing pressure at home to pull the IDF out, as guerrilla forces, led primarily by the Shiite, Iranian backed, 'Party of God' or *Hizbullah*, was emerging to take its toll in dead soldiers[90]. In May 1983, Israel and the Lebanese Government signed an agreement that sought to end the state of war between them, which had existed since 1948, and called on Israel to withdraw beyond its border. The withdrawal, however, was predicated on Syria doing likewise. While Israel sought a means of extracting itself from Lebanon, *Hizbullah* would force the MNF out of Lebanon by February 1984, by means of suicide bomb attacks against the United States and French military compounds on 23 October 1983, which killed 300 soldiers[91]. For much the same reasons, Benny Morris writes: the 'primary engine of Israel's gradual withdrawal from Lebanon was the increasingly violent guerrilla campaign against the IDF presence'. He goes on to note:

> The guerrilla war soon donned the usual features. The population was warned off cooperating with the Israelis; collaborators were shot and Israeli troops were sporadically attacked, from ambush and with mines. The Israeli reactions also followed the timeworn patterns of curfews, searches, mass arrests, torture of suspects, vandalism, looting, and occasional on-the-spot execution—all fueling local anger and support for the guerrillas. [...] At the same time, the alternative—an abrupt, unilateral withdrawal back to the Security Zone without an agreement with, or guarantees by Shi'ites—was rejected by Jerusalem as amounting to an admission that the whole project had been folly[92].

Morris then notes that the cycle of repression and insurgency 'spun out of control'. He notes the IDF and Israel's General Security Services or Shin Bet, would retaliate after attacks by the guerrilla forces:

---

[88]   UN General Assembly Resolution 37/123, 16 December 1982, A/RES/37/123(A-F), and United Nations Security Council Resolution 521, 17 September 1982, S/RES/521, 1982, para. 1. For the events see Robert Fisk, *Pity the Nation: Lebanon at War*, 2001, pp. 359–400; for an analysis from the perspective of international law see International Commission (Seán MacBride, Chair), *Israel in Lebanon: The Report of the International Commission to enquire into reported violations of International Law by Israel during its invasion of Lebanon*, 1983, pp. 162–186.
[89]   Morris, *op. cit.* n. 57, p. 549.
[90]   For an evolution of Hezbollah see Magnus Ranstrop, *Hizb'Allah in Lebanon: The Politics of the Western Hostage Crisis*, 1997, pp. 25–59.
[91]   Note that on 29 February 1984, the Soviet Union vetoed a UN Security Council resolution calling for a United Nations Force to fill the vacuum of the retreating Multi-National Force. See Patil, *op. cit.* n. 28, pp. 303–305.
[92]   Morris, *op. cit.* n. 57, pp. 522 and 553.

During the first year of the occupation [1982 (sic)], the primary target of Israeli security operations had been the remnants of the PLO infrastructure and leadership; from autumn 1983 it was the Shi'ites. Initially, the counterinsurgency efforts were largely defensive and in the hands of the IDF. Mass arrests were the main measure (in August 1982, for example, the Israelis were holding some ten thousand mostly Palestinian prisoners [...] and Shin Bet's input became more critical and multifaceted. Injecting more and more agents into the area [...]. Extortion, intimidation, beatings, and torture became the norm, and Shi'ite militants from time to time were liquidated in their homes and villages by locally hired assassins or Shin Bet operatives[93].

On 6 September, Lebanon brought forward a draft Security Council resolution citing the Universal Declaration on Human Rights, the Fourth Geneva Convention dealing with civilians in armed conflicts, and the 1907 Hague Convention regulations; and sought to have the Council call upon 'Israel, the occupying Power, to respect strictly the rights of the civilians population in the areas under its occupation in southern Lebanon, the western Bekaa and Rashaya district'. The draft, which was vetoed by the United States, demanded 'that Israel immediately lift all restrictions and obstacles to the restoration of normal conditions in the area under its occupation in violation of the Fourth Geneva Convention of 1949, particularly concerning the closing of roads and crossing, the limitations of freedom [...] between those areas and the rest of Lebanon, and the obstruction to the normal conduct of Lebanese Government institutions and personnel'[94]. A similar worded draft resolution, again submitted by Lebanon was vetoed by the United States on 12 March 1985; this time the draft sought to condemn 'the Israeli practices and measures against the civilian population in southern Lebanon, the western Bekaa and Rashaya district which are in violation of the rules and principles of international law, in particular the provisions of the Geneva Convention of 12 August 1949', and demanded that Israel 'desist forthwith' from violating the Geneva Convention and 'other norms of international law'[95]. On 17 January the 1986, a draft resolution was once again introduced by Lebanon and vetoed by the United States. This time, the Resolution sought to curb Israeli conduct towards civilian populations, demanding 'that Israel desist forthwith from its practices and measures against the civilian population in southern Lebanon'[96].

The vetoed resolution of 1986 is instructive, as Lebanon dropped its mention of the western Bekaa and Rashaya district as, by June 1985, the IDF had received enough attacks from *Hizbullah* that it, in fact, retreated unilaterally to its self-declared 'Security Zone' in Southern Lebanon. The United Nations reported that in Southern Lebanon, since 1985, the IDF was 'gradually established a civilian administration in the area it controls. That administration has assumed responsibilities for police, intelligence, the collection of taxes [... it] also issues permits required for residents of the Israel-controlled area to travel to other parts of

93 *Id.*, p. 555.
94 Patil, *op. cit.* n. 28, pp. 305–306.
95 *Id.*, pp. 306–307.
96 *Id.*, p. 309.

Lebanon'[97]. For its part, from 1985 until 2000, the Security Council would no longer deal with Israeli occupation *per se*, instead when it did consider Lebanon, it was through its renewal of the UNIFIL mandate at six month intervals, at which time it inevitability repeated the operative paragraph which read that the Security Council:

> Reiterates its strong support for the territorial integrity, sovereignty and independence of Lebanon within its internationally recognized boundaries.

From its self-proclaimed 'Security Zone' of Southern Lebanon, Israel with its proxy, the Southern Lebanon Army, continued to undertake incursions north. In 1988, '2000 troops, supported by tanks and helicopter gun ships [were used] against "terrorist" positions in a operation that lasted three days'[98]. As a result, six non-aligned States brought a draft resolution condemning 'the recent invasion by Israeli forces of southern Lebanon' noting its deep concern 'by the recent action of those forces causing heavy casualties, displacement of civilian populations, the destruction of houses and property, and in particular the devastation of the entire village of Meidoun'[99]. The United States vetoed the Resolution, as it would one tabled on 14 December 1988, strongly deploring 'the recent Israeli attack against Lebanese territory by naval, air, and land forces'[100]. This incursion was aimed at the base of the Popular Front for the Liberation of Palestine near Beirut.

From the end of the Cold War, which was marked by the implosion of the Soviet Empire in 1989, till Israel was forced to quit Lebanon by *Hizbullah* in 2000, the Security Council did not act to deter what, by reference to General Assembly Resolution 3314 of 1974, remained an act of aggression. It will be recalled that among the enumerated examples of acts of aggression found in the Definition of Aggression, Article 3 not only mentions 'invasion or attack by the armed forces of a State of the territory of another State', but also 'any military occupation, however temporary, resulting from such invasion or attack'. Though a 'New World Order' would be herald by the United Nations response to the 1991 Gulf War, that order would not affect the occupation of Southern Lebanon. During the 1990s, in fact, while the Security Council authorised enforcement actions, under Chapter VII, in Iraq, Somalia, Yugoslavia, Haiti, Rwanda, the African Great Lakes region, Albania, Central African Republic, Sierra Leone, Kosovo, and East Timor, it failed to do so with respect Lebanon[101]. In fact, the Security Council, outside of renewing the UNIFIL mandate, would only deal with one further item—though in a quite muted manner—with respect to Israel's presence in Southern Lebanon: the 1996 massacre at Qana.

---

[97]   United Nations, *The Blue Helmets: A Review of United Nations Peace-keeping*, 1990, p. 150.
[98]   Edgar O'Ballance, *Civil War in Lebanon, 1975–92*, 1998, p. 184.
[99]   Patil, *op. cit.* n. 28, pp. 316.
[100]   Patil, *op. cit.* n. 28, pp. 317.
[101]   See Christine Gray, 'From Unity to Polarization: International Law and the Use of Force against Iraq', *European Journal of International Law*, 2002, Vol. 13, pp. 3–4.

When, on 18 April 1996, the IDF undertook, as part of its 'Grapes of Wrath' campaign, an operation to 'root out terrorists' in Southern Lebanon, approximately eight hundred civilians sought refuge in the headquarters of the Fijian battalion of UNIFIL in the village of Qana. More than one hundred of these Lebanese civilians were killed, by what UN Secretary-General, Boutros-Boutros Ghali considered— though he used diplomatic language—a deliberate Israeli artillery attack. In his cover letter to the Security Council of a report of the incident, the Secretary-General highlighted the finding in the Report nothing that 'the pattern of impacts in the Qana area makes it unlikely that the shelling of the United Nations compound was the result of technical and/or procedural errors' though 'the possibility cannot be ruled out completely'[102]. While the Security Council sat that day and considered the issue, its first attempt at passing a resolution failed, not because of the United States' veto, but because the resolution could not muster enough votes. As the draft sought to condemn 'the Israeli aggression against Lebanon which has brought about high tolls of civilian casualties, led to the displacement of hundreds of thousands of civilians and a massive destruction of Lebanon's infrastructure', it is not surprising given the Council's history regarding using the term 'aggression' that the resolution could muster only four positive votes, with all other members of the Council casting abstentions[103]. Following this, the Security Council did manage to pass a resolution regarding Qana, though it failed to mention it by name. Resolution 1052 expressed that the Council was 'gravely concerned [...] at actions which seriously threaten the safety of UNIFIL and impede the implementation of its mandate, and *deploring* in particular the incident of 18 April 1996 in which shelling resulted in the heavy loss of life among civilians at a UNIFIL site'[104].

As noted earlier, it was not the Security Council which forced Israel to end its aggression, manifest in both its invasion and subsequent occupation, against Lebanon; instead it was the casualties which the IDF suffered at the hands of the guerrilla forces of *Hizbullah*. In April 2000, the Israeli Foreign Minister notified the UN Secretary-General that Israel would 'withdraw its forces present in Lebanon by July 2000, in full accordance with Security Council resolutions 425 (1978) and 426 (1978)'[105]. On 16 May 2000, the IDF and its proxy army started to vacate Lebanon:

> The withdrawal [...] was carried out mainly at night, under cover of artillery fire. At the same time a large number of the [Southern Lebanon Army], together with their families, crossed into Israel. Others surrendered to the Lebanese authorities. Within a few days, those forces had completely disbanded. On 25 May, Foreign Minister [David]

---

[102]   See Security Council, Letter Dated 7 May 1996 from the Secretary-General addressed to the President of the Security Council, 7 May 1996, S/1996/337.
[103]   See S/PV.3654, for the draft resolution, see S/1996/292, 18 April 1996.
[104]   United Nations Security Council Resolution 1052, 18 April 1996, S/RES/1052, 1996, preambular para. 7.
[105]   See Security Council, Report of the Secretary-General on the United Nations Interim Force in Lebanon (for the period from 17 January to 17 July 2000), 20 July 2000, S/2000/718, para. 6.

Levy notified the Secretary-General that Israel had redeployed its forces in compliance with Security Council resolutions 425 (1978) and 426 (1978)[106].

The UN Secretary-General confirmed this, on 16 June, after UNIFIL had completed its verification process. Thus ended the Israeli occupation of Lebanon. During the period of Israeli occupation in Lebanon, the United Nations Security Council underwent major changes in its ability to deal with threat to international peace and security. No longer a paper tiger, the Council, from the 1990s onward, demonstrated that it could reverse acts of aggression and was willing and able to invoke Chapter VII to restore international peace and security through coercive measures. The Israeli invasion of 1982 and its subsequent occupation straddle the period between the Cold and post-Cold War eras, yet the manner in which the United Nations Security Council dealt with the act of Israeli aggression remained constant.

Through the use of its veto power, the United States forfeited the Security Council's ability to seek to reverse the Israeli invasion of Lebanon. Well within its right under the UN Charter, the United States sought (and managed) to shield its ally from the coercive measures, inherent in Chapter VII, regarding aggression. When compared to the manner in which the Security Council dealt with much of the Iran-Iraq War, the Israeli invasion and occupation of Lebanon is different only in form, not in substance. During both episodes, the Security Council did not act as a collective security mechanism, though during the war in the Persian Gulf, this was due, for the longest time, to indifference; while in Lebanon is was a result of the veto power granted to the permanent members. However, when one compares the manner in which the UN Security Council dealt with the 1990 Iraqi occupation of Kuwait and the manner in which it dealt with the Israeli occupation, it becomes obvious that the enforcement of international law—in this case seeking to reverse acts of aggression—has been a selective process. While it is true that the very nature of the Security Council, which is called on to determine whether threats or breaches of the peace or acts of aggression have transpired by a majority vote, will be selective; this does not take away from the perception which emanates from the Middle East that international law is instrumental in nature and is a tool to be used not so much in a just manner, but in a manner aligned with the interests of the powerful and to the detriment of the region.

IV. Response to the Iraqi Invasion and Annexation of Kuwait

Iraq, having seen its war with Iran end, and having suppressed the Kurdish uprising, turned toward the task of reconstruction. Having portrayed itself in the war against Iran as stemming the influence of the Islamic Revolution in the Persian Gulf region and the greater Middle East, the Hussein Administration sought to have $40 billion dollars of aid it received during the war reconstituted from loans to grants. Iraq's debt burden after its war with Iran was such that fifty percent of its

---

[106]   *Id.*, para. 8.

oil income in 1990 was used to service its payments[107]. This, coupled with its attempt at reconstruction and the demobilization of military after the Iran-Iraq War, destabilised the Baghdad administration. While more than half of the Iraqi debt was owed to Kuwait, Saudi Arabia, and the United Arab Emirates, the Government of Iraq pointed the finger at Kuwait, which it accused of having pumped $10 billion dollars worth of oil from disputed territory during the 1980s, of being unwilling to renegotiate loans, and of having deliberately 'flooded the oil market in violation of OPEC production quotas', depressing the price of oil, thus further inhibiting Iraq's ability to recover from the Iran-Iraq War[108]. The Hussein Administration responded by rattling its sabres, and when that failed, on 2 August 1990, Iraq invaded Kuwait.

In an unprecedented move, the United Nations Security Council determined the same day, that there existed 'a breach of international peace and security', and invoked Chapter VII, noting Articles 39 and 40 and demanded that 'Iraq withdraw immediately and unconditionally' from Kuwait[109]. As Matthew Craven of the University of London noted, the 'response of the United Nations to the Iraqi invasion of Kuwait is regarded by many as marking the dawn of a new era for the [UN] Organization as regards its role in maintaining international peace and security'[110]. In a true sense, the invasion of Kuwait was a watershed for the Security Council which, from this point onward, was willing to assert itself by acting to attempt to ensure international peace and security. As noted earlier, it has been willing to authorise the use of force in more than a dozen instances since 1990, while, from this period onward, the Security Council has imposed sanctions, of one form or an other, on Iraq, Libya, the former Yugoslavia, the Federal Republic of Yugoslavia, Haiti, Somalia, Angola, Rwanda, Liberia, Sudan, Sierra Leone, Cambodia, Afghanistan, and Eritrea and Ethiopia[111]. However, the UN Security Council has been most active where Iraq is concerned, reacting to Iraqi aggression against the Emirate in a comprehensive and far-reaching manner.

The vigorous manner in which the UN Security Council dealt with Iraq's invasion of Kuwait is manifest in Resolution 661, which was passed on 6 August 1990. That Resolution, coming four days after the Iraqi invasion, expressed the Council's determination 'to bring the invasion and occupation of Kuwait by Iraq to an end and to restore the sovereignty, independence and territorial integrity of Kuwait'. Through Resolution 661, the Council sanctioned Iraq for failing to comply with the original Resolution 660, by imposing an overall import and export embargo[112]. The Resolution further affirmed the 'inherent right of individual or

---

[107] Tripp, *op. cit.* n. 19, pp. 251–252.

[108] Bishara Bahbah, 'The Crisis in the Gulf—Why Iraq Invaded Kuwait', *Beyond the Storm: A Gulf Crisis Reader*, 1991, p. 52.

[109] See United Nations Security Council Resolution 660, 2 August 1990, S/RES/660, 1990, para. 2. See Appendix 10.

[110] Matthew Craven, 'Humanitarianism and the Quest for Smarter Sanctions', *European Journal of International Law*, 2002, Vol. 13, p. 43.

[111] *Id.*, p. 44.

[112] United Nations Security Council Resolution 661, 4 August 1990, S/RES/661, 1990, para. 3(a). See Appendix 11. Note that the trade sanctions did originally allow for a

collective self-defence, in response to the armed attack by Iraq against Kuwait, in accordance with Article 51 of the Charter'. Iraq, failing to heed the Security Council demand to quit Kuwait, instead annexed its southern neighbour, declaring its 'comprehensive and eternal merger with Kuwait'; a move that the Security Council considered lacked 'legal validity' and thus constituted it, 'null and void'[113]. The Council further responded to Iraq's intransigence by another turn of the screw—it allowed for a naval flotilla to enforce the embargo and banned all flights going in or coming out of Iraq[114]. By late November, with Iraq showing no indication of wishing to reverse its act of aggression, the Security Council provided one final opportunity for it to withdraw from Kuwait. Resolution 678 noted, that 'despite all efforts by the United Nations, Iraq refuses to comply with its obligation to implement resolution 660 [...] in flagrant contempt of the Security Council'. As such, the Council demanded compliance with its resolutions, but provided 'Iraq one final opportunity, as a pause of good will, to do so'[115].

This last reprieve was not, however, open ended, as Resolution 678 authorised 'Member States co-operating with the Government of Kuwait, unless Iraq on or before 15 January 1991 fully implements, [...] the foregoing resolutions, to use *all necessary means* to uphold and implement resolution 660 (1990) and all subsequent relevant resolutions and to restore international peace and security in the area'[116]. The use of the term 'all necessary means' is the trigger, by which the UN Security Council invokes Article 42 of the Charter, allowing for the use of force. While Yoram Dinstein, from the Max Planck Institute in Heidelberg, makes a case that Resolution 678 legitimised an act of 'collective self-defence (Article 51), as opposed to collective security', future action would come to demonstrate that the Council's role in the collective security regime was, in essence, to authorise States to act on its behalf[117]. As such, as Oscar Schacter notes, the resolution was fluid enough to allow for both bases of actions; though the Council need not sanction actions under Article 51, it being a part of a State's inherent right to act in self-defence[118]. Where there is no argument is that the Security Council sanctioned, under Chapter VII, the use of force to reverse the Iraqi aggression against Kuwait; something that the United States-led United Nations Coalition forces undertook on 17 January and completed, by a military cease-fire on 2 March

---

exception for medical supplies, and the possibility for an exception under 'humanitarian circumstances' for foodstuff. For the evolution of the United Nations Iraqi sanctions regime see Chapter Six.

[113] United Nations Security Council Resolution 662, 9 August 1990, S/RES/662, 1990, para. 1.

[114] See respectively, United Nations Security Council Resolutions 665 and 670, 25 August 1990, 25 September 1990, S/RES/665 and S/RES/670, 1990, para. 1 and 3.

[115] United Nations Security Council Resolution 678, 29 November 1990, S/RES/678, 1990, para. 1. See Appendix 12.

[116] *Id.* Emphasis added.

[117] Yoram Dinstein, *War, Aggression and Self-Defence*, 2001, p. 243.

[118] See Oscar Schacter, 'United Nations Law in the Gulf War', *American Journal of International Law*, Vol. 85, 1991, p. 462, where he writes: 'Resolution 678 may be read as consistent with both Article 51 and Article 42'.

1991[119]. Resolution 686 of 2 March set out the terms of the cease-fire, including the obligations found in the Council's previous resolutions, along with the need to rescind 'its actions purporting to annex Kuwait' and to accept 'in principle its liability under international law for the loss, damage or injury [...] as a result of the invasion and illegal occupation of Kuwait'[120].

A month later, the UN Security Council passed Resolution 687, its· most comprehensive resolution to date, meant to restore 'international peace and security in the area'[121]. Seeking to be assured of 'Iraq's peaceful intentions in the light of its unlawful invasion and occupation of Kuwait', the Council set out a list of demands and declared that 'upon official notification by Iraq to the Secretary-General and to the Security Council of its acceptance of the provisions above, a formal cease-fire is effective between Iraq and Kuwait and the Member States cooperating with Kuwait in accordance with resolution 678'. Iraq accepted the provisions of Resolution 687 on 6 April 1991, which included the imposing of the border between itself and Kuwait as established in 1963, to have it demarcated, and to have the Security Council guarantee its inviolability[122]. The Resolution establishes a demilitarised zone on either side of the Iraq-Kuwait border and the deployment of UN observers to ensure its status. It also mandated that 'Iraq shall unconditionally accept the destruction, removal, or rendering harmless, under international supervision' all chemical and biological weapons and ballistic missiles with a range greater than one hundred and fifty kilometres, as well as requiring that 'Iraq shall unconditionally agree not to acquire or develop nuclear weapons'[123]. Finally, beyond issues such as the repatriation of Kuwaitis, both civilian and prisoners of war, Resolution 687 provided for the establishment of a regime to deal with reparations, by way of a compensation commission that was established to deal with losses or damages resulting from the Iraqi invasion[124]. These various elements

---

[119]   The Coalition forces totalled 737,000 men, 190 vessels and 1,800 aircrafts, of which the United States provided 532,000 men (72 percent), 120 vessels (80 percent), and 1,700 aircrafts (94 percent). In all, 35 States provided personnel or equipment to the Coalition during the Second Gulf War; they were: Afghanistan, Argentina, Australia, Bahrain, Bangladesh, Belgium, Canada, Czechoslovakia, Denmark, Egypt, France, Germany, Greece, Hungary, Honduras, Italy, Kuwait, Morocco, The Netherlands, Niger, Norway, New Zealand, Oman, Pakistan, Poland, Portugal, Qatar, Saudi Arabia, Senegal, Spain, Syria, Turkey, United Arab Emirates, United Kingdom, and the United States of America. See Arthur Blair, *At War in the Gulf: A Chronology*, 1992, p. 125.
[120]   United Nations Security Council Resolution 686, 2 March 1991, S/RES/686, 1991, para. 1.
[121]   United Nations Security Council Resolution 687, 3 April 1991, S/RES/687, 1991, para. 33. See Appendix 13.
[122]   See Section A, Resolution 687, *id.* For the Iraqi acceptance of Resolution 687 see Letters from the Deputy Prime Minister and Minister for Foreign Affairs of Iraq to the President of the Security Council and to the Secretary-General stating that Iraq has no choice but to accept the provisions of Security Council resolution 687 (1991), 6 April 1991, S/22456, in United Nations, *The United Nations and the Iraq-Kuwait Conflict, 1990–1996*, pp. 203–206.
[123]   See Section C, Resolution 687, *id.*, paras. 8 and 12.
[124]   See Section E, Resolution 687, *id.*, para. 18.

will now be considered in more detail, as they demonstrate the tools that the Council used to attempt to restore international peace and security.

The one area in which it is clear that Iraq fulfilled it obligations under Resolution 687, is in regard to the establishment of its border with Kuwait. This was undertaken, despite the fact, as Frederic Kirgris, former Vice-President of the American Society of International Law noted, having considered the *travaux preparatoires* of the United Nations Charter, that the 'negotiating history, buttressed by the absence of any Security Council practice to the contrary from 1945 until 1991, casts strong doubt on the propriety of the Council's imposition of the Kuwait-Iraq boundary upon Iraq'[125]. As a follow up to Resolution 687, the Security Council passed Resolution 689 on 9 April 1991, approving a plan by the Secretary-General which established the United Nations Iraq-Kuwait Observation Mission (UNIKOM), a peace-keeping force meant to monitor a demilitarised zone, extending ten kilometres on the Iraqi and five kilometres on the Kuwaiti side of their international border[126]. UNIKOM also provided 'logistical support to the United Nations Iraq-Kuwait Boundary Demarcation Commission' meant to establish a border 'for the first time, in precise geographic coordinates of latitude and longitude [...] and to make arrangements for the physical representation of the boundary through the erection of boundary pillars or monuments'[127]. Though Iraq ceased to participate in the activities of the Demarcation Commission considering that the Commission's undertakings were not technical put political, the Commission concluded its work in 1993. On 27 May 1993, the Security Council reminded Iraq of its obligations under Resolution 687 and demanded 'Iraq and Kuwait, in accordance with international law and relevant Security Council resolutions, respect the inviolability of the international boundary, as demarcated by the Commission [...]'[128].

While Iraq did so, Kuwait failed to respect the boundary which the international community established for it, as it allowed the United States-led coalition to use the its territory as the launching pad for its invasion of March 2003. The UN Secretary-General reported to the Security Council that:

> From 5 March, [...] UNIKOM observed contractors for Kuwaiti authorities cutting numerous openings in the electric fence. While these were later closed, bulldozers were also observed levelling the berm and filling in the ditch along the south demilitarized zone boundary to create possible vehicle passageways. By 16 March, the total number of gaps in the fence had reached 31 and UNIKOM had observed 38 breaches in the berm.

---

[125]   Frederic L. Kirgis, 'The United Nations at Fifty: The Security Council's First Fifty Years', *American Journal International Law*, Vol. 89, 1995, p. 531,

[126]   See United Nations Security Council Resolution 689, 9 April 1991, S/RES/689, 1991.

[127]   See Introduction by Boutros Boutros-Ghali, Secretary-General of the United Nations, United Nations, *The United Nations and the Iraq-Kuwait Conflict 1990–1996*, 1997,   paras. 128 and 149.

[128]   See United Nations Security Council Resolution 833, 27 May 1993, S/RES/883, 1993, para. 5.

The Secretary-General went on to say that the military 'build-up on the Kuwaiti side of the demilitarized zone posed serious potential challenges to UNIKOM in fulfilling its mandate and in ensuring the security of its personnel'[129]. As such, on 17 March 2003 its operations were suspended. On 3 July 2003, the UN Security Council recognised that the 'continued operation of UNIKOM and a demilitarized zone established under resolution 687 (1991) are no longer necessary to protect against threats to international security posed by Iraqi actions against Kuwait' and thus ended both the demilitarised zone and the mandate of UNIKOM as of 6 October 2003[130].

By contrast to the settling of the international border between Iraq and Kuwait, in 1993, the regime of disarmament established by Resolution 687 was the most contentious issue as between Iraq and the Security Council. That regime, not only required an end to Iraq's ability to acquire or possess weapons of mass destruction, it also provided for the UN Secretary-General to establish a plan to 'carry out immediate on-site inspection of Iraq's biological, chemical, and missile capabilities', and ensure their destruction[131]. On the basis of the plan received, the UN Security Council established a Special Commission (UNSCOM) to undertake the work mandated by Resolution 687[132]. However, cooperation between the United Nations and Iraq already looked to be tenuous before the establishment of UNSCOM, as the Security Council, in its Resolution 707 condemned 'Iraq's serious violation of a number of its obligations under [the weapons control provisions] of resolution 687'[133]. UN weapons inspectors played a cat and mouse game with Iraq, finding more than ten times the number of chemical shells than were declared to have existed in Iraq, by October 1991[134]. The confrontation between Iraq and the Commission came to a head over the inspection of 'presidential sites', which led to Iraq expelling United States nationals from UNSCOM, accusing them of spying. When, in 1998, the Commission noted that it was 'not able to conduct the substantive disarmament work mandated by the Security Council', the United Kingdom and the United States responded with their December 'Operation Desert Fox'. Though not authorised by the Security Council, the two permanent members sought to respond to 'the withdrawal by Iraq of cooperation with the UN weapons inspectors; this was a major operation lasting

---

[129] United Nations *Security Council, Report of the Secretary-General on the United Nations Iraq-Kuwait Observation Mission (for the period from 16 September 2002 to 21 March 2003)*, 31 March 2003, S/2003/393.
[130] See United Nations Security Council Resolution 1490, 3 July 2003, S/RES/1490, 2003.
[131] Resolution 687, *op. cit.* n. 121, para. 8(b). For an overview of this disarmament regime see Dieter Fleck, 'Developments of the Law of Arm Control as a Result of the Iraq-Kuwait Conflict', *European Journal of International Law*, 2002, Vol. 13, pp. 105–119.
[132] See United Nations Security Council Resolution 715, 11 October 1991, S/RES/715, 1991, para. 2.
[133] United Nations Security Council Resolution 707, 15 August 1991, S/RES/707, 1991, para. 2.
[134] Chantal de Jonge Oudraat, 'UNSCOM: Between Iraq and a Hard Place', *European Journal of International Law*, 2002, Vol. 13, p. 142.

four days and nights and involving more missiles than used in the entire 1991 conflict'[135].

The operation effectively ended the mandate of UNSCOM, which was replaced by the UN Monitoring, Verification, and Inspection Commission (UNMOVIC) in late 1999[136]. In September 2002, as war appeared imminent, the Iraqi Foreign Minister agreed to allow both UNMOVIC and the International Atomic Energy Agency (IAEA) to return 'to Iraq without conditions'[137]. While details were being worked out between these two international bodies and Iraq, the United Nations Security Council passed Resolution 1441 on 8 November 2002 which determined that 'Iraq has been and remains in material breach of its obligations under relevant resolutions, including resolution 687 (1991), in particular through Iraq's failure to cooperate with United Nations inspectors'. As a result, the Council decided 'to afford Iraq, by this resolution, a final opportunity to comply with its disarmament obligations under relevant resolutions of the Council' and gave it seven days to demonstrate that it was prepared to 'cooperate immediately, unconditionally, and actively with UNMOVIC and the IAEA'[138]. Five days later, Iraq answered this ultimatum by indicating that it was ready to allow the inspectors to once again return to Iraq, which they did on 27 November 2002. Both UNMOVIC and the IAEA were allowed to resume their inspections and did so for three and a half months until they were withdrawn on 16 March 2003, as it was plain that an imminent attack led by the United States was to take place. On 20 March 2003, the United States-led a 'Coalition of the Willing'—a shadow of the 1991 United Nations Coalition[139]—using as its justification for military action the threat which Iraq posed as a result of its position of weapons of

---

[135]   Gray, *op. cit.* n. 101, p. 11.

[136]   See United Nations Security Council Resolution 1284, 17 December 1999, S/RES/1284, 1999, para. 1.

[137]   See International Atomic Energy Agency, Report For The Security Council Pursuant To Resolution 1441 (2002), 27 January 2003, as found at www.iaea.org. Note that the IAEA had been mandated early on to consider whether Iraq was involved in the manufacturing of nuclear weapons. Its conclusion has as follows: 'There were no indications to suggest that Iraq had been successful in its attempt to produce nuclear weapons'. See *id.*, paras 3 and 24.

[138]   United Nations Security Council Resolution 1441, 8 November 2002, S/RES/1441, 2002.

[139]   Of the thirty-five UN Coalition partners that participated in the 1991 Gulf War, twenty did not participate in the 2003 operation. The following are the 'Coalition of the Willing':

Afghanistan, Albania, Angola, Australia, Azerbaijan, Bulgaria, Colombia, Costa Rica, the Czech Republic, Denmark, Dominican Republic, El Salvador, Eritrea, Estonia, Ethiopia, Georgia, Honduras, Hungary, Iceland, Italy, Japan, Kuwait, Latvia, Lithuania, Macedonia, Marshall Islands, Micronesia, Mongolia, The Netherlands, Nicaragua, Palau, Panama, Philippines, Poland, Portugal, Romania, Rwanda, Singapore, Slovakia, the Solomon Islands, South Korea, Spain, Tonga, Turkey, Uganda, Ukraine, United Kingdom, United States, Uzbekistan.

See Office of the President, 'Who are the current coalition members?', Press Release, April 3, 2003, as found at www.whitehouse.gov. Consider *supra.*, n. 119, to compare to the UN Coalition partners.

mass destruction[140]. In contrast, Dr. Hans Blix, the Chairman of UNMOVIC, noted in his final briefing to the United Nations Security Council in June 2003 that his Commission 'has not at any time during the inspections in Iraq found evidence of the continuation or resumption of programmes of weapons of mass destruction or significant quantities of proscribed items—whether from pre-1991 or later'[141].

As opposed to the confrontational nature of the disarmament process, the regime for dealing with responsibility for war damages transpired smoothly. Resolution 687 noted that Iraq 'is liable under international law for any direct loss, damage—including environmental damages and the depletion of natural resources—or injury to foreign Governments, nationals and corporations as a result of its unlawful invasion and occupation of Kuwait'[142]. On the basis of that Resolution and a report prepared by the Secretary-General, the Council passed Resolution 692, which established both a Fund and the United Nations Compensation Commission[143]. The Commission drew on twenty-five percent of the money gained from the 'oil-for-food' programme—meant to mitigate the effects of UN sanctions—and paid out claims of compensation for war damages. As a result of the removal of the Hussein Administration by the US-led 'Coalition of the Willing', the United Nations Security Council moved to end the 'oil-for-food' programme—which funded the Commission's work—within six months. By way of Resolution 1483 of 22 May 2003, the Council decided that during this intermediate period five percent of the money allotted to the programme would be deposited into the Compensation Fund from which the Commission was to draw. As for what would transpire afterwards, the Resolution decided that the requirements to pay into this Fund and to settle all outstanding claims would be 'binding on a properly constituted, internationally recognized, representative

---

[140] See United States President George W. Bush, Address to the Nation, Press Release, March 17, 2003, at http://www.whitehouse.gov/news/releases/2003/03/20030317–7.htmlv, where he stated:

> Intelligence gathered by this and other governments leaves no doubt that the Iraq regime continues to possess and conceal some of the most lethal weapons ever devised. This regime has already used weapons of mass destruction against Iraq's neighbors and against Iraq's people.
> The regime has a history of reckless aggression in the Middle East. It has a deep hatred of America and our friends. And it has aided, trained and harbored terrorists, including operatives of al Qaeda.
> The danger is clear: using chemical, biological or, one day, nuclear weapons, obtained with the help of Iraq, the terrorists could fulfill their stated ambitions and kill thousands or hundreds of thousands of innocent people in our country, or any other.

[141] United Nations Monitoring, Verification, and Inspection Commission, Briefing of the Security Council, 5 June 2003: Oral introduction of the 13th quarterly report of UNMOVIC, 5 June 2003, as found at www.unmovic.org. Note that Blix went on to say: 'As I have noted before, this does not necessarily mean that such items could not exist. They might—there remain long lists of items unaccounted for—but it is not justified to jump to the conclusion that something exists just because it is unaccounted for'.
[142] See Section E, Resolution 687, *op. cit.* n. 121, para. 16.
[143] See United Nations Security Council Resolution 692, 20 May 1991, S/RES/692, 1991, para. 3.

government of Iraq and any successor thereto'[144]. By the end of the 'oil-for-food' programme in November 2003, the Compensation Commission had dealt with ninety-eight percent of all claims—over forty-eight thousand—and awarded more than eighteen billion dollars[145].

Beyond the various elements meant to restore 'international peace and security in the area', as found in Resolution 687, mention should be made of the sanctions imposed by Resolution 661 which were in place from 1991 until 2003[146]. Although Chapter 6 considers the punitive nature of the UN sanctions imposed on Iraq, mention here should be made of the use of sanctions as a coercive tool of compliance, within the framework of collective security. The sanctions were originally established to get Iraq to quit Kuwait, when that failed, its purpose was tied to Iraqi compliance with the cease-fire provisions as spelled out in Resolution 687. However, as has been noted in the study, *The Sanctions Decade*, '[l]arger and more powerful states [...], have tended historically to steer or capture the sanctions enterprise to meet their particular foreign policy objectives'[147]. This was made evident through the actions of the United States and the United Kingdom in the Sanctions Committee—the Security Council body established to oversee the sanctions regime—where they imposed their will to, in the words of a former UN employee, 'inflict economic hardship on Iraq'[148]. By 1997, the declared aim of the United States was to remove Iraqi President Saddam Hussein; as such it was declared by the United States Secretary of State that the sanctions would remain in place until that objective was achieved[149]. The US-led attack of March 2003 proved the Secretary of State right.

Despite the end of hostilities of the 1991 campaign, it may be said that this War has persisted throughout the 1990s, through to the United States-led assault of 2003, and beyond. Though the use of force nominally ended in 1991, the United Kingdom and the United States of America maintained a 'no-fly zone', using military aircraft to exclude the Iraqi air force from parts of northern and southern

---

[144]   United Nations Security Council Resolution 1483, 22 May 2003, S/RES/1483, 2003, para. 21. See Appendix 15.

[145]   See United Nations Compensation Commission, Status of Claims at www.unog.ch/uncc/status.

[146]   The former UN Humanitarian Coordinator for Iraq has noted that, between the suffering which has befallen on the Iraq people because of UN sanctions, and the lack of relief which has been provided by the 'oil-for-food' programme, 'can only lead to one conclusion: humanitarian exemptions, as in the case of Iraq, have not adequately protected the population from the impact of comprehensive economic sanctions', See Graf Sponeck, 'Sanctions and Humanitarian Exemptions: A Practioner's Commentary', *European Journal of International Law*, 2002, Vol. 13, p. 82.

[147]   David Cortright and George Lopez, *The Sanctions Decade: Assessing UN Strategies in the 1990s*, 2000, p. 6.

[148]   Conlon, *United Nations Sanctions Management: A Case Study of the Iraq Sanctions Committee, 1990–1994*, 2000, p. 74.

[149]   See de Jonge Oudraat, *op. cit.* n. 134, p. 144, n. 16.

Iraq, without UN Security Council authorization[150]. The use of military force outside the control of the Security Council increased in December 1998 when the two Western States undertook 'Operation Desert Fox' in response to Iraq's unwillingness to cooperate with UNSCOM, and came to a climax on 20 March 2003 when the United States-led its 'Coalition of the Willing' in an all out attack which eliminated the Hussein Administration by force of arms. That attack and the subsequent occupation meant that most of the measures put in place as a regime intended to restore international peace and security become superfluous. The death-knell of the regime was sounded on 22 May 2003 by way of United Nations Security Council Resolution 1482 which ended the sanctions, moved to put an end to the 'oil-for-food' programme, reduced the amount of money provided to the United Nations Compensation Commission, and professed the intension of the Council to revisit the mandate of UNMOVIC at some future date[151]. As mentioned earlier, UNIKOM folded its tents and left on 6 October 2003.

V. Conclusion

The ten-year period that witnessed Iraq invade first Iran then Kuwait, as well as Israel's invasion and occupation of Lebanon, demonstrates the power dynamics that are at the heart of any legal system. The legitimacy of law is based on its supposed impartial nature, wherein it is meant to be applied on a non-discriminatory basis. If, as it has been in these cases, international law is applied in a selective manner, its very legitimacy is challenged. The instrumental manner in which the United States of American sought to deal with violations to the most fundamental principle of international relations—the prohibition against aggression—brings into focus the qualitatively different manner in which international law is applied in the Middle East. This Chapter has demonstrated the three different ways by which the United Nations, through the Security Council sought to deal with acts of aggression. During the Iran-Iraq War, the Security Council allowed Iran and Iraq to continue battling for nearly eight years before acting under Chapter VII. This wilful neglect was in contrast to the manner in which the United States actively excluded the UN Security Council from the Lebanese conflict which saw Israel invade in 1982 and remain in occupation until the year 2000. Through the use of its veto power, the United States blocked all

---

[150] The United Kingdom and the United States have sought to justify their actions 'in support of Resolution 688' which condemned Iraq for its repression of 'civilian population in many parts of Iraq, including most recently in Kurdish populated areas' and insisted that Iraq 'allow immediate access by international humanitarian organizations to all those in need of assistance'. For her part, Christine Gray from Cambridge University notes that 'Security Council Resolution 688 was not passed under Chapter VII and it did not authorize the use of force'. See Gray, *op. cit.* n. 101, p. 9. Note that France was also party to patrolling the 'no-fly zones' from 1991 until December 1998.
[151] United Nations Security Council Resolution 1483, 22 May 2003, S/RES/1483, 2003. See Appendix 15.

attempts by the Council to take measures to seek to restore international peace and security in relation to these two Mediterranean States.

The irony, as has been mentioned previously, was that while Israel remained in occupation of southern Lebanon, the UN Security Council was witnessing a renaissance under the mantel of a 'New World Order' by seeking to expel Iraq, which had annexed Kuwait in late 1990. The length to which the Security Council was to go to attempt to restore international peace, through the use of force and by way of sanctions with respect to Iraq, while turning a blind eye to Israel's occupation, for many simply confirmed what has been apparent since the inception of the modern Middle East—that international law is meant to ensure the interests of the powerful at the expense of a just outcome for the people of the region.

Chapter 6

Punitive *in extremis*:
United Nations' Iraqi Sanctions

The United Nations-imposed Iraqi sanctions were a clear manifestation of international law being applied in a punitive manner. Almost from its inception, the sanction regime instituted by UN Security Council Resolution 661 was meant to meet the larger geopolitical objectives of the United States of America than to simply restore international peace and security. The nature of the sanctions regime, along with the requirements of the UN Coalition Forces' imposed 1991 cease-fire, had the cumulative effect of causing hundreds of thousands, if not millions, of deaths in Iraq. The debilitating effect of sanctions when married to the destruction that was caused by the air campaign of the UN Coalition Forces, which targeted the electrical system of Iraq, meant that this Fertile Crescent State had been, and continues to be, 'relegated to a pre-industrial age'. The question to be asked is whether the nature of the UN sanctions were of such an extreme nature; going beyond being punitive to transgressing norms of *jus cogens* regarding the protection of civilians? If so, can a case be made that the cumulative effect of such sanctions constitutes an international crime such as genocide or a crime against humanity? If it can be demonstrated that the UN sanctions had, in fact, crossed that threshold, then the very validity of the sanction regime is brought into question, as are issues of culpability for transgressing a *jus cogens* imperative and the responsibility that this would entail.

The following chapter considers the manner in which the Coalition air campaign generally, and its targeting of the Iraqi electrical system specifically, set the table for the hardship that was to come, as the effects of the United Nations-imposed Iraqi sanctions took hold. Through an examination of reports by UN personnel, various intergovernmental, as well as non-governmental, organizations, a clear picture emerges of the mass violations of human rights which transpired in Iraq as a direct result of the UN-imposed sanctions regime. The death toll remains unconscionable; UNICEF reported that children under five years of age were dying at a rate of 4,500 a month from preventable hunger and disease. This children's holocaust was not only limited to children dying, as one-third were, according to a 1997 report by the UN Secretary-General, malnourished, their growth having been stunted. Having examined the effects of the sanctions regime, consideration then turns to characterizing those effects in law and to attributing responsibility for what amounts to a violation of a *jus cogens* norm by the United Nations.

I. The Coalition Air Campaign

The United States-led UN Coalition Forces, in seeking to end the aggression of
Iraq against Kuwait, undertook a military campaign that commenced on 17 January
1991[1]. The strategy utilised by American military planners who sought to remove
Iraqi forces from the Emirate was summarised by the then US Joint Chief of Staff,
General Colin Powell, as follows, 'Our strategy for dealing with this [Iraqi] army is
very, very simple. First we're going to cut it off, then we're going to kill it'[2]. Thus,
the initial aerial attacks against Iraqi forces did not transpire in and around Kuwait,
but targeted, instead, Iraqi infrastructures in Baghdad and southern Iraq in an
attempt to sever links between the central command and the troops which were
occupying Kuwait. The Coalition war was primarily an air campaign, which lasted
thirty-nine days, setting the table for a 'one hundred hour' ground war that resulted
in the reinstatement of 'the Emir as ruler of sovereign Kuwait'[3]. While the military
campaign was ultimately successful, the methods of warfare used by the Coalition
Forces and their long-term consequences appear, as Roger Normand and Chris af
Jochnick of Harvard Law School's Center for Economic and Social Rights have
noted, 'to have been aimed at achieving broad political and economic objectives
rather than specific military goals'[4]. Yet the lack of specificity in the laws of war
are such that while the targeting by Coalition Forces may not amount to a violation
of the laws of war, such destruction would compound the hardship of the sanction
regime instituted by the United Nations and push it to levels which transgressed
norms of *jus cogens*.

The two fundamental tenets of the laws of war—those laws which govern the
conduct of State in warfare—are the 'Geneva Law' and 'Hague Law'. Geneva Law
seeks to protect civilian and military persons who are not party to the conflict and
fall into the hands of an enemy State. While Geneva Law has a long history, having
its genesis in the work of Henry Dunant and the establishment of the International
Committee of the Red Cross in 1863; its most oblivious manifestation is
incorporated in the 1949 Geneva Conventions which relates to protected persons
including: prisoners of war, the sick and the wounded, and to civilians in times of
armed conflict[5]. For its part, Hague Law relates to methods and means of warfare
by seeking to impose humanitarian considerations on military action. The starting
point of Hague Law is to be found in the principles outlined in the preamble of the
Declaration of St. Petersburg of 1868. While the substantive provisions of the
Declaration have become obsolete, the principle that 'the only legitimate object
which States should endeavour to accomplish during war is to weaken the military

---

[1]   See Arthur Blair, *At War in the Gulf: A Chronology*, 1992, p. 125.
[2]   As quoted in Dilip Hiro, *Desert Shield to Desert Storm: The Second Gulf War*, 1992,
p. 319.
[3]   Roger Normand and Chris af Jochnick, 'The Legitimation of Violence: a Critical
Analysis of the Gulf War', *Harvard International Law Journal*, Vol. 35, 1994, p. 388.
[4]   *Id.*, p. 387.
[5]   See generally Caroline Moorehead, *Dunant's Dream: War, Switzerland and the History
of the Red Cross*, 1998.

forces of the enemy' remains intact[6]. Such a principle, which requires the balancing of military necessity with humanitarian consideration, would, in the 1907 Hague Convention Respecting the Laws and Customs of War on Land, find fuller expression; as well as ensuring that future means and methods of warfare would not escape the dictates of humanity.

Two fundamental principles of the laws of war find source in the 1907 Hague Convention; the first, in the annex to the Convention which provides for Regulations Respecting the Laws and Customs of War on Land. At Article 22, States affirmed that 'the right of belligerents to adopt means of injuring the enemy is not unlimited'[7]. Second, in the preamble to the 1907 Hague Convention, State Parties sought 'to diminish the evils of war, as far as military requirements permit', and thus were unwilling to allow the evolution of the art of warfare to escape the obligations to act in a humane manner. Noting that until 'a more complete code of the laws of war has been issued', States:

> deem it expedient to declare that, in cases not included in the Regulations adopted by them, the inhabitants and the belligerents remain under the protection and the rule of the principles of the law of nations, as they result from the usages established among civilized peoples, from the laws of humanity, and the dictates of the public conscience[8].

This provision, known as the 'Martens Clause' named after the Russian jurist Fyodor Martens who proposed its inclusion in the preamble, coupled with Article 22, established that future warfare would be governed by limited humanitarian considerations. The most recent manifestation of this principle is to be found in the 1977 Additional Protocol (I) to the Geneva Conventions and Relating to the Protection of Victims of International Armed Conflicts.

In part three of the Additional Protocol, States Parties established that in 'any armed conflict, the right of the Parties to the conflict to choose methods or means of warfare is not unlimited'[9]. On the basis of this general principle, States negotiating the Additional Protocol (I) sought to place restriction on the methods of warfare by requiring that warring States distinguish between the targeting of

---

[6]   Henry Meyrowitz, 'The Principle of Superfluous Injury or Unnecessary Suffering', *International Review of the Red Cross*, Number 299, 1994, p. 99.
[7]   'Annex to the Convention: Regulations Respecting the Laws and Customs of War on Land' in Adam Roberts and Richard Guelff (eds.), *Documents on the Laws of War*, 2000, p. 77. Note the editorial by Roberts and Guelff, where they point to the customary nature of these provisions by stating that the 'International Military Tribunal at Nuremberg in 1946, and a report of the UN Secretary-General to the Security Council in May 1993 concerning the establishment of the International Criminal Tribunal for the former Yugoslavia, expressly recognised 1907 Hague Convention IV as declaratory of customary international law', *id.*, p. 68.
[8]   See Convention Respecting the Laws and Customs of War on Land. *id.*, pp. 69–72.
[9]   Article 35, International Committee of the Red Cross, *Protocols Additional to the Geneva Conventions of 12 August 1949*, 1997, p. 27. See also Roberts and Guelff, *op. cit.*, n. 7 at pp. 422–479.

military and civilian objectives. Article 48 of the Additional Protocol sets out the basic rule as follows:

> In order to ensure respect for and protection of the civilian population and civilian objects, the Parties to the conflict shall at all times distinguish between the civilian population and combatants and between civilian objects and military objectives and accordingly shall direct their operations only against military objectives.

The Protocol then goes on to detail the protection afforded civilian populations and objectives, the precautionary measures to be taken to ensure the safety of such populations, and the need to protect objects which are 'indispensable to the survival of the civilian population'. Before considering the application of these provisions to the case of the UN Coalition air campaign, mention should be made as to the legal applicability of the provisions of Additional Protocol (I) as binding on members of that coalition: Bahrain, Canada, France, Italy, Kuwait, Qatar, Saudi Arabia, the United Arab Emirates, the United Kingdom, and the United States of America. At the time of the 1991 War; Bahrain, Canada, Italy, Kuwait, Qatar, Saudi Arabia, and the United Arab Emirates were party to Additional Protocol (I)[10]. Though subsequently France and the United Kingdom acceded to the Additional Protocol, at the time of the Coalition air war they were not party; the United States, for its part, is not party to the Protocol[11]. As a result, to find the lowest common denominator as to whether there were violations of the laws of war regarding methods utilised by Coalition Forces, one must turn to customary norms, which are considered as having been subsumed in the relevant provisions of Additional Protocol (I)[12].

Article 48 of the Additional Protocol (I), which establishes a general obligation on warring parties to distinguish, at all times, between civilian and military populations and objectives, appears to have simply enunciated existing customary international law which had, by the eve of the start of the War against Iraq in

---

[10]   See the International Humanitarian Law Database of the International Committee of the Red Cross at www.icrc.org.

[11]   The United Kingdom acceded in 1998, France in 2001. See the website of the International Committee of the Red Cross at *id.*

[12]   The existence of a legal norm can, of course, manifest itself in both conventional and customary form. Consider the pronouncement of the International Court of Justice on the subject:

> The existence of identical rules in international treaty law and customary law has been clearly recognized by the Court in the *North Sea Continental Shelf* cases. To a large extent, those cases turned on the question whether a rule enshrined in a treaty also existed as a customary rule, either because the treaty had merely codified the custom, or caused it to 'crystallize', or because it had influenced its subsequent adoption. The Court found that [...] certain [...] articles of the treaty in question 'were ... regarded as reflecting, or as crystallizing, received or at least emergent rules of customary international law'.

Nicaragua case (Merits), *I.C.J. Reports, 1986*, 27 June 1986, para. 177.

1991, clearly entered the corpus of customary international law[13]. Flowing from this general obligation, States party to the Additional Protocol (I) to the Geneva Conventions have an obligation which is to be 'observed in all circumstances': not to undertake indiscriminate attacks[14]. Indiscriminate attacks being defined, at Article 51(4), as primarily those 'not directed at a specific military objective', and those 'which employ a method or means of combat which cannot be directed at a specific military objective' and, as a result, 'strike military objectives and civilians or civilian objects without distinction'. In the same vein, the Protocol, at Article 52, notes that civilian objects are off limits:

> 2.   Attacks shall be limited strictly to military objectives. In so far as objects are concerned, military objectives are limited to those objects which by their nature, location, purpose or use make an effective contribution to military action and whose total or partial destruction, capture or neutralization, in the circumstances ruling at the time, offers a definite military advantage.
>
> 3.   In case of doubt whether an object which is normally dedicated to civilian purposes, such as a place of worship, a house or other dwelling or a school, is being used to make an effective contribution to military action, it shall be presumed not to be so used.

Finally, Article 54, which deals with the 'protection of objects indispensable to the survival of the civilian population', makes it plain that 'starvation of civilians as a method of warfare is prohibited'. Beyond that, it prescribes, *inter alia*, that:

> 2.   It is prohibited to attack, destroy, remove or render useless objects indispensable to the survival of the civilian population, such as food-stuffs, agricultural areas for the production of food-stuffs, crops, livestock, *drinking water installations and supplies and irrigation works*, for the specific purpose of denying them for their sustenance value to the civilian population or to the adverse Party, whatever the motive, whether in order to starve out civilians, to cause them to move away, or for any other motive. [Emphasis added.]

While it may appear clear that the Coalition air campaign violated the spirit of Additional Protocol (I); making a determination as to a violation of the customary norms regarding the methods of warfare as they played out in the 1991 War is a tougher proposition. In *retrospect*, the destruction of Iraqi civilian infrastructures had a catastrophic effect on the population—not during the hostilities themselves—but because of the maintenance of United Nations sanctions in the aftermath of the war. Judging the actions of the United States and its junior partners during the air

---

[13]   Middle East Watch points to the unanimous 1969 UN General Assembly Resolution 2444 related to Respect for Human Rights in Armed Conflict, from which, the provisions would be paraphrased into the Article 48. Further Middle East Watch reports that 'the U.S. government has expressly recognised this Resolution as declaratory of existing customary international law'. Middle East Watch, *Needless Deaths in the Gulf War: Civilian Causalities during the Air Campaign and Violations of the Laws of War*, 1991, p. 31.

[14]   See Article 51(1) and (4), Additional Protocol, *op. cit.*, n. 7.

campaign, seems to indicate that these States were, at least *prima facie*, in violation of the general provision to distinguish between civilian objects and military objectives. Yet such obligations are always to be weighed against military necessity, and from this perspective, it is difficult to assess whether actions by the Coalition Forces were in violation of the laws of war, or for that matter, whether an attack which causes civilian deaths is 'excessive in relation to the concrete and direct military advantage anticipated'[15]. The weighing of humanitarian considerations against military assessments gives much leeway to commanders in the field to determine what is of military necessity and thus subordinates the humanitarian elements of the laws of war. Normand and Jochnick take this line of reasoning when, having examined the historical development of the laws of war, they conclude that 'despite noble rhetoric to the contrary, the laws of war have been formulated deliberately to privilege military necessity at the cost of humanitarian values. As a result, the laws of war have facilitated rather than restrained wartime violence'[16].

i. The Targeting of the Iraqi Electrical System

The air war undertaken by the Coalition Forces was a 'three-phase operation: a strategic bombing campaign, followed by the establishment of air superiority in the Kuwaiti military theater, followed by attacks on Iraqi troops in the Kuwaiti military theater'[17]. Leaving aside the planning and carrying out of attacks in the Kuwait proper, what was relevant to the future toll of United Nations sanctions against Iraq was the strategic bombing campaign. In their *The Gulf War 1990–1991: Diplomacy and War in the New World Order*, Laurence Freedman and Efraim Karsh, both professors at King's College, University of London, devote a chapter to the strategic bombing campaign. Freedman and Karsh note that the air campaign 'had objectives independent of the expulsion of Iraqi forces from Kuwait: reducing the long-term ability to exert a regional military influence and weakening the regime's hold on power'[18]. Motives beyond pure military necessity thus found their way into the targeting philosophy of United States' planners of the air campaign who, on the one hand, focused on the Air Force's wish to 'concentrate on the sources of Saddam's [Hussein] power and the Army desire to see his ground forces cut down to size before it launched its offensive'[19]. Freedman and Karsh state that, as a result, 'the campaign was not geared solely to military targets' and as such, it was inevitable that 'the strategic approach meant attacking structures that were relevant to both civilian and military affairs'[20]. During the 1991 War, Coalition

---

[15]   See Article 41(5)(b), Additional Protocol, *id*.
[16]   Chris af Jochnick and Roger Normand, 'The Legitimation of Violence: A Critical History of the Laws of War', *Harvard International Law Journal*, Vol. 35, 1994, p. 50.
[17]   Middle East Watch, *op. cit.*, n. 13, p. 71.
[18]   Laurence Freedman and Efraim Karsh, *The Gulf War 1990–1991: Diplomacy and War in the New World Order*, 1993, p. 314.
[19]   *Id.*, p. 317.
[20]   *Id.*, pp. 318–319.

Forces undertook nearly 120,000 *sorties* dropping 84,000 tons of bombs; of those *sorties*, approximately 32,000 took place away from the Kuwaiti theatre of war and, hence, as part of the strategic air war against Iraq proper[21].

In its report entitled *Needless Deaths in the Gulf War*, Middle East Watch noted that the air war 'wreaked major destruction' on Iraqi infrastructures. It reported, 'by the end of the war only two of Iraq's 20 electricity-generating plants were functioning, generating less than four percent of the pre-war output'[22]. 'Predictably', Middle East Watch continues, stressing that electricity was required to maintain basic public utilities, 'the effects of this massive destruction on Iraq's water supply, sewage-treatment system, agricultural production and food distribution systems, and public-health system were severe and continue to be felt'[23]. Note that the emphasis of Middle East Watch is not only on the effects of the destruction *per se*, but its continued impact. But during the war itself, Freedman and Karsh note that depriving 'Iraq of its energy sources undoubtedly had an effect on the ability to sustain its army in the field and operate its air defence and military communications'[24]. This type of military justification was balanced by the United States' military commander, when he noted that 'we never had any intention of destroying 100 per cent of all Iraqi electrical power, because of our interest in making sure that civilians did not suffer unduly'[25]. By the end of the air campaign, the electrical system in Iraq was the most damaged component of Iraqi infrastructures targeted; it having been estimated that it would require 'five to nine years' to recover[26].

Middle East Watch pointed out that as 'a modern, electricity-dependent country, Iraq was reliant on electrical power for essential services such as water purification and distribution, sewage removal and treatment, the operation of hospitals and medical laboratories, and agricultural production'[27]. However, it would fall to a high-ranking United Nations official and not a non-governmental human rights organization to put into words the type of destruction that was visited upon Iraq. Less than a week after the cease-fire of 28 February 1991, the United Nations dispatched a UN mission, headed by Under-Secretary-General Mr. Martti Ahtisaari, to assess the need for urgent humanitarian assistance in both Iraq and Kuwait. In regards to Iraq, Mr. Ahtisaari reported that:

> It should be said at once that nothing that we had seen or read had quite prepared us for the particular form of devastation which has now befallen the country. The recent conflict has wrought near-apocalyptic results upon the economic infrastructure of what had been, until January 1991, a rather highly urbanized and mechanical society. Now,

---

21   Middle East Watch, *op. cit.*, n. 13, pp. 72–73.
22   *Id.*, p. 152. Note that Middle East Watch was the former regional component of the non-governmental human rights organization Human Rights Watch, which today has been subsumed within the larger organization.
23   *Id.*, p. 180.
24   Freedman and Karsh, *op. cit.*, n. 18, p. 321.
25   *Id.*, p. 322 quote from the United States General, Norman Schwarzkopf.
26   *Id.*
27   Middle East Watch, *op. cit.*, n. 13, p. 172.

most means of modern life support have been destroyed or rendered tenuous. Iraq has, for some time to come, been relegated to a pre-industrial age, but with all the disabilities of post-industrial dependency on an intensive use of energy and technology[28].

Mr. Ahtissari's report went on to note that underlying the mission's analysis of the various sectors of Iraqi society was 'the inexorable reality that, as a result of war, virtually all previously viable sources of fuel and power [...] are now, essentially defunct'. He then concluded his general remarks by stating that having 'regard to the nature of Iraq's society and economy, the energy vacuum is an omnipresent obstacle to the success of even a short-term, massive effort to maintain life-sustaining conditions'[29]. In the Report's concluding observations, Mr. Ahtissari stated that 'I, together with all my colleagues, am convinced that there needs to be a major mobilization and movement of resources to deal with aspects of this deep crisis in the fields of agriculture and food, water, sanitation and health'. He then highlights a more long-term, underlying, concern:

> Yet the situation raises, in acute form, other questions. For it will be difficult, if not impossible, to remedy these immediate humanitarian needs without dealing with the underlying need for energy, on an equally urgent basis. The need for energy means, initially, emergency oil imports and the rapid patching up of a limited refining and electricity production capacity, with essential supplies from other countries. Otherwise, food that is imported cannot be preserved and distributed; water cannot be irrigated; medicaments cannot be conveyed where they are required; needs cannot even be effectively assessed. It is unmistakable that the Iraqi people may soon face a further imminent catastrophe, which could include epidemic and famine, if massive life-supporting needs are not rapidly met[30].

In its Report, Human Rights Watch was critical of the targeting by Coalition Forces of the Iraqi power grids. It argued that US military planners, based on a Second World War strategic bombing survey, should have 'readily anticipated' the 'immediate and longer-term consequences of denying almost the entire civilian population of an energy-dependent country an essential service such as electricity'[31]. While Human Rights Watch recognised that incidental death or deprivation of civilians needs could result from attacks to legitimate military targets, it took issue with the sustained attacks, throughout the duration of the air campaign, against the Iraqi electrical system. It saw the actions of the Coalition breaching the standards expressed in Article 54 of the Additional Protocol (I) related to 'protection of objects indispensable to the survival of the civilian

---

[28]   United Nations Security Council, *Report to the Secretary-General on humanitarian needs in Kuwait and Iraq in the immediate post-crisis environment by a mission to the area led by Mr. Martti Ahtisaari, Under-Secretary-General for Administration and Management, dated 20 March 1991*, annexed to a letter from the Secretary-General addressed to the President of the Security Council, UN Doc. S/22366, dated 20 March 1991, para. 8.

[29]   *Id.*, para. 10.

[30]   *Id.*, para. 37.

[31]   Middle East Watch, *op. cit.*, n. 13, p. 177.

population'. Human Rights Watch noted that insofar 'as the civilian population is concerned, it makes little or no difference whether a drinking water facility is attacked and destroyed, or is made inoperative by the destruction of the electrical plan[t] supplying it power. In either case, civilians suffer the same effects—they are denied the use of a public utility indispensable for their survival'. Human Rights Watch then raised a serious issue as to making a distinction between military and civilian targets:

> This destruction is all the more problematic given the allied air forces' supremacy and control of the skies, which enable them to attack with virtual impunity any production or communication facility supporting Iraq's military effort. The apparent justification for attacking almost the entire electrical system in Iraq was that the system functioned as an integrated grid, meaning that power could be shifted countrywide, including to military functions such as command-and-control centers and weapons-manufacturing facilities. But these key military targets were attacked in the opening days of the war. The direct attacks by the allies on military targets should have obviated the need simultaneously to destroy the fixed power sources thought to have formerly supplied them. If these and other purely military targets could be attacked at will, then arguably the principle of humanity would make the wholesale destruction of Iraq's electrical-generating capability superfluous to the accomplishment of legitimate military purpose[32].

To this end, Middle East Watch called on the Coalition States to justify 'under the rules of proportionality and the principle of humanity' the destruction aimed at the Iraqi electrical system, 'particularly as attacks on the system grew increasingly redundant in light of the allies' targeting of indisputable military targets [... and] in view of the crippling impact the destruction of the electrical power system immediately had and continues to have on the health of the Iraqi civilians'[33].

Where Middle East Watch loses the thread of its legal argument is in attempting to call to account the Coalition Forces for the effect of their actions beyond the cease-fire of 28 February 1991. While there may be a customary prohibition against destroying objects indispensable to the survival of the civilian population, such a prohibition is meant to apply only during hostilities wherein it is outlawed as a means of warfare. No evidence has come to light to suggest that US military planners targeted the Iraqi electrical system in an attempt to starve the Iraqi people into submission as a means of winning the war. Beyond that, what was required by military planners was to target only those 'objects which by their nature, location, purpose or use make an effective contribution to military action and [...] offers a definite military advantage'[34]. Middle East Watch quotes the 1991 report of the United States Department of Defense, whereby the 'Pentagon states that attacks on 'electricity production facilities that power military and military-related industrial systems' were related to the goal of isolating and incapacitating the Iraqi regime'. The Defense Department went on to say that it 'was recognized

---

[32] *Id.*, p. 187.
[33] *Id.*, pp. 190–191.
[34] Article 52(2), Additional Protocol, *op. cit.*, n. 7.

at the outset that this campaign would cause some unavoidable hardships for the
Iraqi populace. It was impossible, for example, to destroy the electrical power
supply to Iraqi command and control facilities or chemical weapons factories, yet
leave untouched that portion of the electricity supplied to the general populace'[35].
At the end of the day, if those who planned the Coalition air campaign could justify
that the electrical system was used by the Iraqi military and that its targeting
provided a definite military advantage, then it was fair game.

II. The United Nations Sanctions

In their book, *The Sanctions Decade: Assessing UN Strategies in the 1990s*, David
Cortright and George Lopez note that where Iraq is concerned, it is 'in a class by
itself' as the recipient of 'the longest, most comprehensive, and most severe
multilateral sanctions regime ever imposed'[36]. Consideration now turns to the
sanction regime established by the United Nations Security Council and to the
manner in which it was modified during the twelve years of its existence. The
necessity of this examination of the United Nations sanctions regime is to set the
table for an assessment of transgressions of international legal norms and
attributing responsibility.

i. The United Nations' Iraqi Sanctions Regime

On 6 August 1990, four days after Iraq invaded Kuwait, the United Nations
Security Council passed Resolution 661. In that Resolution, the Council invoked
Chapter VII, and acted within its authority under Article 41 of the UN Charter—
though it did not mention it by name—which provides:

> The Security Council may decide what measures not involving the use of armed force
> are to be employed to give effect to its decisions, and it may call upon the Members of
> the United Nations to apply such measures. These may include complete or partial
> interruption of economic relations and of rail, sea, air, postal, telegraphic, radio, and
> other means of communication, and the severance of diplomatic relations.

The measures which were introduced were meant to 'secure compliance' with the
Security Council's demand regarding Iraq's immediate and unconditional
withdrawal from Kuwait as found in Resolution 660. As a sanction for failing to
comply with its decision, the Council imposed an embargo on all Iraqi and
occupied Kuwaiti imports and exports. This total embargo was limited in one
manner; it was not to include 'supplies intended strictly for medical purposes, and,
in humanitarian circumstances, foodstuffs'[37]. To ensure respect for Resolution 661,

---

[35]   Middle East Watch, *op. cit.*, n. 13, pp. 171–172.
[36]   David Cortright and George Lopez, *The Sanctions Decade: Assessing UN Strategies in
the 1990s*, 2000, p. 8.
[37]   United Nations Security Council Resolution 661, 6 August 1990, S/RES/661, 1990,
para. 3(c). See Appendix 11.

the Council decided to establish a Committee consisting of the members of the Security Council which was to report on the progress and seek information from States as to the actions they had taken regarding the 'effective implementation of the provisions laid down in the present resolution'[38]. In September, the Council decided that the limitation to the embargo regarding foodstuffs would not be open ended, but would be controlled by the Sanctions Committee which would have to make a determination 'that the circumstances have arisen in which there is an urgent humanitarian need to supply foodstuffs to Iraq or Kuwait in order to relieve human suffering'[39]. Thus, during the period leading up to, and throughout the 1991 War, Iraq was denied access to imported food.

On 3 April 1991, the Security Council passed Resolution 687 establishing the conditions which Iraq was required to accept to give effect to the cease-fire offered by the UN Coalition Forces[40]. While the original aim of the sanctions regime was to have Iraq 'withdraw immediately and unconditionally' from Kuwait, its failure to do so, of its own avail, led the Council, via Resolution 687, to attempt to ensure that Iraq had 'peaceful intentions in light of its unlawful invasion and occupation of Kuwait'. Thus, in seeking to restore international peace and security, the Council decided that Iraq would have to accept the demarcation of the border between itself and Kuwait and a demilitarised zone contiguous it; the monitoring and dismantling of its chemical and biological weapons, and its long-range ballistic missiles; and the unconditional renunciation of attempting to acquire or develop nuclear weapons. Further, Iraq was required to service its foreign debt, which it had earlier repudiated; to pay compensation for its war damage; to co-operate with the International Committee of the Red Cross in repatriating non-nationals; and to renounce international terrorism. Resolution 687 also modified the sanction regime, having taken into consideration the report by Mr. Ahtisaari. The Resolution exempts foodstuffs from the embargo, and allowed for a simplified 'no-objection' procedure before the Sanctions Committee to deal with 'materials and supplies for essentially civilian needs'[41]. The 'no-objection' procedure allowed for notification of items mentioned in the Ahtisaari Report to the members of the Sanctions Committee and, if within an established period of time no objection was

---

[38] *Id.*, para. 6.
[39] United Nations Security Council Resolution 666, 13 September 1990, S/RES/666, 1990, para. 5 (see also para. 1).
[40] United Nations Security Council Resolution 687, 3 April 1991, S/RES/687, 1991, para. 33. See Appendix 13. Note also that Resolution 687 sets out, in the preamble, that 'resolution 686 (1991) marked the lifting of the measures imposed by resolution 661(1990) in so far as they applied to Kuwait'.
[41] *Id.*, para. 20. Note that two days after the Ahtissari Report the Sanctions Committee made a determination, as prescribed by Resolution 666, para. 5, that, 'In light of the new information available to it [...] a general determination that humanitarian circumstances apply with respect to the entire civilian population of Iraq'. See Abbas Alnasrawi, 'Iraq: Economic Sanctions and Consequences, 1900–2000', *Third World Quarterly*, Vol. 22, p. 211.

heard, the items were considered to have passed muster of the Committee[42]. Such items include agricultural equipment and supplies, as well as items related to water purification, sanitation, and medicinal needs[43].

By August 1991, it became evident to those working within the humanitarian agencies of the United Nations that the scale of relief that was needed in Iraq was beyond the Organization's capacities. As such, the Security Council passed Resolution 706 allowing Iraq to sell oil which was to be used to purchase 'foodstuffs, medicines, and materials and supplies for essential civilian needs [...] in particular health related materials'[44]. However, this Resolution and Resolution 712, which established the structure for the 'oil-for-food' programme, was stillborn, as Iraq asserted 'that the proposed procedures for providing humanitarian relief were in violation of [its] sovereignty'[45]. It took until April 1995, for new modalities of an 'oil-for-food' programme to be accepted by Iraq, and until December 1996 for the programme to come into force. Under Resolution 986, Iraq was allowed to export one billion dollars worth of oil every ninety days and to provide for an 'equitable distribution of humanitarian relief to all segments of the Iraqi population', though it would fall to the United Nations to administer the programme in the Kurdish areas of northern Iraq[46]. Funds generated by the sale of oil were deposited in a UN controlled escrow account, with the purchase of all imports requiring the prior approval of the Sanctions Committee.

Originally, the 'oil-for-food' programme required that thirty percent of oil sale revenues be handed over to the UN Compensation Committee which administers reparations payments related to war damages; five percent of revenues were shared equally between Turkey, for the transportation costs of oil and to the United Nations for its administration and operational cost related to Iraq. A further thirteen percent of revenues paid for the administration of the Kurdish vilayets. During its existence, the Security Council modified the 'oil-for-food' programme on four occasions, first, by virtue of Resolution 1153, it increased the amount of oil that Iraq was allowed to export to a total worth of just over five billion dollars; and, with Resolution 1284, it lifted the cap on the amount of oil that could be sold for the programme[47]. Resolution 1284 dealt in a more substantive manner with humanitarian concerns in Iraq, although the Security Council placed these concerns within a Resolution that introduces a new disarmament regime (UNMOVIC). The

---

[42]   See Paul Conlon, *United Nations Sanctions Management: A Case Study of the Iraq Sanctions Committee, 1990–1994*, 2000, p. 60–64.

[43]   Ahtisaari Report, *op. cit.*, n. 28, paras. 18 and 27.

[44]   United Nations Security Council Resolution 706, 15 August 1991, S/RES/706, 1991, para. 1(c).

[45]   Cortright and Lopez, *op. cit.*, n. 36, p. 48.

[46]   United Nations Security Council Resolution 986, 14 April 1995, S/RES/986, 1995, para. 8(b).

[47]   United Nations Security Council Resolution 1153, 20 February 1998, S/RES/1153, 1998, para. 1; and United Nations Security Council Resolution 1284, 17 December 1999, S/RES/1284, 1999, para. 15. The renewal of the 'oil-for-food' programme from 1995 till 2002 are found at Resolutions 1111, 1129, 1143, 1153, 1158, 1210, 1242, 1281, 1302, 1330, 1352, 1360, 1382, 1409, 1443, 1447, 1454, 1472, 1476, and 1483.

Resolution removed the 'no-object' provisions and instead noted that 'lists of humanitarian items, including foodstuffs, pharmaceutical and medical supplies, as well as basic or standard medical and agricultural equipment and basic or standard educational items [...] will not be submitted for approval of [the] Committee'[48]. During the year 2000, the allocation of percentage of revenues was changed by virtue of Resolution 1330, which reduced from thirty to twenty-five percent the amount of money to be allocated to the Compensation Committee[49]. Thus, under the 'oil-for-food' programme, the Hussein Administration received fifty-eight percent of the revenues which were to be distributed to eighty-seven percent of the Iraqi population.

In the summer of 2002, as United States troops were amassing on Iraq's borders, little notice was taken of the radical alteration which transpired to the 'oil-for-food' programme. The sanctions regime which, up to that point, had been exclusive in nature: generally speaking, all items were to be deemed excluded unless it was established that they were exempt or had been authorised by the Sanctions Committee. Although it transpired with little fanfare, the sanctions regime was fundamentally modified by Resolution 1402 on 14 May 2002. That Resolution established what amounted to an inclusive regime: all products imported into Iraq were to be allowed unless they were found to be on a 419-page 'Goods Review List'[50]. It will never be known whether this fundamental change to the sanctions regime would have had an effect on the plight of Iraqis as, in the aftermath of the United States-led attack and occupation of Iraq, the sanctions regime was put to an end. Resolution 1483, of 22 May 2003, decided that 'with the exception of prohibitions related to the sale or supply to Iraq of arms and related material' that 'all prohibitions related to trade with Iraq and the provision of financial or economic resources to Iraq established by resolution 661 (1990) and subsequent relevant resolutions, including resolution 778 (1992) of 2 October 1992, shall no longer apply'[51]. The Resolution called for the 'oil-for-food' programme to continue for six months with the aim of facilitating 'as soon as possible the shipment and authenticated delivery of priority civilian goods', but also with a look to establishing the possible costs on the United Nations' involvement in the transition period[52].

---

[48] United Nations Security Council Resolution 1284, 17 December 1999, S/RES/1284, 1999, para. 17.
[49] United Nations Security Council Resolution 1330, 5 December, S/RES/1330, 2000, para. 12.
[50] United Nations Security Council resolution 1402, 14 May 2002, S/RES/1402, 2002. Note that I have argued elsewhere that the overhaul of the sanctions regime had more to do with the coming into force of the statue of the International Criminal Court which criminalises genocide and crimes against humanity than a willingness of the United States to ease the sanctions regime. See Jean Allain,' Iraq Sanctions Distanced from ICC Jurisdiction', *World Editorial and International Law*, 20 October 2002, pp 2–3.
[51] United Nations Security Council, Resolution 1483, 22 May 2003, S/RES/1483, 2002, para. 10. See Appendix 15.
[52] *Id.*, para. 16.

For the longest time, the United Nations regime of Iraqi sanctions retained an overall import and export embargo, with the exception, by virtue of Resolution 661, of 'supplies intended strictly for medical purposes', foodstuffs and 'material supplies for essentially civilian needs' (i.e. 'no-objections' items) as allowed by Resolution 687[53]. Despite these items having received a humanitarian waiver from the sanctions, the ability to get them to Iraq was made cumbersome and ineffective by the functioning of the Sanctions Committee. Although Resolution 1284 called on the UN Secretary-General to take steps to maximise 'the effectiveness of the arrangements set out in resolutions 896 (1995) and related resolutions', these efforts were not enough to deal with the humanitarian issues affecting Iraq[54]. In a March 2000 report, the UN Secretary-General himself stated that even 'if it is implemented perfectly, it is possible that the efforts will prove insufficient to satisfy the population's needs'[55]. Even more to the point was a Report by a Security Council panel meant to examine the humanitarian situation in Iraq which noted in March 1999 that 'the magnitude of the humanitarian needs is such that they cannot be met within the context of the parameters set forth in resolution 986 (1995) and succeeding resolutions [...]'[56]. In large part, this may be attributed to the fact that the Committee's stated objectives had taken a backseat to the agendas of its individual members[57]. The Sanctions Committee moved from ensuring that sanctions were respected, to what was, in effect, a licensing bureau that authorised items to be exported to Iraq on a case-by-case basis. This micro-level of case-by-

---

[53]   There was one further exception to the overall embargo. In 1998, the Security Council allowed States to import 'the necessary parts and equipment to enable Iraq to increase the export of petroleum and petroleum products, in quantities sufficient to produce the sum established [by] resolution 1153'. United Nations Security Council Resolution 1175, 19 June 1998, S/1175/1998, para. 1.

[54]   United Nations Security Council Resolution 1284, 17 December 1999, S/RES/1284, 1999, para. 21.

[55]   As quoted in Commission on Human Rights, *The Adverse Consequences of Economic Sanctions on the Enjoyment of Human Rights: Working Paper prepared by Mr. Marc Bossuyt*, UN Doc. E/CN.4/Sub.2/2000/33, 21 June 2000, para. 62.

[56]   United Nations Security Council, *Report of the second panel established pursuant to the note by the president of the Security Council of 30 January 1999 (S/1999/100), concerning the current humanitarian situation in Iraq*, 30 March 1999, UN Doc. S/1999/356, Annex II, para. 46.

[57]   Consider the assessment made by Cortright and Lopez in the introduction to their book, *The Sanctions Decade: Assessing UN Strategies in the 1990s*, 2000, at p. 6:

   Larger and more powerful states, especially the five permanent members of the Security Council [...], have tended historically to steer or capture the sanctions enterprise to meet their particular foreign policy objectives, which may or may not match the goals of the broader UN community. The history of the Iraqi and Libyan case in particular reflects tensions between UN objectives and those of major states like the United States and Great Britain, A related concern is the manner in which major states tend to 'move the goalposts' regarding criteria for the removal of sanctions once a Security Council resolution is in place. The letter of the law, as imbedded in the text of resolutions, loses prominence, while the most powerful states, especially the United States, interpret the spirit of the resolutions to meet their own particular interests.

case control exerted by the Committee had allowed the United States of America and its junior partners, France and the United Kingdom, to pursue, what Paul Conlon, the author of the sole book on the Sanctions Committee, called 'economic warfare' against Iraq.

'To some extent' Conlon writes, the three Permanent Members' positions were 'merely logical outgrowths of their basic strategy, which was to inflict economic hardship on Iraq'[58]. By 1997, the United States made plain that the aims of the sanctions were no longer those expressed in Resolution 687; instead, the 'larger objective has become the political and military containment of the regime of Saddam Hussein'[59]. With this as a backdrop, the representatives of the three Permanent Members of the Security Council on the Sanctions Committee sought to interpret the exceptions to the embargo in the narrowest of terms. Conlon, who before penning his book worked as a UN Security Council Official, writes that Resolution 687 spoke of 'basic' or 'essential' humanitarian needs and as such a 'host of normal everyday products (wristwatches, cosmetics, video equipment) were blocked'[60]. The Committee was also quick to put a hold on products which they considered of dual (civilian/military) use, to the ire of the UN Director of the humanitarian programme for Iraq who, in 1999, expressed concerns about the 'excessive number of holds placed on supplies and equipment for water and sanitation and electricity'[61]. Of the items which had been given the green light, only a third reached Iraq. As Graf Sponeck, the former UN Humanitarian Coordinator for Iraq noted: out of 'a total of $44.4 billion of oil revenue earned by Iraq from 16 December 1996, when the oil-for-food programme was initiated, to 13 July 2001, only $13.5 billion worth of humanitarian supplies actually arrived in Iraq'[62]. Once in Iraq, it was not guaranteed that items would be distributed in a timely fashion due to the fact that the transportation and communication networks which had been destroyed in 1991 had yet to be re-established as a consequence of the sanction regime. A 1999 UN Report noted that nearly half of medical supplies which had been imported to Iraq 'remained in warehouses and had not been distributed to local clinics and hospitals'[63].

ii. The Effect of United Nations Sanctions on Iraq

As the sanctions against Iraq make plain, despite much noble rhetoric to the contrary, the United Nations Organization was established in 1945 as a coercive collective security arrangement. Though caught in the deep-freeze of the Cold War

---

[58]   Conlon, *op. cit.*, n. 42, p. 74.

[59]   David Cortright and George Lopez, 'Are Sanctions Just? The Problematic Case of Iraq', *Journal of International Affairs*, Vol. 52, 1999, p. 749. The authors go on to note a statement by the President of the United States, Bill Clinton, 'sanctions will be there until the end of time, or as long as [Hussein] lasts'.

[60]   Conlon, *op. cit.*, n. 42, p. 72.

[61]   Cortright and Lopez, *op. cit.*, n. 36, p. 49.

[62]   H. C. Graf Sponeck, 'Sanctions and Humanitarian Exemptions: A Practitioner's Commentary', *European Journal of International Law*, Vol. 13, 2002, p. 82.

[63]   Alnasrawi, *op. cit.*, n. 41, p. 213.

for the better part of its first fifty years, the UN Security Council has been able, since the demise of the Soviet Union, to assert its primary responsibility toward ensuring international peace and security. Although the United Nations has busied itself with other tasks including human rights promotion, the decolonization process and the progressive development of international law; at its core, the UN was established to ensure the international peace. The twin pillars of settling disputes by pacific means as enshrined in Chapter VI of the UN Charter and the internationalization of the use of force found at Chapter VII set the foundations of both the Organization and the international system at large. By becoming parties to the United Nations Charter, States have agreed that if they cannot settle their dispute by peaceful means, and such disputes are considered by the Security Council to challenge the peace, they may find themselves on the wrong side of coercive measures in an attempt repair the breach. The United Nations, it needs to be emphasised, is not about human rights or humanitarianism—these issues are peripheral—its primary purpose is as a coercive tool of international relations[64]. The extent to which the United Nations can coerce is found in the effect which UN sanctions imposed against Iraq had on that State's population. 'As has been documented by United Nations agencies, NGOs, humanitarian and human rights organizations, researchers and political leaders', writes a United Nations human rights specialist, 'the sanctions upon Iraq have produced a humanitarian disaster comparable to the worst catastrophes of the past decades'[65].

Iraq was especially vulnerable to the sanctions imposed by the United Nations, as ninety-five percent of its foreign currency earnings and sixty percent of its gross domestic product was based on oil exports[66]. At the same time, the autocratic nature of the Hussein Administration meant that sanctions would have limited effect on the ruling elite. Marc Bossuyt, in a Working Paper prepared for the UN Sub-Commission on the Promotion and Protection of Human Rights, has noted that:

Under sanctions, the middle class is eliminated, the poor get poorer, and the rich get richer as they take control of smuggling and the black market. The Government and elite can actually benefit economically from sanctions, owing to this monopoly on illegal trade. As many commentators have pointed out, in the long run, as democratic participation, independent institutions and the middle class are weakened, and as social disruption leaves the population less able to resist the Government, the possibility of democracy shrinks. In sum, the civilian suffering that is believed to be the effective factor in comprehensive economic sanctions renders those sanctions ineffectual, even reinforcing the Government and its politics[67].

---

[64]   UN Secretary-General Kofi Annan writes that 'Humanitarian and human rights policy goals cannot easily be reconciled with those of a sanction regime'. See Cortright and Lopez, *op. cit.*, n. 36, p. 23.
[65]   Bossuyt, *op. cit.*, n. 55, para. 63.
[66]   Cortright and Lopez, *op. cit.*, n. 36, p. 43.
[67]   Bossuyt, *op. cit.*, n. 55, para. 50.

The academic studies, says Bossuyt, support the proposition regarding the lack of effectiveness of sanctions *vis-à-vis* authoritarian regimes with the most optimistic assessment being that they are effective one third of the time, and the most pessimistic being 'a dismal 2 per cent success rate for sanctions against 'authoritarian regimes'[68].

Between the United States' avowed purpose of toppling Saddam Hussein as the *sine qua non* for removing sanctions, and the entrenched nature of the Iraqi administration, it were not surprising that the sanctions lasted more than a decade. The result of sanctions have not only been devastating in their nature, but by their cumulative effect very quickly came to constitute a violation of a *jus cogens* imperative. Cortright and Lopez, the leading specialists on sanctions, have noted that the 'social impact of the Iraq crisis reveal a shocking human tragedy. Hundreds of thousands of people have died prematurely from the health disaster that has swept Iraq in the wake of war and during the [...] years of comprehensive sanctions'[69]. The effects of sanctions have been of such a magnitude that they have prompted, not once but twice, the resignation of the highest-ranking UN officials dealing with Iraq:

> Denis Halliday, former United Nations Assistant Secretary-General and Humanitarian Coordinator in Iraq, resigned in September 1998, declaring, 'We are in the process of destroying an entire society. It is a simple and terrifying as that. It is illegal and immoral'. Hans von Sponeck, Halliday's successor as Humanitarian Coordinator in Iraq, resigned on 13 February 2000, explaining that he could not any longer be associated with a program that prolonged the suffering of the people and which had no chance of meeting even the basic needs of the civilian population[70].

Not only did the UN embargo prohibit all but 'basic' humanitarian imports, it denied the repair and rebuilding of the damage of the UN Coalition's air campaign which, recalling the words of Mr. Ahtisaari's 1991 Report, 'wrought near-apocalyptic results upon the economic infrastructure'. Yet nearly a decade after the sanctions were imposed Marc Bossyut noted that the 'situation at present is extremely grave. The transportation, power, and communication infrastructures were decimated by the Gulf War, and have not been rebuilt owing to the sanctions. The industrial sector is also in shambles and agricultural production has suffered greatly. But most alarming is the health crisis that has erupted since the imposition of sanctions'[71].

Studies in the aftermath of the 1991 War chronicled the manner in which the devastation visited upon Iraqi public utilities resulted in conditions which would lead to the premature death of hundreds of thousands of Iraqi civilians. A 1991

---

[68]   *Id.*, para. 51. Note that Cortright and Lopez examine the success from a more nuanced perspective, considering sanction not as a means of punishing a recalcitrant State but as a means of bargaining. See chapter 2 entitled: 'How to Think about the Success and Impact of Sanctions' in Cortright and Lopez, *op. cit.*, n. 36, pp. 13–35.

[69]   Cortright and Lopez, *op. cit.*, n. 59, p. 741.

[70]   *Id.*, para. 68. Footnotes in the original omitted.

[71]   Bossuyt, *op. cit.*, n. 55, para. 59.

joint World Health Organization/United Nations Children's Fund (UNICEF) mission found that the destruction of the electrical generation capacity and pumping stations led to a virtual collapse of the water supply system:

> Waste treatment plants also ceased to function, and raw sewage was pumped directly into the Tigris River, the main source of Iraq's drinking water. Many people were thus forced to rely on water contaminated with untreated sewage. The result was a public health crisis, leading to a major increase in infectious diseases, including cholera and typhoid[72].

By 1995, water production was at fifty percent of its pre-War level with most families continuing to 'consume contaminated water from damaged systems or from untreated local sources'. While 1995 also found 'approximately half of all sewage produced by Baghdad's 4 million people was still being discharged untreated into the Tigris which downstream becomes the principal source of drinking water for most of the densely populated governorates in southern Iraq'[73].

Five years into the United Nations' Iraqi sanctions regime, Erik Hoskins, a physician and member of the Center for International Health at McMaster University in Canada, noted that 'the breakdown in water and sanitation that occurred during the 1991 War, and the Iraqi government's inability to effectively repair these services, have been responsible for outbreaks of cholera, hepatitis, and other infectious diseases'. He went on to state:

> Contaminated water supplies and poor sanitation have created health conditions enabling diarrhea to emerge as the leading child killer during the postwar period. [...] Cholera, which during the 1980s was scarcely detected, reached epidemic levels in 1991 with more than 1,200 confirmed cases. Typhoid also spread rapidly, and during 1991 the number of cases was more than ten times the number of case reported during 1990. [...] The incidents of malaria increased more than tenfold owing to the lack of aerial and ground spraying'[74].

In a background paper prepared for its Executive Committee on Humanitarian Affairs in September 2000, the UN Office of the High Commissioner for Human Rights indicated that:

> Hospitals and health centers have largely remained without repair and maintenance. The functional capacity of the health care system has degraded further due to shortages of water and power supply, lack of transportation and the collapse of the telecommunications system. Furthermore, communicable diseases, such as water borne

---

[72]   Cortright and Lopez, *op. cit.*, n. 36, p. 45.
[73]   Eric Hoskins, 'The Humanitarian Impact of Economic Sanctions and War in Iraq', Tomas Weiss et al. (eds.), *Political Gain and Civilian Pain: Humanitarian Impacts of Economic Sanctions*, 1997, pp. 117–118.
[74]   *Id.*, p. 122.

diseases and malaria have become part of the endemic pattern of the precarious health situation[75].

In its evaluation of activities in Iraq during the year 1999, the International Committee of the Red Cross (ICRC) assessed the near decade of Iraqi sanctions. It noted that the 'oil-for-food' programme had 'not halted the collapse of the health system and the deterioration of water supplies, which together pose one of the gravest threats to the health and well-being of the civilian population'[76].

The breakdown in the health system as a result of the United Nations sanctions had, not surprisingly, affected the most vulnerable of Iraqi society. International agencies recorded the holocaust which befell the infant population of Iraq during the sanctions. In 1991 UNICEF noted an 'alarming and rising incidence of severe and moderate malnutrition among the population of children under age five'[77]. In August 1991, a Harvard study team undertook a comprehensive study of child deaths and estimated that during the first eight months of 1991, 47,000 excess deaths had taken place, while UNICEF found the mortality rate to be more than twice that of the pre-War level[78]. By 1995, the mortality rate of children had risen to five times the rate prior to the sanctions, with the UN Food and Agriculture Organization finding that 'large numbers of Iraqis now have food intakes lower than those of the populations in disaster-stricken African countries'[79]. In 1996, UNICEF put a number on the children dying as a result of the United Nations sanctions regime; it found that 4,500 children were dying every month from preventable hunger and disease[80]. Richard Garfield, a Professor of Nursing at Columbia University, in his study of mortality among Iraqi children found that, between 1991 and 1998, at least 100,000 but more likely 227,000 excess deaths took place, of which three quarters resulted from the consequences of United Nations sanctions[81].

The Panel constituted by the UN Security Council to report on the humanitarian situation in Iraq noted in 1999 that in 'marked contrast to the prevailing situation prior to the events of 1990–1991, infant mortality rates in Iraq today are among the highest in the world, low infant birth weight [of less than 2.5 kilograms] affects at least 23 percent of all births, chronic malnutrition affects every fourth child under five years of age'[82]. The Panel, taking its lead from a 1998

---

[75] Office of the High Commissioner for Human Rights, *The Human Rights Impact of Economic Sanctions on Iraq*, (Background Paper prepared by the Office of the High Commissioner for Human Rights for a meeting of the Executive Committee on Humanitarian Affairs), 5 September 2000, p. 4.
[76] International Committee of the Red Cross, *Iraq: A Decade of Sanctions: ICRC activities on behalf of Iraqi civilians 1999–2000*, 14 December 1999, p. 4.
[77] As quoted in Hoskins, *op. cit.*, n. 73, p. 114.
[78] *Id.*, p. 120.
[79] *Id.*, p. 114.
[80] Cortright and Lopez, op. cit., n. 36, p. 46.
[81] Cortright and Lopez, *id.*
[82] See the Report of the humanitarian panel of the United Nations Security Council, *op. cit.*, n. 56, para. 43.

UNICEF report, made clear that 'almost the whole young child population was affected by a shift in their nutritional status towards malnutrition'[83]. The stunting of the growth of children became widespread; with the UN Secretary-General noting in 1997 that chronic malnutrition had resulted in thirty-one percent of children having had their growth stunted, and twenty-six percent being underweight'[84]. Kofi Annan concluded his 1997 Report to the Security Council by stating that 'one-third of children under five years of age [...] are malnourished'[85]. Garfield notes that by 1998, no improvement in nutritional conditions could be found among children under five, despite the 'oil-for-food' programme. 'Essentially', Garfield writes, 'the nutritional conditions for children in Iraq plateaued [in 1996] and remain at that level a year after the influx of considerably improved rations from the Oil-for-Food programme. And it's only in 1999 that nutritional improvements are starting to be recognized'[86].

The Panel that has been reporting to the Security Council regarding the humanitarian situation in Iraq provided an overall assessment in the following terms:

> The gravity of the humanitarian situation of the Iraqi people is indisputable and cannot be overstated. Irrespective of alleged attempts by the Iraqi authorities to exaggerate the significance of certain facts for political propaganda purposes, the data from different sources as well as qualitative assessments of *bona fide* observers and sheer common sense analysis of economic variables converge and corroborate this evaluation[87].

The overall effect of the United Nations' Iraqi sanctions regime has been, in the words of Richard Garfield, 'the only instance of a sustained, large increase in mortality in a stable population of more than two million in the last two hundred years'[88]. Marc Bossuyt quotes a UN Development Programme field report which states that 'the country has experienced a shift from relative affluence to massive poverty'[89]. The ICRC, which had people on the ground in Iraq throughout the 1990s, reported in 1999 that 'now, after nine years of trade sanctions, imposed by the UN after Iraq's invasion of Kuwait in August 1990, the situation of the civilian population is increasingly desperate'[90]. In its annual report for 2000, the ICRC notes that:

---

[83]   *Id.*, para. 19.
[84]   Cortright and Lopez, *op. cit.*, n. 59, p. 742.
[85]   As cited at *id.*
[86]   Richard Garfield, 'Changes in Health and Well-Being in Iraq during the 1990s: What do We Know and How do We Know it?', *Sanctions on Iraq: Background, Consequences, Strategies (Proceedings of the Conference)*, 2000, p. 45; available at www.cam.ac.uk/societies/casi/conf99/proceedings.html.
[87]   Report of the humanitarian panel of the United Nations Security Council, *op. cit.*, n. 53, para. 49.
[88]   Garfield, *op. cit.*, n. 86, p. 36.
[89]   Bossuyt, *op. cit.*, n. 55, para. 67.
[90]   International Committee of the Red Cross, *op. cit.*, n. 76, p. 2.

Ten years after the Gulf war and the imposition of international trade sanctions, daily life for ordinary Iraqis was a struggle for survival. The tragic effects of the embargo were seen in the steady deterioration of the health system and the breakdown of public infrastructure. Despite the increase availability of food, medicines and medical equipment, following a rise in oil prices and the extension of the 'oil-for-food' programme, suffering remains widespread[91].

The combination of the Coalition air campaign and comprehensive sanctions proved to be a deadly cocktail for Iraq. While the trade embargo made way for foodstuffs, medicine, and humanitarian items, it prevented Iraq from rebuilding its infrastructures with the result that during the period in which the sanctions were in place, it was unable to develop the public utilities required of a modern, urban society. Instead, sanctions increasingly took their toll, not on the Hussein Administration, which in large part remained immune to its effects, but on the Iraqi general public and, more specifically, on Iraqi children. The introduction of the 'oil-for-food' programme failed to provide relief, it having simply stabilised a health catastrophe in free fall. As the authors of *The Sanction Decade* note, 'some degree of civilian pain is probably inevitable with the application of sanctions. The question is not whether humanitarian impacts occur but how serious they are and whether they exceed ethical bounds of proportionality and civilian immunity'. Cortright and Lopez go on to say, 'UN sanctions against the Baghdad regime have grievously violated these ethical standards'[92]. This study, will now turn to the question of whether the United Nations sanctions regime have transgressed not ethical standards, but were they in violation of legal norms?

III. United Nations' Iraqi Sanctions and Norms of *Jus Cogens*

It is clear that the effects of the United Nations' Iraqi sanctions regime were in violation of international human rights law. Yet to characterise these violations brings into doubt the legality of the very nature of the sanctions regime. If it can be demonstrated that the sanctions violated norms of *jus cogens*, then the UN Security Council imposed sanctions breached a peremptory norm of international law and thus should have been rendered null and void. Further, by the standards of the International Criminal Court, such violations of *jus cogens* norms carry with them not only State responsibility but entail individual criminal responsibility. While leaving questions of individual responsibility to the side, the question turns on whether the United Nations' Iraqi sanctions regime did indeed violate a norm of *jus cogens*; and if so, to whom is imparted responsibility for such actions: the United Nations, the Members of the Security Council, or individual Member States?

---

[91]   International Committee of the Red Cross, *Annual Report 2000*, 2000, p. 196.
[92]   Cortright and Lopez, *op. cit.*, n. 36, p. 25.

i. Peremptory Norms of International Law

There exists, in international law, a clear hierarchy of legal rules which finds at its pinnacle *jus cogens* norms[93]. Such norms are considered to be of such fundamental importance to the maintenance of the international legal order that they are peremptory—they are not to be transgressed and no circumstance could preclude the wrongfulness of a State. Thus, within the realm of international law, there is a clear distinction between *jus cogens* where violations of the law automatically incur State responsibility and *jus dispositivum* where there may be circumstances which preclude the wrongfulness of a breach. The concept of *jus cogens* is given voice at the international level, in part, through Articles 53 and 64 of the 1969 Vienna Convention on the Law of Treaties[94]. These provisions provide that treaties may be invalidated or terminated if their content 'conflicts with a peremptory norm of general international law' when it is 'accepted and recognized by the international community of States as a whole as a norm from which no derogation is permitted'. Further, the notion of *jus cogens* appears in the Draft Articles on State Responsibility which were adopted by the International Law Commission in 2001. The Draft Articles, which have been forwarded to the General Assembly for consideration, include provisions related to serious breaches of obligations under peremptory norms of general international law and its consequences, the relation of the concept to countermeasures, and as a circumstance that precludes the wrongfulness of an otherwise illegal act[95].

The existence of a *jus cogens* norm means that no international law, be it conventional or customary, may override such an existing peremptory norms. As a result, such *jus cogens* norms trump even the United Nations Charter which is to be understood as the highest manifestation of *jus dispositivum* on the international plane. The United Nations Charter can be considered the constitution of the

---

[93]   For consideration of *jus cogens* in another context see Jean Allain, 'The *Jus Cogens* Nature of *Non-Refoulement*', *International Journal of Refugee Law*, Vol. 13, 2001, pp. 533–558.
[94]   Articles 53 of the Vienna Convention on the Law of Treaties reads:

A treaty is void if, at the time of its conclusion, it conflicts with a peremptory norm of general international law. For the purposes of the present Convention, a peremptory norm of general international law is a norm accepted and recognized by the international community of States as a whole as a norm from which no derogation is permitted and which can be modified only by a subsequent norm of general international law having the same character.

While Article 64 reads:

If a new peremptory norm of general international law emerges, any existing treaty which is in conflict with that norm becomes void and terminates.

[95]   See Articles 26, 40, 41, and 50, International Law Commission, State Responsibility: Titles and Texts of the Draft Articles on Responsibility of States for Internationally Wrongful Acts adopted by the Committee on Second Reading, A/CN.4/L.602/Rev.1, 26 July 2001.

international system, in part, because States have endowed it with hierarchical supremacy over any other ordinary legal undertaking by virtue of Article 103 which states that if there is a conflict between Member States' United Nations obligations and its 'obligations under any other international agreement, their obligations under the present Charter shall prevail'. Yet, there appear to be two limitations to this application of Article 103, the first, which to some extent was played out before the International Court of Justice in the *Lockerbie* case, requires that action taken on the basis of the UN Charter be in conformity with its provisions[96]. Second, that such actions not be in conflict with norms of *jus cogens*. While there is a clear obligation emanating from Article 25 for States to 'carry out the decisions of the Security Council', and thus to ensure respect for the United Nations' Iraqi sanctions regime, such an obligation would be overridden by an obligation to respect a norm of *jus cogens*. To paraphrase the Draft Articles on State responsibility—a State, which did not carry out the decision of the Security Council to maintain the sanction regime against Iraq, would be precluded from wrongfulness if the sanctions were 'not in conformity with an obligation arising under a peremptory norm of general international law'[97].

Judicial pronouncements and the 'teaching of the most highly qualified publicists' give credence to the overriding nature of *jus cogens* where the Security Council action is considered[98]. Alain Pellet, for instances, notes that the Security Council 'has an absolute obligation to respect *jus cogens*'[99]. Likewise Bardo Fassbender states that 'obligations of States arising from decisions of the Security Council only lawfully arise 'under the present Charter' (Article 103) if those decisions are in accordance with the constitutional law of the international community, including the peremptory norms [...]'[100]. Acting as *Ad Hoc* Judge in the *Genocide* case, pitting Bosnia-Herzegovina against Yugoslavia, Elihu Lauterpacht gave voice to the issue of *jus cogens* as it pertains to genocide and its relationship to Article 103 of the Charter:

> The concept of *jus cogens* operates as a concept superior to both customary international law and treaty. The relief which Article 103 of the Charter may give the Security Council in case of a conflict between one of its decisions and an operative treaty obligation cannot—as a matter of simply hierarchy of norms—extend to a

---

[96] Tomas Franck, Editorial Comment: 'The 'Power of Appreciation': Who is the Ultimate Guardian of UN Legality?', *American Journal of International Law*, Vol. 86, 1992, p. 521.

[97] Article 26, *id.*

[98] Here, of course, one is quoting Article 38(1)(d) of the Statute of the International Court of Justice which reads in full, 'subject to the provisions of Article 59, judicial decisions and the teachings of the most highly qualified publicists of the various nations, as subsidiary means for the determination of rules of law'.

[99] 'Là, je pense, s'arrête le balancier: Le Counseil de sécurité a l'obligation absolue de respecter le *jus cogens* et la Charte des Nations Unies. Ce sont les limites, et les seules limites, à son action'. Alain Pellet, Société Française pour le droit international, *Le Chapitre VII de la Charte des nations unies*, Colloque de Rennes, 1995, p. 237.

[100] Bardo Fassbender, *UN Security Council Reform and the Right of Veto: A Constitutional Perspective*, 1998, p. 126.

conflict between a Security Council resolution and *jus cogens*. Indeed, one only has to state the opposite proposition thus—that a Security Council resolution may even require participation in genocide—for its unacceptability to be apparent[101].

ii. *Characterising the Effects of the Sanctions*

Dennis Halliday, who resigned from his post as UN Assistant Secretary-General and Humanitarian Coordinator in Iraq in September 1998 in protest over the sanctions regime, characterised the UN sanctions in early 1999 as constituting 'genocide'[102]. He notes that, 'With or without original intent, the impact of economic sanctions constitute genocide. Whether it is *de jure* or *de facto* genocide, the semantics are irrelevant [...]'[103]. And, yet for the purposes of this study, semantics are relevant. Obligations which flow from a *de jure* violation of the *jus cogens* imperative not to commit genocide include not only State and individual responsibility, but place obligations on States to desist from actively participating in the type of sanctions which were imposed on Iraq. Consideration will now turn to whether the effect of United Nations sanctions could be considered a *de jure* violation of the prohibition against genocide or, alternatively, whether sanctions could be considered 'part of a widespread or systematic attack directed against any civilian population' and thus be construed as a 'crime against humanity'. While no authoritative decisions have been rendered regarding genocide or crimes against humanity as they relate to State acts, international adjudication has taken place with respect to individual criminal responsibility for such acts[104]. By examining various pronouncements of the international criminal tribunals for the former Yugoslavia and Rwanda and by making reference to the constituting documents of the International Criminal Court, an authoritative understanding of what constitutes 'genocide' and 'crimes against humanity' emerges.

---

[101] Further Request for the Indication of Provisional Measures, *Application of the Convention on the Prevention and Punishment of the Crime of Genocide* (Bosnia and Herzegovina v. Yugoslavia), Order (Separate Opinion, Judge Lauterpacht), 13 September 1993, p. 440.

[102] Dennis Halliday, 'The Deadly and Illegal Consequences of Economic Sanctions on the People of Iraq', *The Brown Journal of World Affairs*, Vol. 7, 2000, pp. 229–233.

[103] *Id.*, p. 232. Halliday goes on to say 'there remains another tragic consequence of the genocide in Iraq—the irreparable damage it has done to the integrity and credibility of the United Nations itself'.

[104] Note that at the time of writing, the International Court of Justice had yet to pronounce itself, on the merits, in the *Application of the Convention on the Prevention and Punishment of the Crime of Genocide* cases brought by Bosnia and Croatia against Yugoslavia. Further, the International Court has rendered an Advisory Opinion regarding the Convention, see *Reservations to the Convention on the Prevention and Punishment of the Crime of Genocide*, *I.C.J. Reports*, 1951.

a. Genocide

It appears that the United Nations' Iraqi sanctions regime falls short of qualifying as an act of genocide within the meaning of the 1948 Convention on the Prevention and Punishment of the Crime of Genocide, as there lacks the required *dolus specialis*. The legal definition of genocide is found at Article 2 of the 1948 Convention, which reads:

> [...] genocide means any of the following acts committed with intent to destroy, in whole or in part, a national, ethnical, racial or religious group, as such:
>
> a) Killing members of the group;
> b) Causing serious bodily or mental harm to members of the group;
> c) Deliberately inflicting on the group conditions of life calculated to bring about its physical destruction in whole or in part;
> d) Imposing measures intended to prevent births within the group;
> e) Forcibly transferring children of the group to another group.

While the crime of genocide is considered the 'crime of crimes' by the International Criminal Tribunal for Rwanda, its definition imposes strict obligations with respect to the intent of the perpetrators[105]. This special intent (or *dolus specialis*) requires that, not only the crimes enunciated in Article 2(a) through (e) be committed, but that such acts be committed with 'intent to destroy, in whole or in part, a national, ethnical, racial or religious group'. William Schabas in his treatise *Genocide in International Law* notes 'in any hierarchy, something has to sit at the top. The crime of genocide belongs at the apex of the pyramid' with respect to international crimes[106]. The United Nations' Iraqi sanctions regime, for its part, lacked the *mens rea* of genocidal intent to make a determination that the Security Council's actions breached the Genocide Convention. As Schabas notes, the crime of genocide has to be conducted with the 'intent to destroy, in whole or in part' a protected group, where that 'specified intent is not established, the act remains punishable, but not as genocide. It may be classified as a crime against humanity or it may be simply a crime under ordinary criminal law'[107].

Despite this, one should not be too quick to discount the possibility that UN Iraqi sanctions did not constitute an act of genocide. In the *Akayesu* case, the first before the International Criminal Tribunal for Rwanda (ICTR), the Trial Chamber noted that it 'considers that intent is a mental factor which is difficult, even impossible, to determine'. It then goes on to say:

> This is the reason why, in the absence of a confession from the accused, his intent can be inferred from a certain number of presumptions of fact. The Chamber considers that it is possible to deduce the genocidal intent inherent in a particular act charged from the general context of the perpetration of other culpable acts systematically directed against

---

[105] William Schabas, *Genocide in International Law*, 2000, p. 9.
[106] *Id.*
[107] *Id.*, p. 214.

that same group, whether these acts were committed by the same offender or by others. Other factors, such as the scale of atrocities committed, their general nature, in a region or a country, or furthermore, the fact of deliberately and systematically targeting victims on account of their membership of a particular group, while excluding the members of other groups, can enable the Chamber to infer the genocidal intent of a particular act[108].

On this basis, can the manner in which the UN Iraqi sanctions were carried out demonstrate genocidal intent? It is clear that the sanctions targeted the Iraqi people, but did they fall into one of the following protected groups: national, ethnic, or racial? In the same manner in which the ICTR had difficulty in determining which of the protected groups Rwandan Tutsis fell into, the same can be said for Iraqis[109]. Traditionally, 'national' groups have been considered as being national minority groups, yet in the case at hand, it is the whole of the Iraqi population which was subject to the sanctions regime[110]. It is clear that Iraqis are not a distinct 'racial' group, as they are part of the larger Arab family which includes Kuwaitis, Saudis, as well as many other citizens of State Members of the League of Arab States. By a process of elimination it appears that Iraqis may well 'fit' the category of 'ethnical' [sic] group which, although taking into consideration 'cultural and linguistic factors' as the 'common denominator', appears to be a catch-all category which is 'largely synonymous with other elements of the enumeration, encompassing elements of national, racial, and religious groups within its scope'[111].

If the Iraqi people are indeed a protected group that was being destroyed then there must be a demonstration that there transpired the *actus reus*, or physical element, of the crime of genocide. Most relevant to the case of the United Nations sanctions imposed on Iraq were the provisions of Article 2 (c) of the 1948 Genocide Convention where it would be considered that there has been an attempt to destroy the Iraqi people by 'deliberately inflicting on the group conditions of life calculated to bring about its physical destruction in whole or in part'. In the *Akayesu* case, the ICTR trial chamber noted that it considered that:

> the expression deliberately inflicting on the group conditions of life calculated to bring about its physical destruction in whole or in part, should be construed as the methods of destruction by which the perpetrator does not immediately kill the members of the group, but which, ultimately, seek their physical destruction.

> For purposes of interpreting [this provision], the Chamber is of the opinion that the means of deliberate inflicting on the group conditions of life calculated to bring about its physical destruction, in whole or part, include, *inter alia*, subjecting a group of people to a subsistence diet, systematic expulsion from homes and the reduction of essential medical services below minimum requirement[112].

---

[108]   *Prosecutor v. Akayesu*, Judgement, 2 September 1998, ICTR-96-4-T, para. 523.
[109]   See Schabas, *op. cit.*, n. 105, pp. 130–133.
[110]   *Id.*, pp. 114–120.
[111]   *Id.*, pp. 126–127.
[112]   *Prosecutor v. Akayesu*, *op. cit.*, n. 108, paras. 505–506.

Where the United Nations' Iraqi sanctions were concerned, it appeares that the denial of foodstuffs during the period between Resolutions 661 and 687 clearly imposed the conditions of life calculated to bring about the physical destruction of the Iraqi people. Beyond that, the humanitarian modification of the sanctions regime had largely failed to ensure the continued existence of the Iraqi people, as the United Nations Secretary-General noted that despite the fact that 'one third of children under five years of age are malnourished', the 'oil-for-food' programme even 'if it is implemented perfectly, it is possible that the efforts will prove insufficient to satisfy the population's needs'[113].

Despite the large-scale deaths in Iraq resulting from the United Nations sanction regime, this closer examination of the law related to the issue of genocide seems to raise more questions than it answers. Despite the possible opening provided by the *Akayesu* case, the provisions of the Convention on the Prevention and Punishment of the Crime of Genocide do not apply to the situation of the UN sanctions as there is no place within its provisions for the possibility of 'negligent' genocide—intent must be demonstrated. As Schabas explains, a 'crime of negligence is one without genuine intent, but resulting from extreme carelessness'[114]. 'Negligence' he states, 'should not be confused with omission' whereby, for instance, an entity denies people the conditions of life. In such a situation there is no negligence: to constitute genocide there must be a purposeful act of omitting to provide the basic food, shelter, clean water, etc. Schabas points to the commentary of the 1996 Code of Crimes against the Peace and Security of Mankind as providing the distinguishing characteristic of genocide as an international crime:

> The prohibited acts enumerated in subparagraph (a) to (c) [of Article 2 of the 1948 Convention] are by their nature conscious, intentional or volitional acts which an individual could not usually commit without knowing that certain consequences were likely to result. These are not the type of acts that would normally occur by accident or even as a result of mere negligence. However, a general intent to commit one of these enumerated acts combined with a general awareness of the probable consequences of such an act with respect to the immediate victim or victims is not sufficient for the crime of genocide. *The definition of this crime requires a particular state of mind or a specific intent with respect to the overall consequences of the prohibited act*[115].

Thus, without being able to demonstrate that the intent of the sanctions was to destroy, in whole or in part, the Iraqi people, the crime of genocide cannot be imputed.

---

[113] *Supra*, see n. 83 and 53.
[114] Schabas, *op. cit.*, n. 105, pp. 226–227.
[115] *Id.*, p. 219. Emphasis added. For more on the 1996 Code see Jean Allain and John R.W.D. Jones, 'A Patchwork of Norms: A Commentary on the 1996 Draft Code of Crimes against the Peace and Security of Mankind', *European Journal of International Law*, Vol. 8, 1997, pp. 100–117.

b. Crimes against Humanity

Short of the intent to commit genocide, consideration now falls to whether the
United Nations sanctions against Iraq can be deemed to have been a 'crime against
humanity'. The leading scholar on the issue of international criminal law, and more
specifically issues of crimes against humanity, M. Cherif Bassiouni, has noted that
this legal concept has 'evolved since 1945 in bits and pieces, fits and bursts, but not
in a cohesive, consistent and comprehensive manner and yet there is still no
specialized convention on crimes against humanity'[116]. Instead, finding its genesis
in the Nuremberg Principles, the concept of crimes against humanity has been
included in a number of legal instruments, and been given its fullest expression in
Article 7 of the Statute of the International Criminal Court. With respect to the
issue at hand, the relevant provisions of Article 7 read:

>   1.   For the purpose of this Statute, 'crime against humanity' means any of the
>   following acts when committed as part of a widespread or systematic attack directed
>   against any civilian population, with knowledge of the attack:
>
>   (b) Extermination;
>
>   2.   For the purpose of paragraph 1:
>
>   (a) 'Attack directed against any civilian population' means a course of conduct
>   involving the multiple commission of acts referred to in paragraph 1 against any
>   civilian population, pursuant to or in furtherance of a State or organizational
>   policy to commit such attack;
>
>   (b) 'Extermination' includes the intentional infliction of conditions of life, *inter
>   alia* the deprivation of access to food and medicine, calculated to bring about the
>   destruction of part of a population;

As secondary legislation, meant to assist the International Criminal Court in
interpreting an applying its subject matter jurisdiction, the State Parties to the
Statute developed an elaboration of the 'Elements of the Crimes'. Flushing out the
manner in which the Court should understand crimes against humanity, the
'Elements of the Crimes' states that an 'attack directed against a civilian
population' requires the commission of multiple acts 'pursuant to or in furtherance
of a State or organizational policy to commit such attack', but that such 'acts need
not constitute a military attack'[117]. The 'Elements of the Crimes' further elaborate
the crime against humanity, to consider the concept of 'extermination' by declaring
that it includes the 'inflicting conditions of life calculated to bring about the
destruction of part of a population'. Added as a footnote to this provision is the

---

[116] M. Cherif Bassiouni, *Crimes against Humanity in International Criminal Law*, 1999,
p. 87.
[117] Article 7, *Elements of the Crimes*, as found in William Schabas, *An Introduction to the
International Criminal Court*, 2001, p. 252.

statement that the 'infliction of such conditions could include the deprivation of access to food and medicine'[118].

Bassiouni notes that the inclusion of this footnote demonstrates that States are in agreement that extermination, 'does not merely occur when a perpetrator executes the material act of, for instance, firing a rifle or wielding a knife which directly results in the killing of another, but also "extermination" occurs when a perpetrator creates "conditions of life" amenable to mass killing'[119]. Bassiouni writes that the 'plain language and ordinary meaning of the word "extermination" implies both intentional and unintentional killing', and that negligence—that is: knowing or should have known and not doing anything—carries with it responsibility for the crime of extermination[120]. It is clear that in the case of the United Nations' Iraqi sanctions that mass killing did take place, the most conservative estimates of deaths resulting from the sanctions are in the hundreds of thousands while the Iraqi Government estimated, in 2001, that over a million and a half people had died as a result of sanctions[121]. While the attribution to UN sanctions as having the effect of 'extermination' appears, *prima facie*, shocking, it should be understood that the legal notion of 'extermination' should be disassociated from the common use of the term. When the definition of extermination in law is considered, that is—'intentional infliction of conditions of life [...] calculated to bring about the destruction of part of a population'—it appears, with all the information available as to the effects of the United Nations sanctions regime imposed on Iraq, during its twelve years; that the United Nations was involved in a campaign of 'extermination', which constituted a crime against humanity.

IV. Responsibility and the United Nations' Iraqi Sanctions

While the sanctions regime was in place, the humanitarian modifications which transpired did not ease the suffering of the Iraqi people, they simply halted the free-fall and capped the continued deaths at their ten-year high. Further, with the UN Secretary-General's acknowledgement that the 'oil-for-food' programme may well 'prove insufficient to satisfy the population's needs', it appears clear that the United Nations knew that the sanctions regime was responsible for mass death, yet failed to take adequate measures to end the consequences of its deliberate act.

---

[118] *Id.*, Article 7(1)(b).

[119] Bassiouni, *op. cit.*, n. 116, p. 305.

[120] *Id.*, see pp. 303 and 305. For judicial pronouncements regarding individual criminal responsibility regarding the crime of extermination see the judgements in the *Akayesu* case (ICTR-96-4-T), 2 September 1998, paras. 591–592; the *Rutaganda* case (ICTR-96-13-T), 6 December 1999, paras. 82–84 and 403–418; and the *Musema* case (ICTR-96-3-T), 27 January 2000, paras. 217–219 and 942–951.

[121] Arabic News quoted the Iraqi News Agency on 12 December 2001 that the Iraqi Permanent Mission at the United Nations 'reported the death of 1.6 million Iraqis as a result of diseases resulting from the sanctions imposed on the country since 1990'. On file with author.

Measured against the standard of the International Criminal Court which gives voice to the customary norm against perpetuating the crime against humanity of extermination, the United Nations' Iraqi sanctions regime falls short. If one is to accept that effects of the United Nations' Iraqi sanctions regime constituted a crime against humanity then issues of responsibility come into focus.

Without a central enforcement system, the international system for dealing with breaches of the law is manifest in the regime of State responsibility. As the noted Swiss Jurist, Max Huber, stated in the 1923 *Spanish Zone of Morocco* claim, 'Responsibility is the necessary corollary of a right. All rights of an international character involve international responsibility. If the obligation in question is not met, responsibility entails the duty to make reparations'[122]. In the case at hand, a violation of a crime against humanity incurs responsibility. Typically, responsibility is conceived of as 'State responsibility', as States remain the primary subjects of international law, while other subjects received their international personality through the filter of the State. This was made plain by the International Court of Justice in its *Reparations for Injuries* opinion, where it found that the United Nations clearly has standing on the international plane:

> the Court has come to the conclusion that the Organization is an international person. That is not the same thing as saying that it is a State, which it certainly is not, or that its legal personality and rights and duties are the same as those of a State. [...] What it does mean is that it is a subject of international law and capable of possessing international rights and duties.

The Court went on to say that the United Nations is a subject of international law with rights and duties, but that those rights and duties 'depend upon its purposes and functions as specified or implied in its constituent documents and developed in practice'[123]. Although the *Reparations for Injuries* case confirmed the United Nations could bring a claim on the international plane invoking the responsibility of a State, the fact that the UN holds not only rights but duties also means that the Organization can be held responsible for violations of international law.

The question of responsibility for the effects of the sanctions regime imposed on Iraq falls squarely on the shoulders of the United Nations. Although it is clear that the United States was the main proponent and, in many ways, crafted the UN sanctions regime against Iraq, responsibility still lies with the UN Organization. The United Nations sanctions regime was undertaken clearly within the framework of the United Nations Charter and persisted in gaining, not only the support of the Permanent Members, but a large number of States that rotated through the other ten seats of the Security Council during the period when the sanctions were in place. It was the unwillingness of the UN Security Council, and its Sanctions Committee, acting collectively to provide adequate relief which caused the humanitarian catastrophe that befell Iraq from 1991 to 2003. Without allowing for the rebuilding

---

[122] As quoted in Ian Brownlie, *Principles of Public International Law*, 1990, p. 434.
[123] International Court of Justice, *Reparation for Injuries Suffered in the Service of the United Nations, I.C.J. Reports, 1950*, 11 April 1949, pp. 178 and 179.

of Iraqi infrastructures destroyed or damaged during the Coalition campaign, Iraq lacked the communication and energy means to undertake proper distribution of humanitarian items, even if such items had proven to be adequate to the needs of Iraqis.

It was disingenuous for the United Nations to blame the Hussein Administration, as it did in 1999, for the deaths which have transpired under its sanctions regime. In 1999, the Strategic Planning Unit of the Office of the UN Secretary-General stated that the 'primary responsibility for the sanctions death-toll clearly lies with the regime. Iraq's deliberate obstructive tactics meant that humanitarian aid under Oil-for-Food did not start to reach those in need until March 1997, despite the fact that the Security Council had made provisions for such aid in 1991'[124]. As it is the United Nations Security Council which imposed the sanctions regime, but then found itself required to modify its provisions for humanitarian reasons, coupled with the fact that it could not reach agreement with the Hussein Administration, and that it finally capitulated to the requirements of the Iraq Government, this can hardly be imputed to Iraq. The UN Security Council was aware of the effects of its sanctions throughout the early 1990s; it had an obligation to seek to mitigate, as far as possible, the excesses of its policy, but instead blamed the hardship of the Iraqi people on the intransigence of the Hussein Administration. As the Committee on Economic, Social and Cultural Rights noted in a General Comment regarding sanctions, 'the inhabitants of a given country do not forfeit their basic [...] rights by virtue of any determination that their leaders have violated norms relating to international peace and security'. As a result, it sought to make plain that just because a State is in violation of the law, does not give license to the Security Council to act, itself, in a lawless manner. The Committee concluded its Comment by stating that 'lawlessness of one kind should not be met by lawlessness of another kind which pays no heed to the fundamental rights that underlie and give legitimacy to any such collective action'[125].

V. Conclusion

While the attribution to UN sanctions as having the effect of 'extermination' appears, at first glance, shocking, it should be understood that the legal notion of 'extermination' should be disassociated from the ordinary meaning of the word. The United Nations Security Council was aware, for more than a decade, of the effects of its sanctions regime on Iraq; though it attempted to mitigate the suffering of Iraqis through its 'oil-for-food' programme, it is made clear by studies carried

---

[124] See 'UN Sanctions: How Effective? How Necessary?', Strategic Planning Unit, Executive Office of the Secretary-General, 1999. Paper prepared for the 2nd Interlaken Seminar on Targeting UN Financial Sanctions, 29–31 March, 1999, Switzerland. Available on the internet at: www.smartsanctions.ch.
[125] Committee on Economic, Social and Cultural Rights, *General Comment 8(1997)—The Relationship between Economic Sanctions and Respect for Economic, Social and Cultural Rights*, para. 16.

out by the Organization itself that these modifications did not reverse the humanitarian catastrophe. When the definition of extermination is considered, that is, 'intentional infliction of conditions of life [...] calculated to bring about the destruction of part of a population' it is clear that for more than twelve years of sanctions, which killed anywhere from hundreds of thousands to nearly two million people, that the United Nations was involved in a campaign of, what can be considered as, in legal terms, 'extermination'; which, in turn, constitutes a crime against humanity. If this characterization of the effects of the United Nations Security Council sanctions imposed on Iraq is correct, then a number of legal obligations flow from it, including the need to adjust the international wrong which transpired through reparations to Iraq and to hold individuals criminally responsible for the committing of this international crime.

The twelve-year period from 1991 to 2003 when the United Nations-imposed sanctions on Iraq were in place has left a dark page for the history of humanity. That the international community was party to, and stood by its ideals when, hundreds of thousands, if not millions, were killed, is reprehensible.   The assessment made by Mr. Ahtissaari in 1991 regarding the air campaign of the UN Coalition Forces, that it had 'wrought near-apocalyptic results upon the economic infrastructure' remained true throughout the sanctions era. The cumulative effect of lack of clean water, proper sanitation, and limited electricity had dire consequences on the Iraq population. While the United Nations 'oil-for-food' programme alleviated some of the suffering, the International Committee of the Red Cross considered, in its 2000 report, that ten years after 'the Gulf war and the imposition of trade sanctions, daily life for ordinary Iraqis was a struggle for survival'. That UN sanctions were legitimate when first imposed goes without saying. Iraq itself understood, when joining the United Nations that if it invaded a neighbouring State it could (although at the time it was unlikely) expect the wrath of the Security Council. However, few could have predicted that the sanctions regime would come to violate a norm of *jus cogens* and amount to, what appeared to be— 'extermination'—a crime against humanity. That being said, the use of international law in such a punitive manner appears to be in line with its instrumentality as it has been played out in the Middle East. It should thus come as little surprise that when the region bore witness to the type of slow death of hundreds of thousands of Iraqis, the legitimacy of international law, upon which the UN sanction regime was based, is brought into question.

Chapter 7

Internalising the Requirements of International Law: Perpetual States of Emergency in Egypt and Syria

So far, this study has concentrated on the influences of outside powers, which have sought to impose their will on the Middle East. Such outside influences remain today, yet their manifestations are more refined than during the colonial era of the inter-War period where the United Kingdom and France imposed their will through direct occupation and administration. Today, while Middle East States are nominally independent, those in power lack the legitimacy of popular support. More often than not, those who maintain control over the State apparatus, do so through authoritarian means of coercion. As a result, a more subtle, 'neo-', colonialism has emerged in many Middle East States whereby foreign control has been ceded to a local elite who govern in their own interest, often at the expense of the overall population. Thus, while having the outward manifestation of democracy—a legislature and periodic elections—a cursory examination of many States in the region will bring to the fore the fact that they maintain their power through force of arms. These semblances of democracy, however, are curtailed by one-party States, where leaders often receive in excess of ninety percent support in elections where they are the only candidates. Lacking the legitimate support to rule, such leaders have developed security apparatuses to ensure their physical, and their administration's, survival. During the Cold War era, the 'enemies' of the State were either 'communists' or 'western imperialists' depending on which side of the divide a Middle Eastern State found itself. Since the demise of the ideological Cold War, Middle East States have developed a new bogeyman in the guise of the 'Islamist'. So-called 'Islamic movements' are a true challenge to a number of Middle East States, because they have proven themselves 'better organized, more efficient and less corrupt than the government administration[s]' in providing, for instance, 'free medicine, distributing school equipment, organizing garbage collection, offering administrative advice'; but also 'emergency relief services [...] guarantee[ing] law and order [and] providing policing'[1].

---

[1]   Lisa Anderson, 'Fulfilling Prophecies: State Policy and Islamist Radicalism', John L. Esposito (ed.), *Political Islam: Revolution, Radicalism or Reform?*, 1997, p. 24.

As a consequence of suppressing legitimate means of political participation, many have turned to religious groups as a means of expressing their disenchantment with illegitimate regimes. The result has been that these States, 'threatened by the challenge to their legitimacy and weakening of their power base, have subjugated the [human] rights that they have readily embraced in written form to repressive measures meant to consolidate and maintain their unrepresentative governments in the wake of popular Islamic challenges'[2]. This Chapter considers the manner in which the leaders of both Egypt and Syria have subjugated their international human rights obligations to ensure maintenance of their power in light of Islamic challenges. The principle manner in which they have sought to suppress such movements has been through the labelling of Islamists as 'terrorists' and maintaining perpetual state of emergency which has given them free rein to deny protection of international human rights law. While it is clear that, having been denied the possibility of change through peaceful, democratic, means, Islamist groups have turned to force of arms in targeting the State apparatus. It should be made plain that these attacks are a result of the State's closing off all other avenues of challenging their authoritarian rule.

While states of emergency exist in Algeria (since 1992), and Israel (since 1948), the cases of Egypt and Syria stand out as being representative of states of emergency which have been maintained quasi-permanently as a means of suppressing popular support in all its guises. Although the case of Algeria is clearly one where the State invoked a state of emergency to suppress the democratic gains of the 1991 election by the *Front Islamique de Salut*; the state of emergency has not traditionally been a tool of suppression in this North African State, though it may be moving toward the Egypto-Syrian model[3]. The exclusion of consideration of the Israeli state of emergency transpires as it has been a means, not so much to suppress its own citizens, but to allow for repressive measures against Palestinians and maintaining its war readiness[4]. Egypt and Syria, by contrast, have maintained states of emergency for extended periods of time, ensuring that their leaders retain unchallenged control over the State apparatus.

Through the use of perpetual states of emergency, the leaders of Egypt and Syria have demonstrated that they have learnt the lessons taught by their former colonial masters—that international law need not be a hindrance to action if one has the power to proceed. The types of human rights abuses and the fact that they are large scale, systematic, and a permanent fixture on the Middle East landscape is a direct result of the persistent devaluation of international law in the region. Having been witness to the manner in which Powers outside the Middle East have

---

[2]   Jean Allain and Andreas O'Shea, 'African Disunity: Comparing Human Rights Law and Practice of North and South African States', *Human Rights Quarterly*, Vol. 24, 2002, pp. 111–112.

[3]   See *id.*, pp. 112–113; and more generally, 'The Shaping of the Civil War' in Luis Martinez, *The Algerian Civil War 1990–1998*, 2000, pp. 23–91.

[4]   For the Israeli state of emergency see John Quigley, 'Israel's Forty-Five Year Emergency: Are there Time Limits to Derogations from Human Rights Obligations?', *Michigan Journal of International Law*, Vol. 15, 1994, pp. 491–518.

acted, unencumbered by the restraints of international law, it should come as little surprise that the administrations in Egypt and Syria do not feel compelled to respect its dictates at the price of their possible unseating. While Egypt and Syria have maintained states of emergency, in part, because they function within nominal democracies, it should be understood that in other parts of the Middle East where, for instance, monarchies rule, the invoking of states of emergency is not necessary as suppression and the maintenance of the *status quo* can transpire through the system of governance already in place. Yet the results are the same: the suppression of individual human rights and the violation of international human rights law as a means of ensuring the maintenance of power by unrepresentative elites.

I. States of Emergency in International Law

In law, human rights are not absolute. There are, in international human rights law, as Rosalyn Higgins wrote in 1977, 'techniques of accommodation', which allow States to dictate the extent to which they will incorporate human rights law into their domestic system[5]. Such techniques include, fundamentally, the ascribing to international human rights instruments, and thereafter withdrawal; less all-encompassing however are such items as reservations, 'claw-back' clauses, and the possibility of derogation from obligations during periods of emergency[6]. The final technique thus allows States to suspend—legally—certain human rights during times of emergency. While it may seem a paradox, the purpose of the suspension of certain human rights in such emergencies is to ensure the enjoyment of the most fundamental rights while seeking to restore the full gamut of human rights as quickly as possible. With this in mind, States were willing, in the drafting of human rights instruments, to accept the insertion of derogation clauses. However, as Professor Jaime Oraá points out, in *Human Rights in States of Emergency in International Law*, the drawing up of a list of which fundamental human rights should never be suspended and thus considered as *non-derogable* rights, did prove

---

[5]   Rosalyn Higgins, 'Derogation under Human Rights Treaties', *The British Yearbook of International Law: 1976–1977*, 1978, p. 281.

[6]   Higgins provides a working definition of a claw-back clause as being 'one that permits, in normal circumstances, breach of an obligation for a specified number of public reasons'. *Id.* An example would be, for instance, Article 12(1) of the International Covenant on Civil and Political Rights which provides that:

Everyone lawfully within the territory of a State shall, within that territory, have the right to liberty of movement and freedom to choose his residence.

But, then, Article 12(3) limits that right by establishing that:

The above-mentioned rights shall not be subject to any restrictions except those which are provided by law, are necessary to protect national security, public order (*ordre public*), public health or morals or the rights and freedoms of others, and are consistent with the other rights recognized in the present Covenant.

more controversial[7]. Although States argued about rights which should be considered non-derogable, the principle emerged that some rights 'can never be suspended; consequently, this principle establishes a clear limitation on the right of [States] to take measures derogating from human rights standards when it faces an emergency'[8].

On this basis emerged a number of universal and regional human rights instruments which have derogation provisions though they also include a core number of non-derogable rights. While the 1980 African Charter of Human and Peoples' Rights does not allow for the possibility of derogation, both the 1969 American Convention on Human Rights and the 1950 European Convention for the Protection of Human Rights and Fundamental Freedoms do have such provisions[9].

---

[7]   Jaime Oraá, *Human Rights in States of Emergency in International Law*, 1992, p. 90.

[8]   *Id.*, p. 124.

[9]   All three regional human rights Conventions can be found in Ian Brownlie and Guy Goodwin-Gill (eds.), *Basic Documents on Human Rights*, 2002; note, however, that the structure of the European system has fundamentally changed as a result of coming into force of Protocol 11. See Protocol No. 11 to the Convention for Protection of Human Rights and Fundamental Freedoms: Restructuring the Control Machinery Established thereby, 1 November 1998, ETS n. 155. Article 27 of the American Convention, entitled 'Suspension of Guarantees', reads:

> 1.   In time of war, public danger, or other emergency that threatens the independence or security of a State Party, it may take measures derogating from its obligations under the present Convention to the extent and for the period of time strictly required by the exigencies of the situation, provided that such measures are not inconsistent with its other obligations under international law and do not involve discrimination on the grounds of race, color, sex, language, religion, or social origin.

> 2.   The foregoing provision does not authorize any suspension of the following articles: Article 3 (Right to Juridical Personality), Article 4 (Right to Life), Article 5 (Right to Humane Treatment), Article 6 (Freedom from Slavery), Article 9 (Freedom from *Ex Post Facto* Laws), Article 12 (Freedom of Conscience and Religion), Article 17 (Rights of the Family), Article 18 (Right to a Name), Article 19 (Rights of the Child), Article 20 (Right to Nationality), and Article 23 (Right to Participate in Government), or of the judicial guarantees essential for the protection of such rights.

> 3.   Any State Party availing itself of the right of suspension shall immediately inform the other States Parties, through the Secretary General of the Organization of American States, of the provisions the application of which it has suspended, the reasons that gave rise to the suspension, and the date set for the termination of such suspension.

By comparison, Article 15 of the European Convention, entitled 'Derogation in Time of Emergency', states:

> 1.   In time of war or other public emergency threatening the life of the nation any High Contracting Party may take measures derogating from its obligations under this Convention to the extent strictly required by the exigencies of the situation, provided that such measures are not inconsistent with its other obligations under international law.

> 2.   No derogation from Article 2 [Right to Life], except in respect of deaths resulting from lawful acts of war, or from Articles 3 [Prohibition of Torture], 4 (paragraph 1) [Prohibition of Slavery and Forced Labour] and 7 [No Punishment without Law] shall be made under this provision.

At the universal level, the possibility to derogate from specific human rights is made possible by Article 4 of the 1966 International Covenant on Civil and Political Rights (ICCPR)[10]. This Article reads:

1.   In time of public emergency which threatens the life of the nation and the existence of which is officially proclaimed, the States Parties to the present Covenant may take measures derogating from their obligations under the present Covenant to the extent strictly required by the exigencies of the situation, provided that such measures are not inconsistent with their other obligations under international law and do not involve discrimination solely on the ground of race, colour, sex, language, religion or social origin.

2.   No derogation from articles 6, 7, 8 (paragraphs 1 and 2), 11, 15, 16 and 18 may be made under this provision.

3.   Any State Party to the present Covenant availing itself of the right of derogation shall immediately inform the other States Parties to the present Covenant, through the intermediary of the Secretary-General of the United Nations, of the provisions from which it has derogated and of the reasons by which it was actuated. A further communication shall be made, through the same intermediary, on the date on which it terminates such derogation.

On the basis of this provision, States party to the ICCPR may, in times of public emergency, make it known that they are suspending specific provisions of the Covenant for a limited period of time; it being understood, by way of subsection 2, that they may not suspend Article 6 related the right to life; Article 7 dealing with torture; Article 8(1)(2) setting out provisions related to the prohibition on slavery and servitude; Article 11 expressing the obligation not to imprison a person for their inability to fulfil a contractual obligation; Article 15, providing protection at trial with respect to the notion of *nullum crimen sine lege*; Article 16 regarding recognition before the law; and finally Article 18, ensuring the right to freedom of thought, conscience, and religion.

Considering the *travaux préparatoires* of the ICCPR, Professor Oraá notes that while there was agreement as to the inclusion of a derogation clause, and within that provision would be enumerated a number of non-derogable rights, it was not clear 'what criteria were adopted in the elaboration of the list' of non-derogable

---

3.   Any High Contracting Party availing itself of this right of derogation shall keep the Secretary General of the Council of Europe fully informed of the measures which it has taken and the reasons therefore. It shall also inform the Secretary General of the Council of Europe when such measures have ceased to operate and the provisions of the Convention are again being fully executed.

[10]   See Ian Brownlie (ed.), *Basic Documents on Human Rights*, 1992, p. 127.

rights which ultimately found its way into Article 4(2)[11]. What emerged were two overarching principles that implicitly were used during the drafting of the treaty:

> First, to include those rights which are absolutely fundamental and indispensable for the protection of the human being. Second, to include those rights the derogation of which by the State in public emergencies would never be justified because they have no direct bearing on the emergency[12].

This second principle goes a long way toward explain why, for instance, it was thought that the obligation not to imprison a person for failing to fulfill a contractual obligation was included as a non-derogable right alongside the right to life and the prohibition against torture.

i. General Comment Number 29

While much has been written about states of emergency, and both the European and the Inter-American human rights courts have made pronouncement in its regard; the most authoritative pronouncement, to date, where the Middle East is concerned, regarding states of emergency, has been made by the treaty monitoring body of the ICCPR[13]. Before entering the labyrinth of the human rights' system of the United Nations, it may be helpful to draw the distinction between the charter-based and treaty-based mechanisms. With respect to the charter-based mechanisms, primary consideration will be given to the UN Commission on Human Rights which is composed of fifty-three UN Member States and its Special Rapporteurs,

---

[11]   *Id.*, p. 90. Note that there are only four non-derogable rights common to the ICCPR, the European Convention, and the American Convention. They are: right to life, freedom from torture, from slavery, and from *ex post facto* laws.

[12]   *Id.*, p. 94.

[13]   Consider the International Commission of Jurists, *States of Emergency: Their Impact on Human Rights*, 1983; Jaime Oraá, *Human Rights in States of Emergency in International Law*, 1992; Joan Fitzpatrick, Human *Rights in Crisis: The International System for Protecting Human Rights during States of Emergency*, 1994. Note also the work of the International Law Association in Richard Lillich, 'Paris Minimum Standards of Human Rights Norms in a State of Emergency', *American Journal of International Law*, Vol. 79, 1985, pp. 1072–1081; and Richard Lillich, 'Queensland Guidelines for Bodies Monitoring Respect for Human Rights during State of Emergency', *American Journal of International Law*, Vol. 85, 1991, pp. 716–720.

Specific to the Inter-American system see Thomas Buergenthal and Dinah Shelton, *Protecting Human Rights in the Americas: Cases and Materials*, 1995, pp. 483–493; and the advisory opinions of the Inter-American Court in the *Habeas Corpus in Emergency Situations* case, Advisory Opinion OC–8, 30 January 1987 and the *Judicial Guarantees in States of Emergency* case, Advisory Opinion OC–9, 6 October 1987. With regard to the European system see R. St. J. Macdonald, 'Derogations under Article 15 of the European Convention on Human Rights', *Columbia Journal of Transnational Law*, Vol. 36, 1997, pp. 225–267; and the leading cases of the European Court: the *Borgan* case, no. 145, 28 November 1988; *Brannigan & McBride*, no. 258, 26 May 1993; and the *Askoy* case, 21987/93, 18 December 1996.

experts acting in their individual capacity with respect to issues such as states of emergency or torture. As regards the UN treaty-based system, monitoring bodies composed of a limited number of independent experts who assist State parties in monitoring compliance of their treaty obligations. Specific to this study is the considerations of the Committee against Torture in monitoring the 1984 Convention against Torture and, as established under Article 28 of the ICCPR, the Human Rights Committee that supervises the manner in which the State Parties have given effect to their obligations under the Covenant.

As part of its mandate to monitor State compliance with the ICCPR, the Human Rights Committee may receive petitions (called 'communications') from States or individuals regarding non-fulfilment of their obligations; beyond this however, the Committee is also mandated to prepare reports and 'such general comments as it may consider appropriate'[14]. On this basis, the Human Rights Committee has adopted dozens of 'General Comments' in which it has sought to give flesh to various provisions of the Covenant so as to assist States in fulfilling their obligations. Such General Comments appear to fall somewhere between 'judicial decisions and the teachings of the most highly qualified publicists' in their juridical value as a subsidiary means of determining international law[15]. Juridically, the legal value of General Comments comes from the fact that they are authoritative pronouncements by experts of international bodies entrusted with the task monitoring compliance of State Parties' obligations under international human rights treaties. For his part, Thomas Buergenthal, when he sat as a member of the Committee, considered General Comments to be:

> distinct juridical instruments, enabling the Committee to announce its interpretation of different provisions of the Covenant in a form that bears some resemblance to the advisory opinion practice of international tribunals. These general comments or 'advisory opinions' are relied upon by the Committee in evaluating the compliance of states with their obligations under the Covenant, be it in examining State reports or 'adjudicating' individual communications under the Optional Protocol[16].

On 24 July 2001, the Human Rights Committee adopted General Comment Number 29 entitled 'Derogations from Provisions of the Covenant during a State of Emergency'[17]. In it, the Committee considered the nature of Article 4 of the Covenant, explaining that, 'on the one hand, it allows for a State party unilaterally to derogate temporarily from a part of its obligations under the Covenant. On the

---

[14]   See Article 40, ICCPR, in Brownlie, *op. cit.*, n. 10. For the possibility of State to State petitions see Article 41; for individual petitions see Article 1 of the 1966 Optional Protocol to the International Covenant on Civil and Political Rights, *id.*, pp. 144–147.
[15]   See Article 38, Statute of the International Court of Justice, in Eric Suy, *Corpus Iuris Gentium*, 1996, p. 40.
[16]   As quoted in Henry Steiner and Philip Alston, *International Human Rights in Context: Law, Politics, Morals*, 2000, p. 732.
[17]   Human Rights Committee, *General Comment Number 29: States of Emergency (article 4)*, CCPR/C/21/Rev.1/Add.11, 31 August 2001. Note that General Comment 29 replaces General Comment 5 of 31 July 1981.

other hand, Article 4 subjects both this very measure of derogation, as well as its material consequences, to a specific regime of safeguards'[18]. With respect to Article 4, it may be said that seven safeguards exist, two procedural and five substantive. The procedural safeguards require a State to have 'officially proclaimed' a state of emergency and to notify its proclamation immediately to the UN Secretary-General. As for the substantive safeguards of Article 4, there is an obligation on States: 1) to proclaim a state of emergency only when the situation 'threatens the life of the nation'; 2) to only take such measures as are 'strictly required by the exigencies of the situation'; 3) to ensure that the measures taken are consistent with their other international obligations; 4) to not discriminate; and finally, 5) to not transgress non-derogable rights[19].

The Human Rights Committee has provided more flesh to the bare bones of Article 4 by noting that there is a 'fundamental requirement' that any measure which derogates from the Covenant be limited by exigencies of the situation in relation to, not only its 'geographical coverage and material scope', but also in its 'duration'[20]. Such limitations are to reflect the 'principle of proportionality' whereby each measure must be shown to be 'strictly required by the exigencies of the situation' to meet the objectives sought. In other words, that the suspension of each right must seek to meet a specific objective, and that the measures undertaken to reach that objective should not go beyond what is absolutely necessary in any given situation. As a result, the Human Rights Committee has noted that 'the legal obligation to narrow down all derogations to those strictly required by the exigencies of the situation establishes both for States parties and for the Committee a duty to conduct a careful analysis under each article of the Covenant based on an objective assessment of the actual situation'[21].

Beyond the duty to limit measures under states of emergency to those strictly required by the exigencies of the situation, the Human Rights Committee has determined that 'enumeration of non-derogable provisions in article 4 is related to, but not identical with, the question whether certain human rights obligations bear the nature of peremptory norms of international law'[22]. As a result, the Committee goes on to list a number of human rights which it considers to have crossed the threshold from simple customary international law to being a norm of *jus cogens* which would, *ipso facto*, be considered as non-derogable. The Committee points to Article 10(1) of the ICCPR, that 'all persons deprived of their liberty shall be treated with humanity and with respect for the inherent dignity of the human person' and states that it 'believes that here the Covenant expresses a norm of general international law not subject to derogation'[23]. Building on this, the Human

---

[18] *Id.*, para. 1.

[19] Here I rework Venkat Iyer's notion of 'controls' on States declaring emergencies. See Venkat Iyer, 'States of Emergency: Moderating their Effects on Human Rights', *Dalhousie Law Journal*, Vol. 22, 1999, p. 135.

[20] See General Comment 29, *op. cit.*, n. 17, para. 4.

[21] *Id.*, para. 6.

[22] *Id.*, para. 11.

[23] *Id.*, para. 13(a).

Rights Committee notes that Article 2(3) of the Covenant requires that State Parties provide a remedy for any violation of a right. As such, even in a state of emergency a State has a 'fundamental obligation […] to provide a remedy that is effective'[24].

In a further step to ensure that non-derogable rights are protected, the Human Rights Committee noted that the rights catalogued in Article 4(2) 'must be secured by procedural guarantees'; in this vein the Committee noted that 'the principles of legality and the rule of law require that fundamental requirements of fair trial must be respected during a state of emergency'[25]. The Committee then goes on to amplify what it sees as being required:

> Only a court of law may try and convict a person for a criminal offence. The presumption of innocence must be respected. In order to protect non-derogable rights, the right to take proceedings before a court to enable the court to decide without delay on the lawfulness of detention, must not be diminished by a State party's decision to derogate from the Covenant.

> The Committee takes as its basis for making the assertion that fundamental fair trial guarantees are to be upheld in emergency situations, the fact that 'certain elements of the right to a fair trial are explicitly guaranteed under international humanitarian law during armed conflict', and, as such, it 'finds no justification for derogations from these guarantees during other emergency situations'[26].

ii. Perpetual States of Emergency

While it has been recognised that often public disturbances, whether man-made or natural, necessitate the imposition of a state of emergency, such an invocation can also 'serve as a smokescreen for repressive governmental policies'[27]. As Professor Jaime Oraá, Director of the *Pedro Arrupe* Institute of Human Rights, University of Deusto, Bilbao, noted in his seminal work on states of emergency, such situations are, by their very nature, meant to be temporary. Professor Oraá states:

---

[24]   Article 2(3) of the ICCPR reads:

Each State Party to the present Covenant undertakes:

(a)   Ensure that any person whose rights or freedoms as herein recognized are violated shall have an effective remedy, notwithstanding that the violation has been committed by persons acting in an official capacity;

(b)   Ensure that any person claiming such a remedy shall have his right thereto determined by competent judicial, administrative or legislative authorities, or by any other competent authority provided for by the legal system of the State, and to develop the possibilities of judicial remedy; […]

[25]   See General Comment 29, *op. cit.*, n. 17, paras. 15 and 16.
[26]   *Id.*, para. 16.
[27]   Allan Rosas, 'Emergency Regimes: A Comparison', Donna Gomien (ed.), *Broadening the Frontiers of Human Rights*: *Essays in Honour of Asbjørn Eide*, 1993, p. 166.

As is well known, one of the greatest problems in situations of emergency is the permanent character that derogations assume in some countries; in other words, the maintenance of the derogating measures for a protracted period even though the emergency has ended[28].

Such states of emergency have become, as the UN Special Rapporteur on states of emergency, Mr. Leandro Despouy, noted in 1997, 'the legal means of "legalizing" the worst abuses and the most pernicious forms of arbitrariness'[29]. In this, his final Report, the Special Rapporteur, 'after 12 years of uninterrupted activity' provides his 'final conclusions as to the protection of human rights during states of emergency'[30]. Mr. Despouy notes that, fundamentally, all legal systems allow for special measures to deal with crises, and that this rationale is 'the backbone of the state of emergency as regulated by contemporary international law and determines its essentially protective rather than repressive nature'[31]. Taking this as the yardstick by which states of emergency are to be measured, it is plain that perpetual states of emergency turn the concept on its head: meant to protect fundamental human rights, perpetual state of emergency are used as a tool of repression.

The Special Rapporteur notes, when speaking about perpetual states of emergency, that this 'anomaly essentially consists in the routine introduction of a state of emergency, followed by its straightforward perpetuation or its repeated renewal or extension'[32]. Mr. Despouy goes on to explain that:

> Such anomalies are particularly serious because they disregard the principle of time limitation which establishes the temporary nature of states of emergency. They also disregard the principle whereby the danger or crisis must be either current or imminent. Discretionary power supplants proportionality.
>
> In a word, what was temporary becomes definitive, what was provisional constant and what was exceptional permanent, *which means that the exception becomes the rule*[33].

Such perpetuations of states of emergency inevitably leads to their sophistication, with the danger that the emergency provisions escape the constitutional structure of the State and became parallel but fall outside the legal framework of accountability. In such situations, the Special Rapporteur explains, 'the normal legal order subsists although, parallel to it, a special, para-constitutional legal order

---

[28] Oraá, *op. cit.*, n. 13, p. 22.

[29] See Commission on Human Rights, *Administration of Justice: Questions of Human Rights of Detainees: Questions of Human Rights and States of Emergency, Tenth Annual Report and List of States which, since 1 January 1985, have proclaimed, extended or terminated a state of emergency, presented by Mr. Leandro Despouy, Special Rapporteur appointed pursuant to Economic and Social Council Resolution 1985/37*, UN Doc. E/CN.4/Sub.2/1997/19, 23 June 1997, para. 3.

[30] *Id.*, para. 16.

[31] *Id.*, para. 42.

[32] *Id.*, para. 127.

[33] *Id.*, para. 129. Emphasis added.

begins to take shape [...] which in most cases set themselves above the Constitution itself, so that the normal legal order only remains in force to the extent that it has not been overridden by the former'[34]. Further, the Special Rapporteur explains, that this new legal order established under a state of emergency spins a web whose:

> complexity becomes impossible to unravel when we find ourselves dealing with laws which, based on this para-constitutional order, appear ordinary inasmuch as they are intended to apply independently of any state of emergency.

> Basically, the logic behind this sophistication is nothing more than the wish to secure an extremely complex legal arsenal allowing the authorities to invoke, according to the needs of the moment, either the normal legal system or the special system, although in practice the former is clearly relinquished in favour of the latter.

> In a word, the perpetuation and sophistication of exceptional regimes are really the two sides of the same coin. In one case, the exception is the rule and in the other normality is the exception[35].

The outcome of such perpetual states of emergency, as will be demonstrated when consideration is given to the human rights situations in Egypt and Syria, is a transformation of the criminal system to allow for the effective suppression of opposition groups often at the expense of violations of non-derogable rights. It will become evident that under the guise of states of emergency the executive organ—personified by the Presidents of Egypt and Syria—has been able to institute measures of criminal law which, on the one hand, limit procedural safeguards through, for instance, referral of cases to military courts; while, on the other hand, broadening the scope of what is considered 'criminal' so as to place many people at risk of being prosecuted/persecuted. In this vein, it is worth noting the 'most valuable lesson' which the Special Rapporteur, Mr. Despouy, has been able to draw from his 'long-term examination of developments in states of emergency' is: 'their dangerous tendency to accumulate anomalies when they are applied abusively and perpetuated. As irregularities are compounded, the number of human rights affected increases and even those fundamental rights from which no derogation is permitted are ultimately affected'[36]. Taking this as a lead, consideration will now turn to situations in Egypt and Syria where violations of, for instance, Article 7, regarding torture, have been found to be widespread and systematic. Further consideration will be given to specific instances, in the Syrian context, where blatant violations of Article 6, the right to life, were perpetrated. Finally, building on the premise of the Human Rights Committee that Article 2(3) of the Covenant is non-derogable to the extend that there is a 'fundamental obligation [...] to provide a remedy that is effective', and that 'the principles of legality and the rule of law require that fundamental requirements of fair trial must

---

[34] *Id.*, para. 131.
[35] *Id.*, para. 132.
[36] *Id.*, para. 169.

be respected during a state of emergency'[37]; consideration will also be given to rights of the accused of crimes under state of emergency legislation in both States.

II. Egypt: Human Rights under a Perpetual State of Emergency

In his 1997 Report the Special Rapporteur on states of emergency, Mr. Leandro Despouy, noted that thirty States where found to be in a perpetual state of emergency[38]. From a cursory examination of the Report of the Office of the High Commissioner for Human Rights which lists the States which, in 2001, had a state of emergency in force, it may be said that perpetual states of emergency have receded from being a world-wide phenomena to a Middle East one[39]. Of the eight States that had proclaimed states of emergency before July 1999 and still had them in force in 2001, five were Middle Eastern States: Algeria, Egypt, Israel, Syria, and Turkey[40]. Beyond permanent states of emergency, it should be highlighted that in the Special Rapporteur's Report of 1997, he notes that beyond the five Middle East States that maintained *declared* states of emergency, there existed in northern Iraq and in Lebanon '*de facto* states of emergency'. Further, reference should be made to emergency legislation dating back to the British Mandate period, which has been used in the Occupied Territories by Israel, as well as the invoking of states of emergency by the Palestinian Authority in areas nominally under its control[41].

---

[37] See General Comment 29, *op. cit.*, n. 17, paras. 15 and 16.

[38] See Tenth Annual Report, *op. cit.*, n. 29 , para. 128.

[39] See Commission on Human Rights, *Administration of Justice: Questions of Human Rights and States of Emergency*, Report of the Office of the High Commissioner for Human Rights submitted in accordance with Commission on Human Rights decisions 1998/108, UN Doc. E/CN.4/Sub.2/2001/6, 12 June 2001.

[40] Of the other three states, the charge of a perpetual state of emergency could only be levelled against Sri Lanka which has had its state of emergency in force since 1983. Beyond that, the other two States, which maintained a state of emergency, had done so, on an on-again/off-again basis: for Indonesia, since 1998 (though annexed East Timor remained under an Indonesian-imposed state of emergency from 1983 to 1999), and for Sierra Leone since 1987. Note that Turkey ended its state of emergency in the predominantly Kurdish areas of south-eastern Turkey in November 2002.

[41] For *de facto* states of emergencies in Lebanon and Iraq see Commission on Human Rights, *The Administration of Justice and the Human Rights of Detainees: Questions of Human Rights and States of Emergency—Addendum: Tenth annual list of States which, since 1985, have proclaimed, extended or terminated a state of emergency*, Final Report of the Special Rapporteur, Mr. Leandro Despouy, appointed pursuant to Economic and Social Council Resolution 1985/37, UN Doc. E/CN.4/Sub.2/1998/19/Add.1, 9 June 1997, pp. 6–7. For Palestine, see Amnesty International, 'Israel and the Occupied Territories', *Annual Report 2001*, 2001; as for the state of emergency called by the Palestinian Authority see for instance: Tracy Wilkinson, 'Facing a Severe Test of Power, Arafat Cracks Down on Dissent; Mideast: Palestinian Leader Declares State of Emergency in Gaza Strip after Deadly Clashes', *Los Angeles Times*, 10 October, 2001, p. 10; and Lamia Lahoud, 'Palestinian Authority Declares State of Emergency', *The Jerusalem Post*, 3 December 2001, p. 2.

Turning specifically to Egypt, although the Special Rapporteur noted that it has maintained a state of emergency since 1981, it should be emphasised that Egypt has functioned under a state of emergency for 63 out of the last 90 years. In other words, since the demise of the Ottoman Empire and the invocation of the first state of emergency at the beginning of the First World War, in 1914, to 2004, Egypt has had only 19 years without a state of emergency being in force. Since the end of British colonial rule and the evacuation of British Forces from Egypt in June 1956, an independent Egypt has found itself almost perpetually under a state of emergency. While there have been gaps in which the states of emergency have been lifted, these periods amount to less than four and a half years, over a 46 year-period. Starting with the 1956 Suez War, Nasser declared a state of emergency on 1 November 1956; since then, the states of emergency have been revoked twice. The 1956 state of emergency was lifted for a period of 40 months from 14 March 1964, until it was reinstated on 5 June 1967, as a result of the 1967 War with Israel. That 1967 state of emergency would be maintained until 15 May 1980, but would be reintroduced 18 months later with the assassination of the Egyptian President Anwar Sadat on 6 October 1981. Since then, for more than 20 years, Egyptians have lived under a permanent state of emergency[42].

As will be demonstrated, the perpetuation of the state of emergency in Egypt, fits, hand in glove, with its violations of the most fundamental of human rights. By the perpetual status of its state of emergency, over more than 20 years, Egypt is in *prima facie* violation of its obligations under Article 4 of the International Covenant on Civil and Political Rights. By its practices, which have been facilitated by its state of emergency legislation, it appears, in no uncertain terms, that Egypt is in violation of the *jus cogens* norm prohibiting torture as found in both its obligations under the ICCPR at Article 7 and under the Convention against Torture. This was confirmed by the UN Special Rapporteur on issues of torture, in his 2001 Report to the UN Commission on Human Rights, where he concluded 'that torture is systematically practiced' in Egypt[43]. Likewise, Egypt appears to be in violation of the rights which are required to safeguard the non-derogable rights regarding Article 6, right to life, and Article 7, prohibition against torture. As the Human Rights Committee noted in its General Comment 29, Article 10(1) providing that all 'persons deprived of their liberty shall be treated with humanity and with respect for the inherent dignity of the human person' is a 'norm of general international law not subject to derogation'[44]. As a result the Committee pointed to the need to 'secure procedural guarantees' including the 'fundamental requirements

---

[42]   The information in this paragraph was taken and updated from: Mohammad El-Ghamry, *Detention and the Emergency Law: A Study of the Constitutional and Legal System of Detention in Egypt*, published by the Center for Human Rights Legal Aid, 1995.
[43]   See Commission on Human Rights, *Civil and Political Rights including the Question of Torture and Detention*, Report of the Special Rapporteur, Sir Nigel Rodley, submitted pursuant to Commission on Human Rights resolution 2000/43, UN Doc. E/CN.4/2001/66, 25 January 2001, para. 476.
[44]   General Comment 29, *op. cit.*, n. 17, para. 13(a).

of fair trial'[45]. In more diplomatic language, the ICCPR's Human Rights Committee expressed its concern about 'the duration and conditions of police custody and administrative detention'. It also raised its concern regarding the 'multitude of special courts', which it noted that 'from the point of view of legal consistency in the judicial procedure and procedural guarantees' should only exist 'as an exceptional measure'[46].

Before examining, in detail, the extent to which Egypt is in violation of its obligations under the International Covenant and the Convention against Torture, it is worth noting the scope of the obligation it has undertaken regarding these two instruments. Egypt signed the International Covenant on Civil and Political Rights in 1967, ratifying it on 14 January 1982. Having become a party to ICCPR and the 1966 International Covenant on Economic, Social and Cultural Rights on the same day, it attached a Declaration, applicable to both covenants. That Declaration reads, '... Taking into consideration the provisions of the Islamic Sharia and the fact that they do not conflict with the text of annexed to the instrument, we accept, support and ratify it ...'[47]. As for the 1984 Convention against Torture and Other Cruel, Inhuman and Degrading Treatment and Punishment, Egypt acceded to it on 25 June 1986 without reservation[48]. While Egypt has *not* attached a reservation to the Convention, neither has it made a declaration to the effect that it accepts the competence of the Committee Against Torture (CAT) to receive communications from either States claiming that Egypt is not fulfilling its obligations under the Convention, or to receive petitions from individuals who claim their rights have been violated[49].

i. State of Emergency

Under Article 40, Egypt, like all States party to the ICCPR, has an obligation to 'submit reports on the measures [it has] adopted which give effect to the rights recognized' within the Covenant and 'on the progress made in the enjoyment of those rights'. Egypt has provided the Human Rights Committee with four

---

[45]   *Id.*, paras. 15 and 16.
[46]   Human Rights Committee, *Concluding Observations of the Human Rights Committee: Egypt*, Consideration of Reports submitted by States Parties under Article 40 of the Covenant: Comments of the Human Rights Committee, UN Doc. A/48/40, paras. 666–710, 9 August 1993, paras. 707 and 708.
[47]   See United Nations, *Multilateral Treaties Deposited with the Secretary-General* (status as of 30 April 1999), 1999, p. 128 for dates of signature and ratification; p. 131 for the referral to p. 118 which provides the Egyptian declaration *qua* reservation. Note that Egypt is not party to either the 1966 Optional Protocol International Covenant on Civil and Political Rights, or to the Second or Third Optional Protocols.
[48]   *Id.*, p. 201.
[49]   See Article 21 and 22, Convention against Torture and Other Cruel, Inhuman and Degrading Treatment and Punishment, 10 December 1984, in Brownlie, *op. cit.*, n. 11, pp. 45–48.

periodical reports, the last, though seven years late, was delivered in 2002[50]. In its previous report provided in 1991, the Members of the Committee noted that the 'state of emergency in Egypt seemed to be a permanent rather than an exceptional situation'; while the Committee as a whole stated that this 'constitutes one of the main difficulties impeding the full implementation of the Covenant'[51]. The Committee noted, with regret, in 1993, that Egypt had failed to notify 'the other State parties to the Covenant, through the Secretary-General, of the provisions from which it has derogated and of the reasons by which it was actuated, as specifically required by article 4, paragraph 3, of the Covenant'[52]. When questioned by the Committee Members, the Egyptian Representative noted that, despite the fact that, by 1991, the state of emergency had been in place for ten years, its non-compliance with Article 4(3) of the ICCPR, 'did not imply bad faith, but had been a mere omission'[53].

More recently, in its concluding observations regarding the 2002 report, the Human Rights Committee stated that it was 'disturbed by the fact that the state of emergency proclaimed by Egypt in 1981 is still in effect, meaning that the State party has been in a semi-permanent state of emergency ever since'. The Committee then called on Egypt to 'consider reviewing the need to maintain the state of emergency'[54]. Instead of having reconsidered its state of emergency, Egypt, one year later, sought to explain how such a review would transpire. In its comments to the observations of the Committee in November 2003, Egypt stated that the 'right of a State to declare a state of emergency [...] is a principle recognized in every legal system'[55]. It went on to acknowledge that, in 'accordance with the principle that a state of emergency is an exceptional circumstance that is not expected to last, since its very existence is dependent on the circumstances that necessitated its proclamation'. Egypt then described the circumstances which did necessitate the latest state of emergency:

In the circumstances that faced the country following the assassination of President Mohamed Anwar al-Sadat, Egypt was forced to declare a state of emergency, which was subsequently extended in order to deal with the phenomenon of terrorism and to protect the security and stability of society. Security efforts have largely succeeded in

[50] See Human Rights Committee, *Combined third and fourth periodic reports: Egypt. (State Party Report)*, UN Doc. CCPR/C/EGY/2001/3. 15 April 2002.
[51] Human Rights Committee, *Concluding Observations of the Human Rights Committee: Egypt*, Consideration of Reports submitted by States Parties under Article 40 of the Covenant: Comments of the Human Rights Committee, UN Doc. A/48/40, paras. 666–710, 9 August 1993, paras. 690 and 704.
[52] Egyptian combined third and fourth reports, *op. cit.*, n. 50, para. 704.
[53] *Id.*, para. 674.
[54] Human Rights Committee, *Concluding observations of the Human Rights Committee: Egypt*, UN Doc. CCPR/CO/76/EGY, 28 November 2002, para. 6.
[55] Human Rights Committee, *Comments by the Government of Egypt on the concluding observations of the Human Right Committee*, UN Doc. CCPR/CO/76/EGY/Add.1, 4 November 2003, para. 3.

eradicating the phenomenon of terrorism, in spite of its spread throughout all other parts of the world[56].

It then noted that under Egyptian law, any reconsideration of the status of the state of emergency depended on its Legislature, which will only give its 'approval for an extension, once it has been determined that the conditions for such an extension have been met, based on evidence resulting from discussions by the elected parliamentary assembly'[57]. Despite this assurance and the request of the Human Rights Committee that Egypt review the necessity of its state of emergency, Human Rights Watch reported, in February 2003, that the Egyptian parliament— the People's Assembly—had abruptly renewed the state of emergency so as to 'quash the growing campaign for the abolition of the law'[58]. The maintenance of perpetual states of emergency and human rights abuses have a direct relationship. Consideration now turns to the issue of torture in Egypt which the Committee considered 'to appear to display a systematic pattern'[59].

ii. Torture

The use of torture in Egypt is so pervasive that the individual charged with considering the issue within the United Nations system, the Special Rapporteur, Sir Nigel Rodley, concluded, in his 2001 report that torture in Egypt is 'habitual, widespread and deliberate'[60]. This determination is made against a backdrop of consistent and long-term monitoring by the Special Rapporteur, as well as the Committee against Torture, not to mention a plethora of reports by non-governmental human rights organizations. More than ten years ago, the Human Rights Committee expressed concern in its 1993 observations to Egypt's periodic report mandated by the ICCPR, that the conditions of detention in Egypt 'are likely to expose accused persons to torture and ill-treatment by police and security forces'[61]. In his 1996 report, the Special Rapporteur on issues of torture noted that he was 'dismayed that there appears to be no let-up in allegations suggesting a widespread, persistent incidence of torture. The observations he made in his previous report [...] regrettably remain fully applicable'[62].

In 1997, the Special Rapporteur 'advised the Government that he had received information indicating that torture of persons detained for political reasons

---

[56] *Id.*, para. 7.

[57] *Id.*, para. 8.

[58] Human Rights Watch, 'Egypt's Emergency without End", Press Release, 25 February 2003.

[59] Human Rights Committee, op. cit. n. 54, para. 13.

[60] See 2001 Report of the Special Rapporteur, Sir Nigel Rodley, *op. cit.*, n. 43, para. 476.

[61] *Id.*, para. 710.

[62] Commission on Human Rights, *Question of the Human Rights of All Persons subjected to any form of Detention or Imprisonment, in particular: Torture and other Cruel, Inhuman or Degrading Treatment or Punishment*, Report of the Special Rapporteur, Mr. Nigel S. Rodley, submitted pursuant to Commission on Human Rights resolution 1995/37, UN Doc. E/CN.4/1996/35, 9 January 1996, para. 63.

continued to take place on a systematic basis. In addition, the use of torture against persons detained in ordinary criminal cases was said to occur with frequency'[63]. At that time, Nigel Rodley went on to say that:

> he continued to receive information according to which conditions of a number of prisons were said to be extremely poor. On the whole, the prison system was said to be characterized by the use of torture and other ill-treatment as a means of discipline and punishment[64].

For instance, in 1997, Rodley transmitted to the Government his concern that some '100 prisoners at the high security prison in Cairo were reportedly subjected to collective punishment by flogging on 17 June 1996, after a watch had been discovered in one inmate's cell and part of a ball-point pen had been found in another cell. They were allegedly stripped and flogged with whips on their backs and feet'[65]. The Special Rapporteur's Final Report of 1997 outlined the following methods of torture reportedly taking place in Egypt, 'electronic shock, suspension by the wrists or ankles, burning the body with cigarettes, threats of rape or sexual abuse to the detainee or to female relatives in his presence'[66].

For its part, the Committee against Torture noted, in 1994, when considering Egypt's second periodic report mandated by the Convention against Torture that in 'light of a good deal of concordant and specific information received [...], the Committee is concerned about the fact that torture is apparently still widespread in Egypt'[67]. Building on the work of the Committee against Torture, Rodley noted, in his 25 January 2001 report that:

> In the light of the continuing failure of the Government to invite the Special Rapporteur to visit Egypt since he first requested such an invitation in 1996 and of its refusal even to grant access to the Committee against Torture when it conducted its 1991–1994 inquiry, the Special Rapporteur feels that he must make an assessment of the situation on the basis of information reaching him over the years.

---

[63] Commission on Human Rights, *Question of the Human Rights of All Persons subjected to any form of Detention or Imprisonment, in particular: Torture and other Cruel, Inhuman or Degrading Treatment or Punishment*, Report of the Special Rapporteur, Mr. Nigel S. Rodley, submitted pursuant to Commission on Human Rights resolution 1997/38, UN Doc. E/CN.4/1998/38, 24 December 1997, para. 87.

[64] *Id.*, para. 88.

[65] Commission on Human Rights, *Question of the Human Rights of All Persons subjected to any form of Detention or Imprisonment, in particular: Torture and other Cruel, Inhuman or Degrading Treatment or Punishment*, Report of the Special Rapporteur, Mr. Nigel S. Rodley, submitted pursuant to Commission on Human Rights resolution 1997/38; Addendum: Summary of cases transmitted to Government and replies received, UN Doc. E/CN.4/1998/38/Add.1, 24 December 1997.

[66] See 1997 Report of the Special Rapporteur, *op. cit.*, n. 63, para. 87.

[67] See General Assembly, *Report of the Committee against Torture*, UN. Doc. A/49/44, 12 June 1994, para. 86.

Regrettably, despite the passage of six years since the inquiry and four years since the adoption of the report of the Committee against Torture [...], the Special Rapporteur can find no better way to express that assessment than to use the language employed by the Committee [...] substituting reference to his own function for that of the Committee:

> ·The Special Rapporteur considers that the information received with regard to allegations of the systematic practice of torture in Egypt appears to be well founded. His conclusion is based on the existence of a great number of allegations, which come from different sources. These allegations largely coincide and describe in the same way the methods of torture, the places where torture is practised and the authorities who practise it. In addition, the information comes from sources that have proved to be reliable in connection with other activities of the Special Rapporteur.
>
> On the basis of this information, the Special Rapporteur is forced to conclude that torture is systematically practised by the security forces in Egypt, in particular by State Security Intelligence, since in spite of the denials of the Government, the allegations of torture submitted by reliable non-governmental organizations consistently indicate that reported cases of torture are seen to be habitual, widespread and deliberate in at least a considerable part of the country[68].

The information upon which this assessment has been made has come from a number of local and international human rights organizations including Amnesty International, which stated in its 2000 Annual Report that 'torture in police stations continued to be widespread'[69]. As a result of the relentless war against 'terrorism' which the Mubarak Administration had been undertaking, Amnesty International noted the 'decrease in arrests of alleged members of armed Islamist groups was reflected in a significant reduction in reports of systematic torture of political suspects'[70]. This, however, did not prevent Amnesty from publishing, in 2001, a report entitled: *Egypt: Torture Remains Rife as Cries for Justice Go Unheeded.* The Report notes that 'widespread torture and ill-treatment continue because the government refuses to acknowledge that torture persists and to take the basic steps necessary to eradicate torture in police stations, prisons and other detention centers'[71]. The Report goes on to note that 'torture and ill-treatment is endemic in

---

[68]   See 2001 Report of the Special Rapporteur, Sir Nigel Rodley, *op. cit.*, n. 43, para. 476. Note that in its 1999 Report, the Committee against Torture persisted in its alarm regarding torture, noting that it was a subject of concern that 'large number of allegations of torture and even death relating to detainees made against both the police and the State Security Intelligence'. See General Assembly, *Report of the Committee against Torture*, UN. Doc. A/54/44, 17 May 1999, para. 207.

[69]   See Amnesty International, *Amnesty International Report 2000 (Egypt)*, available on the internet at www.amnesty.org.

[70]   *Id.*

[71]   Amnesty International, *Egypt: Torture Remains Rife as Cries for Justice Go Unheeded*, MDE 12/001/2001, 28 February 2001, p. 2. Amnesty International backs its report, stating:

many detention centers throughout Egypt' and that the root cause of 'widespread torture and ill-treatment over the past two decades has been facilitated by prolonged incommunicado detention, the state's failure to investigate torture allegations, and the almost total impunity of the security forces responsible for these crimes'[72].

iii. Lack of Judicial Oversight

The link between perpetual states of emergency and torture appears as a result of the imbalance which is created by power being usurped by the executive organ at the expense of the judiciary, which, as a result, loses its ability to oversee the administration of the criminal system. As was noted by the Special Rapporteur on states of emergency, Mr. Leandro Despouy, in his final report, 'as a result of the growing sophistication and institutionalization of states of emergency, extensive powers have generally been exercised by those in charge of the executive branch'. He goes on to note that the:

> judiciary, whether *de facto* or *de jure*, lacks the authority to monitor the timeliness and legality of the introduction of the state of emergency (a power that is reserved for the political authorities), being equally powerless to oppose the specific measures affecting individual human rights, whether detentions, expulsions from the territory, relegation to or confinement in a particular part of the territory, etc.[73].

Mr. Despouy makes reference to a colleague who, having been asked by the Commission on Human Rights to report on issues of the independence of the judiciary, noted that the 'promulgation of decrees instituting a state of emergency often leads to [...] the establishment of special courts and the restriction or suspension of judicial review'. He concludes that, 'These irregularities ultimately bring about an actual institutional transformation, the main affect of which is to replace the concept of the separation and independence of powers with that of a hierarchy of powers, favouring the executive [...]'[74].

In a 1993 report, Human Rights Watch considered the 'major shift of policy' whereby Egyptian President Mubarak decreed his ability to refer civilians to be tried before military courts. As of October 1992, military courts started to try 'civilians accused of "terrorism" offences, bypassing the security-court system staffed by civilian judges that has been in place under Egypt's long-standing

---

Information gathered by Amnesty International over the past two decades as well as by other Egyptian and international human rights organizations through interviews with victims and their relatives, medical examinations and judgments by Egypt's own criminal and civil courts constitutes an irrefutable body of evidence of the entrenched nature of the pattern of torture in Egypt. Over the past decade Amnesty International has published numerous reports documenting torture in Egypt. Egyptian and other international human rights organizations have similarly documented the widespread practice of torture in Egypt. *Id.*

[72] *Id.*, p. 4.
[73] See Tenth Annual Report, *op. cit.*, n. 29, para. 147.
[74] *Id.*, para. 149.

emergency law'[75]. Human Rights Watch considers that such military trials of
civilians violates the right to equality before the law (Article 14(1) of the ICCPR)
'because civilians sentenced to death by military courts are not afforded the same
rights as civilians condemned to death by criminal courts'; and violate the right to
appeal to a higher tribunal according to law as found in Article 14(5), because 'the
verdicts and sentences of the three-judges [...] cannot be appealed to a higher
court', only to the President[76]. In its 1993 Report regarding the measures which
Egypt had undertaken regarding its obligations under the ICCPR, the Human
Rights Committee noted that 'under the Emergency Act, the President of the
Republic is entitled to refer cases to the State security courts, to ratify judgements
and to pardon. The President's role as both part of the executive and part of the
judiciary system is noted with concern by the Committee, notwithstanding that in
the matter of appeal it was explained that it would act only to reduce sentences. On
the other hand, military courts should not have the faculty to try cases which do not
refer to offences committed by members of the armed forces in the course of their
duties'[77].

While such referrals of civilians to military courts had subsided in the late
1990s, reappeared in late 2001, when President Mubarak referred '94 civilians
charged in connection with their alleged affiliation with armed Islamist groups' to
military courts, while some '170 other defendants are also due to appear before a
military court on similar charges following their referral by a presidential decree on
16 October 2001. Many of this group have reportedly been held for several years in
administrative detention'[78]. Amnesty International went on to state that:

> Trials before these military courts violate fundamental requirements of international
> law for fair trial, including the right to be tried before a competent, independent and
> impartial court established by law and the right to appeal to a higher court[79].

In 1997, the UN Special Rapporteur on issues of extrajudicial, summary, or
arbitrary execution, Mr. Bacre Waly Ndiaye, reiterated 'his concern that civilians
continue to be tried before military courts whose procedures fall short of
international fair trial standards, particularly since these courts cannot be
considered impartial and independent and the defendants have no right to appeal
sentences. The Special Rapporteur call[ed] upon the Government of Egypt to bring

[75] Human Rights Watch, *Egypt: Trials of Civilians in Military Courts violate
International Law*, Vol. 5, 1993, p. 1, available at www.hrw.org/mideast/index.php.
[76] *Id.* Note generally Michael Farhang, 'Terrorism and Military Trials in Egypt:
Presidential Decree No. 375 and the Consequences For Judicial Authority', *Harvard
International Law Journal*, Vol. 35, 1994, pp. 225–237.
[77] See 1993 Human Rights Committee Report, *op. cit.*, n. 46, para. 706.
[78] See Amnesty International, *Egypt: Trials of Civilians before Military Courts violate
Human Rights Standard*, MDE 12/032/2001, 19 November 2001, available on the internet at
www.amnesty.org.
[79] *Id.*

its laws into conformity with the International Covenant on Civil and Political Rights'[80].

The imbalance created by concentration of power in the executive branch in Egypt for which the use of military trials as against civilians is only the most obvious manifestation of the disregard by the Mubarak Administration for the rule of law. Although caught up in an undeclared civil war against the Muslim Brotherhood, during the 1990s, Human Rights Watch rightly pointed out that acts of 'murder and attempted murder committed by armed opposition groups' do not give the Egyptian State 'a license to abandon the human rights standards that it has pledged to uphold under Egyptian and international law'[81]. Human Rights Watch continues:

> In disregard of these standards, Egyptian security forces, particularly State Security Investigation (SSI), the internal-security apparatus attached to the Ministry of Interior, have been permitted to operate in a lawless manner. Human rights abuses by these forces include arbitrary arrest, incommunicado detention, and torture of suspects during interrogation[82].

This lawlessness by the Egyptian security apparatus has been manifest in what Human Rights Watch has called a 'particularly reprehensible security force practice: the detention and intimidation of innocent family members [...] in order to pressure fugitive relatives to surrender'[83]. Beyond this, political prisoners have been detained, without charge or, worse still, following acquittal. In its 2001 report on torture in Egypt, Amnesty International stated that:

> Thousands of alleged members or members of armed Islamist groups have been detained, often for years without charge or trial, or following acquittal, under provisions of the emergency legislation. It is estimated that today, several thousand political detainees, including possible prisoners of conscience, remain in administrative detention under Article 3 of the emergency legislation despite having been issued release orders by the courts. Administrative detention is ordered by the executive branch of a government without a judicial warrant, without the filing of any criminal charges, and without the intention of bringing the detainee to trial[84].

Administrative detention, as mentioned, can transpire by virtue of the 1958 Emergency Law, which provides, at Article 3, that the Minister of the Interior can

---

[80] See Commission on Human Rights, *Question of the Violation of Human Rights and Fundamental Freedoms in any part of the World, with Particular Reference to Colonial and other Dependent Countries and Territories: Extrajudicial, Summary or Arbitrary Executions*, Report of the Special Rapporteur, Mr. Bacre Waly Ndiaye, submitted pursuant to Commission on Human Rights Resolution 1997/61, Addendum: Country Situation, UN Doc. E/CN.4/1998/68/Add.1, 19 December 1997, paras. 152–153.

[81] Human Rights Watch, *Egypt: Hostage-Taking and Intimidation by Security Forces*, Vol. 7, 1995, p. 1, available at www.hrw.org/mideast/index.php.

[82] *Id.*

[83] *Id.*

[84] Amnesty International, *Egypt: Torture Remains Rife, op. cit.*, n. 71, p. 26.

order the arrest and detention *without charge or trial* of 'suspected persons or those who endanger public order or security'[85]. In its 2000 Annual Report, Amnesty International reported that 'hardly any new cases of administrative detention under emergency legislation were reported'. 'However', it noted 'thousands of suspected members or supporters of banned Islamist groups arrested in previous years [...] remained administratively detained without charge or trial. Some had been held for more than a decade. Others were acquitted by military or (Emergency) Supreme State Security Courts, but remain in detention'[86].

Much in the same manner that the perpetuation of the state of emergency has allowed the Mubarak Administration to maintain power and to violate human rights with impunity, consideration will now turn to the Syrian State which has followed a parallel course in suppressing internal dissent. The establishment of a state security apparatus under the state of emergency in Syria has also allowed for systematic violations of the non-derogable rights enshrined in Article 4(2) of the ICCPR with impunity. While the lack of judicial supervision developed in Syria under the perpetual state of emergency in force since 1963 has allowed for systematic violations to the rights of detainees, political prisoners, as in Egypt, have been targets of systematic violations of human rights including torture. While Egypt's violations of the prohibition against torture as a non-derogable right under the ICCPR and its obligation under the Convention against Torture remains rife; in the Syrian context, consideration will go beyond violations of Article 7, to also consider violation of Article 6—the right to life—as it relates to extrajudicial killings. As we shall see, during the administration of former President Hafez Asad, what was required before the state of emergency apparatus could become fully operational, was the removal of the opposition by all means at his disposal.

III. Syria: Human Rights under a Perpetual State of Emergency

The Syrian Arab Republic, like most States of the Middle East, is the creation of European Powers as a result of their triumph over the Ottoman Empire during the First World War. Much in line with the Sykes-Picot Agreement of 1916—as part of the parcelling out of the spoils of victory which transpired at San Remo in 1920—Great Britain received its Mandate for Palestine in exchange for France receiving the Mandate for Syria and the Lebanon[87]. While Lebanon was detached from the Mandate with Syria in 1926, Syria, proper, gained independence in 1946. Led by the Baath, a pan-Arabist political party, Syria joined with Egypt in 1958 to form the United Arab Republic (UAR). The UAR, a result of Egyptian President

---

[85]   Article 3, Emergency Law Number 162 of 1958. Translation provided by the Author.

[86]   See Amnesty International, *Amnesty International Report 2000 (Egypt)*, available at www.amnesty.org.

[87]   See Daniel Pipes, *Greater Syria: The History of an Ambition*, 1990, p. 28. Pipes notes that the 'laconic [Sykes-Picot] agreement merely stated that 'the mandates chosen by the principles Allied Powers are: France for Syria, and Great Britain for Mesopotamia and Palestine.', see p. 28, n. 70.

Gamal Abdel Nasser's growth in popularity in the wake of the Suez War of 1956, would only survive until 1961, when Syria ceded from the Union. One of Nasser's requirements for having established the Union was that Syrian political parties would dissolve themselves; as such, the Baath Party officially closed shop. Although the Baath Party lost ground with Syria's general public as a result of the 'UAR débâcle', the members from minority groups—primarily the Alawis— 'remained faithful and kept the party structure intact when the formal apparatus had disappeared'[88]. Constituting between ten and fifteen percent of the population and concentrated near the Mediterranean, between Lebanon and Turkey, the Alawis, a derivative of Shiite Islam[89], were instrumental in the ability of the Baath Party to rise to power after the demise of the UAR, through its instigation of a *coup d'état* in March 1963. The Alawis found themselves not only controlling the Baath Party, but came to dominate the armed forces slowly, from 1948 onward, as a failed *coup d'état* by Sunni officers led to purges and counter-purges of their military ranks.

It was only in 1970, as a result of political machinations revolving around the *Black September* operations in Jordan meant to rid itself of the Palestinian Liberation Organization, that power in Syria was consolidated by a Alawi military leader, Hafez Asad. President Asad would rule Syria for thirty years before his death in June 2001, only to be replaced by his son, Bashar Asad, in a referendum a month later. Although emergency legislation had been passed in 1962, it came into effect as a result of Legislative Decree No.1 of 9 March 1963, issued when the Alawis took control of the Syrian State apparatus. Since then, for nearly forty years, Syria has lived under what the UN Human Rights Committee has termed a 'quasi-permanent state of emergency'[90]. It, like Egypt, is in *prima facie* violation of its obligations under Article 4 of the International Covenant on Civil and Political Rights due to the perpetual nature of its state of emergency. Further, much like Egypt, Syria has been in flagrant violation of obligations to respect the non-derogable rights of Article 4, such as those regarding the right to life found at Article 6 of the ICCPR. With this in mind, the Human Rights Committee noted that it was 'deeply concerned about allegations of extrajudicial executions and disappearances'[91]. Beyond the violations of the right to life, the UN Special Rapporteur dealing with torture, Sir Nigel Rodley, noted in 1996, that he had received 'information indicating that torture of persons detained for political reasons in the country was systematic'[92], in violation of Article 7 of the ICCPR.

---

[88] *Id.*, p. 156.
[89] The term 'Alawis' was imposed by the French during the Mandate on the Nusayris or Ansaris. Pipes writes that the 'Alawi doctrines date from the ninth century A.D. and derive from the Twelver or Imami branch of Shi'i theology' but notes that 'by almost any standard they must be considered non-Muslims.', *id.*, p. 159.
[90] See the 2001 Human Rights Committee Report, *op. cit.*, n. 50, para. 81(2).
[91] *Id.*, para. 81(10).
[92] Commission on Human Rights, *Question of the Human Rights of All Persons subjected to any form of Detention or Imprisonment, in particular: Torture and other Cruel, Inhuman or Degrading Treatment or Punishment*, Report of the Special Rapporteur, Mr. Nigel S. Rodley, submitted pursuant to Commission on Human Rights resolution 1995/37;

Before turning to consider the perpetual nature of the state of emergency in Syria, it is worth noting that while Syria is a party to the International Covenant on Civil and Political Rights, having acceded to it on 21 April 1969[93], it is not a party to the 1984 Convention against Torture.

i. State of Emergency

When the Human Rights Committee considered Syria's second periodic report, in 2001, regarding its adherence to the ICCPR, the Committee welcomed the 'opportunity to resume the dialogue with the State party *after an interval of 24 years*'[94]. The Committee, in its introduction went on to say:

> It regrets the considerable delay in submitting the report, which was due in 1984, and the lack of information on the human rights situation in actual fact, which makes it

---

Addendum: Summary of communications transmitted to the Government and replies received, UN Doc. E/CN.4/1996/35/Add.1, 16 January 1996, para. 663.

[93] Note that Syria did make a reservation to the ICCPR which reads as follows:

> 1. The accession of the Syrian Arab Republic to these two Covenants shall in no way signify recognition of Israel or entry into a relationship with it regarding any matter regulated by the said two Covenants.

> 2. The Syrian Arab Republic considers that paragraph 1 of article 26 of the Covenant on Economic, Social and Cultural Rights and paragraph 1 of article 48 of the Covenant on Civil and Political Rights are incompatible with the purpose and objectives of the said Covenants, inasmuch as they do not allow all States, without distinction or discrimination, the opportunity to become parties to the said Covenants.

See United Nations, *Multilateral Treaties Deposited with the Secretary-General* (status as of 30 Apr. 1999), 1999, p. 128, for dates of signature and ratification; p. 136 for the referral to p. 121 where the Syrian reservation is found. Note that Syria, like Egypt, is not party to any of the protocols to the Covenant on Civil and Political Rights.

Attached to the Syrian Reservation is a footnote that indicates that Israel, having received notification of provisions like those made in sub-section 1 in reservations from Iraq and Libya as well, noted that in its view 'the two Covenants are not the proper place for making such political pronouncements. The Government of Israel will, in so far as concerns the substance of the matter, adopt towards the Government of [Syria] an attitude of complete reciprocity'. Israel went on to say that the declaration concerned 'cannot in any way affect the obligations of the [Syrian Arab Republic] already existing under general international law'. See United Nations, *Multilateral Treaties Deposited with the Secretary-General* (status as of 30 April 1999), 1999, p. 126.

As for sub-section 2, the reservation, Syria sought to point to the awkwardness of Articles 26 of the ICCPR and Article 48 of the ICESCR as these provisions meant that only Members of the United Nations could become party to the Covenants, while the preamble of both spoke of the 'equal and inalienable rights of all members of the human family.', see Brownlie, *op. cit.*, n. 11.

[94] See the 2001 Human Rights Committee Report, *op. cit.*, n. 50, para. 81(2). Emphasis added.

difficult for the Committee to determine whether the State party's population is able fully and effectively to exercise its fundamental rights under the Covenant[95].

The Committee expressed its concern that the 'state of emergency has remained in force ever since [9 March 1963], placing the territory of the Syrian Arab Republic under a quasi-permanent state of emergency, thereby jeopardizing the guarantees of article 4 of the Covenant'[96]. The basis upon which the state of emergency was invoked in Syria in 1963 is Legislative Decree Number 51 of 22 December 1962 which provides under Article 1, *inter alia*, that:

> a) State of Emergency may be declared in wartime or in the event of a war-threatening condition or in the event that security or public order in the territories of the Republic or in part thereof is subjected to danger because of internal riots or public disasters.

Upon such a declaration, a military governor is to be appointed by the Prime Minister and may, by virtue of Article 4, 'issue written directives' to take the following steps, which may include referral to military courts: restrictions on freedom of movement, speech, assembly, and detainee individuals; the monitoring of mail, telephones and the press; establish curfews; and limit firearms through licensing[97].

As the Human Rights Committee noted in its General Comment 29, while such states of emergency may be invoked, the 'restoration of a state of normalcy where full respect for the Covenant can again be secured must be the predominant objective of a State party derogating from the Covenant'[98]. With this in mind, the Committee, in its final observations of 5 April 2001 regarding Syria's second periodical Report, noted that the information regarding 'the conditions for proclaiming a state of emergency is still not sufficiently precise'[99]. The Committee questioned the validity of the proclamation of a state of emergency as Syria, in its Report, noted that since 1948, it has been subjected,

> like other neighbouring Arab States, to a real threat of war by Israel and, on many occasions, this threat of war has culminated in actual aggression against the territory, territorial waters and air space of the Syrian Arab Republic, particularly in 1967 when Israel seized part of the territory of the Syrian Arab Republic, which it is still occupying, and expelled a large portion of the population[100].

---

[95] *Id.*

[96] *Id.*, para. 81(6).

[97] See Emergency Law, Legislative Decree Number 15, 22 December 1962 as found on the Syrian Committee of Human Rights website at: http://www.shrc.org/english/reports/2001/repressive_laws/10.htm.

[98] See General Comment 29, *op. cit.*, n. 17, para. 1.

[99] See the 2001 Human Rights Committee Report, *op. cit.*, n. 53, para. 81(7).

[100] Human Rights Committee, *Consideration of Reports submitted by States Parties under Article 40 of the Covenant: Second periodic report States Parties due in 1984: Syrian Arab Republic*, UN Doc. CCPR/C/SYR/2000/2, 25 August 2000, para. 49.

The state of emergency, however, did not come into effect in 1948, but as a product of the *coup d'état* which witnessed the Alawis' ascent to power in 1963.

While General Comment 29 notes that a fundamental condition required for invoking the derogation provisions of Article 4 is that the 'situation must amount to a public emergency which threatens the life of the nation'[101], the Syrian Report argues that this is, in fact, the situation. 'This state of affairs' the Report reads, referring to the threat posed by Israel:

> consisting in a real threat of war [...] gave rise to an exceptional situation that
> necessitated the rapid and extraordinary mobilization of forces [...] and, consequently,
> the promulgation of legislation to ensure the Administration's ability to act rapidly in
> the face of these imminent threats when application of the ordinary legislation cannot
> guarantee rapid action in such circumstances. Accordingly, there was a need to
> promulgate this Act and maintain it in force[102].

Clearly, the need to institute the state of emergency in 1963 had more to do with an attempt to consolidate power within Syria than the 'real threat of war' posed, at that time, by Israel. It will become plain, when consideration turns shortly to human rights violations in Syria, that the threat which is sought to be diminished by the evocation of a state of emergency is not external and does not threaten the nation; instead, it is internal and threatens the governing administrations: both the Asad dynasty and the privileged position of the Alawis minority. In its dialogue with the Human Rights Committee, the Syrian Representative sought to de-emphasis the state of emergency informing the UN Human Rights Committee that the 'state of emergency is rarely put into effect [sic]'. Despite this, the Committee recommended that 'it be formally lifted as soon as possible'[103]. To that end, the Committee stated that Syria 'should indicate within one year [...] the measures it has taken or envisages to take to lift the state of emergency'[104].

ii. Extra-Judicial Killings

It may be said that the reason why the state of emergency legislation is rarely invoked today, is because the challengers to the Asad dynasty are either languishing in jail, or are dead. In a generally positive biography of Hafez Asad written in 1988, Partick Seale noted that:

> The regime which Asad had intended to be humane was brutalized. Habits of arbitrary
> rule acquired in the struggle for survival proved addictive, the relatively liberal
> atmosphere of the beginning of his presidency could not easily flourish again in the
> shadow of the powerful instruments of repression which had grown up.
>   Asad did not revel in killing, but resorted to it only for *raison d'état* [...].
> Unleashing Special Forces on whole communities, using tank fire against residential

---

[101] See General Comment 29, *op. cit.*, n. 17, para. 2.
[102] See the 2001 Human Rights Committee Report, *op. cit.*, n. 50, para. 81(6).
[103] *Id.*
[104] *Id.*, para. 81(29).

quarters, slaughtering prisoners, arming civilian supporters, shooting suspects or, what was scarcely better, hauling them in batches before field courts—this slide into brutality swept aside any semblance of due process of law[105].

Indeed, the 1980s saw wholesale massacres perpetuated by the Syrian State in response to terrorist attacks against the ruling elite and the Alawis minority. As Partick Seale points out, these 'acts of terror did not erupt in a vacuum': the former merchant class had been disposed and the new leadership 'began to amass considerable wealth' as 'Alawi fortunes resulting from the community's political ascent' started to become evident[106]. Seale continues by stating that by the mid-1970s for 'the first time since the Baath takeover in 1963, Asad and the ruling group of officers and party functionaries, overwhelmingly from country and small-town backgrounds, stood on a foundation of real wealth'[107]. The resulting change in the social order brought with it a 'groundswell of complaints about corruption and unfairness', further, the 'have-nots were beginning to stir' as, for instance, the cost of a flat had, between 1970 and 1977 increased by a factor of eight[108]. That stirring was manifest not only in protest but violent attacks against the new ruling class.

As Seale explains, 'the authorities identified the terrorists as 'the Muslim Brothers',

> a blanket phrase they were to use throughout the five-year crisis to describe the Muslim or Muslim-spearheaded opposition which manifested itself in a variety of guerrilla groups with different leaders and histories and operating in different parts of Syria. The movement of dissent was wider than the guerrillas, but they were the sharp end of the grave internal challenge Asad faced from 1977 to 1982[109].

Open defiance by opposition groups in the northern cities of Aleppo, Hama, and Homs challenged the Administration. In the wake of the murder of thirty-two Alawis officer cadets at the Aleppo Artillery School in 1979, it was decided that President Asad's younger brother Rifat would lead a 'drive to wage all-out war against the terrorists'. Rifat Asad professed his willingness to fight 'a hundred wars, demolish a million strongholds, and sacrifice a million martyrs'. 'It was not', as Patrick Seale would write, 'a programme inviting restraint'[110]. When, on 26 June 1980, President Asad narrowly escaped an assassination attempt, the gloves were removed. In less than 24 hours, military units were flown by helicopter to Tadmur Prison where many Islamist and Muslim Brothers were being held. The Middle East component of Human Rights Watch reported that between 600-1100 prisoners were murdered while in their prison cells by the Syrian army, in what a London-

---

[105]   See Patick Seale, *Asad: The Struggle for the Middle East*, 1988, p. 338.
[106]   *Id.*, pp. 317 and 319.
[107]   *Id.*, p. 320.
[108]   *Id.*
[109]   *Id.*, pp. 321–322.
[110]   *Id.*, p. 327.

based, Syrian human rights organization called the 'Tadmur Jail Slaughter'[111]. Less than a month later, on 7 July 1980, the Syrian National Assembly passed a law, making membership of the Muslim Brotherhood—which had already been outlawed—punishable by death[112].

'Asad's long war with the Islamic underground was approaching its *dénouement*. In the autumn of 1980 his enemies regrouped' as an 'Islamic Front' which 'promised free speech, free elections, an independent judiciary, land reform, and much else, under the banner of Islam'[113]. The war unravelled for the Islamists in the wake of the Syrian government attacks against the city of Hama in 1981 and especially in 1982. In 1981, as a result of an ambush at a 'security checkpoint near the Alawis village on the outskirts of Hama [...] Special Forces and the 47th Brigade moved into the city and began house-to-house searches'. Middle East Watch, in its book entitled *Syria Unmasked: The Suppression of Human Rights by the Asad Regime*, continued, 'security forces dragged men out of their homes and shot them in the street without even an identify check [...], they killed at least 350 people'[114]. However, as horrifying as these events may seem, its was deemed a 'minor slaughter' by a Syrian human rights organization, when considered against what transpired in 1982[115].

Hama, the fourth largest city in Syria with a population of over 200,000 people was the locus of the last stand of the Islamic Front and the end to open warfare in Syria between the Government and opposition groups—but at what cost. Middle East Watch notes that sometime 'in late January 1982, the administration decided to end Hama's intransigent opposition'[116]. As a brigade of commandos entered the city, in early February, to round up the opposition, the Islamists decided they would make their stand. Middle East Watch explained what transpired in the following terms:

> For two days fighting raged as security forces could not penetrate the old city. Then, on the third day, government forces gained the initiative as some of the toughest and most reliable military units—Defense Brigades, Special Forces, unites of Shafiq Fayadh's 3rd Armored Division, as well as the 47th Armored Brigade—joined the battle. Commandos seasoned by the battlefields of Lebanon blasted the city with helicopter-launched bombs and rockets, artillery, and tank fire. [... Fewer] than a thousand rebels held out against more than thirty thousand troops.
>
> Hama now endured a fierce collective punishment. For three days, security forces killed hundreds of people in a series of mass executions near the municipal stadium and at other sites. [...] Army sappers blew up many of the buildings that still stood, sometimes with tens of people inside.

---

[111] See Middle East Watch, *Syria Unmasked: The Suppression of Human Rights by the Asad Regime*, 1991, pp. 15–16; and Syrian Human Rights Committee, *Report of the Human Rights Situation in Syria over a 20-Year Period: 1979–1999*, 2001, pp. 17–37.
[112] Middle East Watch, *id.*, p. 16.
[113] See Patick Seale, *op. cit.*, n. 105, p. 331.
[114] Middle East Watch, *op. cit.*, n. 111, p. 18.
[115] See Syrian Human Rights Committee, *op. cit.*, n. 111, pp. 37–46.
[116] Middle East Watch, *op. cit.*, n. 111, p. 19.

[…] Estimates of the number killed vary widely, but the most credible analysts put the number at between five and ten thousand people. Many, many thousands more were injured. With a third or more of the city's housing completely destroyed, between sixty and seventy thousand were left homeless[117].

While the massacre transpired, 'pictures of Hama were shown throughout Syria as an object lesson for Asad's other enemies'[118]. Although this would be the last major offensive against Islamists by the Syrian military, extrajudicial killings persist to this day, though on a more minor scale than visited upon Hama. The UN Human Rights Committee in its 2001 Report noted, with respect to Syria, that it was 'deeply concerned about the allegations of extrajudicial executions and disappearances' and as such called on Syria to establish an independent commission of inquiry to look into these allegations[119].

iii. Torture

The Human Rights Committee having expressed itself on extrajudicial killings; turned to the issue of torture and the violation of the non-derogable Article 7 of the International Covenant, and noted:

> The Committee is deeply concerned about the constant and duly substantiated allegations of violations of Article 7 of the Convention, to which the delegation did not respond, which are attributed to law enforcement personnel. It notes with concern the many allegations that torture is practiced in Syrian prisons, particularly Tadmur military prison[120].

In 2001, Amnesty International reported that 'the level of brutality endured by prisoners in Tadmur Prison is shocking. It is hard to believe that the kind of torture and ill-treatment described in this report is still taking place today'[121]. Since the invocation of the state of emergency 'tens of thousand of people have been rounded up in successive waves of mass arrests targeted at suspected members of left-wing, Islamist or Arab nationalist organizations […] or at anyone engaged in activities opposed to the government and its policies'[122]. These individuals, more often than not were taken to Tadmur Prison which, according to Amnesty International,

> appears to have been designed to inflict the maximum suffering, humiliation and fear on prisoners and to keep them under the strict control by breaking their spirit. Prisoners

---

[117] *Id.*, p. 20. It should be noted that in Middle East Watch acknowledge that before the events of 1982, 'Hama was Syria's most beautiful city. Some say it was the most lovely city in the Middle East.', p. 19.
[118] See Daniel Pipes, *op. cit.*, n. 87, p. 183.
[119] See the 2001 Human Rights Committee Report, *op. cit.*, n. 53, para. 81(10)
[120] *Id.*, para. 81(12).
[121] See Amnesty International, *Syria: Torture, despair and dehumanization in Tadmur Military Prison*, 19 September 2001, MDE 24/014/2001, p. 1.
[122] *Id.*, p. 2.

are not only completely isolated from the outside world, they are also prevented from communicating with each other. Every aspect of life in Tadmur Prison is a dehumanizing experience[123].

Amnesty International voiced concerns similar to those noted earlier by the UN Special Rapporteur dealing with torture, whereby Sir Nigel Rodley reported, in 1996, that 'he had received information indicating that torture of persons detained for political reasons in the country was systematic'[124]. The Special Rapporteur, went on to say:

Emergency legislation brought into force in 1963 allowed for the preventive detention of persons suspected of endangering public security and order. These powers were said to be exercised outside any judicial control by a number of security branches, most often by *al-Amn al-Siyassi* (Political Security) and *al-Mukhabarat al-'Askariyya* (Military Intelligence).

The Special Rapporteur noted that when these people were brought before the Supreme Security Court, which deals with 'political and security cases', the defendants

reportedly stated in court that they had been tortured. None of these persons, however, was known to have been medically examined and no investigations into their allegations were known to have been carried out.

Torture is allegedly practiced to extract information or 'confessions' and as a form of punishment. The methods of torture reported include: *falaqa* (beating on the soles of the feet); *dullab* (tyre), whereby the victim is hung from a suspended tyre and beaten with sticks and cables; pouring cold water over the victim's body; and *al-Kursi al-Almani* (the German Chair), consisting of bending a metal chair on which the victim is seated so as to cause extension of the spine, severe pressure on the neck and limbs, respiratory difficulties, loss of consciousness and possible fracturing of the vertebrae[125].

Taking the lead of the 1996 Report of the Special Rapporteur, Amnesty International noted, in 2001, that it 'remains concerned that the mechanisms, provided for under the Emergency Legislation of 1963, which facilitate human rights violations, remain intact'. 'As a result', Amnesty International went on to say, 'any member or suspected member of an opposition group risks arrest, detention, and torture'[126]. Although Amnesty reports that since 1991, Government amnesties have reduced the number of political prisoners from several thousand to several hundreds, it was still concerned that:

---

[123] *Id.*

[124] Commission on Human Rights, *Question of the Human Rights of All Persons subjected to any form of Detention or Imprisonment, in particular: Torture and other Cruel, Inhuman or Degrading Treatment or Punishment*, Report of the Special Rapporteur, Mr. Nigel S. Rodley, submitted pursuant to Commission on Human Rights resolution 1995/37; Addendum: Summary of communications transmitted to the Government and replies received, UN Doc. E/CN.4/1996/35/Add.1, 16 January 1996, para. 663.

[125] *Id.*, paras. 663–665.

[126] See Amnesty International, *op. cit.*, n. 121, p. 3.

thus far, no steps have been taken by the authorities to provide redress for past and continuing human rights violations; there have been no investigations into 'disappearances', extrajudicial executions, or torture and ill-treatment, including deaths in custody. Despite numerous allegations of torture, some of which were made in court by the victims themselves, no proper investigations appear to have been carried out by the Syrian authorities. Although the bulk of these violations took place in the 1980s and early 1990s, their impact continues to be felt by the victims and their families and friends[127].

In its Annual Country Report on Syria in 2000, Amnesty noted that there were 'fewer reports of torture during 2000, but the system allowing for its application remained intact'. It then continued, stating that 'torture and ill-treatment of political detainees continued to be systematically applied in Tadmur Prison and other detention centers'[128]. Amnesty goes on to provide an example of the torture endured in Syria, 'one prisoner, held incommunicado for seven days in December in *lieu of his exiled relative*, was reported to have been tortured by the method known as *dullab*, beating with sticks and cables while hanging from a suspended tyre'[129].

iv. Lack of Judicial Oversight

Much in the same manner that human rights NGOs and UN human rights monitors have expressed their concern about Syrian violations of Article 7, they have also considered issues centred around the rights of individuals detained. It should be emphasised here that in General Comment 29, the UN Human Rights Committee noted that it 'is inherent in the protection of rights explicitly recognized as non-derogable' that they be assured, often times by 'judicial guarantees'[130]. When such guarantees are not available to an individual detainee, it is a recipe for violations, abuse, ill-treatment, and the type of immunity that breeds torture. Some years ago, for instance, the International Federation of Human Rights sought to draw the attention of the UN Commission on Human Rights to the fact that, in Syria, 1994 marked the 'twenty-fifth anniversary of the arrest of Mr. Ahmad Swaidani and the twenty-fourth year of detention of 11 other political prisoners, all of whom are currently detained without trial under the state of emergency'[131]. Such a flagrant abuse of power was been made possible in Syria by recourse to the Legislative Decree of 1962 which allows, during a state of emergency, for a Military Governor

---

[127] *Id.*
[128] See Amnesty International, *Amnesty International Report 2000 (Syria)*, available on the internet at www.amnesty.org.
[129] *Id.* Emphasis added.
[130] See General Comment 29, *op. cit.*, n. 17, para. 15.
[131] See Commission on Human Rights, *Question of the Human Rights of all Persons subjected to any Form of Detention or Imprisonment: Written Statement submitted by the International Federation of Human Rights, a non-governmental organization in consultative status (category II)*, UN Doc. E/CN.4/1994/NGO/25, 8 February 1994, para. 1.

to be appointed by the Prime Minister, who may, by virtue of Article 4(a), take the following action:

> Impose restrictions on the freedom of persons in terms of holding meetings, residence, transport, movements, and *detaining suspects* or people threatening public security and order on a temporary basis, authorizing the conducting of investigations related to both persons and places at any time, and requesting any person to perform any task[132].

In his 1996 Report, the Special Rapporteur on the issue of torture noted that 'persons arrested by the security branches were said usually to be held incommunicado, without access to lawyers, medical doctors, relatives, or the courts. [...] Incommunicado detention was reported to occur for lengths ranging from a few weeks to years'. The Special Rapporteur further noted that the courts established to deal with these individuals—the State Security Courts—'reportedly lack independence from the executive branch. It is accountable only to the Minister of the Interior and does not have the power to supervise the activities of the security forces with respect to the treatment of detainees'[133]. The result of the fact that these forces are immune from the Syrian constitutional order means that they may act with impunity. 'Under the state of emergency' Amnesty International reports 'different branches of the security forces have been able to arbitrarily detain political suspects at will for as long as they please'[134]. As a result of this extra-constitutional framework of 'justice' established by the security forces, persons 'detained have frequently been tortured while held in total isolation from the outside world for months or years without charge or trial'[135].

In its 2001 Report, the UN Human Rights Committee considered the report prepared by Syria regarding the measures it has taken to give effect to the rights recognised in the ICCPR. It expressed its concern 'about the number of people held in pre-trial detention'. It went on to say that hundreds 'of people have reportedly been arrested and detained without an arrest warrant or indictment, only to be released without judicial procedures having been initiated and, in many cases, after many years in detention'[136]. Despite its diplomatic language, the Committee was most taken aback by the State Security Courts, whose procedures it considers 'incompatible with [certain] provisions of Article 14'[137]. The Committee was critical of Syria *vis-à-vis* its State Security Courts with reference to: Article 14(1) related to individuals being 'entitled to a fair and public hearing by a competent, independent and impartial tribunal established by law'; Article 14(3) setting out the rights of the accused; and Article 14(5) establishing a right to an appeal 'by a higher tribunal according to law'. The lack of judicial oversight allowed for by the state of emergency and reflected in the procedures of the State Security Courts has allowed Syrian security forces to perpetuate the type of systematic torture and

---

132 See Emergency Law, *op. cit.*, n. 97. Emphasis added.
133 Report of the Special Rapporteur, *op. cit.*, n. 63, paras. 663–665.
134 See Amnesty International, *op. cit.*, n. 121, p. 2.
135 See Amnesty International, *op. cit.*, n. 121, p. 2.
136 See the 2001 Human Rights Committee Report, *op. cit.*, n. 50, para. 81(14).
137 *Id.*, para. 81(16).

extrajudicial killings as a means of ensuring the 'stability' of President Asad's administration and its Alawis ruling class.

IV. Conclusion

Perpetual states of emergency have transpired in Egypt and Syria to ensure the *status quo* of the governing administrations of Mubarak and Asad. These rulers, like others in the region, understand the qualitatively different manner of the applicability of international law in the Middle East. Despite having subscribed to human rights treaties, both Egypt and Syria have witnessed a mutation of their domestic order that allows for violation of non-derogable rights as State policy. In much the same manner as Western States have allowed their interests to trump international law in the region, leaders in the Middle East, such as Mubarak and Asad, have not seen human rights obligations as an encumbrance to consolidating and maintaining their rule. Having stifled peaceful means of dissent, both Egypt and Syria were faced with an armed insurrection seeking to topple their unrepresentative leaders. Both administrations acted in similar manners, although Hafez Asad turned to mass murder before he could effectively consolidate his powerbase. In both Egypt and Syria, torture remains a live State policy in prisons, while the lack of judicial oversight of the executive organ means that the security apparatuses are working outside a legal framework—effectively outlaws. This chapter clearly demonstrates that the malaise of the Middle East is not solely the result of outside actors who have treated those in the region as an underclass of the international society, but also results from leaders who have internalised the qualitative exceptionalism of international law.

Chapter 8

A Stream Apart:
Peaceful Settlements in the Middle East

As the preceding chapters have shown, the qualitatively different manner in which international law has been applied has left the region the locus of conflict. The use of State violence as either a means of external aggression or internal control has been a hallmark of the Middle East. Yet, despite the bloodshed which has been characteristic of the evolution of the modern Middle East, there exists the peaceful settlement of international disputes running parallel to the formative events of Middle Eastern history. Thus, until Middle East States gained their independence, cases of judicial settlement or arbitration which transpired regarding the region took place within the context of European colonialism and were the purview of colonial States. For example, in 1904, the Permanent Court of Arbitration dealt with the issue of slavery as it pertained to the ships of the sultan of present-day Oman in the *Muscat Dhows* case, a dispute between France and Great Britain. In the same vein, the Permanent Court of Justice dealt with the *Mavrommatis* cases in the 1920s, regarding the revoking of concessions in Palestine between Greece, the State invoking diplomatic protection of one of its nationals, and Great Britain, the mandatory power. As Middle East States rid themselves of the yoke of colonialism, dispute settlement by legal means went through a transition phase whereby cases often involved the former colonial master and the newly independent State. Since the end of this period, Middle East States have quietly been using judicial settlement and arbitration as a tool of statecraft. Examples of such intra-Middle East cases include the 1989 *Taba* Arbitration pitting Egypt against Israel, and the 2001 *Maritime Delimitation and Territorial Question* as between Qatar and Bahrain.

Though the peaceful settlement of dispute can in no way be considered the cure for what ails the region, its emphasis can assist in seeking to invigorate international law with the legitimacy it so clearly lacks. What necessitates the need to invigorate international law in the Middle East with this sense of legitimacy is the fact that States, for the most part, do not feel compelled to heed its imperatives which, at the end of the day, makes them vulnerable and suspicious of one another. Without the controls imposed on their conduct by the dictates of international law, Middle Eastern States find themselves required to fend for themselves with no ability to rely on past practice or established norms. When this reality is superimposed on a region that is the most militarised in the world, what emerges is a powder keg with an extremely short fuse. Emphasizing the recourse to the pacific settlement of disputes is the primary manner by which those within the domain of public international law can best attempt to lengthen that fuse.

I. The Most Militarised Region in the World

Over the last eighty years—the period of the existence of the modern Middle East—the Middle East has been a primary locus of war. While the previous chapters have not sought to mention all conflicts which have transpired, this study has dealt with—in varying degrees of depth—the Middle East as a theatre of both the First and Second World Wars; the 1948 War (Egypt, Jordan, Iraq, Israel, Lebanon and Syria); the 1956 War (Egypt, France, Israel, and the United Kingdom); the Iran-Iraq (1980–88); Lebanese War (Israel, Lebanon and Syria (1980–2001), the 1991 War (Iraq and 35 UN Coalition Forces), and the 2003 War (Iraq and the United States-led coalition of 41 States). Beyond these conflicts, mention should also be made of the following wars which simply add to the litany of armed conflicts which have transpired in the region: the Yemeni War (Egypt, Saudi Arabia, and Yemen (1962–70)), the 1967 War (Egypt, Jordan, Iraq, Israel, and Syria); and the 1973 War (Egypt, Israel, and Syria). It should thus come as little surprise, given the number of times that States have had recourse to the use of force, that the Middle East has maintained from the 1950s onward, the dubious distinction of being the 'most militarized region in the world'[1]. Such a distinction is manifest, not only in the proliferation of conventional weapons, but also in the acquisition—or attempted acquisition—of weapons of mass destruction, including nuclear, biological and chemical weapons.

The Stockholm International Peace Research Institute, in its annual consideration of the arms industry, estimates that for the year 2002, worldwide military expenditures amounted to US$ 794 billion, or an average of 128 dollars per person[2]. During the period 1996–2000, Middle East States received just twenty-five percent of all major conventional weapons transferred internationally, though their accumulated population makes up but five percent of total world population[3]. This transfer of weaponry has allowed five Middle East States—Turkey (4), Saudi Arabia (5), Egypt (8), Israel (10), and the United Arab Emirates (13),—to rank among the top fifteen recipients of arms during the same five-year

---

[1]   Anthony Cordesman, 'The Most Militarized Region in the World', *The Military Balance in the Middle East*, Executive Summary: Region-Wide Trends, 2001, pp. 33.

[2]   Elisabeth Sköns et al., 'Military expenditure', Stockholm International Peace Research Institute, *SIPRI Yearbook 2003: Armaments, Disarmament and International Security*, 2003, p. 301.

[3]   See Table 13.1, 'Transfer of major conventional weapons from the largest suppliers to the 38 largest recipients, 1998-2002, *id.*, pp. 442-443. Of the 92.5 billion dollars of arms transferred worldwide, the Middle East received 22.5 billion. The *SIPRI Yearbook* considers the following States as constituting the Middle East: Bahrain, Egypt, Iran, Iraq, Israel, Jordan, Kuwait, Lebanon, Oman, Saudi Arabia, Syria, Turkey, United Arab Emirates, and Yemen. The *Yearbook* considers Algeria, Libya, Morocco, and Tunisia as the separate entity of 'North Africa'.

period[4]. In the case of the Gulf States, the financing of their arms procurement has been made possible through the use of oil revenues; while both Egypt and Israel have received annual billion-dollar military subsidies from the United States of America to offset their military costs. From 1993 to the year 2002, the military expenditures of Egypt was over two billion US dollars annually; Iran, from six to sixteen billion annually; Israel from seven to nearly ten billion annually; Kuwait, from a high of more than eleven billion in 1991 to an average of approximately three and a half billion annually thereafter. Oman, surprisingly, has spent, on average, nearly two billion a year over the 1993–2002 period; while Saudi Arabia remains the largest spender on military stuffs, with expenditures of nearly twenty-nine billion during 1991, the year of the Coalition war against Iraq, while its expenditures since then have fluctuated between thirteen and twenty-one billion dollars a year. The final States worth mentioning are Syria, which has spent on average approximately four billion annually, though as of 2001, this has increased to over five billion; Turkey which saw its annual spending increase from 1991 when it stood at six billion to just over ten billion for the year 2002; and the United Arab Emirates, which spend on average one and a half billion dollars on its military annually[5].

What makes the Middle East the most militarised region on the globe is the relevance of military expenditures and their relation to overall spending of the States. For instance, while overall military expenditures make up an average of two percent of the Gross National Product of the accumulation of all States in 1997; for Middle East States it approached eight percent of GNP. Arms imports made up about one percent of total imports worldwide, while in the Middle East they constituted more than ten percent all of imports. Most telling, though, of the militarization of the Middle East is that while, on average, States of the international community use up just over ten percent of their central government expenditures on the military, for Middle East States that percentage jumps to twenty-three percent of their total budget[6]. Such expenditures are manifest in the number of troops, which Middle East States maintain at the ready, and the amount of sophisticated weaponry that they have at their command. With respect to arm force numbers, Egypt maintains nearly 450,000 men at the ready, Israel over 167,000, while Iran has 540,000 soldiers, Saudi Arabia over 124,000, and Syria 319,000[7]. As for sophisticated weaponry, from the end of the Cold War until 1997 the Middle East saw the delivery, to the region, of over 4,000 tanks, 820 supersonic combat aircraft, and more than 450 attack helicopters[8].

---

[4]   See Table 13A, 'The volume of transfers of major conventional weapons: by recipients and suppliers, 1998–2002', *id.*, p. 466.

[5]   See Table 10A.4, 'Military expenditures by region and country, in constant US dollars, 1993–2002', *id.*, p. 350.

[6]   Anthony Cordesman, 'The Most Militarized Region in the World', *op. cit.* n. 1, p. 37.

[7]   See International Institute for Strategic Studies, The *Military Balance: 2003–2004*, 2003, pp. 105–122. Note that Iraq had 389,000 soldiers pre-2003 conflict; while Morocco at 196,000 and Algeria at 127,000 men also maintain large armed forces. *Id.*

[8]   Anthony Cordesman, 'Total Middle Eastern Arms Deliveries by Major Weapon: 1986–1997', *op. cit.* n. 1, p. 48.

Beyond this abundance of conventional weapons in the region, Middle East States have sought to acquire and, in various instances, have used weapons of mass destruction. On the one hand, Israel regards 'Arab states as hostile to the very existence of their state and are determined to make every attempt to destroy it'[9]. This, coupled with the fact that it believes that Arab countries enjoy 'a quantitative advantage [...] in the size of populations and armed forces, in territory and strategic depth, in natural resources—primarily oil—and the resulting financial capacity to pay for advanced arms, and in the number of states and the ability to influence international organizations', means that Israel feels vulnerable to attack[10]. Israel's lack of 'strategic depth'—its size does not allow it much room to sustain or absorb an attack on its territory—has led it to establish a deterrence strategy which includes nuclear weapons. While the Stockholm International Peace Research Institute notes that establishing 'the size and composition of the Israeli nuclear stockpile is extremely difficult', it goes on to say that it 'is estimated that Israel may have as many as 200 warheads, consisting of aircraft bombs, missile warheads and non-strategic/battlefield types'[11]. It is believed that Israel has been a *de facto* nuclear State since 1966, having received assistance from France in establishing its nuclear program.

On the other hand, the 'Arab world regard[s] Israel as the common enemy and view[s] it as dangerously aggressive and expansionist, seeking to achieve regional hegemony while pretending to strive for peace'[12]. Arab States believe that Israel has a 'qualitative military advantage' which is manifest in advanced technology, its strategic relationship with the United States, and its nuclear capability[13]. While Arab States have been advocating adherence to the nuclear Non-Proliferation Treaty, and calling for not only a Middle East nuclear weapons-free zone, but also a weapons of mass destruction-free zone, they have sought to link nuclear non-proliferation to the disarmament of other unconventional arms. As Shai Feldman of the John F. Kennedy School of Government, notes, 'The late 1992 decision of the Arab League not to sign the Chemical Weapons Convention (CWC) until Israel joins the Nuclear Non-Proliferation Treaty (NPT) provides clear evidence of this linkage'[14]. As Abdullah Toukan, an advisor to the King of Jordan, has written, in a piece which accompanies Shai Feldman's, 'Israel's nuclear capability and ambiguous nuclear policy are still considered by Arab states as a major destabilizing factor in the Middle East and a driving force for the proliferation of nuclear weapons and other weapons of mass destruction'. Toukan goes on to state

---

[9]   Shai Feldman, 'Israel's National Security: Perceptions and Policy', Shai Feldman and Abdullah Toukan, *Bridging the Gap: A Future Security Architecture for the Middle East*, 1997, p. 8.

[10]   *Id.*, p. 9.

[11]   See Stockholm International Peace Research Institute, *SIPRI Yearbook 2001: Armaments, Disarmament and International Security*, 2001, p. 483.

[12]   Abdullah Toukan, 'Arab National Security Issues: Perceptions and Policies', Shai Feldman and Abdullah Toukan, *Bridging the Gap: A Future Security Architecture for the Middle East*, 1997, p. 34.

[13]   *Id.*, p. 37.

[14]   Shai Feldman, *Nuclear Weapons and Arms Control in the Middle East*, 1997, p. 264.

that this 'strategic capability drove a number of regional Arab states to declare that some form of an 'in-kind' deterrence should be developed or acquired. As a result, some Arab states resorted to a poor nation's atomic bomb: chemical and biological weapons'[15].

Thus, not only has the Middle East been the focal point for the build-up of conventional weapons, it has also been a centre for the accumulation and, in two specific instances, the use of non-conventional weapons. The first such use was during the 1960s, when Egypt used chemical weapons against Yemeni villages while intervening on the side of Yemeni Republicans against Royalists. In the wake of the 1956 War at Suez, with the forced withdrawal of the British, French, and Israeli forces from Egyptian soil, President Gamal Abdel Nasser emerged as the personification of Arab nationalism. So powerful was the allure of pan-Arabism that it led to the establishment, in 1958, of the United Arab Republic, whereby Syria was effectively incorporated into a political union dominated by Egypt. That same year, Yemen joined the United Arab Republic in a loose federation known as the United Arab States. The Arab federation would last only three years; the termination of the United Arab States by Nasser in 1961, for its part, led first to a cold war, which was followed, in 1962, by a *coup d'état* apparently 'engineered and pre-arranged by President Nasser of Egypt'[16]. The *coup* leaders, in dethroning the Yemeni leadership, sought to establish a republic and, to that end, requested Egyptian military intervention. Despite the influx of tens of thousands of Egyptian troops, the Republicans were unable to consolidate their power against the Royalists who had support from Saudi Arabia; the conflict only ending when Egypt withdrew its forces in the wake of the 1967 War. Though Egypt was party to the 1925 Protocol prohibiting the use of chemical warfare, it appears that it did, indeed, use gas against both civilian and military targets during late 1966 and 1967[17]. During that period, a number of Yemeni hamlets were gassed, including the village of Kitaf, where 'more than two hundred people were killed by toxic gas'[18].

The second occasion when non-conventional weapons have been used in the region, as mentioned earlier, was during the Iran-Iraq War, when Iraq used chemical weapons against Iran and 'became the first in history to attack its own

---

15 Toukan, *op. cit.*, n. 12, p. 47.

16 Saeed Badeeb, *The Saudi-Egyptian Conflict over North Yemen, 1962–1970*, p. 34.

17 For confirmation of gas attacks see International Committee of the Red Cross, 'ICRC and the Yemen Conflict', *International Review of the Red Cross*, Number 75, 1967, p. 317, which reads in part, 'the International Committee of the Red Cross again received from its delegates in the Yemen reports of bombing by toxic gas. A medical team, led by the head of the ICRC mission in the Yemen, went on May 15 and 16 [1967] to a village [...], the ICRC doctors on arrival at the site immediately gave treatment to some of the wounded and collected various indications pointing to the use of poison gas'. See also Gerhard von Glahn, *Law Among Nations*, 1981, pp. 648–649.

18 Meir Ossad, 'Legal Aspects of the Egyptian Intervention in Yemen', *Israeli Law Review*, Vol. 5, 1970, p. 244.

civilian population with chemical weapons'[19]. The Iraqi use of gas against its own population transpired during the February-September 1988 *Anfal* Campaign meant to suppress, once again, Iraqi Kurdish resistance, and was made most noteworthy by the attack on the town of Halabja, where five thousand Iraqi Kurds were gassed to death[20]. Likewise, during its war against Iran, 'Iraq used both nerve gas and mustard gas on an increasing scale for at least five years killing and injuring thousands of solders and civilians'[21]. As Frits Kalshoven, Professor Emeritus of Public International and Humanitarian Law at Leiden University, noted, 'too many words need not be wasted on the legal side of the matter: in the relations between Iraq and Iran, the 1925 Geneva Protocol was fully applicable, and the reported Iraqi employment of chemical weapons, whether against Iranian combatants (as it may have been in most instances) or civilians, was indubitably unlawful'[22].

On the horns of the dilemma, which finds Israel seeking nuclear weapons for its security, and Arab States seeking chemical weapons for theirs, and while both increase their conventional weapons, we find further arms races in the Middle East which are in no way connected to the Arab-Israeli conflict. As Anthony Cordesman, a senior Fellow at the Washington-based Center for Strategic and International Studies, wrote in 1991, both 'the proliferation of weapons of mass destruction and the conventional arms race in the Middle East [... is] shaped by a series of smaller and inter-related arms races within the region'[23]. Cordesman notes, for instance, that the Moroccan, Mauritanian, and Algerian dispute over South Sahara, or disputes in the Gulf which include Iran, Iraq, and Kuwait are reflective of this reality. Though the building up of conventional and non-conventional weapons is meant to bring security to each State, viewed from a historical perspective, States of the Middle East have not been dissuaded from the use of force by issues of balance of forces, deterrence, or compliance; instead militarism has simply shortened the fuse of an already explosive situation. While it

---

[19] See Middle East Watch, *Iraq's Crime of Genocide: The Anfal Campaign against the Kurds*, 1995, p. 6. For previous mention of Iraqi use of chemical weapons see Chapter 5, Section II.

[20] Consider the following excerpt from the Human Rights Watch report; 'Most notable perhaps among our findings is the unequivocal evidence we have been able to accumulate of Iraq's repeated use of chemical weapons against the Kurds. To summarise the evidence: we have found several documents that report on specific air and artillery attacks carried out by Iraqi forces with chemical agents against Kurdish villages in 1987 and 1988. These documents match in precise detail testimonial and forensic evidence collected by Middle East Watch in northern Iraq in 1992. The documents are crystal clear, for example, on the issue of culpability for the chemical attack on Halabja on March 16, 1988, in which some 5,000 Kurdish civilians were killed'. Middle East Watch, *Bureaucracy of Repression: The Iraqi Government in its Own Words*, 1994, p. 10.

[21] Timothy McCormack, 'International Law and the Use of Chemical Weapons in the Gulf War', *California Western International Law Journal*, Vol. 21, 1990–1991, p. 29.

[22] Frits Kalshoven, 'Prohibitions or Restriction on the Use of Methods and Means of Warfare', *The Gulf War of 1980–1988: The Iran-Iraq War in International Legal Perspective*, 1992, p. 101.

[23] Anthony Cordesman, *Weapons of Mass Destruction in the Middle East*, 1991, pp. 5–6.

may be said that States in the region have had a predilection to resolve disputes by force, there does exist a stream of peaceful settlement of disputes that has occurred throughout the era of the modern Middle East. Recourse to the pacific settlement of disputes, especially the legal means of dispute settlement, can act as a foundation for seeking to infuse legitimacy into international law in the Middle East. To emphasise the peaceful settlement of disputes at this juncture of a consideration of international law in the Middle East is meant to demonstrate instances of success, and to emphasise that such examples of pacific settlement can only assist in bringing the region under the control of the rule of law and the modern law of nations, which has as its fundamental pillars, the prohibition of the use of force and the peaceful settlement of disputes.

II. The Peaceful Settlement of Disputes

The growth of the international system has been predicated on an attempt by States to put an end to the use of force in their mutual relations. Over the last century, as States have moved to limit the use of force, they have also sought to provide an alternative: the pacific settlement of their differences. Both the limitations on the use of force and the peaceful settlement of international disputes—two sides of the same coin—are a product of the twentieth century, having emerged as result of advances in the technology of communication and warfare which rendered war too costly to the Statist-system[24]. In the aftermath of the First World War, it became obvious to statesmen, that with the dismantling of the Ottoman and Austro-Hungarian empires and the overthrow of the Czarist regime in Russia, the price of war had become too high. That, if Great Powers were to go to war, the end product might well be their reduction to little more than modern-day Austria; or a regime change, like that of the Bolsheviks, might well threaten the very existence of State-based international systems. Thus, during the twentieth century, States established, and further honed, various means of dispute settlement by non-belligerent means. These various methods find their modern expression in the United Nations Charter which establishes that States are to seek a solution to their disputes through 'negotiation, enquiry, mediation, conciliation, arbitration, judicial settlement, resort to regional agencies or arrangements, or other peaceful means of their own choice'.

The notion that the limitation of the use of force and the peaceful settlement of disputes are two sides of the same coin is reinforced by the manner in which the UN Charter itself was drafted. Further, a reading of the Charter makes it clear that these two concepts are the fundamental pillars of the international system; as Article 1(1) reads, the purpose of the United Nations is, first and foremost:

> To maintain international peace and security, and to that end: to take effective collective measures for the prevention and removal of threats to the peace, and for the suppression of acts of aggression or other breaches of the peace, and to bring about by

---

[24] See Jean Allain, *A Century of International Adjudication: The Rule of Law and its Limits*, 2000.

peaceful means, and in conformity with the principles of justice and international law, adjustment or settlement of international disputes or situations which might lead to a breach of the peace.

Using this as its benchmark, the Charter then establishes a number of principles which are meant to allow the Organization to pursue such a purpose. At Article 2, the Charter seeks to give expression to both the peaceful settlement of disputes and limitations on the use of force. Article 2(3), reads that 'All Members shall settle their international disputes by peaceful means'; while Article 2(4) makes it plain that 'All Members shall refrain in their international relations from the threat or use of force against the territorial integrity or political independence of any state'. More flesh is given to these bare bones principles, as the Charter devotes its Chapter VI to peaceful settlements and Chapter VII to the manner in which the United Nations may act collectively in attempting to respond to threats or breaches of the peace, or acts of aggression. Emphasis here will be given to Chapter VI, which is entitled the 'Pacific Settlement of Disputes', whereas the elements of Chapter VII of the United Nations Charter have been dealt with, in detail, previously[25].

While the UN Charter grants the Security Council the 'primary responsibility for the maintenance of international peace and security' and obliges States to 'carry out the decisions of the Security Council', its executory role does not extend to the area of pacific settlement of international disputes. Considered in another manner, while procedures are spelled out for attempting to re-establish international peace and security through the coercive measures imparted to the Security Council by Chapter VII, the provisions of Chapter VI are more akin to a framework treaty than setting out the manner of actions which States should follow, free from the compulsion of the Security Council (or any other State for that matter). This fundamental distinction is manifest in the fact that while States have an obligation to negotiate over a difference, there is no obligation whatsoever to settle the disputes[26]. As a result, States may, and have, allowed disputes to linger indefinitely instead of seeking to settle a conflicting claim. This is very much the situation, for instance, regarding the dispute over the Abu Musa and Tumbs islands which were seised from, respectively, the Emirates of Sharjah and Ras Al-Khaimah by the Shah of Iran on 30 November 1971, the day before these Emirates gained their independence from the United Kingdom. While neither Iran nor the two Emirates, which now form part of the United Arab Emirates, has resorted to all-out warfare, neither have they been successful in any marked manner in seeking to settle their dispute by peaceful means—thus the *status quo* of Iranian occupation has persisted for over thirty years[27].

---

[25] See Chapter 5, Section I, and Chapter 6, Section II.

[26] See Patrick Dailler and Alain Pellet, *Droit International Public*, 1994, p. 784. The noted exception being if the dispute threatens international peace and security thus allowing the UN Security Council to evoke Chapter VII of the Charter.

[27] For consideration of the disputed islands see: Jalil Roshandel, 'On the Persian Gulf Islands', pp. 135–153; Hassan H. al-Alkin, 'The Island Question: An Arabian Perspective', pp. 155–170; and Richard Schofield, 'Anything but Black and White: A Commentary on the

If States, however, are prepared to seek peaceful settlement, then the framework of Chapter VI of the Charter, to a large extent, leaves it to the parties themselves to decide the means of settlement. While Chapter VI notes the various means of dispute settlement, it also makes it clear that the Security Council will not impose a settlement, but may instead act to facilitate such a settlement. As a result, it is left to the parties through direct negotiation, or with the assistance of a third party, to seek a resolution of their dispute. Such third-party settlement may be as benign as simply offering one's good offices, but may also include mediation or conciliation. Beyond these diplomatic *qua* political means of dispute settlement, States have advanced two means of legal settlement which entail both a process of binding decisions whereby States, having given their consent to settle, have agreed that they will abide by the award of the arbitration panel or judgement of the judicial bench. The fundamental limitation to the use of legal means of dispute settlement, is the need for both parties to consent to appear before an adjudicative body. Where a binding decision as to competing claims is in the offering, States— especially those that perceive themselves to be on the wrong side of the law—are often times disinclined to participate. To remedy such a situation, States have been given the opportunity, through a compromissory clause or the 'optional clause system' of the International Court of Justice, to give their consent beforehand to settle future dispute by legal means. For its part, a compromissory clause is a provision of a treaty (i.e. an article) which notes that if there is a dispute about the interpretation or application of that legal instrument, then recourse will be had to dispute settlement. Such a compromissory clause may—though it need not— include recourse to either/or arbitration or judicial settlement depending on the preference which the parties expressed when negotiating the instrument. Whereas, the 'optional clause' system, as found at Article 36(2) of the Statute of the International Court of Justice, for its part, allows States to make a declaration accepting as compulsory, the jurisdiction of the Court regarding future disputes. Such declarations, it should be noted, are for the most part limited by provisions which, in effect, place reservations on the scope of disputes to which the State grants consent to appear before an international court[28].

As between arbitration and judicial settlement, the difference between these two means of adjudication is to be found in the manner in which they are constituted and carry out their function. It is clear that of the two forms, arbitration provides the most leeway for the parties in seeking to impact on the manner of proceeding. This is due to the fact that the agreement to arbitrate entails the necessity to establish the mechanism and the parameters upon which a third party—the arbitrator(s)—will adjudge the various claims. An agreement by States to arbitrate requires an intermediate step before an arbitration panel can contemplate a settlement: States must come to an agreement on the means and modalities to be utilised by a panel. In other words, once States have agreed to

---

Lower Gulf Islands Dispute' pp. 171–187, which all appear in Lawrence Potter and Gary Sick (eds.), *Security in the Persian Gulf: Origins, Obstacles, and the Search for Consensus*, 2002.

[28] See Allain, *op. cit.* n. 24, pp. 36–66.

settle their dispute via arbitration, they must negotiate, starting from a blank page, a *compromise*—in effect, a treaty—which will establish who and how many arbitrators will take part, the procedures they will follow, the laws they will apply, the questions they will answer, and the manner in which the parties will fund this *ad hoc* mechanism. While the use of arbitration was a mainstay on the international stage during the nineteenth century, it was felt at the time that negotiating such a *compromis* from a blank page was itself an encumbrance to the peaceful settlement of international disputes; as such during the Hague Peace Conference of 1899, States agreed to establish the Permanent Court of Arbitration. In essence, the Permanent Court of Arbitration was meant to fill in many of the blanks to facilitate the establishment of a *compromis*; thus the Court of Arbitration, which has been in existence for more than a century, maintains, for example, a list of arbitrators from which States can choose their own rules of procedure. In essence, the Permanent Court of Arbitration can be considered 'a device for facilitating the creation of tribunals and a machinery for aiding in the conduct of arbitral proceedings'[29].

In contrast to the room granted to States to negotiate the framework by which an arbitration proceeding will deliver a binding decision based on law, States, when having recourse to judicial settlement, have very little say in the manner in which a court will proceed toward giving a final judgement. States, having consented to settle their dispute by recourse to a court of law, have agreed to lay their claim before a pre-existing institution which has judges sitting in permanence, an established means of proceeding, and a pre-determined budget allowing it to carry out its work. Once States have agreed to appear before such a court, it is for the court to decide the parameters of the dispute and to render judgement on the issues it sees as being pertinent to putting an end to the conflict between the States. Such a court, open to all States, has been a fixture at the international level for just over eighty years, with the establishment, in 1920, of the Permanent Court of International Justice. The Permanent Court, while remaining the same in substance, would be incorporated into the United Nations system and reconstituted as the International Court of Justice in 1945. This Court, housed at the Peace Palace with the Permanent Court of Arbitration, in The Hague, The Netherlands, was used to great effect during the inter-War years, saw a decline in use during the Cold-War and Decolonization eras, but now finds its docket, in the early years of the twenty-first century, busier than at any time previously[30]. Throughout the various eras of the existence of these two organs—the Permanent Court of Arbitration and the Permanent Court of International Justice/International Court of Justice—Middle East States have been involved, in varying degrees, in disputes which have been settled by recourse to legally binding, final settlement, by peaceful means.

[29]   Manley Hudson, 'The Permanent Court of Arbitration', *American Journal of International Law*, Vol. 27, 1933, p. 445. For more on the Permanent Court of Arbitration , see Allain, *id.*, pp. 6–35. The website of the Permanent Court of Arbitration is www.pca-cpa.org.
[30]   For discussion of the Permanent Court of Justice and the International Court of Justice, see Allain, *id.*, pp. 36–66. The website of the International Court of Justice is www.icj-cij.org.

III. Peaceful Settlement of Disputes in the Middle East

Recourse to arbitration and judicial settlement has been a mainstay of international relations in the Middle East, though this approach has been neglected as a result of war which has been the dominant reality of the region's modern history. Consideration now turns to the various instances of legal dispute settlement that have transpired during the era of the modern Middle East to demonstrate that the region has an established record of pacific settlement of international disputes, and that recourse to such mechanisms should be promoted, not only to ensure a more peaceful co-existence in the region, but also as a means of invigorating legitimacy into international law in the Middle East. The latter would, in turn, provide States with a sense of security, which would allow them to stand down from their militarist outlook, providing the possibility for a peaceful co-existence; and the dividends of development which might well flow from such a transformation of their international relations. Seen from this perspective, the compounding of instances of peaceful settlement of disputes in the Middle East is worth emphasising.

i. The Colonial Era

Over a century ago, when dispute settlement by peaceful means emerged as a tool of statecraft, large swaths of the present-day Middle East were under the colonial yoke of the Ottoman Empire as it had been since the twelfth century. When, during the nineteenth century, the Ottoman Empire declined in relative strength *vis-à-vis* the Great Powers of Europe, those northern States made inroads into the region and ensured their privileged position, not by outright colonialism or occupation, but by virtue of capitulation agreements. As they were originally conceived, such agreements were meant to grant special privileges to European merchants to allow them to do business in the Muslim world. The first such capitulation agreement is said to have been extended by Saladin in 1171 to merchants of the Commonwealth of Pisa[31]. Such agreements extended:

> permission for merchants to enter the grantor's territory and trade there; freedom to exercise their own religion, without [...] regulations as to dress; the grant of special quarters in which to live in and carry out their trade; freedom from all taxes except customs dues; immunity to some extent from local jurisdiction, and the privilege of being tried by their own consuls according to their own law; and lastly, the right to have their succession regulated by their own rules of inheritance[32].

Allowing Europeans the possibility of immunity from local jurisdiction meant that issues of their violation of local laws were to be dealt with, not by the legal system of the Ottoman vessel, but by their own local representative on trade issue—their

---

[31] Jasper Yeates Brinton, *The Mixed Courts of Egypt*, 1968, p. 2.
[32] James Harry Scott, *The Law Affecting Foreigners in Egypt: As the Result of the Capitulations, with an Account of their Origin and Development*, 1908, pp. ix–x.

Consul—which exercised extraterritorial jurisdiction over their State's subjects. Much as Europeans were immune from local jurisdiction, States of the Middle East had yet to be introduced into the club of 'civilized nations', and thus did not have standing to bring claims against European Powers. As a result, as the following two cases before the Permanent Court of Arbitration attest, disputes regarding Middle East issues were brought by European States against one another. On 8 August 1905, the Permanent Court of Arbitration rendered an award in the *Muscat Dhows* case, wherein Great Britain sought to establish the parameters of French privileges and immunities granted to subjects of the Sultan of Muscat who owned or sailed dhows flying French flags. Though both European Powers had agreed in 1862 'to engage reciprocally to respect the independence of His Highness the Sultan of Muscat', they sought—in a reflection of the colonial times—to arbitrate, to determine the status of certain of his subjects[33]. The dispute arose over *dhows* that were thought to be involved in the slave trade which were immune from visitation from British ships, as they flew French flags.

The Permanent Court dealt with two questions; the first concerned the nature of the privileges which such sailing ships maintained under French flags. The Panel found that while subjects of the Sultan of Muscat could be authorised by France to fly its flag, this privilege was modified by the General Act of Brussels of 1890 which sought to suppress the slave trade. Thus, though France could allow any subject of the Sultan to fly its flag before it ratified the General Act on 2 January 1892, afterward, such an authorization was modified to only include those specifically designated as *'protégé'*. The decision, in effect, ended the flagging of *dhows* of subjects of the Sultan of Muscat with the *tricolore* as an Ottoman law had rescinded the status of *protégé* in 1863. Thus, only those individuals who could demonstrate that they had this status before 1863—in other words, more than forty years previously—were still entitled to fly the French standard. The second question which the French-Great Britain arbitration answered, dealt with the status of subjects of the Sultan of Muscat on vessels flying French flags. The Permanent Court of Arbitration found that *dhows*, which met the above criteria of being *protégé*, were 'entitled in the territorial waters of Muscat to the inviolability provided by the French-Muscat treaty of November 17, 1844'. While the *dhows* flying the French standard were exempt from the jurisdiction of the Sultan, his subjects, be they owners, masters, crew members or their families, were found not to enjoy 'any right of extra-territoriality [such as were granted to Europeans under capitulation agreements], which could exempt them from the sovereignty, especially from the jurisdiction, of His Highness the Sultan of Muscat'[34].

A second case dealt with by the Permanent Court of Arbitration of a dispute, which transpired in the Middle East, was the 1909 *Casablanca Arbitration Award*[35]. This case, which pitted Germany against France, revolved around an

---

[33] See 'Decision of the Permanent Court of Arbitration in the matter of the Muscat dhows', *American Journal of International Law*, Vol. 2, 1908, p. 923.

[34] *Id.*, p. 928.

[35] 'France v. Germany: The Casablanca Arbitration Award', *American Journal of International Law*, Vol. 3, 1909, pp. 755–760.

attempt by the German consulate in Casablanca, Morocco—which was under French occupation—to board various individuals, including German nationals, who had deserted from the French Foreign Legion, onto a German steamship. Despite having been given safe conduct by the German consulate, which exercised exclusive jurisdiction over German nationals due to extraterritorial jurisdiction vested in a capitulation agreement, they were 'arrested by agents of France, and that on this occasion, agents of Germany were attacked, maltreated, outraged, and threatened by the agents of France'[36]. The Court of Arbitration found, in its award of 22 May 1909, that the German consulate was 'wrong and a grave and manifest error' had been committed in attempting to load non-German nationals on the German steamship[37]. Though unwilling to impute an international wrongful act on the German consulate, the Permanent Court of Arbitration also found that Germany did not have the 'right to grant its protection to the deserters of German nationality'[38]. The unwillingness of the Court to find fault with the German consulate may have had to do with the manner in which the French authorities acted. The Court noted it 'was wrong for the French military authorities not to respect, as far as possible, the actual protection being granted to these deserters in the name of the German consulate', it earlier having noted that the French could have offered 'to leave them in sequestration at the German consulate until the question of the competent jurisdiction had been decided'[39]. The outcome of the case was the simple pronouncement of the Court of Arbitration; no reparation payments were awarded.

Beyond cases dealt with by the Permanent Court of Arbitration, in what amounted to the pre-European colonial period, the Permanent Court of International Justice rendered a number of judgements in the aftermath of the First World War, during the period in which France and Great Britain gained mandate status over much of the territory of the Middle East as a result of the dissolution of the Ottoman Empire. The Permanent Court of International Justice came into being as an outcome of the First World War, it having been conceived in the provisions of Article 14 of the Covenant of the League of Nations[40]. Thus, both the World Court—this combination of the Permanent Court of International Justice and the International Court of Justice—and the modern Middle East came into being at the same time, more than eighty years ago, as an outcome of the First World War. During the period of its existence, from its inauguration at the Hague Peace Palace in 1922, to its last public sitting in December 1939, the Permanent Court of International Justice rendered judgement in eleven cases which, although related to the Middle East, were brought forward as against a mandate *qua* colonial powers,

---

[36]   *Id.*, p. 757.
[37]   *Id.*, p. 760.
[38]   *Id.*
[39]   *Id.*, pp. 760 and 759. As for violence used by the French, the Permanent Court went on to say that 'the circumstances did not warrant, on the part of the French soldiers, either the threat made with a revolver or the prolongation of the shots fired at the Moroccan soldiers of the consulate'. *Id.*, p. 760.
[40]   See Article 14, Covenant of the League of Nations, 1922.

or resulted from an advisory opinion rendered by the Court at the behest of the Council of the League of Nations.

The first such case was, in fact, a referral by the Council of the League of Nations regarding the *Nationality Decrees issued in Tunis and Morocco*[41]. In that case, the Permanent Court of International Justice was asked to render an opinion regarding a dispute between France and Great Britain over French degrees issued in Tunis and Morocco. The Court was not asked to consider the merits of the case, but instead to consider whether the dispute referred to 'is or is not by international law solely a matter of domestic jurisdiction' as prescribed in Article 15(8) of the Covenant of the League of Nations[42]. Among the various grounds which were found to be susceptible to consideration under international law was the 'interpretation of international engagements' as they related to capitulatory rights of British subjects in Tunis and Morocco[43]. The dispute regarded treaties concluded by Great Britain with Morocco and Tunis that granted the former extraterritorial rights *vis-à-vis* its subjects in perpetuity. France, for its part, argued that these instruments had 'lapsed by virtue of the principle known as the *clausula rebus sic stantibus* because the establishment of a legal and juridical regime in conformity with French legislation has created a new situation which deprives the capitulatory regime of its *raison d'être*'[44]. The Permanent Court found, on a number of grounds, including this one, that the dispute could be deemed to be of an international nature and thus did not fall solely within France's domestic jurisdiction.

The next issue, for which the Permanent Court of International Justice would render three judgements, was the previously mentioned *Mavrommatis Concessions* cases, which were brought forward by Greece, on behalf of one of its nationals, against Great Britain in its capacity as the Mandatory Power over Palestine[45]. By virtue of its first judgement, the Court found, in 1924, that it had jurisdiction to deal with the matters though it narrowed the claim to only those regarding Jerusalem. When, in March 1925, the Permanent Court considered the merits, it found that public works concessions which had been granted to Euripide Mavrommatis in 1914 by the City of Jerusalem were valid, while the overlapping

---

[41]   Permanent Court of International Justice, *Collection of Advisory Opinion*, Series B, Number 4, 7 February 1923.

[42]   Article 15(8) of the Covenant of the League of Nations reads:

> If the dispute between the parties is claimed by one of them, and is found by the Council, to arise out of a matter which by international law is solely within the domestic jurisdiction of that party, the Council shall so report, and shall make no recommendation as to its settlement.

[43]   Permanent Court of International Justice, *op. cit.*, n. 41, p. 30.

[44]   *Id.*, p. 29.

[45]   Three cases regarding this matter were dealt with by the Permanent Court: *Mavrommatis Palestine Concessions* case, Permanent Court of International Justice, *Collection of Judgments*, Series A, No. 2, 30 August 1924; *Mavrommatis Jerusalem Concessions* case, Permanent Court of International Justice, *Collection of Judgments*, Series A, No. 5, 26 March 1925; and, case of the *Readaptation of the Mavrommatis Jerusalem Concessions* (Jurisdiction), Permanent Court of International Justice, *Collection of Judgments*, Series A, No. 10, 10 October 1927.

rights granted to Pinhas Rutenberg were 'not in conformity with the international obligations accepted by the Mandatory for Palestine'[46]. In 1927, the Court considered for the final time issues related to this case. Mavrommatis claimed that the British Government was not complying with the 1925 Judgment through its inaction, which caused delays coupled with 'the hostility displayed toward him by certain British authorities'. This, Greece contended, rendered it 'materially and morally impossible for M. Mavrommatis to obtain the financial assistance indispensable for the formation of the company for the operation of his concessions'[47]. For its part, the Permanent Court found that this issue was not within its jurisdiction as it did not relate to a violation of the Mandate for Palestine but was of a lower legal order and, as a result, put an end to the Greek claim.

In a case which has also been discussed previously, the Permanent Court, in 1925, provided the Council of the League of Nations with an Advisory Opinion regarding the modalities by which the Council could determine the fate of the vilayet of Mosul. As the delegates at the Conference of Lausanne could not come to an agreement on its fate, they inserted, in the Treaty of Lausanne, a provision that mandated that the frontier between Turkey and Iraq should be 'laid down in friendly agreement' or, after a pregnant pause, be 'referred to the Council of the League of Nations'[48]. The Permanent Court of International Justice, it will be recalled, was of the opinion that the decision taken by the Council in regard to the attaching of Mosul to either Iraq or Turkey was of a binding nature[49]. As such, the Court paved the way for the Council of the League to adopt the proposal of a report of a Committee of Enquiry which had previously determined that the vilayet should be attached to the British Mandate of Iraq, on condition that the Mandate remain in force for twenty-five years, and provide certain guarantees regarding the

---

[46] *Mavrommatis Jerusalem Concessions* case, Permanent Court of International Justice, *Collection of Judgments*, Series A, No. 5, 26 March 1925, p. 51.
[47] The case of the *Readaptation of the Mavrommatis Jerusalem Concessions* (Jurisdiction), Permanent Court of International Justice, *Collection of Judgments*, Series A, No. 10, 10 October 1927, p. 5.
[48] *Article 3, Paragraph 2, of the Treaty of Lausanne (Frontier between Turkey and Iraq)*, Permanent Court of International Justice, *Collection of Advisory Opinions*, Series B, No. 12, 21 November 1925, p. 14. Article 3 of the Treaty of Peace between the Allied and Associated Powers and Turkey, 24 July 1923, reads:

The frontier between Turkey and Iraq shall be laid down in friendly arrangement to be concluded between Turkey and Great Britain within nine months.

In the event of no agreement being reached between the two Governments within the time mentioned, the dispute shall be referred to the Council of the League of Nations.

The Turkish and British Governments reciprocally undertake that, pending the decision to be reached on the subject of the frontier, no military or other movement shall take place which might modify in any way the present state of the territories of which the final fate will depend upon that decision.

[49] Id., *Article 3, Paragraph 2, of the Treaty of Lausanne*, p. 33.

Kurdish population[50]. Those conditions, as noted in the opening Chapter of this study, were never fulfilled, as Iraq gained its independence in 1932.

Again in 1925, the Permanent Court provided another advisory opinion, this time on an issue that derived from the Treaty of Lausanne, related to the powers of a Mixed Commission which was meant to oversee the exchange of Greek and Turk populations[51]. The Permanent Court was asked to consider what the term 'established' meant in Article 2 of the Treaty concerning the Exchange of Greek and Turkish Populations, which reads:

> The following persons shall not be included in the exchange provided for in Article I:
>
> > The Greek inhabitants of Constantinople.
> > The Moslem inhabitants of Western Thrace.
>
> All Greeks who were already *established* before the 30th October, 1918, within the areas under the Prefecture of the City of Constantinople, as defined by the law of 1912, shall be considered as Greek inhabitants of Constantinople.
>
> All Moslems established in the region to the east of the frontier line laid down in 1913 by the Treaty of Bucharest shall be considered as Moslem inhabitants of Western Thrace[52].

The Court determined that 'established' meant all Greeks and Muslims who had a 'residence of lasting nature' in the areas under consideration and that Greek inhabitants of Constantinople were exempt from being expelled if they could demonstrate that they arrived before October 1918, and had the 'intention of residing there for an extended period'[53].

Two further cases should be noted in passing as they involve Turkey, but lack a Middle East component. The first, is the well-known 1927 case of the *S.S. 'Lotus'*, wherein the Permanent Court declined to judge in France's favour in its attempt to have Turkey institute criminal proceedings against the officer on watch during the collision of the *Lotus* with the Turkish steamer *Boz-Kourt*, with regard to violations of both the Treaty of Lausanne and the principles of international

---

[50] Commission of Enquiry, Question of the Frontier between Turkey and Iraq: Report to the Council by the Commission instituted by the Council Resolution of September 30th, 1924, *Documents distributed to Council and State Members*, C. 400, M. 147, 20 August 1925, p. 88.

[51] Treaty concerning the Exchange of Greek and Turkish Populations, 30 January 1923. See also Article 142, Treaty of Peace between the Allied and Associated Powers and Turkey, 24 July 1923, which reads, 'The separate Convention concluded on the 30th January, 1923, between Greece and Turkey, relating to the exchange of the Greek and Turkish populations, will have as between these two High Contracting Parties the same force and effect as if it formed part of the present Treaty'.

[52] Article 2, Treaty concerning the Exchange of Greek and Turkish Populations, 30 January 1923. Emphasis added.

[53] *Exchange of Greek and Turkish Populations,* Court of International Justice, *Collection of Advisory Opinions*, Series B, No. 10, 21 February 1925, p. 26.

law[54]. The second case dealt with issues of delimitation between Turkey and Italy; although it was placed on the docket of the Permanent Court, in 1933, it was never dealt with, as the parties, by mutual agreement, requested its removal[55]. While the above two cases did not directly affect the Middle East, the 1938 *Phosphates in Morocco* case did, *ratione loci*, though the case itself did not reach the merits phase[56]. Italy made an application to the Court regarding the loss, by some of its nationals, of phosphates prospecting licenses to French nationals in Morocco, which, it will be recalled was a French Protectorate at the time. The Permanent Court was unable to consider the merits as it found, during its preliminary phase, that the dispute dealt with 'situations or facts' which had transpired before France had declared its acceptance of the compulsory jurisdiction of the Court. This fact, in and of itself, would not have made the issue *ultra vires*, however, when accepting the jurisdiction of the Permanent Court of International Justice, France had indicated in its Declaration that it would only accept 'disputes which may arise after the ratification of the present declaration with regard to situations or facts subsequent to such ratification'[57].

The final case to be dealt with during the watch of the Permanent Court was very much an anomaly as it dealt with two Middle East 'States', though both under foreign occupation. With the exception of cases related to Turkey—which was considered part of the international community—all other cases mentioned thus far have been disputes between European States over issues transpired in the Middle East region. The 1940 *Suspension of the Operation of the French Company Radio-Orient in Egypt* was the first such case which dealt with two nominally independent Middle East States—though Egypt was, and would remain, under British Occupation until the mid-1950s, while the other party in the suit was the State of the Levant (present day Lebanon and Syria), which was under the French Mandate[58]. The case, which transpired as an arbitration under the auspices of the Permanent Court of Arbitration had to do with the suspension of telegraph services by Egypt belonging to the French company '*Radio-Orient*' which was located in Beirut. The Panel determined that Egypt had been in violation of its obligation, under the 1932 Madrid International Telecommunications Conventions, and determined that it had to revoke the order prohibiting 'Egyptian telegraph offices from accepting telegrams' from *Radio-Orient*[59]. The move from this case, which saw the settlement of a dispute by pacific means of two nominally independent

---

[54] The case of the *S.S. 'Lotus'*, Permanent Court of International Justice, *Collection of Judgments*, Series A, No. 9, 7 September 1927, p. 5.

[55] Case concerning *The Delimitation of the Territorial Waters between the Island of Castellorizo and the Coasts of Anatolia*, Permanent Court of International Justice, *Collection of Judgments*, Series A/B, No. 51, 26 January 1933.

[56] *Phosphates in Morocco*, Permanent Court of International Justice, *Collection of Judgments*, Series A/B, No. 74, 14 June 1938.

[57] *Id.*, p. 22.

[58] Permanent Court of Arbitration, *In the Matter of the Suspension of the Operation of the French Company Radio-Orient in Egypt*, 2 April 1940, as found in *American Journal of International Law*, Vol. 37, 1943, pp. 341–349.

[59] *Id.*, p. 348.

States under foreign domination, to two independent Middle East states seeking recourse to arbitration or judicial settlement would take a period of nearly forty years. This *intermezzo* of four decades, brought on by the decolonization process and suspicions about the International Court of Justice, however, did not mean that dispute settlement in the region came to a halt. Dispute settlement again was a reflection of the times as it would deal with claims between newly independent States and the interests of the former colonial masters.

ii. The Decolonization Process

The Permanent Court of International Justice would find itself dormant during the Second World War, as the Court moved from the occupied Netherlands to neutral Geneva, Switzerland, during the war years. Yet, when the Court was reconstituted, it was as the 'International Court of Justice'. The International Court, in substance, was the same as the Permanent Court, though with cosmetic changes required to allow it to become an organ of the newly established United Nations Organization[60]. From 1945 until the collapse of the Soviet Union and the end of the Cold War in 1989, the use of legal means of dispute settlement in the Middle East was a reflection of the decolonization process whereby claims were brought forward either by European States against other European States where colonialism still existed, or by such States against newly independent States as a means of settling claims arising out of the decolonization process. Further, this period witnessed a hesitancy on the part of newly independent States of the region to bring claims, in part because of the handling by the International Court of Justice of the South-West Africa/Namibia affair.

The first referral to the International Court of Justice of an issue which arose in the Middle East was a request brought forward by the United Nations General Assembly for an advisory opinion regarding the ability of the United Nations Organizations to bring claims forward at the international level. The General Assembly had been prompted to request such an opinion in the aftermath of the assassination, in September 1948, of the UN Mediator for Palestine, Count Folke Bernadotte. Bernadotte had been unpopular both with Arabs and Israelis as he sought to reach a compromise during the ceasefires of the 1948 War, his fate having been sealed at gunpoint by the Zionist terror group, the Stern Gang, as he was driven through the streets of Jerusalem. In its 1949 advisory opinion on *Reparations for Injuries Suffered in the Service of the United Nations*, the International Court found that the Organization did, indeed, possess objective international personality and could thus 'bring an international claim against' not only members of the United Nations, but also non-members such as Israel as it was at the time[61]. While this case did not expressly touch on the decolonization process, the UN General Assembly did establish, in 1950, the United Nations Tribunal for

---

[60]   For the transition from the Permanent Court of International Justice to the International Court of Justice, see Allain, *op. cit.*, n. 24, pp. 49–51.

[61]   International Court of Justice, *I.C.J. Reports, 1949*, 11 April 1949, p. 187.

Libya, which sought to deal specifically with the settling of claims regarding Italian property in a newly independent Libya.

On 21 November 1949, the UN General Assembly resolved that Libya 'shall be constituted a united, independent and sovereign State', thus escaping the control of its former colonial master, Italy[62]. This was as a result of the Treaty of Peace which had been signed between Italy and the Four Powers which called for the 'disposal of the former Italian colonies'. France, Great Britain, the Soviet Union, and the United States, had handed over this issue to the General Assembly for its consideration. On 15 December 1950, the UN General Assembly passed Resolution 388, which sought to deal with economic and financial issues before power was handed over to an independent Libya. To facilitate the settling of various financial claims, the General Assembly established a United Nations Tribunal, which was mandated with the jurisdiction to 'decide all disputes arising between the said authorities [Italian and Libyan] concerning the interpretation and application of the present resolution'[63]. This United Nations Tribunal for Libya handed down three awards during its existence, the first, *Italy v. Libya* was rendered in 1955. The case revolved around the property of thirteen institutions, such as the Bank of Naples and the Royal Automobile Club of Italy, and their status as either Italian public property and thus susceptible to seizure by Libya; or private property which would allow them to remain in Italian hands. The Tribunal, in rendering its award, considered the character of these institutions and found that some were, indeed, completely private, others public, while still others of a mixed public/private character[64].

The second award was made by the United Nations Tribunal for Libya in the *Italy v. United Kingdom of Great Britain and Northern Ireland and the United Kingdom of Libya* case, and consisted of a decision on interim measures in 1952 and an award in 1953[65]. Though the interim measures sought by Italy regarding its wish to have certain property reinstated were turned down, so too was a Libyan claim regarding the lack of jurisdiction of the Tribunal to deal with the matter[66]. As to the merits, the Tribunal dismissed the majority of Italian claims, only holding that where there was a doubt concerning moveable property which was thought to be of cultural significance (*patrimonio disponibile*), such property should be held in custodianship by Libya until authorised to dispose of it by the Tribunal or by mutual agreement with Italy[67]. The final award by the UN Tribunal for Libya was

---

[62]   General Assembly Resolution 289 A (IV), 21 November 1949.
[63]   General Assembly Resolution 388(V), 15 December 1950. See the section on 'The Question of the Former Italian Colonies', United Nations, *Yearbook of the United Nations*, 1950, pp. 345–362.
[64]   United Nations Tribunal for Libyan, *Italy v. Libya*, 27 June 1955. See Hersch Lauterpacht (ed.), *International Law Reports: Year 1955*, 1958, pp. 103–113.
[65]   See United Nations Tribunal for Libya, *Italy v. United Kingdom of Great Britain and Northern Ireland and the United Kingdom of Libya* (Interim Measures), 18 February 1952, in Hersch Lauterpacht (ed.), *International Law Reports*, Vol. 25, 1958–I, pp. 517–522; and the Merits at *id.*, 31 January 1953, pp. 3–13.
[66]   *Id.* (Interim Measures), p. 522.
[67]   International Court of Justice, *op. cit.* n. 48 (Merits), p. 12.

rendered in 1954; it dealt with 'Italian property in Libya which had been in the custody of the British Military Occupation Administration'[68]. The Tribunal found that various properties had been disposed of properly; that is, either having been released to liquidators, handed over to representatives of the institutions in question, or settled by agreement[69]. The United Nations Tribunal for Libya was dissolved in 1955 with the creation by the General Assembly of its successor, the Italian-Libyan Mixed Arbitration Commission[70].

Moving from the north of Africa to the Persian Gulf, in the early 1950s, two arbitrations transpired between British petroleum companies and two Trucial Principalities: Abu Dhabi and Qatar (at the time, these States were protectorates of the United Kingdom, independent in internal matters, but their foreign relations were controlled by the United Kingdom). Although it can not be said that these arbitrations transpired at the international level, as in neither case did the companies have international personality, such State/company arbitrations, as will be discussed, would become common in later years as Middle East States sought to assert their sovereignty within the framework of the 'New International Economic Order' by, inter alia, nationalizing their petroleum industries. In the first of these two arbitrations, the 1950 Petroleum Development (Qatar) LTD. v. Ruler of Qatar case, the arbitration panel decided that the concessions owned by the Petroleum Development company included islands that were not previously charted as well as the sea-bed and sub-soil beneath the territorial water and beneath the high seas contiguous to the territorial waters[71]. The second arbitration was the 1951 Petroleum Development LTD. v. Sheikh of Abu Dhabi case related to similar claims by the company over concession which also touched upon the maritime environment. In that Award, the single umpire determined that the company succeeds 'as to the subsoil of the territorial waters (including the territorial waters) of islands)', and that the Sheikh succeeds as to the subsoil [of] the submarine area contiguous with Abu Dhabi outside the territorial zone'[72]. It should be noted that the Petroleum Development Company had initially received its concessions via the Anglo-Iranian Oil Company Limited. The Anglo-Iran Oil Company, for its part, would also run into conflict within its area of operation, as opposed to the two previous cases, the United Kingdom would step in and invoke diplomatic protection to seek to have the rights of the oil company respected at the international level.

In 1951, the United Kingdom sought and received interim measures as against Iran so as to ensure that 'no measures of any kind should be taken designed to

---

[68]   See United Nations Tribunal for Libyan, Italy v. Libya, 3 July 1954, in Hersch Lauterpacht (ed.), International Law Reports, Vol 25, 1958–I, pp.13–25.
[69]   Id., p. 24.
[70]   See General Assembly Resolution 988(X), 6 December 1955, as reproduced in the section entitled: 'The Italian-Libyan Mixed Arbitration Commission', United Nations, Yearbook of the United Nations, 1955, pp. 340–343.
[71]   See Petroleum Development (Quatar) LTD. v. Ruler of Quatar, April 1950, in Hersch Lauterpacht (ed.), International Law Reports: Year 1951, 1961, p. 163.
[72]   Petroleum Development LTD. v. Sheikh of Abu Dhabi, September 1951, id., p. 148.

hinder the carrying on of the industrial and commercial operations of the Anglo-Iranian Oil Company, Limited'[73]. While such interim measures were meant to ensure that Iran did not give effect to the nationalization of the Anglo-Iranian Oil Company, this only held until the International Court of Justice made a final judgement on the matter. In 1952, the Court rendered judgement when it decided, in the preliminary phase, that it lacked jurisdiction to proceed to the merits phase. The Court found that the limitations subscribed to by Iran, the successor to the State of Persia, by way of its 1932 declaration accepting the jurisdiction of the Court only 'in regard to situations or facts relating directly or indirectly to the application of treaties or conventions accepted by Persia and subsequent to the ratification of this Declaration' held sway[74]. As such, the United Kingdom was unable to show any treaty related to the dispute which had come into force after 1932, and, as a result, the International Court not only put an end to proceedings, but noted that the interim measures ceased 'to be operative upon the delivery of this Judgment'[75].

In 1952, the International Court had occasion to again deal with an issue which transpired in the Middle East; this time the case was a throwback to the capitulations cases dealt with by the Permanent Court of International Justice. In its application to the Court, France argued, *inter alia*, that the United States of America was no longer 'entitled to claim that the application of all laws and regulations to its nationals in Morocco requires its express consent'[76]. While the United States of America sought to have its capitulations rights in the French Zone of Morocco upheld, the International Court found that, due to the fact that those rights had been based on a most-favoured-nations clause that had elapsed, it could not do so. The Court considered that European Powers had renounced their capitulatory rights during the early part of the twentieth century, and that, as of

---

[73] *Anglo-Iranian Oil Co.* case, International Court of Justice, *I.C.J. Reports, 1951*, 5 July 1951, pp. 93–94.
[74] *Anglo-Iranian Oil Co.* case (Preliminary Objection) International Court of Justice, *I.C.J. Reports, 1952*, 22 July 1952, p. 113.
[75] *Id.*, p. 114. Note that in various other cases involving Middle East States, the International Court did not have the opportunity, for various reasons, to render judgement on the merits. In the case concerning *The Aerial Incident of July 17th, 1955*, Israel vs. Bulgaria (Preliminary Objections), International Court of Justice, *I.C.J. Reports, 1959*, 26 May 1959, pp. 127–147, the Court found that it lacked jurisdiction. In the case concerning *The Compagnie du port, des quais et des entrepôts de Beyrouth and the Société Radio-Orient*, France vs. Lebanon, the Court ordered the removal of the case from its docket at the Parties' request. See International Court of Justice, *Yearbook 1960–1961*, 1961, p. 83. In the *Aegean Sea Continental Shelf* case, Greece vs. Turkey, the Court found that it was without jurisdiction to consider the dispute over the delimitation of the continental shelf. See International Court of Justice, *Yearbook 1978–1979*, 1979, p. 124. In the *Aerial Incident of 3 July 1988* case, which dealt with the destruction of an Iranian civil airliner by the American warship USS *Vincennes* over the Persian Gulf in 1988, the Court discontinued proceeding as a result of the mutual consent of the parties. See International Court of Justice, *Yearbook 1995–1996*, 1996, pp. 161–163.
[76] *Case concerning Rights of Nationals of the United States of America in Morocco*, International Court of Justice, *I.C.J. Reports, 1951*, 5 July 1951, pp. 93–94.

1937, 'no Power other than the United States has exercised consular jurisdiction in the French Zone of Morocco and none has been entitled to exercise such jurisdiction'[77]. As a result, the Court determined that the United States could not maintain an overall capitulations regime, granting its consular in the French Zone of Morocco jurisdiction to act in all disputes regarding its nationals, be they civil or criminal matters[78]. While this case was truly a throwback to a past era, the cases that followed it heralded the arrival of a new era wherein Middle East States sought to assert their new-found independence as sovereign States.

A manifestation of sovereignty by a newly independent State of the Middle East as against their former colonial Power made an appearance in the dubious award made by the French presiding judge in the 1957 *Re Franco-Tunisian Arbitration* case. As the facts of this award indicate, as part of the decolonization process, France and Tunisia had agreed, in 1955, to a number of treaties granting the latter internal autonomy; one of which provided for a mixed arbitral tribunal. In March 1956, the States signed a protocol 'providing for the complete independence of Tunisia', though the Protocol had 'a clause to the effect that for the time being the Conventions of June 3, 1955, were to remain in force, with the exception of those provisions which were incompatible with the status of Tunisia as an independent sovereign State'[79]. When, in 1956, France filed an application regarding a dispute before the Franco-Tunisian Arbitral Tribunal, the Tunisian arbitrators were of the view that the Tribunal no longer had jurisdiction to act as a result of the 1956 Protocol. 'As a result, the Tribunal was unable to function', wrote the presiding judge in this award made on behalf of the Tribunal in 1957[80]. The president of the Tribunal, clearly overstepping his power to act, held that the Tunisian members of the Tribunal had resigned and thus it fell to the Parties to the 1955 Convention to appoint their replacements. In the end, Tunisia did not replace the arbitrators, and the Franco-Tunisian Arbitral Tribunal ceased to function[81].

As States such as Tunisia started to assert their sovereignty in the midst of the decolonization process, the role of international law generally, and recourse to the International Court of Justice specifically, was stunted by the rendering of the 1966

---

[77] *Id.*, p. 190.

[78] *Id.*, p. 212. Note, however, that by the 1836 Treaty with Morocco and the 1906 General Act of Algeciras, the United States did retain limited consular jurisdiction where they were mentioned in the provisions of those instruments.

[79] *Re Franco-Tunisian Arbitration* case, 2 April 1957, in Hersch Lauterpacht and Ehuli Lauterpacht (eds.), *International Law Reports: Year 1957*, 1961, p. 768.

[80] *Id.*

[81] Consider the similarities between this case and the *Interpretation of Peace Treaties with Bulgaria, Hungary and Romania*, International Court of Justice, *I.C.J. Reports, 1950*, 30 March 1950, pp. 65–78, where these three States failed to appoint representatives to a mixed Commission, thus not allowing it to fulfil its mandate. Note another arbitration panel, in 1955, though constituted, failed to deliver an award because of the resignation of the three arbitrators, including the president of the panel, Charles de Visscher, brought on by the apparent lack of independence of the Saudi Arabian arbitrator in the case of the *Oasis of Buraimi*. See Raymond Goy, 'L'Affaire de l'oasis de Buraimi', *Annuaire Français de droit international*, Vol. 3, 1957, pp. 189–205.

South West Africa Advisory Opinion[82]. In that Opinion, the Court effectively overturned its 1962 judgement regarding preliminary objections which had found that Ethiopia and Liberia had, as members of the League of Nations, 'a legal right or interest in the observance by the Mandatory of its obligations'[83]. Though the Court had found, in 1962, that these two States could bring a claim seeking to end South Africa's Mandate because of its racial policies in South-West Africa; in 1966, the Court decided against, effectively bring to an end the merits phase of proceedings by determining that 'the Applicants cannot be considered to have established any legal right or interest appertaining to them in the subject-matter of the present claims, and that accordingly, the Court must decline to give effect to them'[84]. The result of this Opinion was not only one of '[d]isillusionment with the Court, but a feeling of betrayal' by the newly independent States which, through their numerical superiority in the UN General Assembly, sought to impact the development of international law[85]. The repercussions of what Professor Georges Abi Saab called the 'disaster of 1966', came to be felt for many years, as few newly independent, and no Middle Eastern, States had recourse to the International Court of Justice during the rest of the 1960s and 1970s. However, while no inter-State dispute was forwarded to the International Court of Justice by Middle Eastern States during this period, a number of disputes as between these States and multi-national corporations were settled by arbitration.

By all accounts, the most far-reaching assertion of sovereignty by Middle East States, in the wake of the decolonization process, was the steps taken by a number of States during the 1960s and 1970s, to nationalise their respective petroleum industries. While it is clear that such nationalizations were well within the sovereign prerogative of independent States, the number of nationalizations gained impetus from the engine of the 'New International Economic Order' (NIEO) being proffered by newly independent States[86]. A fundamental pillar of the New International Economic Order was that the right of self-determination meant little if newly independent States did not have control over their natural resources. To this end, in 1960, the United Nations General Assembly made plain in its *Declaration on the Granting of Independence to Colonial Countries and Peoples* that 'All peoples have the right to self-determination; by virtue of that right they freely determine their political status and freely pursue their economic, social and cultural

---

[82]   *South West Africa* case, International Court of Justice, *I.C.J. Reports, 1966*, 11 July 1966.
[83]   *South West Africa* case (Preliminary Objections), International Court of Justice, *I.C.J. Reports, 1962*, 21 December 1962, p. 343.
[84]   *South West Africa* case, *op. cit.* n. 84, p. 51. For an overall consideration of the issue of South Africa and its Mandate for South West Africa see John Dugard (ed.), *The South West Africa/Namibia Dispute: Documents and Scholarly Writings on the Controversy between South Africa and the United Natiosn*, 1973.
[85]   Michla Pomerance, 'The ICJ and South West Africa (Namibia): A Retrospective Legal/Political Assessment', *Leiden Journal of International Law*, Vol. 12, 1999, p. 430.
[86]   As for the legality of the right to nationalise, see the discussion in Chapter 2, Section III, regarding the nationalization of the Suez Canal Company.

development'[87]. Building on this, the General Assembly passed a further resolution two years later, entitled: *Permanent Sovereignty over Natural Resources*, which noted that:

> 1.   The right of peoples and nations to permanent sovereignty over their natural wealth and resources must be exercised in the interest of their national development and of the well-being of the people of the State concerned.

The Resolution further stated that:

> 4.   Nationalization, expropriation or requisitioning shall be based on grounds or reasons of public utility, security or the national interest which are recognized as overriding purely individual or private interests, both domestic and foreign. In such cases the owner shall be paid appropriate compensation, in accordance with the rules in force in the State taking such measures in the exercise of its sovereignty and in accordance with international law. In any case where the question of compensation gives rise to a controversy, the national jurisdiction of the State taking such measures shall be exhausted. However, upon agreement by sovereign States and other parties concerned, settlement of the dispute should be made through arbitration or international adjudication[88].

Though the concepts within the New International Economic Order would be among the primary contributions to the discipline of international law during the 1960s and 1970s; the NIEO would, in effect, lose much of its momentum as a

---

[87]   United Nations General Assembly, Resolution 1514 (XV), 14 December 1960.

[88]   United Nations General Assembly, Resolution 1803 (XVII), 14 December 1962. Note that, in 1973, the General Assembly passed a *Charter of Economic Rights and Duties of States*, which states at Article 1 that, 'Every State has and shall freely exercise full permanent sovereignty, including possession, use and disposal, over all its wealth, natural resources and economic activities'. While the Charter provided for a clause related to nationalization, it determined that settlement of disputes would be settled only by reference to international law, and that instead domestic law should hold. Article 2(c) states that each State has a right:

> To nationalize, expropriate or transfer ownership of foreign property, in which case appropriate compensation should be paid by the State adopting such measures, taking into account its relevant laws and regulations and all circumstances that the State considers pertinent. In any case where the question of compensation gives rise to a controversy, it shall be settled under the domestic law of the nationalizing State and by its tribunals, unless it is freely and mutually agreed by all States concerned that other peaceful means be sought on the basis of the sovereign equality of States and in accordance with the principle of free choice of means.

United Nations General Assembly, Resolution 3281 (XXIX), 12 December 1974. In his 'Preface to the First Edition' of Milan Bulajić, *Principles of International Development Law: Progressive Development of the Principles of International Law Relating to the New International Economic Order*, 1993, p. x; the author writes that 'basic point of controversy relating to the Charter concerns the implementation of the principle of permanent sovereignty over natural resources, particularly with regard to compensation for expropriated foreign property'.

result of the unwillingness of industrial States to participate in this new Order. The New International Economic Order's ultimate demise, as a conceptualization meant to bring about a more equitable distribution of the planet's resources, can be traced to the collapse of the Soviet Union, from which so-called 'Third World' States had gained much of their support[89]. However, during the 1960s and 1970s, the notions of self-determination and permanent sovereignty over one's natural resources were very much alive and were felt acutely in the Middle East. It follows, as Philippe Cahier noted in his General Course before the Hague Academy of International Law, that, as a corollary of a States' right over its natural resources being a manifestation of its sovereignty, a State could move to nationalise those sectors that sought to exploit such natural resources[90]. Iran was the first State in the Middle East to nationalise its petroleum industry in 1951. Though the United Kingdom sought to settle the dispute by recourse to the International Court of Justice, it failed on jurisdictional grounds to have its claim heard[91]. By contrast, the 1971 Libyan nationalization of British Petroleum (BP) and the 1974 nationalization of California Asiatic Company and Texaco Overseas Petroleum Company, resulted in arbitral awards.

In both the 1974 award in the *BP Exploration Company (Libya) Limited vs. the Government of the Libyan Arab Republic* and the 1977 *Texaco Overseas Petroleum Company and California Asiatic Company v. Government of the Libyan Arab Republic* cases, the arbitrators found that Libya had breached the concession agreements with these foreign companies through its nationalization process[92]. In both the *BP vs. Libya* and *Texaco v. Libya* awards, the arbitrator found that *restituto in integrum* was due by Libya to the companies. These awards were never carried out however, as Libya—asserting its sovereignty—did not recognise the procedures as between it and a foreign company. The Ministry of Petroleum explaining it position in a letter to the British Petroleum company in 1978 in the following terms:

> We would like to take this opportunity to reemphasize the long standing position of the Libyan Government of not recognizing as valid, or of any legal value, actions taken by certain oil companies in challenging of nationalization laws decrees by competent legislative authorities in the Jamahiriya. We consider such nationalization an absolute sovereign right of the State, to be exercised according to its discretion, and may not be subject to adjudication in any court of law, let alone an arbitration proceeding[93].

---

[89] For an intellectually quite stimulating account of issues surrounding the aims and purposes of the New International Economic Order see Mohammed Bedjaoui, *Towards a New International Economic Order*, 1979.

[90] See Phillipe Cahier, 'Cour général', *Collected Courses of The Hague Academy of International Law*, Vol. 195, 1985, p. 53.

[91] See above, n. 75. For the justification brought forward by Iran see Chapter 1, 'La nationalization du petrole Iranien, "acte de liberation nationale"', Dominique Rosenberg, *Le Principe de souveraineté des États sur leur resources naturelles*, 1983, pp. 94–100.

[92] See Hersch Lauterpacht (ed.), *International Law Reports*, Vol. 53, 1979, pp. 297–388 and 389–512.

[93] *Id.*, p. 297, n. 1.

That having been said, Libya did, in short order, settle its outstanding claims emanating from petroleum companies by agreeing to provide them with crude oil in compensation for their loses as result of its having taken control over the oil sector[94]. The last case of nationalization measures taken against the petroleum sector which led to arbitration resulted from the 1977 Kuwaiti Decree Law No. 124 which nationalised the assets of the American Independent Oil Company (Aminoil)[95]. As a result of agreement between the Parties, an arbitration panel was established which rendered an award in 1982 that determined that the amount of compensation due to Aminoil was, as Fernando Tesón notes, to be found on a balance 'between the interest of the host countries and their need for foreign capital, and the understandable desire for private investment to be protected against major risk', and awarded Aminoil US $179 million[96].

Before moving on to the post-colonial era and considering cases in which Middle East States sought recourse to adjudication to settle their own disputes, one final case should be mentioned that touched on the decolonization process: the 1975 *Western Sahara* Advisory Opinion. In this Opinion, requested by the UN General Assembly, the International Court of Justice proved to be of little assistance in settling the dispute, by providing its opinion as to the legal ties of the colonised area of Spanish Western Sahara, as between Morocco and Mauritania[97]. The Court found that:

> there existed legal ties of allegiance between the Sultan of Morocco and some of the tribes living in the territory of Western Sahara. They equally show the existence of rights, including some rights relating to the land, which constituted legal ties between the Mauritanian entity [...]. On the other hand, the Court's conclusion is that the materials and information presented to it do not establish any tie of territorial sovereignty between the territory of Western Sahara and the Kingdom of Morocco or the Mauritanian entity[98].

As a result of a protest march by Moroccans which transpired on the day when this Opinion was made public, Spain was placed under pressure to leave Western Sahara. It did, whereby Morocco and Mauritania occupied the area, which, to this day, remains under this alien occupation[99]. The case for Western Sahara appears to be an anomaly, as, by 1975, most of the Middle East was constituted as

---

[94]   See Rudolf Dolzer, 'Libya Oil Companies Arbitration', Rudolf Berhardt (ed.), *Encyclopedia of Public International Law*, Vol. 3, 1997, pp. 215–218. For a consideration of legal issues surrounding oil concessions generally, see Henry Cattan, *The Law of Oil Concessions in the Middle East and North Africa*, 1967.

[95]   *Government of Kuwait v. American Independent Oil Company(Aminoil)*, 24 March 1982, Hersch Lauterpacht (ed.), *International Law Reports*, Vol. 66, 1984, pp. 519–627.

[96]   Fernando Tesón, 'State Contracts and Oil Expropriations; The Aminoil-Kuwait Arbitration', *Virginia Journal of International Law*, Vol. 24, 1984, p. 358.

[97]   *Western Sahara* (Advisory Opinion), International Court of Justice, *I.C.J. Reports, 1975*, 22 May 1975.

[98]   *Id.*, p. 68.

[99]   See Karin Oellers-Frahm, 'Western Sahara (Advisory Opinion)', Rudolf Berhardt (ed.), *Encyclopedia of Public International Law*, Vol. 4, 2000, pp. 1463–1465.

independent States that asserted themselves as subjects of international law by, *inter alia*, bringing claims forward on the international plane.

iii. The Post-Colonial Era

It was not until the early 1980s that Middle East States turned to the legal means of dispute settlement to deal with their inter-State claims. No longer was the Middle East to be the incidental locus of dispute settlement by vying European States, or were newly-independent States to be involved in claims with their former colonial masters or their oil companies. Instead, Middle Eastern States turned to adjudication as a means of seeking to settle disagreements amongst themselves; or as against third States. Middle Eastern States thus, during the last quarter of the twentieth century, became true subjects of international law, seeking to have their claims respected on the international plane, while having their disputes settled by peaceful means. Generally speaking, inter-Middle Eastern recourse to instances of adjudication have centred on an issue that is fundamental to State sovereignty— seeking to establish the boundaries of where their sovereignty may be asserted. The first case of international adjudication involving two independent Middle East States resulted in the 1981 award *In the matter of arbitration concerning the border between the Emirates of Dubai and Sharjah*[100]. The arbitration panel was asked to demarcate the boundaries between these two States, federated within the United Arab Emirates, and delivered a technical award that established the maritime boundary by making plain the Universal Transverse Mercator co-ordinates of the line which was to divided them[101].

In 1982, the International Court of Justice dealt with the issue of boundaries in the Middle East for the first time, rendering judgement in the *Continental Shelf* case between Libya and Tunisia[102]. In that case, the Court was asked to set out 'the principles and rules of international law which may be applied for the delimitation of the areas of the continental shelf' of Libya and Tunisia, so that the Parties might

---

[100] See *Dubai-Sharjah Border Arbitration*, 19 October 1981, Ehuli Lauterpacht and Christopher Greenwood (eds.), *International Law Reports*, Vol. 91, 1993, pp. 549–701.

[101] For a commentary on the case, see D.W. Bowett, 'The Dubai/Sharjah Boundary Arbitration', *The British Yearbook of International Law*, Vol. 65, 1994, pp. 103–134; where he concludes by saying:

> Yet perhaps the most significant aspect of the award is that it demonstrates the falsity of the assumption, all too easily made in some quarters, that the established rules of international law are the product of practice by the developed, Western nations, and are designed to serve their interests and not those of the newer, developing nations. For there is an award in which Dubai, relying on quite traditional rules, successfully challenged a land boundary laid down by Great Britain as Protecting Power. It is to be hoped that the award will therefore serve as an encouragement to the newer nations to use arbitration, or reference to the International Court, as a means of settling disputes. *Id.*, p. 133.

[102] *The Continental Shelf* (Tunisia/Libyan Arab Jamahiriya), International Court of Justice, *I.C.J. Reports, 1982*, 24 February 1982.

utilise these principles 'with a view to conclusion of a treaty in this matter'[103]. Despite the Court's 1982 judgement wherein it sought to fulfill the request of the parties, Tunisia sought, shortly thereafter, to have the Court reconsider its Judgment. In the 1985 *Application for Revision and Interpretation of the Judgment of 24 February 1982 in the Case concerning the Continental Shelf*, the Court found that while it was inadmissible that it would revise the Judgment, the Court accepted Tunisia's request for interpretation of the meaning of such technical parts of the earlier Judgment as, for instance, 'the most westerly point of the Gulf of Gabes'[104]. In 1981, before the International Court had a chance to render judgement on the dispute between Tunisia and Libya, Malta sought unsuccessfully to intervene in the case[105]. Though the Court would find the Maltese request *ultra vires*, as the island State was unwilling to participate as a party in the proceedings, Malta ultimately did have a say in this delimitation. This was as a result of the 1985 *Continental Shelf* case, whereby Libya had agreed to bring its dispute with Malta over the continental shelf to the International Court of Justice for settlement. In that case, the parties sought, in essence, the same thing that was requested of the Court by Tunisia and Libya regarding their continental shelf dispute[106]. The Court determined that Libya and Malta were to delimit their continental shelf 'in accordance with equitable principles and taking into account all relevant circumstances', including, *inter alia*, the 'general configuration of the coasts', the 'disparity in the lengths of the relevant coasts of the Parties and the distance between them'[107].

While the previous cases here dealt within the framework of Arab solidarity, the next issues that were brought to settlement were conducted within a climate of great consternation, not only for the States involved, but the international community as a whole. The seeking of settlement between the United States of America and Iran over the affairs that transpired in the aftermath of the 1978 Revolution which brought Ayatollah Khomeini to power, persist to this day. Although the International Court of Justice was to render judgement in 1979 in the *United States Diplomatic and Consular Staff in Tehran* case, the true settlement of claims by both Iran and the United States of America came as a result of the 1981 Algerian Accords which, among other things, established the Iran-United States Claims Tribunal. The 1979 Judgment resulted from an application brought by the United States as against Iran for failing to ensure the protection of its diplomatic premises, which had been overrun by demonstrators protesting the providing of sanctuary by the United States to the overthrown former Shah of Iran, Reza

[103] *Id.*, pp. 21 and 22.
[104] *Application for Revision and Interpretation of the Judgment of 24 February 1982 in the case concerning the Continental Shelf*, (Tunisia/Libyan Arab Jamahiriya), International Court of Justice, *I.C.J. Reports, 1985*, 10 December 1985, pp. 230 and 231.
[105] *The Continental Shelf* (Tunisia/Libyan Arab Jamahiriya) *Application by Malta for Permission to Intervene*, International Court of Justice, *I.C.J. Reports, 1981*, 14 April 1981.
[106] *The Continental Shelf* (Libyan Arab Jamahiriya/Malta), International Court of Justice, *I.C.J. Reports, 1985*, 3 June 1985, p. 16.
[107] *Id.*, p. 57.

Pahlevi. The Court found that while the attack on the United States Embassy and holding hostage of its staff did not originally involve agents of Iran; that, when Ayatollah Khomeini gave his blessing to the maintenance of the situation, this incurred the responsibility of the State[108]. However, no reparations where paid by Iran as a result of the judgement of the Court, as these obligations were superseded by the Algerian Accords of 19 January 1981[109]. One of three instruments emanating from the North African city was the Declaration of the Democratic and Popular Republic of Algeria concerning the Settlement of Claims by the Government of the United States and the Government of the Islamic Republic of Iran, established the Iran-US Claims Tribunal which is still in existence today[110].

On the basis of Article 2 of the 1981 Declaration, the Iran-US Claims Tribunal, has had jurisdiction to decide

> 1. [...] claims of nationals of the United States against Iran and claims of nationals of Iran against the United States, and any counterclaim which arises out of the same contract, transaction, or occurrence that constitutes the subject matter of that national's claim, if such claims and counterclaims are outstanding on the date of this Agreement, whether or not filed with any court, and arise out of debts, contracts (including transactions which are the subject of letters of credit or bank guarantees), expropriations or other measures affecting property rights, excluding [...].

> 2. The Tribunal shall also have jurisdiction over official claims of the United States and Iran against each other arising out of contractual arrangements between them for the purchase and sale of goods and services[111].

Of the nearly four thousand cases that had been filed with the Tribunal, by June 2001, all but twenty had been settled[112]. David Caron and John Crook explain the work of the Tribunal thus:

> By the mid-1990s, virtually all of the Tribunal's docket either had been resolved or transferred to another forum. Most of the approximately 2,800 small claims were settled by an agreement between the two Governments in August 1990, moving the task of adjudicating them to the Tribunal to the Foreign Claims Settlements Commission of the United States. Awards or settlements resolved most of the large commercial claims during the 1980s. [... As] of December 1999, only seven large private claims remain; six by U.S. claimants and one by an Iranian claimant.

---

[108] *United States Diplomatic and Consular Staff in Tehran*, International Court of Justice, *I.C.J. Reports, 1980*, 24 May 1980.

[109] See International Court of Justice, *Yearbook 1980–1981*, 1981, p. 126.

[110] See 'Declaration of the Democratic and Popular Republic of Algeria concerning the Settlement of Claims by the Government of the United States and the Government of the Islamic Republic of Iran', David Caron and John Crook (eds.), *The Iran-United States Claims Tribunal and the Process of International Claims Resolution*, 2000, pp. 379–382 (Appendix 2).

[111] *Id.*

[112] See Maurizio Brunetti, 'The Iran-United States Claims Tribunal', *Hague Yearbook of International Law*, 2001, pp. 249–250.

This disappearance of small claims and the resolution of most of the large commercial claims brought into clear focus what had not been widely appreciated before. By handling the docket as it did during its first decade, the Tribunal had either not touched, or only dealt with the edges of, a small category of very big and politically difficult cases. Thus, although the Tribunal faced far fewer cases as it went into the 1990s, they also were the cases that would be the most difficult to complete[113].

Although the Iran-US Claims Tribunal, which is established in The Hague, The Netherlands, is in its waning years, and has had difficulty in resolving the few cases still remaining on its docket, the Tribunal has been a major achievement in settling claims by pacific means between States that have been, in a number of instances, openly hostile toward each other.

While Iran and the United States of America have been at odds from the 1978 Revolution onward; Egypt and Israel, which fought each other in the 1948, 1956, 1967, and 1973 Wars, moved, in the late 1970s, toward a peaceful co-existence. This change of heart was given its first legal manifestation in the September 1978 Camp David Accords, which set out a framework to achieve peace in the Middle East. While the Accords failed to achieve the greater aim for peace in the region, they did lead to the March 1979 Treaty of Peace between the Arab Republic of Egypt and the State of Israel[114]. While this agreement has been the basis of peace between these two States for nearly twenty-five years, it was originally met with hostility by other Arab States that perceived the Treaty as an Egyptian break with Arab solidarity and an abandonment of the Palestinian cause. The most obvious manifestation of this was the decision to expel Egypt from the League of Arab States and to move its headquarters from Cairo to Tunis. As part of this attempt to isolate Egypt, 'the majority of States of the Eastern Mediterranean Region made clear that they wished to transfer the [World Health Organization] Regional Office from Alexandria to the territory of another Arab State'[115]. The UN General Assembly sought an advisory opinion on this matter as the World Health Organization (WHO) and Egypt had agreed, in 1951, on the modalities which would be required any modification to the host agreement. In rendering its Advisory Opinion in 1980, the International Court of Justice stated that if the WHO Regional Office was to leave Egypt prematurely, there was 'a duty both upon the Organization and upon Egypt to consult together in good faith as to the question under what conditions and in accordance with what modalities a transfer

---

[113]   David Caron and John Crook, 'Moving to End Game', David Caron and John Crook (eds.), *The Iran-United States Claims Tribunal and the Process of International Claims Resolution*, 2000, p. 334. Further works of note on the Tribunal include Richard Lillich and Daniel Barstow Magraw (eds.) *The Iran-United States Claims Tribunal: Its Contribution to the Law of State Responsibility*, 1998; and Mohsen Mohebi, *The International Law Character of the Iran-United States Claims Tribunal*, 1999.

[114]   Treaty of Peace between the Arab Republic of Egypt and the State of Israel, 26 March 1979.

[115]   Ehuli Lauterpacht and Christopher Greenwood (eds.), *International Law Reports*, Vol. 62, 1982, p. 452.

of the Regional Office from Egypt may be effected'[116]. Such obligations also extended to ensuring that the work of the WHO and the interest of Egypt were not prejudiced in the period of transition and that a reasonable time of notice was given before a move was effectuated.

Despite isolation within the Arab world, Egypt, like Israel, was committed to ensuring that the 1979 Peace Treaty became the basis for peaceful co-existence. This became apparent when the parties agreed to arbitrate a dispute over the demarcation of their common border. Although the issue was somewhat insignificant—regarding a limited amount of territory adjacent to the Gulf of Aqaba—the settling of the dispute by peaceful means was of major symbolic significances, as it demonstrated to both parties that they were serious in wishing to maintain the peace. Article 7 of the Peace Treaty noted that if there was a dispute between the parties then, ultimately, that disagreement would be 'submitted to arbitration'. As Israel sought to withdraw its occupying forces from the Sinai Peninsula, it became apparent that the issue of location of the border in the coastal region of Taba was disputed. In 1986 a *compromis* was signed, and in 1988, an arbitral panel rendered an award that established the location of fourteen border pillars which a Joint Boundary Commission had failed to agree upon[117]. As Ruth Lapidoth, the sole dissenting arbitrator has noted in the *Encyclopaedia of Public International Law*, despite the panel having found in Egypt's favour, the 'Award was promptly implemented'[118].

Since the settling of the *Taba* Arbitration in 1988, a number of disputes regarding Middle Eastern States have been referred to various international *fora* for settlement by legal means. Of those, some are still pending before in the International Court of Justice, including the *Question of Interpretation and Application of the 1971 Montreal Conventions arising from the Aerial Incident at Lockerbie* cases involving Libya on the one hand and the United Kingdom and United States of America on the other. A further case which is pending is the *Oil Platforms* case pitting Iran against the United States. Beyond these disputes, the International Court of Justice has, as has the Permanent Court of Arbitration, had the opportunity to render a number of final decisions regarding Middle East States. In 1994 and 1995 the International Court of Justice rendered two judgements wherein it established that Qatar and Bahrain had consented to the jurisdiction of the Court to settle a dispute concerning territorial claims and maritime delimitation. In 1994, the International Court was clear in determining that an exchange of letters between the Parties, which had been facilitated by the King of Saudi Arabia,

---

[116] *Interpretation of the Agreement of 25 March 1951 between the WHO and* Egypt, International Court of Justice, *I.C.J. Reports, 1980*, 20 December 1980, p. 178.
[117] *Arbitral Award in the Dispute concerning Certain Boundary Pillars between the Arab Republic of Egypt and the State of Israel*, 29 September 1988, Ehuli Lauterpacht and Christopher Greenwood (eds.), *International Law Reports*, Vol. 80, 1989, pp. 226–312.
[118] Ruth Lapidoth, '*Taba* Arbitration', Rudolf Berhardt (ed.), *Encyclopedia of Public International Law*, Vol. 4, 2000, p. 751.

constituted an 'international agreement creating rights and obligations'[119]. The 1995 Judgment found that it, indeed, had both jurisdiction to deal with the issue and that the dispute was admissible[120]. The Court finally dealt with the merits in 2001, deciding the sovereignty of a number of islands and establishing a 'single maritime boundary that divides the various maritime zones of the State of Qatar and the State of Bahrain' [121].

A similar case, which dealt with one Middle East State, regarded Yemen in a case revolving around Red Sea islands which had been the locus of armed conflicts between it and its African neighbour. While the Permanent Court of Arbitration has been in existence for more than a hundred years, it has only rendered six inter-State awards since 1932, two of which deal with this dispute between Eritrea and Yemen[122]. As the Permanent Court moved toward celebrating its centenary in 1999, more attention was paid to its existence. This was manifest not only in the settlements of October 1998 and December 1999 as between Eritrea and Yemen, but also in the fact that as of 2004 there were four more inter-State disputes pending. In the 1998 Award, the Permanent Court of Arbitration established the sovereignty as between Eritrea and Yemen over a number of islands, islets and rocks in the Red Sea[123]. On that basis the Panel, in a second award in 1999, set a series of geodetic lines establishing the maritime boundary between the African and Arabian State in the region of Bab el-Mandeb, the strait separation the Red Sea from the Gulf of Aden[124].

IV. Conclusion

The compounding of instances of the peaceful settlement of disputes that have been presented here are meant to demonstrate that an alternative exists in the Middle East. Though the main stream of historical discourse around the evolution of the modern Middle East has been focused on war and bloodshed, this concluding chapter has sought to demonstrate the various instances when dispute

---

[119] *Case concerning Maritime Delimitation and Territorial Questions between Qatar and Bahrain* (Jurisdiction and Admissibility), 1 July 1994, para. 41. See the website of the International Court of Justice at: www.icj-cij.org.

[120] *Case concerning Maritime Delimitation and Territorial Questions between Qatar and Bahrain* (Jurisdiction and Admissibility), 15 February 1995, *id.*

[121] *Case concerning Maritime Delimitation and Territorial Questions between Qatar and Bahrain* (Merits), 16 March 2001, *id.* Bahrain was awarded sovereignty over Qit'at Jaradah and the Hawar Islands while Qatar received Zubarah and Janan islands. The Court also found that 'low-tide elevation of Fasht ad Dibal falls under the sovereignty of the State of Qatar'. *Id.*, para. 252.

[122] See Allain, *op. cit.* n. 24, p. 33.

[123] See *Award of the Arbitral Tribunal in the First Stage (Territorial Sovereignty and Scope of the Dispute)*, 9 October 1998, at the web site of the Permanent Court of Arbitration: http://pca-cpa.org.

[124] See Award of the Arbitral Tribunal in the Second Stage (Maritime Delimitation), 17 December 1999, id.

settlement by pacific means has transpired. This stream apart has run parallel to the historical narrative which weaves throughout this study—a narrative that seeks to demonstrate the manner in which international law has been applied in a quantitatively different manner in the Middle East. This exceptionalism, which sees international law applied more often than not in a subjective manner, that is, in tune with the wishes of those with power to make it so, means that international law has never really gained legitimacy in the region. Whether the issue is Kurdish, wherein positive law has failed to accommodate their aspirations for a semblance of self-determination; or that of British imperial policies as manifest in its management of the Suez Canal or Palestine; or issues revolving around the abandonment of the Palestinian Refugees, the selective enforcement or the punitive nature of Security Council actions in the region, or perpetuation of states of emergency in Egypt and Syria; the reality remains constant: that international law in the Middle East is aligned closer to power than justice.

Having examined the Middle East through the lens of international law, it is impossible to escape the reality that, due to its subjective, repressive, and punitive application, international law can not be divorced from the dictates of power. International law in the Middle East can not slip the claim of subjectivity; however, while this may be true in other parts of the world, the exceptionalism which is found in this region is predicated on the fact that its cumulative effect has impacted negatively on literally millions of people—be it nearly thirty million Kurds, twenty million Iraqis, or four million Palestinian Refugees, etc. That international law lacks legitimacy means that no normative framework has emerged in the region from which States can hang future expectations of behaviour. Thus, international law can not be expected to ensure restraint of action when its precepts and principles have been de-legitimised to such an extent that its currency is of little value. Instead, what has emerged from the manner in which international law has been applied and enforced is the creation of the region of the Middle East as the underclass of the international legal order whereby law is used as a sword against it, as opposed to a shield to protect it. By the various means highlighted in this study, where international law was manipulated, set aside, or simply violated, to meet the interests of the powerful, it becomes evident that international law in the Middle East is qualitatively different.

While advocating pacific means of dispute settlement in seeking to breath life into the legitimacy of international law, it should be emphasised that the legitimacy of the law in the Middle East must be found beyond the limits of the legal order— in the realm of international relations. If international law is to play a role in lengthening the fuse on the powder keg which is the Middle East, what will be required is an international system that seeks to interpret and apply international law in a objective manner. That is, to ensure that, having established a normative order, its principles are applied to the Middle East in the same manner as elsewhere. The alignment of international law with the dictates of powerful States has left a bitter legacy that requires addressing. That various political machinations have been at the root of the malaise of the Middle East raises questions as to how long an international system can persist wherein a strategically important part of the globe is treated as an underclass of society. By seeking to bring to the fore the experience of the people in the Middle East, to focus on suppressed narratives, and to highlight the manner in which international law has been misapplied in the region is meant to allow for an expanded space in which international law can be both considered and critiqued. In this manner, an attempt can be made to first acknowledge, then seek to redress, the balance which currently finds international law in the Middle East aligned closer to power than justice.

Epilogue

The conceptual framework of this study and its drafting originated in September 2000. A conscious decision was made in writing this monograph to ensure that it was up-to-date, but at the same time not to incorporate events that transpired which appeared to have affected the meta-narrative of the region. History has demonstrated that the region is volatile and that changes can come fast and furious. The period of 2000–2004 has been monumental in this respect. Over the past four years, much has changed in the Middle East; sadly, events have confirmed the overall thesis which is developed in this book. The so-called 'Oslo Peace Process' between the State of Israel and the Palestinian Authority imploded, leading to the start of the second—*Al Asqa—Intifada*. The election of Ariel Sharon as Prime Minister of Israel brought in its wake an all-out military campaign, initiated to once again take full control over the Occupied Territories. More consequential to the region as a whole were the events of 11 September 2001, when nineteen young men, Egyptians and Saudi Arabians, hijacked four commercial airliners over the United States of America and used them as missiles against targets in New York City and Washington, D.C. Over three thousand people, both those on board and in the World Trade Centre and Pentagon buildings, were killed[1]. Having identified the radical Islamist Osama bin Laden and his *al-Qaeda* network as the masterminds of the attacks of September 11, the United States, less than a month later, commenced a war against bin Ladan's host State: Taliban-ruled Afghanistan.

The final event to transpire which has greatly affected the region was the United States-led March 2003 attack against Iraq, which ousted the administration of Suddam Hussein. The manner, in which these events have played out, although the epicentre has been in the Middle East, have had repercussions beyond the region and affected international relations to its core. Although it is too early to say with any firm conviction, the lack of respect for the rule of law which has been a hallmark of the Middle East, appears to be moving from a regional toward becoming a universal phenomena. The United States' use of force against Iraq, without a United Nations Security Council mandate, has placed the fundamental pillar of the international system of governance—the multilateral control over the projection of force—into question. This Epilogue considers these events and seeks to demonstrate the manner in which they have affected the narrative presented in this study.

---

[1] Eric Lipton, 'Death toll is near 3,000, but some uncertainty over the count', *The New York Times*, 11 September 2002, p. 47.

I. The Continued Withering of Palestine

The fundamental premise of this study has been that the application and interpretation of international law has, for the vast majority of people in the Middle East, made them the underclass of the international system. Although this study has not focused specifically on the plight of Palestinians under Israeli occupation, the events that have transpired since the elapsing of the interim period set by the Oslo Accords are worth recounting, as they bear witness to a people under occupation who were subjected to, and remain subject to, military attack by the most powerful military force in the region. The agreement initiated in the Norwegian capital came about as a result of two dynamics: the first was the original *intifada*—the popular Palestinian uprising against the Israeli Occupation—which made the Occupied Territories uncontrollable; the second, the support by Yasser Arafat of the Hussein Administration during the Iraqi occupation of Kuwait and the subsequent 1991 War. These events caused the Palestinian leader to become further isolated, as a result of which, he lost support among the oil-rich Persian Gulf States. The original Oslo Accords signed on 13 September 1993, were meant to lead, after 'a transitional period not exceeding five years [...] to a permanent settlement based on Security Council Resolutions 242 and 338'[2]. United Nations Security Council Resolution 242 established two principles, that Israel should withdraw its 'armed forces from territories occupied in the recent [1967] conflict', while there was to be 'acknowledgment of the sovereignty, territorial integrity and political independence of every state in the area and their right to live in peace'[3]. Security Council Resolution 338 called for an end to the 1973 Egypt-Syrian war against Israel and for the parties to negotiate with an aim to establish 'a just and durable peace in the Middle East'[4].

The Oslo Accords, however, sought to shift issues of international law to the permanent status of negotiations by excluding them from its own framework: the status of 'Jerusalem, refugees, settlements', as well as 'security arrangements, borders, relations and cooperation with other neighbors, and other issues of common interest' would be considered after this interim agreement had been implemented[5]. This agreement, in essence, created a situation of Palestinian servitude toward Israel, as the Palestinian Authority was given the responsibility, as the Israeli Defence Forces left the Territories, of controlling the population, by guaranteeing 'public order and internal security for the Palestinians of the West Bank and the Gaza Strip', through the establishment of 'a strong police force'[6]. By way of an agreement signed in September 1995, the parties decided, by reference to areas designated on maps, to establish three zones within which jurisdiction

---

[2]   Walter Laqueur and Barry Rubin (eds.), 'Declaration of Principles on Interim Self-Government Arrangements', *The Israel-Arab Reader: A Documentary History of the Middle East Conflict*, 2001, p. 413.

[3]   *Id.,* 'UN Security Council: Resolution 242', p. 116.

[4]   *Id.,* 'UN Security Council: Resolution 338', p. 152.

[5]   See Article V, Declaration of Principles, Laqueur and Rubin, *op. cit.* n. 2, p. 414.

[6]   *Id.,* Article 7.

would be transferred from Israel to the Palestinian Authority. The executive organ of the Palestinian Authority—its Council—was, within a phased period of eighteen months, to assume jurisdiction in all three areas. However, this never transpired; instead, the Occupied Territories were made into various, non-contiguous, cantons which were separated, for the most part, by by-pass roads which had been constructed exclusively to allow Israeli settlers to travel to and from their enclaved settlements to Israel proper. The phasing period never truly got beyond the first stage, whereby, in Area 'A', the Palestinians assumed the 'powers and responsibilities for internal security and public order', in Area 'B', while the Palestinians were responsible for 'public order' the Israelis retained 'the overriding responsibility for security for the purpose of protecting Israelis and confronting the threat of terrorism'; and in Area 'C', which was the territory on which Israeli settlements are found, where the Israelis relinquished no control[7].

As the five-year interim period of the Oslo Accords came to an end, Israeli Prime Minister Binyamin Netanyahu who had been obstinate in moving the 'Oslo Peace Process' forward was replaced in a general election by Ehud Barak. Prime Minister Barak and Palestinian Authority Chairman Yasser Arafat met with outgoing US President Bill Clinton in what amounted to a last attempt at mediating—this time an overarching agreement—at Camp David, the US presidential retreat in Thurmont, Maryland, in July 2000. While the English-language press was quick to criticise Chairman Arafat; what was on offer at Camp David did not amount to peaceful co-existence, but further servitude, with an eye to overall Israeli annexation. The continuing withering of Palestine was demonstrated by *Le Monde Diplomatique*[8] which, on the basis of the Camp David negotiations, produced a map of what has been termed Prime Minister Barak's 'generous offer' at Camp David. The map separated the West Bank into three Palestinian enclaves; one to the south and two to the north of Jerusalem. As H.D.S. Greenway, a regular contributor to *The Boston Globe* noted in an editorial/opinion piece:

> Israel's offer at Camp David was indeed the most generous offer Israel had ever made, but it was not an offer of a viable Palestinian state. The Palestine on offer was chopped up into sectors with no access to each other—separated by Israeli settlements, settlement roads, and Israeli-controlled areas. The same was true of East Jerusalem, where Israelis have been trying to force Palestinians to leave. It was as if the Palestinian state were to get the spots while the rest of the leopard would remain in Israeli hands[9].

---

[7]   *Id.*, Article 13, 'Interim Agreement on the West Bank and Gaza Strip', p. 511. The 'Wye River Memorandum' mediated by United States President Bill Clinton, as between Yasser Arafat, and in the wake of the assassination of Yitzak Rabin, Prime Minister Binyamin Netanyahu, was primarily related to the redeployment of Israeli troops and its security concerns. See pp. 529–534. Note also the redeployment mandated by the Sharm El-Sheikh Memorandum of 3 September 1999 found at http://www.monde-diplomatique.fr/cahier/proche-orient/charm99-en.

[8]   See 'Cartographie des 'concessions' israéliennes', *Le Monde diplomatique*, Décembre 2000, avalable at http://carto.eu.org/article651.html.

[9]   H.D.S. Greenway 'How Middle East Peace Process was Killed', *The Boston Globe*, 3 May 2002, p. 23.

These landmasses were to be completely separated from one another and from Jordan by a ring of Israeli controlled land with the justification that it connected various Israeli settlements. In many ways, Camp David further revealed the overall strategic attempt by Israel to slowly squeeze the establishment of a Palestinian State of out existence. Although rarely recognised, or spoken of, an examination of Israeli actions since 1948 demonstrates a persistent attempt to wither Palestine so that an Israeli State can take hold of all territory west of the Jordan River.

Israel is in the process of State formation much in the same manner as States of the Western Hemisphere were involved in their colonial conquests during the nineteenth century. Where the case of Israel differs is that, in the latter part of the twentieth and the beginning of the twenty-first centuries, the State system no longer allows for such ventures as various principles of international law attests— at least in theory. Pitted against Israel's colonial venture are the dictates of international law as manifest in the right which Palestinians have to self-determination and in the so-called 'Stimson Doctrine', which speaks of the unwillingness of States to recognise the acquisition of territory by force. Consider the parallels between the creation and growth of the State of Israel and the formation of States in the 'New World'. Both started as colonial ventures, often times the justification was religious; but just as important was the economic migration that took place, whereby the under-classes of many societies were moved out or forced out of their country of origin toward the new satellite. Classic colonial State building, in which Israel fits the mould along with the States of North, Central, and South America, finds the successful imposition of a European population with a parallel disposition of the indigenous population. From their colonial outposts, these populations, through natural growth and a continuous influx of new settlers, were able to expand their territorial gains, isolating the native populations, and systematically changing the nature of the social landscape to consolidate a hold on the land.

Israel's policies have thus far mirrored the North American experience by instituting a number of legal instruments over a period of time consolidating its continuous territorial gains. Thus, in North America, treaties providing vast tracks of land in the early 1800s were replaced after the 'Indian Wars' with a number of isolated cantons of 'reserved land' by the late 1800s. Such an experience has also been visited upon the Palestinians, who under the British Mandate provided by the League of Nations legalised the colonialism of European Jewry and legitimised the Zionist venture. From Mandate Palestine, the European settlers were able to establish themselves, not over all of historical Palestine, but in various enclaves and increase their numbers from approximately 66,000 in 1918 to 460,000 by 1945. The 1947 UN Partition Plan provided the basis for establishing an Israeli State in those areas—with some transfer of populations—where Jewish people made up the majority. The outcome of the 1948 War was the consolidation by Israeli forces, of not only the areas allotted to a Jewish State by the United Nations, but once that had transpired, the conquering of Galilee and the Negev.

It was not until 1967, with UN Security Council Resolution 242, that the international community accepted the 1948 gains by Israel, *de jure*. Although the Security Council emphasised 'the inadmissibility of the acquisition of territory by war', it simply required that Israel withdraw 'from territories occupied in the recent conflict'. Under what was meant to be an interim agreement, the Oslo Accords further reduced Palestinian control to Area 'A'. Thus, within a forty-five year period (1922–1967), Palestinians went from having a nominally independent State under British tutelage, to being offered forty-five percent of historical Palestine under the Partition Plan, only to be further reduced by the Israeli occupation and the Olso Agreements to Palestinian control over what amounts to eighteen percent of Mandate Palestine. The Israeli occupation, as is evident if one reads reports produced by the International Committee of the Red Cross, the United Nations, or various non-governmental human rights organizations, has not been benign. Through land confiscation, house demolition, and the strategic use of colonial settlements, Israel has managed to command much of the land of the West Bank and Gaza Strip. This isolation of various Palestinian communities was legitimised through their canonization in the Oslo Accords, though with the promise that the agreements were an interim measure which would pave the way toward a final settlement.

When it became clear that this promise would not materialise at Camp David in the summer of 2000, the visceral reaction of the Palestinian people was manifest in *Al Asqa Intifada*. Granted, the uprising was sparked by the visit of Ariel Sharon and more than a hundred IDF soldiers to the Temple Mount, the third most revered site in Islam; but the sense that the 'Peace Process' had failed to improve the daily lives of Palestinians meant that an armed uprising once again took hold in the Occupied Territories[10]. On the back of the insecurity felt by Israelis as a result of the start of the uprising, Ariel Sharon was elected Prime Minister of Israel in February 2001 and later re-elected in January 2003. Prime Minister Sharon's popularity with Israelis stemmed from his hard-line approach to Palestinians, as he moved shortly after his first election victory to effectively end the control of the Palestinian Authority over areas where it had established jurisdiction as a result of the Oslo Accords: Area 'A'. In essence, the Prime Minister moved to re-occupy the Territories and establish overall IDF military control over both the West Bank and the Gaza Strip. The Israelis undertook a pacification campaign that included imposing various collective punishments on the Palestinians, as well as curfews and roadblocks. Further, they undertook a campaign of assassination against various Palestinian leaders, which the IDF euphemistically called 'targeted killings'. Three months into the *intifada*, the Palestinians responded to these wholesale attacks (the IDF's use of tanks, helicopter gunships, and F-16 fighter planes against targets in residential areas) in a retail manner: through suicide bombings[11].

---

[10] See Suzanne Goldenberg, 'Rioting as Sharon Visits Islam Holy Site', *The Guardian* (London), 29 September 2000, p. 16.
[11] See Human Rights Watch, *Erased in a Moment: Suicide Bombing Attacks Against Israeli Civilians*, 2002. Note that while there was an attack on January 2001, it was not truly until six months into the *intifada* that suicide bombings became part of the limited arsenal of the Palestinians.

The culmination of violence would come with the undertaking, by the IDF, of 'Operation Defensive Shield' in March 2002. The London *Guardian* detailed a report of the military operation which was presented to the Security Council by United Nations Secretary-General Kofi Annan:

> Operation Defensive Shield began on March 29 with an incursion into Ramallah, during which the Israeli Defence Force (IDF) seized most of the buildings in the headquarters compound of Yasser Arafat. Operations followed in Tulkarem and Qalqilya on April 1, Bethlehem on April 2, and in Jenin and Nablus on April 3. By then, six of the largest cities in the West Bank, and their surrounding towns, villages and refugee camps, were occupied by the Israeli military. The IDF announced the official end of the operation on April 21. The withdrawals were, in general, not to pre-March 29 positions, but to positions encircling the cities. Since then, the IDF has made more incursions.
>
> Operation Defensive Shield involved Israeli troops and vehicles entering cities and imposing curfews. The incursions were accompanied by the entry into nearby villages and refugee camps. Cities were declared 'special closed military areas'.
>
> [...] The IDF arrested Palestinians who they believed were involved in armed action against Israel. In most of these incursions the IDF also destroyed infrastructure they believed to be part of the operating capacity of militant groups, and infrastructure of the Palestinian Authority security services.
>
> The sealing off of areas during the operation meant that humanitarian workers were unable to deliver assistance. There were also cases of Israeli forces not respecting the neutrality of medical and humanitarian workers and attacking ambulances.
>
> There were numerous reports of the IDF compelling Palestinian civilians to accompany them during house searches, check suspicious subjects, stand in the line of fire from militants, and in other ways protect soldiers. Soldiers have acknowledged that they forced Palestinians to knock on doors for house searches, but they and the government deny the deliberate use of civilians as human shields.
>
> According to local human rights groups, more than 8,500 Palestinians were arrested between February 27 and May 20. Reportedly, most of the 2,500 Palestinians arrested during the first wave of incursions in February and March were released within a week, whereas many of the more than 6,000 Palestinians arrested during Operation Defensive Shield after March 29 were held for longer periods without any outside contact.

The report went on to note that a total of '497 Palestinians were killed [and 1,447 wounded] in the IDF reoccupation of Palestinian area A from March 1 to May 7 2002 and immediately afterwards' while more 'than 2,800 refugee homes [were] damaged and 878 were destroyed, leaving more than 17,000 people homeless or in need of shelter rehabilitation'[12].

---

[12]   Foreign Staff, 'UN Report Details West Bank Wreckage: Banned by Israel, Kofi Annan's Fact-Finders were Left with Only Second-Hand Accounts of the Spring Invasion', *The Guardian* (London), 2 August 2002, p. 14. From the start of the *Intifada* in September 2000 to June 2004, more than four thousand people have been killed. The overall numbers are, '3,437 Palestinians and 942 Israelis killed, with 33,776 Palestinians and 6,008 Israelis

II. September 11 and its Repercussions

The events of 11 September 2001, wherein young men, citizens of Middle Eastern States, hijacked civilian aircrafts and crashed them into buildings in New York and Washington, D.C., has had a fundamental impact on the region. Where Palestine is concerned, Israel was quick to equate—and the United States to acquiesce—the acts of Palestinians with those of *al-Qaeda*. As was noted in the Chapter 1 of this study, self-determination—as a right—has been defined as being applicable in quite narrow terms: as against colonialism, racist regimes, and foreign occupation. With the de-colonisation process having run its course, and the racist regimes of the South African type having disappeared, the only situation in which a *right* of self-determination exists today may be said to be in situations of foreign occupation. The willingness of Palestinians to target Israeli civilians outside of the Occupied Territories has hurt their struggle, as they have transgressed fundamental tenets of international law regarding the distinction between civilian and military targets. They have done themselves a disservice by failing to make it plain to all the difference between 'freedom fighter' and 'terrorist'. This distinction is quite easy; as freedom fighters, Palestinians have the right to use all means available to challenge the IDF in the Occupied Territories[13]. Short of this, the international community might well decide, as part of the United States, 'war on terror', that the right of self-determination no longer holds and that the likes of Palestinians no longer have a legal right to struggle against foreign domination of the type which has been imposed on them since 1967.

The other major ramification for the Middle East was the willingness of the United States, after having toppled the Taliban Administration in Afghanistan in late 2001, to turn its sights toward the Hussein Administration of Iraq. In so doing, not only did the United States invade and occupy Iraq in 2003, it did so in such a way as to challenge, in a fundamental manner, the United Nations system of international governance. The Bush Administration sought to equate Saddam Hussein with *al-Qaeda* and Iraq as a 'rogue State' with weapons of mass destruction. In his annual address to the United States legislature in 2002, President George W. Bush identified Iraq along with Iran and North Korea as constituting an 'axis of evil':

> Iraq continues to flaunt its hostility toward America and to support terror. The Iraqi regime has plotted to develop anthrax, and nerve gas, and nuclear weapons for over a decade. This is a regime that has already used poison gas to murder thousands of its own citizens—leaving the bodies of mothers huddled over their dead children. This is a regime that agreed to international inspections—then kicked out the inspectors. This is a regime that has something to hide from the civilized world.

---

wounded. See briefing of 23 June 2004, by Under-Secretary-General for Political Affairs, Kieran Prendergast, to the UN Security Council, UN Doc. S/PV.4994, p. 2.

[13] See Jean Allain, *On Achieving Palestinian Statehood: Concepts, Ends and Means from the Perspective of International Law*, 2002 (booklet), 40 pp.

States [i.e. North Korea, Iran and Iraq] like these, and their terrorist allies, constitute an axis of evil, arming to threaten the peace of the world. By seeking weapons of mass destruction, these regimes pose a grave and growing danger. They could provide these arms to terrorists, giving them the means to match their hatred. They could attack our allies or attempt to blackmail the United States. In any of these cases, the price of indifference would be catastrophic.

We will work closely with our coalition to deny terrorists and their state sponsors the materials, technology, and expertise to make and deliver weapons of mass destruction. [...] And all nations should know: America will do what is necessary to ensure our nation's security.

We'll be deliberate, yet time is not on our side. I will not wait on events, while dangers gather. I will not stand by, as peril draws closer and closer. The United States of America will not permit the world's most dangerous regimes to threaten us with the world's most destructive weapons[14].

From this point forward, it became evident that the Bush Administration was bent on forcibly removing President Saddam Hussein from power. Where the international community had been unwilling to challenge the United States' apparent prerogative to attack Afghanistan, any capital of goodwill which had been accumulated during the aftershock of the events of 11 September 2001 was spent by the time the issue of Iraq was considered. The Bush Administration's final diplomatic success as an outgrowth of the events of September 11 took place in November 2002, when it managed to pass unanimously UN Security Council Resolution 1441 which determined that 'Iraq has been and remains in material breach of its obligations under relevant resolutions, including resolution 687 (1991), in particular through Iraq's failure to cooperate with United Nations inspectors'. As a result the Council decided 'to afford Iraq, by this resolution, a final opportunity to comply with its disarmament obligations under relevant resolutions of the Council; and accordingly decides to set up an enhanced inspection regime with the aim of bringing to full and verified completion the disarmament process'[15]. While British Prime Minister Tony Blair remained steadfast throughout the build-up toward war, other States, including the other Permanent Members of the Security Council, sought to give the UN inspection regime the opportunity to undertake its work.

It was on the issue of the inspections by the United Nations Special Commission and the International Atomic Energy Agency that the battle-lines were drawn. In January 2003, once again during this State of the Union address to the congress of American legislators, President Bush noted:

Almost three months ago, the United Nations Security Council gave Saddam Hussein his final chance to disarm. He has shown instead utter contempt for the United Nations,

---

[14]   George W. Bush, State of the Union Address, 29 January 2002. See www.whitehouse.gov /news/releases/2002/01/20020129-11.html.
[15]   United Nations Security Council Resolution 1441, 8 November 2002, S/RES/1441, 2002.

and for the opinion of the world. [...] The dictator of Iraq is not disarming. To the contrary; he is deceiving. From intelligence sources we know, for instance, that thousands of Iraqi security personnel are at work hiding documents and materials from the U.N. inspectors, sanitizing inspection sites and monitoring the inspectors themselves. Iraqi officials accompany the inspectors in order to intimidate witnesses.

The President then went on to provide the justification for acting:

Before September the 11th, many in the world believed that Saddam Hussein could be contained. But chemical agents, lethal viruses and shadowy terrorist networks are not easily contained. Imagine those 19 hijackers with other weapons and other plans—this time armed by Saddam Hussein. [...] Some have said we must not act until the threat is imminent. Since when have terrorists and tyrants announced their intentions, politely putting us on notice before they strike? If this threat is permitted to fully and suddenly emerge, all actions, all words, and all recriminations would come too late. Trusting in the sanity and restraint of Saddam Hussein is not a strategy, and it is not an option.

He further announced that he would seek a convening of the Security Council so that his Secretary of State, Colin Powell, could 'present information and intelligence about Iraqi's illegal weapons programs, its attempt to hide those weapons from inspectors, and its links to terrorist groups'[16].

In the lead-up to this meeting, the rift which formed between the United States on the one hand, and France and Germany on the other, became public, over the American move toward the use of its military might. While the diplomatic groundwork was being set to seek to invoke the North Atlantic Treaty to protect Turkey in case of a military intervention into Iraq, the United States Defence Secretary, Donald Rumsfeld, dismissed the need to have the two Continental Powers on board. He chided France and Germany for seeking to block the move within NATO, terming them 'old Europe'[17]. In a very terse display of public diplomacy, the German Foreign Minister, Joschka Fischer, noted that his country was not abandoning its obligation to defend Turkey, but wanted to wait on the report of the weapons inspector before seeking to increase the military build-up in the region. The *Daily Telegraph* of London reported that Fischer had not yet heard a case put forward by the United States as justifying the scuttling of the inspection regime and going to war. The *Telegraph*'s reporter described the scene as follows:

Mr Fischer discarded a speech which had been written for him, and referred instead to his own brief notes. In German, he referred to Saddam Hussein as a 'horrible dictator' who had weapons of mass destruction and had bombed his neighbours.

---

[16] George W. Bush, State of the Union Address, 28 January 2003. See http://www.whitehouse.gov /news/releases/2003/01/20030128-23.html.

[17] Defence Secretary Rumsfeld was quoted as saying: 'You're thinking of Europe as Germany and France. I don't', he said. 'I think that's old Europe. If you look at the entire NATO Europe today, the centre of gravity is shifting to the east and there are a lot of new members'. See John Hooper and Ian Black, 'Threat of War: Anger at Rumsfeld Attack on 'old Europe': Transatlantic Row Berlin and Paris Hit Back at US Defence Chief', *The Guardian*, 24 January 2003, p. 5.

But that, he said, was not argument enough for going to war. 'My generation learned you must make a case, and excuse me, I am not convinced,' the Green politician shouted in English while directing his gaze, teacher-like, over silver half-moon frames, at the United States defence secretary.

'That is my problem,' he said. 'I cannot go to the public and say, 'these are the reasons', because I don't believe in them'[18].

The lines having been drawn, the United States moved to the UN Security Council to seek to get a mandate to allow its 150,000 strong troops in the region to commence their invasion. However, the real threat of a French veto coupled with the inability of the United States to muster a simple majority of the UN Security Council to support waging its war against Iraq meant that United States' diplomacy had come to an end. Instead of forcing the issues at the United Nations in New York, the Bush Administration simply walked away. By insisting on using force outside of the United Nations System, it made it clear that the multilateral controls on the use of force which had been the hallmark of world order since 1945 no longer held.

On 20 March 2003, the United States led an attack that was multilateral in name only, as part of 'The Coalition of the Willing'[19]. Although the United Kingdom provided a large number of troops, what amounted to an act of aggression was clearly conceived and carried out under the umbrella of United States' leadership and military dominance. While the apparent breakdown of the international control of the use of force as established by the United Nations System transpired in March 2003, it should be made clear that this was not an abrupt rupture. The stage was set by Western States four years previously for a breakdown of the international order which had been conceived in San Francisco in 1945. That system of international governance, which has been considered at various times in this study, relates to the international control of the use of force by way of the Security Council's powers under Chapter VII of the UN Charter. The breakdown of the UN System of international governance is found in an embryonic form starting in 1999 with the Kosovo crisis and the willingness of NATO to circumvent the Security Council by attacking Yugoslavia. Before this, the limitations of the use of force were established and agreed upon—self-defence or through the Security Council. Yet, through its actions, NATO States uncorked the genie's bottle.

By acting outside of the United Nations system, and predicating their intervention on a new pretext: 'humanitarian intervention', they sent the message that one need not act with UN Security Council approval. The consensus regarding NATO's intervention among international lawyers is that it was illegal—

[18]   Kate Connolly, 'I am not convinced, Fischer tells Rumsfeld', *The Daily Telegraph*, 10 February 2003, p. 4.
[19]   For the members of this Coalition, see Chapter 5, n. 139. For a comparison to the United Nations Coalition which undertook the 1991 War, see Chapter 5, n. 119.

tantamount to aggression[20]. Yet, questions were raised: though illegal was it not legitimate? Such was the conclusion of the Independent International Commission on Kosovo, a non-governmental body of eminent persons including the former Prosecutor at the ICTY, Richard Goldstone and Princeton University Law Professor Richard Falk[21]. This opening of the possibility for recourse to the use of force outside of the control of Security Council was further widened in the aftermath of the attacks of 11 September 2001, when the international community stood idle as the United States of America undertook its attack against Afghanistan with the tacit support of the United Nations. Shortly after September 11, the UN Security Council recognised the United States' 'inherent right of self-defence', thus giving it the green light to project force despite having been consistent for decades in establishing that self-defence is to take place on one's own territory—not halfway around the world—and not weeks after an attack has taken place[22]. The bottle having been uncorked with regard to Kosovo and having let the genie out of the bottle by actions toward Afghanistan, the international community had to sit idle, unable to command the genie to return when the United States Administration sought to apply the 'Bush Doctrine'.

In September 2002, George W. Bush put forward *The National Security Strategy of the United States of America* in which he declared that 'We must be prepared to stop rogue states and their terrorist clients before they are able to threaten or use weapons of mass destruction against the United States and our allies and friends'. He went on to say that 'the United States can no longer solely rely on a reactive posture as we have in the past. [...] We cannot let our enemies strike first'. To justify this position, the US President wrote that for 'centuries, international law recognized that nations need not suffer an attack before they can lawfully take action to defend themselves against forces that present an imminent danger of attack. Legal scholars and international jurists often condition the legitimacy of preemption on the existence of an imminent threat [...]'. The Bush Doctrine thus emerges as the following, 'To forestall or prevent such hostile acts by our adversaries, the United States will, if necessary, act preemptively'[23]. Yet to say that international law recognises the notion of pre-emptive self-defence is over-stating one's case. If there is any consensus about the use of force in pre-emptive

---

[20] Consider for instance: Francesco Francioni, 'Of War, Humanity and Justice: International Law After Kosovo', *Max Planck Yearbook of United Nations Law*, Vol. 4, 2000, pp. 107–126; Jens Elo Rytter, 'Humanitarian Intervention without the Security Council: From San Fransico to Kosovo—and Beyond', *Nordic Journal of International Law*, Vol. 70, 2001, pp. 121–160; and Nicholas Tsagourias, 'Humanitarian Intervention after Kososvo and Legal Discourse: Self-Deception or Self-Consciousness?', *Leiden Journal of International Law*, Vol. 13, 2000, pp. 11–32.
[21] The Independent International Commission on Kosovo, *The Kosovo Report (Conflict, International Response, Lessons Learned)*, 2000; and United Nations Security Council Resolution 661, 6 August 1990, S/RES/661, 1990, para. 3(c).
[22] United Nations Security Council Resolution 1373, 28 September 2001, S/RES/1373, 2001.
[23] George W. Bush, *The National Security Strategy of the United States of America*, September 2002; available at www.whitehouse.gov/nsc/nss.pdf.

self-defence it is to be found not in State practice and *opinio juris*, but in the writings of Anglo-American jurists.

The source of where such jurists have sought to give voice to the 'law' which gives a State the right to attack another in self-defence is to be found not in established law, but in correspondence between the foreign ministers of Great Britain and the United States over the *Caroline* incident which took place on the Niagara River in 1837. In that correspondence, the British argued that their destruction of the US ship, the *Caroline*, was justifiable; this then was accepted by the US Secretary of State, Daniel Webster, who recognised that self-defence could transpire in a pre-emptive manner if 'that self-defense is instant, overwhelming, and leav[es] no choice of means, and no moment of deliberation'[24]. Yet, such correspondence does not establish international law, nor have events since 1837 transpire so as to allow the Webster pronouncement to enter the corpus of the law of nations. As Professor Antonio Cassese, the first President of the International Criminal Tribunal for former Yugoslavia (ICTY) has noted in examining the manner in which countries have reacted to claims of pre-emptive self-defence, 'it is apparent that such practice does not evince agreement among States [...] with regard to anticipatory self-defence'[25]. In other words, having examined previous cases in which States have sought to justify their use of force on the basis of pre-emptive self defence, Cassese determines that there is a lack of consensus and as such no customary law has emerged with respect to the notion of pre-emption. Yet, English and American jurists such as Malcolm Shaw are prepared to say that the 'traditional definition of the right of self-defence in customary international law occurs in the *Caroline* case'[26]. Likewise, Oscar Schachter puts it, 'The conditions of the right of anticipatory defence under customary law were expressed generally in an eloquent formulation by the US Secretary of State Daniel Webster in a diplomatic note to the British in 1842'[27]. It is on the back of such a *faux* consensus that the Bush Doctrine lies.

III. Conclusion

The events of the past four years have further confirmed the underlying thesis of this study: that international law has been applied and interpreted in such a manner as to weigh in, where the Middle East is concerned, closer to power than justice. Both the continued withering of Palestine and the manner in which the United

---

[24]   See John Bassett Moore, 'Destruction of the *Caroline*', *A Digest of International Law*, Vol. 2, 1906, p. 412. Note that in the correspondence between Webster and Lord Ashburton of Great Britian it was recognised that what has come to be known as the Caroline Doctrine was a principle established as between only these two States. Further, it was recognised that a violation of the laws of nations had transpired in the case at hand, a violation of the territorial sovereignty of the United States of America, for which Great Britain apologised. See also Robert Jennings, 'The *Caroline* and McLeod Cases', *American Journal of International Law*, Vol. 32, 1938, pp. 82–99.

[25]   Antonio Cassese, *International Law*, 2001, p. 309.

[26]   Malcolm Shaw, *International Law*, 1997, p. 787.

[27]   Louis Henkin et al.(eds.), *International Law: Cases and Materials*, 1993, p. 927.

States attacked Iraq, in 2003, speak volumes as to the lack of an effective restraint on actors in the region. Whether the Middle East will continue to slide down the slippery slope of lawlessness or various actors will reverse directions and seek to breathe legitimacy into a normative framework of international relations remains to be seen.

Or put another way, are we doomed to simply stand by—at our peril—and allow the Athenian dictate to hold: that the 'strong do what they have the power to do and the weak accept what they have to accept'?

Cairo, Egypt
1 July 2004

Appendix 1

1888 Constantinople Convention

CONVENTION BETWEEN GREAT BRITAIN, GREMANY, AUSTRIA-HUNGARY,
SPAIN, FRANCE, ITALY, THE NETHERLANDS, RUSSIA AND TURKEY,
RESPECTING THE FREE NAVIGATION OF THE SUEZ MARITIME CANAL

Article I

The Suez Maritime Canal shall always be free and of commerce or of war, without
distinction of flag.

Consequently, the High Contracting Parties agree not in any way to interfere with the
free use of the Canal, in time of war as in time of peace.

The Canal shall never be subjected to the exercise of the right of blockade.

Article II

The High Contracting Parties, recognizing that the Fresh-Water Canal is indispensable to the
Maritime Canal, take note of the engagements of His Highness the Khedive towards the
Universal Suez Canal Company as regards the Fresh-Water Canal; which engagements are
stipulated in a Convention bearing the date of 18th March, 1863, containing an expose and
four Articles.

They undertake not to interfere in any way with the security of that Canal and its
branches, the working of which shall not be exposed to any attempt at obstruction.

Article III

The High Contracting Parties likewise undertake to respect the plant, establishments,
buildings, and works of the Maritime Canal and of the Fresh-Water Canal.

Article IV

The Maritime Canal remaining open in time of war as a free passage, even to ships of war of
belligerents, according to the terms of Article I of the present Treaty, the High Contracting
Parties agree that no right of war, no act of hostility, nor any act having for its object to
obstruct the free navigating of the Canal, shall be committed in the Canal and its ports, even
though the Ottoman Empire should be one of the belligerent Powers.

Vessels of war of belligerents shall not revictual or take in stores in the Canal and its
ports of access, except in so far may be strictly necessary. The transit of the aforesaid
vessels through the Canal shall be effected with the least possible delay, in accordance with
the Regulations in force, and without any intermission than the resulting from the necessities
of the service.

Their stay at Port Said and in the roadstead of Suez shall not exceed twenty-four hours, except in case if distress. In such case they shall be bound to leave as soon as possible. An interval of twenty-four hours shall always elapse between the sailing of a belligerent ship from one of the ports of access and the departure of a ship belonging to the hostile Power.

Article V

In time of war belligerent Powers shall not disembark nor embark within the Canal and its ports of access either troops, munitions, or materials of war. But in case of an accidental hindrance in the Canal, men may be embarked or disembarked at the ports of access by detachments not exceeding 1,000 men, with a corresponding amount of war material.

Article VI

Prizes shall be subjected, in all respects, to the same rules as the vessels of war of belligerents.

Article VII

The Powers shall not keep any vessel of war in the waters of the Canal (including Lake Timsah and the Bitter Lakes).

Nevertheless, they may station vessel of war in the ports of access of Port Said and Suez, the number of which shall not exceed two for each power.

This right shall not be exercised by belligerents.

Article VIII

The agents in Egypt of the Signatory Powers of the present Treaty shall be charged to watch over its execution. In case of any event threatening the security or the free passage of the Canal, they shall meet on the summons of three of their number under the presidency of their Doyen, in order to proceed to the necessary verifications. They shall inform the Khedivial Government of the danger which they may have perceived, in order that that Government may take proper steps to insure the protection and the free use of the Canal. Under any circumstances, they shall meet once a year to take note of the due execution of the Treaty.

The last mentioned meetings shall take place under the presidency of a Special Commissioner nominated for that purpose by the Imperial Ottoman Government. A Commissioner of the Khedive may also take part in the meeting, and may preside over it in case of the absence of the Ottoman Commissioner.

They shall especially demand the suppression of any work or the dispersion of any assemblage on either bank of the Canal, the object or effect of which might be to interfere with the liberty and the entire security of the navigation.

Article XI

The Egyptian Government shall, within the limit of its powers resulting from the Firmans, and under the conditions provided for in the present Treaty, take the necessary measures for insuring the execution of the said Treaty.

In case the Egyptian Government shall not have sufficient means at its disposal, it shall call upon the Imperial Ottoman Government, which shall take the necessary measures to respond to such appeal, shall give notice thereof to the Signatory Powers of the Declaration of London of the 17th March, 1885, and shall, if necessary, concert with them on the subject.

The provisions of Articles IV, V, VII and VIII shall not interfere with the measures which shall be taken in virtue of the present Article.

Article X

Similarly, the provisions of Articles IV, V, VII and VIII shall not interfere with the measures which His Majesty the Sultan and His Highness the Khedive, in the name of His Imperial Majesty, and within the limits of the Firmans granted, might find it necessary to take for securing by their own forces the defence of Egypt and the maintenance of public order.

In case His Imperial Majesty the Sultan, or His Highness the Khedive, would find it necessary to avail themselves of the exceptions for which this article provides, the Signatory Powers of the Declaration of London shall be notified thereof by the Imperial Ottoman Government.

It is likewise understood that the provisions of the four Articles aforesaid shall in no case occasion any obstacle to the measures which the Imperial Ottoman Government may think it necessary to take in order to insure by its own forces the defence of its other possessions situated on the eastern coast of the Red Sea.

Article XI

The measures which shall be taken in the cases provided for by Article IX and X of the present Treaty shall not interfere with the free use of the Canal. In the same cases, the erection of permanent fortifications contrary to the provisions of Article VIII is prohibited.

Article XII

The High Contracting Parties, by application of the principle of equality as regards the free use of the Canal, a principle which forms one of the bases of the present Treaty, agree that none of them shall endeavour to obtain with respect to the Canal territorial or commercial advantages or privileges in any international arrangements which may be concluded. Moreover, the rights of Turkey as the territorial Power are reserved.

Article XII

With the exception of the obligations provided for in this treaty, no encroachment is legalised on the rights of sovereignty or prerogatives deriving from the firmans.

Article XIV

The High Contracting Parties agree that the engagements resulting from present Treaty shall not be limited by the duration of the Acts of Concession of the Universal Suez Canal Company.

Article XV

The stipulations of the present Treaty shall not interfere with the sanitary measures in force in Egypt.

Article XVI

The High Contracting Parties undertake to bring the present Treaty to the knowledge of the States which have not signed it, inviting them to accede to it.

Article XVII

The present Treaty shall be ratified, and the ratifications shall be exchanged at Constantinople, within the space of one month, or sooner, if possible.

In faith of which the respective Plenipotentiaries have signed the present Treaty, and have affixed to it the seal of their arms.

Done at Constantinople, the 29th day of the month of October, in the year 1888.

Appendix 2

l'Entente Cordiale:
The 1904 Franco-British Declaration

Article 1

His Britannic Majesty's Government declare that they have no intention of altering the political status of Egypt.

The Government of the French Republic, for their part, declare that they will not obstruct the action of Great Britain in that country.

It is agreed that the post of Director-General of Antiquities in Egypt shall continue, as in the past, to be entrusted to a French savant.

The French schools in Egypt shall continue to enjoy the same liberty as in the past.

Article 2

The Government of the French Republic declare that they have no intention of altering the political status of Morocco.

His Britannic Majesty's Government, for their part, recognise that it appertains to France, more particularly as a Power whose dominions are conterminous for a great distance with those of Morocco, to preserve order in that country, and to provide assistance for the purpose of all administrative, economic, financial, and military reforms which it may require.

They declare that they will not obstruct the action taken by France for this purpose, provided that such action shall leave intact the rights which Great Britain, in virtue of treaties, conventions, and usage, enjoys in Morocco, including the right of coasting trade between the ports of Morocco, enjoyed by British vessels since 1901.

Article 3

His Britannic Majesty's Government for their part, will respect the rights which France, in virtue of treaties, conventions, and usage, enjoys in Egypt, including the right of coasting trade between Egyptian ports accorded to French vessels.

Article 4

The two Governments, being equally attached to the principle of commercial liberty both in Egypt and Morocco, declare that they will not, in those countries, countenance any inequality either in the imposition of customs duties or other taxes, or of railway transport charges. The trade of both nations with Morocco and with Egypt shall enjoy the same treatment in transit through the French and British possessions in Africa. An agreement between the two Governments shall settle the conditions of such transit and shall determine the points of entry.

This mutual engagement shall be binding for a period of thirty years. Unless this stipulation is expressly denounced at least one year in advance, the period shall be extended for five years at a time.

Nevertheless the Government of the French Republic reserve to themselves in Morocco, and His Britannic Majesty's Government reserve to themselves in Egypt, the right to see that the concessions for roads, railways, ports, etc., are only granted on such conditions as will maintain intact the authority of the State over these great undertakings of public interest.

Article 5

His Britannic Majesty's Government declare that they will use their influence in order that the French officials now in the Egyptian service may not be placed under conditions less advantageous than those applying to the British officials in the service.

The Government of the French Republic, for their part, would make no objection to the application of analogous conditions to British officials now in the Moorish service.

Article 6

In order to ensure the free passage of the Suez Canal, His Britannic Majesty's Government declare that they adhere to the treaty of the 29th October, 1888, and that they agree to their being put in force. The free passage of the Canal being thus guaranteed, the execution of the last sentence of paragraph 1 as well as of paragraph 2 of Article of that treaty will remain in abeyance.

Article 7

In order to secure the free passage of the Straits of Gibraltar, the two Governments agree not to permit the erection of any fortifications or strategic works on that portion of the coast of Morocco comprised between, but not including, Melilla and the heights which command the right bank of the River Sebou.

This condition does not, however, apply to the places at present in the occupation of Spain on the Moorish coast of the Mediterranean.

Article 8

The two Governments, inspired by their feeling of sincere friendship for Spain, take into special consideration the interests which that country derives from her geographical position and from her territorial possessions on the Moorish coast of the Mediterranean. In regard to these interests the French Government will come to an understanding with the Spanish Government. The agreement which may be come to on the subject between France and Spain shall be communicated to His Britannic Majesty's Government.

Article 9

The two Governments agree to afford to one another their diplomatic support, in order to obtain the execution of the clauses of the present Declaration regarding Egypt and Morocco.

In witness whereof his Excellency the Ambassador of the French Republic at the Court of His Majesty the King of the United Kingdom of Great Britain and Ireland and of the British Dominions beyond the Seas, Emperor of India, and His Majesty's Principal Secretary of State for Foreign Affairs, duly authorised for that purpose, have signed the present Declaration and have affixed thereto their seals.

Secret Articles

Article 1

In the event of either Government finding themselves constrained, by the force of circumstances, to modify their policy in respect to Egypt or Morocco, the engagements which they have undertaken towards each other by Articles 4, 6, and 7 of the Declaration of today's date would remain intact.

Article 2

His Britannic Majesty's Government have no present intention of proposing to the Powers any changes in the system of the Capitulations, or in the judicial organisation of Egypt.

In the event of their considering it desirable to introduce in Egypt reforms tending to assimilate the Egyptian legislative system to that in force in other civilised Countries, the Government of the French Republic will not refuse to entertain any such proposals, on the understanding that His Britannic Majesty's Government will agree to entertain the suggestions that the Government of the French Republic may have to make to them with a view of introducing similar reforms in Morocco.

Article 3

The two Governments agree that a certain extent of Moorish territory adjacent to Melilla, Ceuta, and other presides should, whenever the Sultan ceases to exercise authority over it, come within the sphere of influence of Spain, and that the administration of the coast from Melilla as far as, but not including, the heights on the right bank of the Sebou shall be entrusted to Spain.

Nevertheless, Spain would previously have to give her formal assent to the provisions of Articles 4 and 7 of the Declaration of today's date, and undertake to carry them out. She would also have to undertake not to alienate the whole, or a part, of the territories placed under her authority or in her sphere of influence.

Article 4

If Spain, when invited to assent to the provisions of the preceding article, should think proper to decline, the arrangement between France and Great Britain, as embodied in the Declaration of today's date, would be none the less at once applicable.

Article 5

Should the consent of the other Powers to the draft Decree mentioned in Article I of the Declaration of today's date not be obtained, the Government of the French Republic will not oppose the repayment at par of the Guaranteed, Privileged, and Unified Debts after the 15th July, 1910.

Done at London, in duplicate, the 8th day of April, 1904.

Appendix 3

1956 Sèvres Protocol

The results of the conversations which took place at Sèvres from 22 to 24 October 1956 between the representatives of the Governments of the United Kingdom, the State of Israel and of France are the following:

The Israeli forces launch in the evening of 29 October 1956 a large-scale attack on the Egyptian forces with the aim of reaching the Canal Zone the following day.

On being apprised of these events, the British and French Governments during the day of 30 October 1956 respectively and simultaneously make two appeals to the Egyptian Government and the Israeli Government on the following lines:

To the Egyptian government

Halt all acts of war.

Withdraw all its troops ten miles from the canal.

Accept temporary occupation of key positions on the canal by vessels of all nations until a final settlement.

To the Israeli government

Halts all acts of war.

Withdraw all its troops ten miles to the east of the canal.

In addition, the Israeli Government will be notified that the French and British governments have demanded of the Egyptian government to accept temporary occupation of key positions along the canal by Anglo-French forces.

It is agreed that if one of the Governments refused, or did not give its consent, within twelve hours the Anglo-French forces would intervene with the means necessary to ensure that their demands are accepted.

The representatives of the three governments agree that the Israeli Government will not be required to meet the conditions in the appeal addressed to it, in the event that the Egyptian Government does not accept those in the appeal addressed to it for their part.

In the event that the Egyptian Government should fail to agree within the stipulated time to the conditions of the appeal addressed to it, the Anglo-French forces will launch military operations against the Egyptian forces in the early hours of the morning of 31 October.

The Israeli Government will send forces to occupy the Western shore of the Gulf of Aqaba and the group of islands Tiran and Sanafir to ensure freedom of navigation in the Gulf of Aqaba.

Israel undertakes not to attack Jordan during the period of operations against Egypt. But in the event that during the same period Jordan should attack Israel, the British Government undertakes not to come to the aid of Jordan.

The arrangements of the present protocol must remain strictly secret.

They will enter into force after the agreement of the three Governments.

Appendix 4

UN General Assembly Resolution 302 (1948)

8 December 1949

The General Assembly,

Recalling its resolutions 212 (III) of 19 November 1948 and 194 (III) of 11 December 1948, affirming in particular the provisions of paragraph 11 of the latter resolutions,

Having examined with appreciation the first interim report of the United Nations Economic Survey Mission for the Middle East and the report of the Secretary-General on assistance to Palestine refugees,

1.   Expresses its appreciation to the Governments which have generously responded to the appeal embodied in its resolution 212 (III), and to the appeal of the Secretary-General, to contribute in kind or in funds to the alleviation of the conditions of starvation and distress among the Palestine refugees;

2.   Expresses also its gratitude to the International Committee of the Red Cross, to the League of Red Cross Societies and to the American Friends Service Committee for the contribution they have made to this humanitarian cause by discharging, in the face of great difficulties, the responsibility they voluntarily assumed for the distribution of relief supplies and the general care of the refugees; and welcomes the assurance they have given the Secretary-General that they will continue their co-operation with the United Nations until the end of March 1950 on a mutually acceptable basis;

3.   Commends the United Nations International Children's Emergency Fund for the important contribution which it has made towards the United Nations programme of assistance; and commends those specialized agencies which have rendered assistance in their respective fields, in particular the World Health Organization, the United nations Educational, Scientific and Cultural Organization and the International Refugee Organization;

4.   Expresses its thanks to the numerous religious, charitable and humanitarian organizations which have materially assisted in bringing relief to Palestine refugees;

5.   Recognizes that, without prejudice to the provisions of paragraph 11 of General Assembly resolution 194 (III) of 11 December 1948, continued assistance for the relief of the Palestine refugees is necessary to prevent conditions of starvation and distress among them and to further conditions of peace and stability, and that constructive measures should

be undertaken at an early date with a view to the termination of international assistance for relief;

6.   Considers that, subject to the provisions of paragraph 9(d) of the present resolution, the equivalent of approximately $33,700,000 will be required for direct relief and works programmes for the period 1 January to 31 December 1950 of which the equivalent of $20,200,000 is required for direct relief and $13,500,000 for works programmes; that the equivalent of approximately $21,200,000 will be required for works programmes from 1 January to 30 June 1951, all inclusive of administrative expenses; and that direct relief should be terminated not later than 31 December 1950 unless otherwise determined by the General Assembly at its fifth regular session;

7.   Establishes the United Nations Relief and Works Agency for Palestine Refugees in the Near East:

a)   To carry out in collaboration with local governments the direct relief and works programmes as recommended by the Economic Survey Mission;

b)   To consult with the interested Near Eastern Governments concerning measures to be taken by them preparatory to the time when international assistance for relief and works projects is no longer available;

8.   Establishes an Advisory Commission consisting of representatives of France, Turkey, the United Kingdom of Great Britain and Northern Ireland and the United States of America, with power to add not more than three additional members from contributing Governments, to advise and assist the Director of the United Nations Relief and Works Agency for Palestine Refugees in the Near East in the execution of the programme; the Director and the Advisory Commission shall consult with each near Eastern Government concerned in the selection, planning and execution of projects;

9.   Requests the Secretary-General to appoint the Director of the United Nations Relief and Works Agency for Palestine Refugees in the Near East in consultation with the Governments represented on the Advisory Commission;

a)   The Director shall be the chief executive officer of the United Nations Relief and Works Agency for Palestine Refugees in the Near East responsible to the General Assembly for the operation of the programme;
b)   The Director shall select and appoint his staff in accordance with general arrangements made in agreement with the Secretary-General, including such of the staff rules and regulations of the United Nations as the Director and the Secretary-General shall agree are applicable, and to the extent possible utilize the facilities and assistance of the Secretary-General;
c)   The Director shall, in consultation with the Secretary-General and the Advisory Committee on Administrative and Budgetary Questions, establish financial regulations for the United Nations Relief and Works Agency for Palestine Refugees in the Near East;
d)   Subject to the financial regulations established pursuant to clause (c) of the present paragraph, the Director, in consultation with the Advisory Commission, shall apportion available funds between direct relief and works projects in their discretion, in the event that the estimates in paragraph 6 require revision;

10. Requests the Director to convene the Advisory Commission at the earliest practicable date for the purpose of developing plans for the organization and administration of the programme, and of adopting rules of procedure;

11. Continues the United Nations Relief for Palestine Refugees as established under General Assembly resolution 212 (III) until 1 April 1950, or until such date thereafter as the transfer referred to in paragraph 12 is affected, and requests the Secretary-General in consultation with the operating agencies to continue the endeavour to reduce the numbers of rations by progressive stages in the light of the findings and recommendations of the Economic Survey Mission;

12. Instructs the Secretary-General to transfer to the United Nations Relief and Works Agency for Palestine Refugees in the Near East the assets and liabilities of the United Nations Relief for Palestine Refugees by 1 April 1950, or at such date as may be agreed by him and the Director of the United Nations Relief and Works Agency for Palestine Refugees in the Near East;

13. Urges all Members of the United Nations and non-members to make voluntary contributions in funds or in kind to ensure that the amount of supplies and funds required is obtained for each period of the programme as set out in paragraph 6; contributions in funds may be made in currencies other than the United States dollar in so far as the programme can be carried out in such currencies;

14. Authorizes the Secretary-General, in consultation with the Advisory Committee on Administrative and Budgetary Questions, to advance funds deemed to be available for this purpose and not exceeding $5,000,000 from the Working Capital Fund to finance operations pursuant to the present resolution, such sum to be repaid not later than 31 December 1950 from the voluntary governmental contributions requested under paragraph 13 above;

15. Authorizes the Secretary-General, in consultation with the Advisory Committee on Administrative and Budgetary Questions, to negotiate with the International Refugee Organization for an interest-free loan in an amount not to exceed the equivalent of $2,800,000 to finance the programme subject to mutually satisfactory conditions for repayment;

16. Authorizes the Secretary-General to continue the Special Fund established under General Assembly resolution 212 (III) and to make withdrawals therefrom for the operation of the United Nations Relief for Palestine Refugees and, upon the request of the Director, for the operations of the United Nations Relief and Works Agency for Palestine Refugees in the Near East;

17. Calls upon the Governments concerned to accord to the United Nations Relief and Works Agency for Palestine Refugees in the Near East the privileges, immunities, exemptions and facilities which have been granted to the United Nations Relief for Palestine Refugees, together with all other privileges, immunities, exemptions and facilities necessary for the fulfilment of its functions;

18. Urges the United Nations International Children's Emergency Fund, the International Refugee Organization, the World Health Organization, the United Nations Educational, Scientific and Cultural Organization, the Food and Agriculture Organization and other appropriate agencies and private groups and organizations, in consultation with the Director

of the United Nations Relief and Works Agency for Palestine Refugees in the Near East, to furnish assistance within the framework of the programme;

19. Requests the Director of the United Nations Relief and Works Agency for Palestine Refugees in the Near East:

a)	To appoint a representative to attend the meeting of the Technical Assistance Board as observer so that the technical assistance activities of the United Nations Relief and Works Agency for Palestine Refugees in the Near East may be co-ordinated with the technical assistance programmes of the United Nations and specialized agencies referred to in Economic and Social Council resolution 222 (IX) A of 15 August 1949;

b)	To place at the disposal of the Technical Assistance Board full information concerning any technical assistance work which may be done by the United Nations Relief and Works Agency for Palestine Refugees in the Near East, in order that it may be included in the reports submitted by the Technical Assistance Board to the Technical Assistance committee of the Economic and Social Council;

20. Directs the United Nations Relief and Works Agency for Palestine Refugees in the Near East to consult with the United Nations Conciliation Commission for Palestine in the best interests of their respective tasks, with particular reference to paragraph 11 of General Assembly resolution 194 (III) of 11 December 1948;

21. Requests the Director to submit to the General Assembly of the United Nations an annual report on the work of the United Nations Relief and Works Agency for Palestine Refugees in the Near East, including an audit of funds, and invites him to submit to the Secretary-General such other reports as the United Nations Relief and Works Agency for Palestine Refugees in the Near East may wish to bring to the attention of Members of the United Nations, or its appropriate organs;

22. Instructs the United Nations Conciliation Commission for Palestine to transmit the final report of the Economic Survey Mission, with such comments as it may wish to make, to the Secretary-General for transmission to the Members of the United Nations and to the United Nations Relief and Works Agency for Palestine Refugees in the Near East.

Appendix 5

UN General Assembly Resolution 3314 (1974)

14 December 1974

The General Assembly,

Having considered the report of the Special Committee on the Question of Defining Aggression, established pursuant to its resolution 2330(XXII) of 18 December 1967, covering the work of its seventh session held from 11 March to 12 April 1974, including the draft Definition of Aggression adopted by the Special Committee by consensus and recommended for adoption by the General Assembly,

Deeply, convinced that the adoption of the Definition of Aggression would contribute to the strengthening of international peace and security,

1.   Approves the Definition of Aggression, the text of which is annexed to the present resolution;

2.   Expresses its appreciation to the Special Committee on the Question of Defining Aggression for its work which resulted in the elaboration of the Definition of Aggression;

3.   Calls upon all States to refrain from all acts of aggression and other uses of force contrary to the Charter of the United Nations and the Declaration on Principles of International Law concerning Friendly Relations and Cooperation among States in accordance with the Charter of the United Nations;

4.   Calls the attention of the Security Council to the Definition of Aggression, as set out below, and recommends that it should, as appropriate, take account of that Definition as guidance in determination, in accordance with the Charter, the existence of an act of aggression.

Annex—Definition of Aggression

The General Assembly,

Basing itself on the fact that one of the fundamental purposes of the United Nations is to maintain international peace and security and to take effective collective measures for the prevention and removal of threats to the peace, and for the suppression of acts of aggression or other breaches of the peace,

Recalling that the Security Council, in accordance with Article 39 of the Charter of the United Nations, shall determine the existence of any threat to the peace, breach of the peace or act of aggression and shall make recommendations, or decide what measures shall be taken in accordance with Articles 41 and 42, to maintain or restore international peace and security,

Recalling also the duty of States under the Charter to settle their international disputes by peaceful means in order not to endanger international peace, security and justice,

Bearing in mind that nothing in this Definition shall be interpreted as in any way affecting the scope of the provisions of the Charter with respect to the functions and powers of the organs of the United Nations,

Considering also that, since aggression is the most serious and dangerous form of the illegal use of force, being fraught, in the conditions created by the existence of all types of weapons of mass destruction, with the possible threat of a world conflict and all its catastrophic consequences, aggression should be defined at the present stage,

Reaffirming the duty of States not to use armed force to deprive peoples of their right to self-determination, freedom and independence, or to disrupt territorial Integrity,

Reaffirming also that the territory of a State shall not be violated by being the object, even temporarily, of military occupation or of other measures of force taken by another State in contravention of the Charter, and that it shall not be the object of acquisition by another State resulting from such measures or the threat thereof,

Reaffirming also the provisions of the Declaration on Principles of International Law concerning Friendly Relations and Cooperation among States in accordance with the Charter of the United Nations,

Convinced that the adoption of a definition of aggression ought to have the effect of deterring a potential aggressor, would simplify the determination of acts of aggression and the implementation of measures to suppress them and would also facilitate the protection of the rights and lawful interests of, and the rendering of assistance to, the victim,

Believing that, although the question whether an act of aggression has been committed must be considered in the light of all the circumstances of each particular case, it is nevertheless desirable to formulate basic principles as guidance for such determination,

Adopts the following Definition of Aggression:

Article 1

Aggression is the use of armed force by a State against the sovereignty, territorial integrity or political independence of another State, or in any other manner inconsistent with the Charter of the United Nations, as set out in this Definition.
Explanatory note: In this Definition the term "State":

a)   Is used without prejudice to questions of recognition or to whether a State is a member of the United Nations;

b)   Includes the concept of a "group of States" where appropriate.

Article 2

The First use of armed force by a State in contravention of the Charter shall constitute prima facie evidence of an act of aggression although the Security Council may, in conformity with the Charter, conclude that a determination that an act of aggression has been committed would not be justified in the light of other relevant circumstances, including the fact that the acts concerned or their consequences are not of sufficient gravity.

Article 3

Any of the following acts, regardless of a declaration of war, shall, subject to and in accordance with the provisions of article 2, qualify as an act of aggression:

a)   The invasion or attack by the armed forces of a State of the territory of another State, or any military occupation, however temporary, resulting from such invasion or attack, or any annexation by the use of force of the territory of another State or part thereof;

b)   Bombardment by the armed forces of a State against the territory of another State or the use of any weapons by a State against the territory of another State;

c)   The blockade of the ports or coasts of a State by the armed forces of another State;

d)   An attack by the armed forces of a State on the land, sea or air forces, or marine and air fleets of another State;

e)   The use of armed forces of one State which are within the territory of another State with the agreement of the receiving State, in contravention of the conditions provided for in the agreement or any extension of their presence in such territory beyond the termination of the agreement;

f)   The action of a State in allowing its territory, which it has placed at the disposal of another State, to be used by that other State for perpetrating an act of aggression against a third State;

g)   The sending by or on behalf of a State of armed bands, groups, irregulars or mercenaries, which carry out acts of armed force against another State of such gravity as to amount to the acts listed above, or its substantial involvement therein.

Article 4

The acts enumerated above are not exhaustive and the Security Council may determine that other acts constitute aggression under the provisions of the Charter.

Article 5

1.   No consideration of whatever nature, whether political, economic, military or otherwise, may serve as a justification for aggression.

2.   A war of aggression is a crime against international peace. Aggression gives rise to international responsibility.

3.   No territorial acquisition or special advantage resulting from aggression is or shall be recognized as lawful.

Article 6

Nothing in this Definition shall be construed as in any way enlarging or diminishing the scope of the Charter, including its provisions concerning cases in which the use of force is lawful.

Article 7

Nothing in this Definition, and in particular article 3, could in any way prejudice the right to self-determination, freedom and independence, as derived from the Charter, of peoples forcibly deprived of that right and referred to in the Declaration on Principles of International Law concerning Friendly Relations and Cooperation among States in accordance with the Charter of the United Nations, particularly peoples under colonial and racist regimes or other forms of alien domination: nor the right of these peoples to struggle to that end and to seek and receive support, in accordance with the principles of the Charter and in conformity with the above-mentioned Declaration.

Article 8

In their interpretation and application the above provisions are interrelated and each provision should be construed in the context of the other provisions.

UN Security Council Resolution 425 (1978)

March 19, 1978

The Security Council,

Taking note of the letters of the Permanent Representative of Lebanon (S/12600 and S/12606) and the Permanent Representative of Israel (S/12607),

Having heard the statements of the Permanent Representatives of Lebanon and Israel,

Gravely concerned at the deterioration of the situation in the Middle East, and its consequences to the maintenance of international peace,

Convinced that the present situation impedes the achievement of a just peace in the Middle East,

Calls for strict respect for the territorial integrity, sovereignty and political independence of Lebanon within its internationally recognized boundaries,

Calls upon Israel immediately to cease its military action against Lebanese territorial integrity and withdraw forthwith its forces from all Lebanese territory,

Decides, in the light of the request of the Government of Lebanon, to establish immediately under its authority a United Nations interim force for southern Lebanon for the purpose of confirming the withdrawal of Israeli forces, restoring international peace and security and assisting the Government of Lebanon in ensuring the return of its effective authority in the area, the force to be composed of personnel drawn from States Members of the United Nations.

Requests the Secretary-General to report to the Council within twenty-four hours on the implementation of this resolution.

Appendix 7

UN Security Council Resolution 479 (1980)

28 September 1980

The Security Council,

Having begun consideration of the item entitled, "The Situation between Iran and Iraq",

Mindful that all Member States have undertaken the Charter obligations to settle their international disputes by peaceful means and in such a manner that international peace and security and justice are not endangered,

Mindful as well that all Members are obliged to refrain in their international relations from the threat of or use of force against the territorial integrity or political independence of any State,

Recalling that under Article 24 of the Charter the Security Council has primary responsibility for the maintenance of international peace and security,

Deeply concerned about the developing situation between Iran and Iraq,

1. Calls upon Iran and Iraq to refrain immediately from any further use of force and to settle their dispute by peaceful means and in conformity with principles of justice and international law;

2. Urges them to accept any appropriate offer of mediation or conciliation or to resort to regional agencies or arrangements or other peaceful means of their own choice that would facilitate the fulfilment of their Charter obligations;

3. Calls upon all other States to exercise the utmost restraint and to refrain from any act which may lead to a further escalation and widening of the conflict;

4. Supports the efforts of the Secretary-General and the offer of his good offices for the resolution of this situation;

5. Requests the Secretary-General to report to the Security Council within forty-eight hours.

UN Security Council Resolution 508 (1982)

5 June 1982

The Security Council,

Recalling Security Council resolution 425 (1978), 426 (1978) and the ensuing resolutions, and more particularly, Security Council resolution 501 (1982),

Taking note of the letters of the Permanent Representative of Lebanon dated 4 June 1982 (S/15161 and S/15162),

Deeply concerned at the deterioration of the present situation in Lebanon and in the Lebanese-Israeli border area, and its consequences for peace and security in the region,

Gravely concerned at the violation of the territorial integrity, independence, and sovereignty of Lebanon,

Reaffirming and supporting the statement made by the President and the members of the Security Council on 4 June 1982 (S/15163), as well as the urgent appeal issued by the Secretary-General on 4 June 1982,

Taking note of the report of the Secretary-General,

1.   Calls upon all the parties to the conflict to cease immediately and simultaneously all military activities within Lebanon and across the Lebanese-Israeli border and no later than 0600 hours local time on Sunday, 6 June 1982;

2.   Requests all Member States which are in a position to do so to bring their influence to bear upon those concerned so that the cessation of hostilities declared by Security Council resolution 490 (1981) can be respected;

3.   Requests the Secretary-General to undertake all possible efforts to ensure the implementation of and compliance with this resolution and to report to the Security Council as early as possible and not later than forty-eight hours after the adoption of this resolution.

UN Security Council Resolution 598 (1987)

20 July 1987

The Security Council,

Reaffirming its resolution 582 (1986)

Deeply concerned that, despite its calls for a cease-fire, the conflict between Iran and Iraq continues unabated, with further heavy loss of human life and material destruction,

Deploring the initiation and continuation of the conflict,

Deploring also the bombing of purely civilian population centers, attacks on neutral shipping or civilian aircraft, the violation of international humanitarian law and other laws of armed conflict, and, in particular, the use of chemical weapons contrary to obligations under the 1925 Geneva Protocol,

Deeply concerned that further escalation and widening of the conflict may take place,

Determined to bring to an end all military actions between Iran and Iraq,

Convinced that a comprehensive, just, honourable and durable settlement should be achieved between Iran and Iraq,

Recalling the provisions of the Charter of the United Nations and in particular the obligation of all member states to settle their international disputes by peaceful means in such a manner that international peace and security and justice are not endangered,

Determining that there exists a breach of the peace as regards the conflict between Iran and Iraq,

Acting under Articles 39 and 40 of the Charter of the United Nations,

1.   Demands that, as a first step towards a negotiated settlement, Iran and Iraq observe an immediate cease-fire, discontinue all military actions on land, at sea and in the air, and withdraw all forces to the internationally recognized boundaries without delay;

2.   Requests the Secretary-General to dispatch a team of United Nations Observers to verify, confirm and supervise the cease-fire and withdrawal and further requests the Secretary-General to make the necessary arrangements in consultation with the Parties and to submit a report thereon to the Security Council;

3.   Urges that prisoners of war be released and repatriated without delay after the cessation of active hostilities in accordance with the Third Geneva Convention of 12 August 1949;

4.   Calls upon Iran and Iraq to cooperate with the Secretary-General in implementing this resolution and in mediation efforts to achieve a comprehensive, just and honourable settlement, acceptable to both sides, of all outstanding issues in accordance with the principles contained in the Charter of the United Nations;

5.   Calls upon all other States to exercise the utmost restraint and to refrain from any act which may lead to further escalation and widening of the conflict and thus to facilitate the implementation of the present resolution;

6.   Requests the Secretary-General to explore, in consultation with Iran and Iraq, the question of entrusting an impartial body with inquiring into responsibility for the conflict and to report to the Security Council as soon as possible;

7.   Recognizes the magnitude of the damage inflicted during the conflict and the need for reconstruction efforts, with appropriate international assistance, once the conflict is ended and, in this regard, requests the Secretary-General to assign a team of experts to study the question of reconstruction and to report to the Security Council;

8.   Further requests the Secretary-General to examine in consultation with Iran and Iraq and with other states of the region measures to enhance the security and stability of the region;

9.   Requests the Secretary-General to keep the Security Council informed on the implementation of this resolution;

10.   Decides to meet again as necessary to consider further steps to insure compliance with this resolution.

Appendix 10

UN Security Council Resolution 660 (1990)

2 August 1990

The Security Council,

Alarmed by the invasion of Kuwait on 2 August 1990 by the military forces of Iraq,

Determining that there exists a breach of international peace and security as regards the Iraqi invasion of Kuwait,

Acting under Articles 39 and 40 of the Charter of the United Nations,

1.   Condemns the Iraqi invasion of Kuwait;

2.   Demands that Iraq withdraw immediately and unconditionally all its forces to the positions in which they were located on 1 August 1990;

3.   Calls upon Iraq and Kuwait to begin immediately intensive negotiations for the resolution of their differences and supports all efforts in this regard, and especially those of the League of Arab States;

4.   Decides to meet again as necessary to consider further steps with to ensure compliance with the present resolution.

UN Security Council Resolution 661 (1990)

6 August 1990

The Security Council,

Reaffirming its resolution 660 (1990) of 2 August 1990,

Deeply concerned that that resolution has not been implemented and that the invasion by Iraq of Kuwait continues with further loss of human life and material destruction,

Determined to bring the invasion and occupation of Kuwait by Iraq to an end and to restore the sovereignty, independence and territorial integrity of Kuwait,

Noting that the legitimate Government of Kuwait has expressed its readiness to comply with resolution 660 (1990),

Mindful of its responsibilities under the Charter of the United Nations for the maintenance of international peace and security,

Affirming the inherent right of individual or collective self-defence, in response to the armed attack by Iraq against Kuwait, in accordance with Article 51 of the Charter,

Acting under Chapter VII of the Charter of the United Nations,

    1.   Determines that Iraq so far has failed to comply with paragraph 2 of resolution 660 (1990) and has usurped the authority of the legitimate Government of Kuwait;

    2.   Decides, as a consequence, to take the following measures to secure compliance of Iraq with paragraph 2 of resolution 660 (1990) and to restore the authority of the legitimate Government of Kuwait;

    3.   Decides that all States shall prevent:

(a)   The import into their territories of all commodities and products originating in Iraq or Kuwait exported there from after the date of the present resolution;

(b)   Any activities by their nationals or in their territories which would promote or are calculated to promote the export or trans-shipment of any commodities or products from Iraq or Kuwait; and any dealings by their nationals or their flag vessels or in their territories in any commodities or products originating in Iraq or Kuwait and exported therefrom after the date of the present resolution, including in particular any transfer of funds to Iraq or Kuwait for the purposes of such activities or dealings;

(c)   The sale or supply by their nationals or from their territories or using their flag vessels of any commodities or products, including weapons or any other military equipment, whether or not originating in their territories but not including supplies intended strictly for medical purposes, and, in humanitarian circumstances, foodstuffs, to any person or body in Iraq or Kuwait or to any person or body for the purposes of any business carried on in or operated from Iraq or Kuwait, and any activities by their nationals or in their territories which promote or are calculated to promote such sale or supply of such commodities or products;

4.   Decides that all States shall not make available to the Government of Iraq or to any commercial, industrial or public utility undertaking in Iraq or Kuwait, any funds or any other financial or economic resources and shall prevent their nationals and any persons within their territories from removing from their territories or otherwise making available to that Government or to any such undertaking any such funds or resources and from remitting any other funds to persons or bodies within Iraq or Kuwait, except payments exclusively for strictly medical or humanitarian purposes and, in humanitarian circumstances, foodstuffs;

5.   Calls upon all States, including States non-members of the United Nations, to act strictly in accordance with the provisions of the present resolution notwithstanding any contract entered into or licence granted before the date of the present resolution;

6.   Decides to establish, in accordance with rule 28 of the provisional rules of procedure of the Security Council, a Committee of the Security Council consisting of all the members of the Council, to undertake the following tasks and to report on its work to the Council with its observations and recommendations:

a)   To examine the reports on the progress of the implementation of the present resolution which will be submitted by the Secretary-General;

b)   To seek from all States further information regarding the action taken by them concerning the effective implementation of the provisions laid down in the present resolution;

7.   Calls upon all States to co-operate fully with the Committee in the fulfilment of its task, including supplying such information as may be sought by the Committee in pursuance of the present resolution;

8. Requests the Secretary-General to provide all necessary assistance to the Committee and to make the necessary arrangements in the Secretariat for the purpose;

9. Decides that, notwithstanding paragraphs 4 through 8 above, nothing in the present resolution shall prohibit assistance to the legitimate Government of Kuwait, and calls upon all States:

a) To take appropriate measures to protect assets of the legitimate Government of Kuwait and its agencies;

b) Not to recognize any regime set up by the occupying Power;

10. Requests the Secretary-General to report to the Council on the progress of the implementation of the present resolution, the first report to be submitted within thirty days;

11. Decides to keep this item on its agenda and to continue its efforts to put an early end to the invasion by Iraq.

UN Security Council Resolution 678 (1990)

29 November 1990

The Security Council,

Recalling, and reaffirming its resolutions 660 (1990) of 2 August (1990), 661 (1990) of 6 August 1990, 662 (1990) of 9 August 1990, 664 (1990) of 18 August 1990, 665 (1990) of 25 August 1990, 666 (1990) of 13 September 1990, 667 (1990) of 16, September 1990, 669 (1990) of 24 September 1990, 670 (1990) of 25 September 1990, 674 (1990) of of 29 October 1990 and 677,(1990) of 28 November 1990.

Noting that, despite all efforts by the United Nations, Iraq refuses to comply with its obligation to implement resolution 660 (1990) and the above-mentioned subsequent relevant resolutions, in flagrant contempt of the Security Council,

Mindful of its duties and responsibilities under the Charter of the United Nations for the maintenance and preservation of international peace and security,

Determined to secure full compliance with its decisions,

Acting under Chapter VII of the Charter,

1. Demands that Iraq comply fully with resolution 660 (1990) and all subsequent relevant resolutions, and decides, while maintaining all its decisions, to allow Iraq one final opportunity, as a pause of goodwil, to do so;

2. Authorizes Member States co-operating with the Government of Kuwait, unless Iraq on or before 15 January 1991 fully implements, as set forth in paragraph 1 above, the foregoing resolutions, to use all necessary means to uphold and implement resolution 660 (1990) and all subsequent relevant resolutions and to restore international peace and security in the area;

3. Requests all States to provide appropriate support for the actions undertaken in pursuance of paragraph 2 of the present resolution;

4. Requests the States concerned to keep the Security Council regularly informed on the progress of actions undertaken pursuant to paragraphs 2 and 3 of the present resolution;

5. Decides to remain seized of the matter.

UN Security Council Resolution 687 (1991)

April 3, 1991

The Security Council,

Recalling its resolutions 660 (1990) of 2 August 1990, 661 (1990) of 6 August 1990, 662 (1990) of 9 August 1990, 664 (1990) of 18 August 1990, 665 (1990) of 25 August 1990, 666 (1990) of 13 September 1990, 667 (1990) of 16 September 1990, 669 (1990) of 24 September 1990, 670 (1990) of 25 September 1990, 674 (1990) of 29 October 1990, 677 (1990) of 28 November 1990, 678 (1990) of 29 November 1990 and 686 (1991) of 2 March 1991,

Welcoming the restoration to Kuwait of its sovereignty, independence and territorial integrity and the return of its legitimate Government,

Affirming the commitment of all Member States to the sovereignty, territorial integrity and political independence of Kuwait and Iraq, and noting the intention expressed by the Member States cooperating with Kuwait under paragraph 2 of resolution 678 (1990) to bring their military presence in Iraq to an end as soon as possible consistent with paragraph 8 of resolution 686 (1991),

Reaffirming the need to be assured of Iraq's peaceful intentions in the light of its unlawful invasion and occupation of Kuwait,

Taking note of the letter sent by the Minister for Foreign Affairs of Iraq on 27 February 1991 and those sent pursuant to resolution 686 (1991),

Noting that Iraq and Kuwait, as independent sovereign States, signed at Baghdad on 4 October 1963 "Agreed Minutes Between the State of Kuwait and the Republic of Iraq,

Regarding the Restoration of Friendly Relations, Recognition and Related Matters", thereby recognizing formally the boundary between Iraq and Kuwait and the allocation of islands, which were registered with the United Nations in accordance with Article 102 of the Charter of the United Nations and in which Iraq recognized the independence and complete sovereignty of the State of Kuwait within its borders as specified and accepted in the letter of the Prime Minister of Iraq dated 21 July 1932, and as accepted by the Ruler of Kuwait in his letter dated 10 August 1932,

Conscious of the need for demarcation of the said boundary,

Conscious also of the statements by Iraq threatening to use weapons in violation of its obligations under the Geneva Protocol for the Prohibition of the Use in War of Asphyxiating, Poisonous or Other Gases, and of Bacteriological Methods of Warfare, signed at Geneva on 17 June 1925, and of its prior use of chemical weapons and affirming that grave consequences would follow any further use by Iraq of such weapons,

Recalling that Iraq has subscribed to the Declaration adopted by all States participating in the Conference of States Parties to the 1925 Geneva Protocol and Other Interested States, held in Paris from 7 to 11 January 1989, establishing the objective of universal elimination of chemical and biological weapons,

Recalling also that Iraq has signed the Convention on the Prohibition of the Development, Production and Stockpiling of Bacteriological (Biological) and Toxin weapons and on Their Destruction, of 10 April 1972,

Noting the importance of Iraq ratifying this Convention,

Noting moreover the importance of all States adhering to this Convention and encouraging its forthcoming Review Conference to reinforce the authority, efficiency and universal scope of the convention,

Stressing the importance of an early conclusion by the Conference on Disarmament of its work on a Convention on the Universal Prohibition of Chemical Weapons and of universal adherence thereto,

Aware of the use by Iraq of ballistic missiles in unprovoked attacks and therefore of the need to take specific measures in regard to such missiles located in Iraq,

Concerned by the reports in the hands of Member States that Iraq has attempted to acquire materials for a nuclear-weapons programme contrary to its obligations under the Treaty on the Non-Proliferation of Nuclear Weapons of 1 July 1968,

Recalling the objective of the establishment of a nuclear-weapons-free zone in the region of the Middle East,

Conscious of the threat that all weapons of mass destruction pose to peace and security in the area and of the need to work towards the establishment in the Middle East of a zone free of such weapons,

Conscious also of the objective of achieving balanced and comprehensive control of armaments in the region,

Conscious further of the importance of achieving the objectives noted above using all available means, including a dialogue among the States of the region,

Noting that resolution 686 (1991) marked the lifting of the measures imposed by resolution 661 (1990) in so far as they applied to Kuwait,

Noting that despite the progress being made in fulfilling the obligations of resolution 686 (1991), many Kuwaiti and third country nationals are still not accounted for and property remains unreturned,

Recalling the International Convention against the Taking of Hostages, opened for signature at New York on 18 December 1979, which categorizes all acts of taking hostages as manifestations of international terrorism,

Deploring threats made by Iraq during the recent conflict to make use of terrorism against targets outside Iraq and the taking of hostages by Iraq,

Taking note with grave concern of the reports of the Secretary-General of 20 March 1991 and 28 March 1991, and conscious of the necessity to meet urgently the humanitarian needs in Kuwait and Iraq,

Bearing in mind its objective of restoring international peace and security in the area as set out in recent resolutions of the Security Council,

Conscious of the need to take the following measures acting under Chapter VII of the Charter,

1.   Affirms all thirteen resolutions noted above, except as expressly changed below to achieve the goals of this resolution, including a formal cease-fire:

A

2.   Demands that Iraq and Kuwait respect the inviolability of the international boundary and the allocation of islands set out in the "Agreed Minutes Between the State of Kuwait and the Republic of Iraq Regarding the Restoration of Friendly Relations, Recognition and Related Matters", signed by them in the exercise of their sovereignty at Baghdad on 4 October 1963 and registered with the United Nations and published by the United Nations in document 7063, United Nations, Treaty Series, 1964;

3.   Calls upon the Secretary-General to lend his assistance to make arrangements with Iraq and Kuwait to demarcate the boundary between Iraq and Kuwait, drawing on appropriate material, including the map transmitted by Security Council document S/22412 and to report back to the Security Council within one month;

4.   Decides to guarantee the inviolability of the above-mentioned international boundary and to take as appropriate all necessary measures to that end in accordance with the Charter of the United Nations;

B

5.   Requests the Secretary-General, after consulting with Iraq and Kuwait, to submit within three days to the Security Council for its approval a plan for the immediate deployment of a United Nations observer unit to monitor the Khor Abdullah and a demilitarized zone, which is hereby established, extending ten kilometres into Iraq and five kilometres into Kuwait from the boundary referred to in the "Agreed Minutes Between the State of Kuwait and the Republic of Iraq Regarding the Restoration of Friendly Relations, Recognition and Related Matters" of 4 October 1963; to deter violations of the boundary through its presence in and surveillance of the demilitarized zone; to observe any hostile or potentially hostile action mounted from the territory of one State to the other; and for the Secretary-General to report regularly to the Security

Council on the operations of the unit, and immediately if there are serious violations of the zone or potential threats to peace;

6.   Notes that as soon as the Secretary-General notifies the Security Council of the completion of the deployment of the United Nations observer unit, the conditions will be established for the Member States cooperating with Kuwait in accordance with resolution 678 (1990) to bring their military presence in Iraq to an end consistent with resolution 686 (1991);

C

7.   Invites Iraq to reaffirm unconditionally its obligations under the Geneva Protocol for the Prohibition of the Use in War of Asphyxiating Poisonous or Other Gases, and of Bacteriological Methods of Warfare, signed at Geneva on 17 June 1925, and to ratify the Convention on the Prohibition of the Development, Production and Stockpiling of Bacteriological (Biological) and Toxin Weapons and on Their Destruction, of 10 April 1972;

8.   Decides that shall unconditionally accept the destruction, removal, or rendering harmless, under international supervision, of:

All chemical and biological weapons and all stocks of agents and all related subsystems and components and all research, development, support and manufacturing facilities;

All ballistic missiles with a range greater than 150 kilometres and related major parts, and repair and production facilities;

9.   Decides, for the implementation of paragraph 8 above, the following:
Iraq shall submit to the Secretary-General, within fifteen days of the adoption of the present resolution, a declaration of the locations, amounts and types of all items specified in paragraph 8 and agree to urgent, on-site inspection as specified below;
The Secretary-General, in consultation with the appropriate Governments and, where appropriate, with the Director-General of the World Health Organization, within forty-five days of the passage of the present resolution, shall develop, and submit to the Council for approval, a plan calling for the completion of the following acts within forty-five days of such approval:

The forming of a Special Commission, which shall carry out immediate on-site inspection of Iraq's biological, chemical and missile capabilities, based on Iraq's declarations and the designation of any additional locations by the Special Commission itself;
The yielding by Iraq of possession to the Special Commission for destruction, removal or rendering harmless, taking into account the requirements of public safety, of all items specified under paragraph 8 (a) above, including items at the additional locations designated by the Special Commission under paragraph 9 (b) (i) above and the destruction by Iraq, under the supervision of the Special Commission, of all its missile capabilities, including launchers, as specified under paragraph 8 (b) above;

The provision by the Special Commission of the assistance and cooperation to the Director-General of the International Atomic Energy Agency required in paragraphs 12 and 13 below;

10. Decides that Iraq shall unconditionally undertake not to use, develop, construct or acquire any of the items specified in paragraphs 8 and 9 above and requests the Secretary-General, in consultation with the Special Commission, to develop a plan for the future ongoing monitoring and verification of Iraq's compliance with this paragraph. to be submitted to the Security Council for approval within one hundred and twenty days of the passage of this resolution;

11. Invites Iraq to reaffirm unconditionally its obligations under the Treaty on the Non-Proliferation of Nuclear Weapons of 1 July 1968;

12. Decides that Iraq shall unconditionally agree not to acquire or develop nuclear weapons or nuclear-weapons-usable material or any subsystems or components or any research, development, support or manufacturing facilities related to the above; to submit to the Secretary-General and the Director-General of the International Atomic Energy Agency within fifteen days of the adoption of the present resolution a declaration of the locations, amounts, and types of all items specified above; to place all of its nuclear-weapons-usable materials under the exclusive control, for custody and removal, of the International Atomic Energy Agency, with the assistance and cooperation of the Special Commission as provided for in the plan of the Secretary-General discussed in paragraph 9 (b) above; to accept, in accordance with the arrangements provided for in paragraph 13 below, urgent on-site inspection and the destruction, removal or rendering harmless as appropriate of all items specified above; and to accept the plan discussed in paragraph 13 below for the future ongoing monitoring and verification of its compliance with these undertakings;

13. Requests the Director-General of the International Atomic Energy Agency, through the Secretary-General, with the assistance and cooperation of the Special Commission as provided for in the plan of the Secretary-General in paragraph 9 (b) above, to carry out immediate on-site inspection of Iraq's nuclear capabilities based on Iraq's declarations and the designation of any additional locations by the Special Commission; to develop a plan for submission to the Security Council within forty-five days calling for the destruction, removal, or rendering harmless as appropriate of all items listed in paragraph 12 above; to carry out the plan within forty-five days following approval by the Security Council; and to develop a plan, taking into account the rights and obligations of Iraq under the Treaty on the Non-Proliferation of Nuclear Weapons of 1 July 1968, for the future ongoing monitoring and verification of Iraq's compliance with paragraph 12 above, including an inventory of all nuclear material in Iraq subject to the Agency's verification and inspections of the International Atomic Energy Agency to confirm that the Agency's safeguards cover all relevant nuclear activities in Iraq, to be submitted to the Security Council for approval within one hundred and twenty days of the passage of the present resolution;

14. Takes note that the actions to be taken by Iraq in paragraphs 8, 9, 10, 11, 12 and 13 of the present resolution represent steps towards the goal of establishing in the Middle East a zone free from weapons of mass destruction and all missiles for their delivery and the objective of a global ban on chemical weapons;

D

15.   Requests the Secretary-General to report to the Security Council on the steps taken to facilitate the return of all Kuwaiti property seized by Iraq, including a list of any property that Kuwait claims has not been returned or which has not been returned intact;

E

16.   Reaffirms that Iraq, without prejudice to the debts and obligations of Iraq arising prior to 2 August 1990, which will be addressed through the normal mechanisms, is liable under international law for any direct loss, damage, including environmental damage and the depletion of natural resources, or injury to foreign Governments, nationals and corporations, as a result of Iraq's unlawful invasion and occupation of Kuwait;

17.   Decides that all Iraqi statements made since 2 August 1990 repudiating its foreign debt are null and void, and demands that Iraq adhere scrupulously to all of its obligations concerning servicing and repayment of its foreign debt;

18.   Decides also to create a fund to pay compensation for claims that fall within paragraph 16 above and to establish a Commission that will administer the fund;

19.   Directs the Secretary-General to develop and present to the Security Council for decision, no later than thirty days following the adoption of the present resolution, recommendations for the fund to meet the requirement for the programme to implement the decisions in paragraphs 16, 17 and 18 above, including: administration of the fund; mechanisms for determining the appropriate level of Iraq's contribution to the fund based on a percentage of the value of the exports of petroleum and petroleum products from Iraq not to exceed a figure to be suggested to the Council by the Secretary-General, taking into account the requirements of the people of Iraq, Iraq's payment capacity as assessed in conjunction with the international financial institutions taking into consideration external debt service, and the needs of the Iraqi economy; arrangements for ensuring that payments are made to the fund; the process by which funds will be allocated and claims paid; appropriate procedures for evaluating losses, listing claims and verifying their validity and resolving disputed claims in respect of Iraq's liability as specified in paragraph 16 above; and the composition of the Commission designated above.

F

20.   Decides, effective immediately, that the prohibitions against the sale or supply to Iraq of commodities or products, other than medicine and health supplies, and prohibitions against financial transactions related thereto contained in resolution 661 (1990) shall not apply to foodstuffs notified to the Security Council Committee established by resolution 661 (1990) concerning the situation between Iraq and Kuwait or, with the approval of that Committee, under the simplified and accelerated "no-objection" procedure, to materials and supplies for essential civilian needs as identified in the report of the Secretary-General dated 20 March 19919, and in any further findings of humanitarian need by the Committee;

21. Decides that the Security Council shall review the provisions of paragraph 20 above every sixty days in the light of the policies and practices of the Government of Iraq, including the implementation of all relevant resolutions of the Security Council, for the purpose of determining whether to reduce or lift the prohibitions referred to therein;

22. Decides that upon the approval by the Security Council of the programme called for in paragraph 19 above and upon Council agreement that Iraq has completed all actions contemplated in paragraphs 8, 9, 10, 11, 12 and 13 above, the prohibitions against the import of commodities and products originating in Iraq and the prohibitions against financial transactions related thereto contained in resolution 661 (1990) shall have no further force or effect;

23. Decides that, pending action by the Security Council Committee established by resolution 661 (1990) shall be empowered to approve, when required to assure adequate financial resources on the part of Iraq to carry out the activities under paragraph 20 above, exceptions to the prohibition against the import of commodities and products originating in Iraq;

24. Decides that, in accordance with resolution 661 (1990) and subsequent related resolutions and until a further decision is taken by the Security Council, all States shall continue to prevent the scale or supply, or the promotion or facilitation of such sale or supply, to Iraq by their nationals, or from their territories or using their flag vessels or aircraft, of:

Arms and related material of all types, specifically including the sale or transfer through other means of all forms of conventional military equipment, including for paramilitary forces, and spare parts and components and their means of production, for such equipment;

Items specified and defined in paragraphs 8 and 12 above not otherwise covered above;

Technology under licensing or other transfer arrangements used in the production, utilization or stockpiling of items specified in subparagraphs (a) and (b) above; Personnel or materials for training or technical support services relating to the design, development, manufacture, use, maintenance or support of items specified in subparagraphs (a) and (b) above;

25. Calls upon all States and international organizations to act strictly in accordance with paragraph 24 above, notwithstanding the existence of any contracts, agreements, licenses of any other arrangements;

26. Requests the Secretary-General, in consultation with appropriate Governments, to develop within sixty days, for the approval of the security Council, guidelines to facilitate full international implementation of paragraphs 24 and 25 above and paragraph 27 below, and to make them available to all States and to establish a procedure for updating these guidelines periodically;

27. Calls upon all States to maintain such national controls and procedures and to take such other actions consistent with the guidelines to be established by the Security

Council under paragraph 26 above as may be necessary to ensure compliance with the terms of paragraph 24 above, and calls upon international organizations to take all appropriate steps to assist in ensuring such full compliance;

28.   Agrees to review its decisions in paragraphs 22, 23, 24 and 25 above, except for the items specified and defined in paragraphs 8 and 12 above, on a regular basis and in any case one hundred and twenty days following passage of the present resolution, taking into account Iraq's compliance with the resolution and general progress towards the control of armaments in the region;

29.   Decides that all States, including Iraq, shall take the necessary measures to ensure that no claim shall lie at the instance of the Government of Iraq, or of any person or body in Iraq, or of any person claiming through or for the benefit of any such person or body, in connection with any contract or other transaction where its performance was affected by reason of the measures taken by the Security Council in resolution 661 (1990) and related resolutions;

G

30.   Decides that, in furtherance of its commitment to facilitate the repatriation of all Kuwaiti and third country nationals, Iraq shall extend all necessary cooperation to the International Committee of the Red Cross, providing lists of such persons, facilitating the access of the International Committee of the Red Cross to all such persons wherever located or detained and facilitating the search by the International Committee of the Red Cross for those Kuwaiti and third country nationals still unaccounted for;

31.   Invites the International Committee of the Red Cross to keep the Secretary-General apprised as appropriate of all activities undertaken in connection with facilitating the repatriation or return of all Kuwaiti and third country nationals or their remains present in Iraq on or after 2 August 1990;

H

32.   Requires Iraq to inform the Security Council that it will not commit or support any act of international terrorism or allow any organization directed towards commission of such acts to operate within its territory and to condemn unequivocally and renounce all acts, methods and practices of terrorism;

I

33.   Declares that, upon official notification by Iraq to the Secretary-General and to the Security Council of its acceptance of the provisions above, a formal cease-fire is effective between Iraq and Kuwait and the Member States cooperating with Kuwait in accordance with resolution 678 (1990);

34.   Decides to remain seized of the matter and to take such further steps as may be required for the implementation of the present resolution and to secure peace and security in the area.

UN Security Council Resolution 688 (1991)

April 5, 1991

The Security Council,

Mindful of its duties and its responsibilities under the Charter of the United Nations for the maintenance of international peace and security,

Recalling of Article 2, paragraph 7, of the Charter of the United Nations,

Gravely concerned by the repression of the Iraqi civilian population in many parts of Iraq, including most recently in Kurdish populated areas, which led to a massive flow of refugees towards and across international frontiers and to cross-border incursions, which threaten international peace and security in the region,

Deeply disturbed by the magnitude of the human suffering involved, Taking note of the letters sent by the representatives of Turkey and France to the United Nations dated 2 April 1991 and 4 April 1991, respectively (S/22435 and S/22442),

Taking note also of the letters sent by the Permanent Representative of the Islamic Republic of Iran to the United Nations dated 3 and 4 April 1991, respectively (S/22436 and S/22447),

Reaffirming the commitment of all Member States to the sovereignty, territorial integrity and political independence of Iraq and of all States in the area,

Bearing in mind the Secretary-General's report of 20 March 1991 (S/22366),

1.   Condemns the repression of the Iraqi civilian population in many parts of Iraq, including most recently in Kurdish populated areas, the consequences of which threaten international peace and security in the region;

2.   Demands that Iraq, as a contribution to remove the threat to international peace and security in the region, immediately end this repression and express the hope in the same context that an open dialogue will take place to ensure that the human and political rights of all Iraqi citizens are respected;

3. Insists that Iraq allow immediate access by international humanitarian organizations to all those in need of assistance in all parts of Iraq and to make available all necessary facilities for their operations;

4. Requests the Secretary-General to pursue his humanitarian efforts in Iraq and to report forthwith, if appropriate on the basis of a further mission to the region, on the plight of the Iraqi civilian population, and in particular the Kurdish population, suffering from the repression in all its forms inflicted by the Iraqi authorities;

5. Requests further the Secretary-General to use all the resources at his disposal, including those of the relevant United Nations agencies, to address urgently the critical needs of the refugees and displaced Iraqi population;

6. Appeals to all Member States and to all humanitarian organizations to contribute to these humanitarian relief efforts;

7. Demands that Iraq cooperate with the Secretary-General to these ends;

8. Decides to remain seized of the matter.

UN Security Council Resolution 1483 (2003)

22 May 2003

The Security Council,

Recalling all its previous relevant resolutions,

Reaffirming the sovereignty and territorial integrity of Iraq,

Reaffirming also the importance of the disarmament of Iraqi weapons of mass destruction and of eventual confirmation of the disarmament of Iraq,

Stressing the right of the Iraqi people freely to determine their own political future and control their own natural resources, welcoming the commitment of all parties concerned to support the creation of an environment in which they may do so as soon as possible, and expressing resolve that the day when Iraqis govern themselves must come quickly,

Encouraging efforts by the people of Iraq to form a representative government based on the rule of law that affords equal rights and justice to all Iraqi citizens without regard to ethnicity, religion, or gender, and, in this connection, recalls resolution 1325 (2000) of 31 October 2000,

Welcoming the first steps of the Iraqi people in this regard, and noting in this connection the 15 April 2003 Nasiriyah statement and the 28 April 2003 Baghdad statement,

Resolved that the United Nations should play a vital role in humanitarian relief, the reconstruction of Iraq, and the restoration and establishment of national and local institutions for representative governance,

Noting the statement of 12 April 2003 by the Ministers of Finance and Central Bank Governors of the Group of Seven Industrialized Nations in which the members recognized the need for a multilateral effort to help rebuild and develop Iraq and for the need for assistance from the International Monetary Fund and the World Bank in these efforts,

Welcoming also the resumption of humanitarian assistance and the continuing efforts of the Secretary-General and the specialized agencies to provide food and medicine to the people of Iraq,

Welcoming the appointment by the Secretary-General of his Special Adviser on Iraq,

Affirming the need for accountability for crimes and atrocities committed by the previous Iraqi regime,

Stressing the need for respect for the archaeological, historical, cultural, and religious heritage of Iraq, and for the continued protection of archaeological, historical, cultural, and religious sites, museums, libraries, and monuments,

Noting the letter of 8 May 2003 from the Permanent Representatives of the United States of America and the United Kingdom of Great Britain and Northern Ireland to the President of the Security Council (S/2003/538) and recognizing the specific authorities, responsibilities, and obligations under applicable international law of these states as occupying powers under unified command (the "Authority"),

Noting further that other States that are not occupying powers are working now or in the future may work under the Authority,

Welcoming further the willingness of Member States to contribute to stability and security in Iraq by contributing personnel, equipment, and other resources under the Authority,

Concerned that many Kuwaitis and Third-State Nationals still are not accounted for since 2 August 1990,

Determining that the situation in Iraq, although improved, continues to constitute a threat to international peace and security,

Acting under Chapter VII of the Charter of the United Nations,

1. Appeals to Member States and concerned organizations to assist the people of Iraq in their efforts to reform their institutions and rebuild their country, and to contribute to conditions of stability and security in Iraq in accordance with this resolution;

2. Calls upon all Member States in a position to do so to respond immediately to the humanitarian appeals of the United Nations and other international organizations for Iraq and to help meet the humanitarian and other needs of the Iraqi people by providing food, medical supplies, and resources necessary for reconstruction and rehabilitation of Iraq's economic infrastructure;

3. Appeals to Member States to deny safe haven to those members of the previous Iraqi regime who are alleged to be responsible for crimes and atrocities and to support actions to bring them to justice;

4. Calls upon the Authority, consistent with the Charter of the United Nations and other relevant international law, to promote the welfare of the Iraqi people through the effective administration of the territory, including in particular working towards the restoration of conditions of security and stability and the creation of conditions in which the Iraqi people can freely determine their own political future;

5. Calls upon all concerned to comply fully with their obligations under international law including in particular the Geneva Conventions of 1949 and the Hague Regulations of 1907;

6. Calls upon the Authority and relevant organizations and individuals to continue efforts to locate, identify, and repatriate all Kuwaiti and Third-State Nationals or the remains of those present in Iraq on or after 2 August 1990, as well as the Kuwaiti archives, that the previous Iraqi regime failed to undertake, and, in this regard, directs the High-Level Coordinator, in consultation with the International Committee of the Red Cross and the Tripartite Commission and with the appropriate support of the people of Iraq and in coordination with the Authority, to take steps to fulfil his mandate with respect to the fate of Kuwaiti and Third-State National missing persons and property;

7. Decides that all Member States shall take appropriate steps to facilitate the safe return to Iraqi institutions of Iraqi cultural property and other items of archaeological, historical, cultural, rare scientific, and religious importance illegally removed from the Iraq National Museum, the National Library, and other locations in Iraq since the adoption of resolution 661 (1990) of 6 August 1990, including by establishing a prohibition on trade in or transfer of such items and items with respect to which reasonable suspicion exists that they have been illegally removed, and calls upon the United Nations Educational, Scientific, and Cultural Organization, Interpol, and other international organizations, as appropriate, to assist in the implementation of this paragraph;

8. Requests the Secretary-General to appoint a Special Representative for Iraq whose independent responsibilities shall involve reporting regularly to the Council on his activities under this resolution, coordinating activities of the United Nations in post-conflict processes in Iraq, coordinating among United Nations and international agencies engaged in humanitarian assistance and reconstruction activities in Iraq, and, in coordination with the Authority, assisting the people of Iraq through:

(a) coordinating humanitarian and reconstruction assistance by United Nations agencies and between United Nations agencies and non-governmental organizations;

(b) promoting the safe, orderly, and voluntary return of refugees and displaced persons;

(c) working intensively with the Authority, the people of Iraq, and others concerned to advance efforts to restore and establish national and local institutions for representative governance, including by working together to facilitate a process leading to an internationally recognized, representative government of Iraq;

(d) facilitating the reconstruction of key infrastructure, in cooperation with other international organizations;

(e) promoting economic reconstruction and the conditions for sustainable development, including through coordination with national and regional organizations, as appropriate, civil society, donors, and the international financial institutions;

(f) encouraging international efforts to contribute to basic civilian administration functions;

(g) promoting the protection of human rights;

(h) encouraging international efforts to rebuild the capacity of the Iraqi civilian police force; and

(i) encouraging international efforts to promote legal and judicial reform;

9. Supports the formation, by the people of Iraq with the help of the Authority and working with the Special Representative, of an Iraqi interim administration as a transitional administration run by Iraqis, until an internationally recognized, representative government is established by the people of Iraq and assumes the responsibilities of the Authority;

10. Decides that, with the exception of prohibitions related to the sale or supply to Iraq of arms and related materiel other than those arms and related materiel required by the Authority to serve the purposes of this and other related resolutions, all prohibitions related to trade with Iraq and the provision of financial or economic resources to Iraq established by resolution 661 (1990) and subsequent relevant resolutions, including resolution 778 (1992) of 2 October 1992, shall no longer apply;

11. Reaffirms that Iraq must meet its disarmament obligations, encourages the United Kingdom of Great Britain and Northern Ireland and the United States of America to keep the Council informed of their activities in this regard, and underlines the intention of the Council to revisit the mandates of the United Nations Monitoring, Verification, and Inspection Commission and the International Atomic Energy Agency as set forth in resolutions 687 (1991) of 3 April 1991, 1284 (1999) of 17 December 1999, and 1441 (2002) of 8 November 2002;

12. Notes the establishment of a Development Fund for Iraq to be held by the Central Bank of Iraq and to be audited by independent public accountants approved by the International Advisory and Monitoring Board of the Development Fund for Iraq and looks forward to the early meeting of that International Advisory and Monitoring Board, whose members shall include duly qualified representatives of the Secretary-General, of the Managing Director of the International Monetary Fund, of the Director-General of the Arab Fund for Social and Economic Development, and of the President of the World Bank;

13. Notes further that the funds in the Development Fund for Iraq shall be disbursed at the direction of the Authority, in consultation with the Iraqi interim administration, for the purposes set out in paragraph 14 below;

14. Underlines that the Development Fund for Iraq shall be used in a transparent manner to meet the humanitarian needs of the Iraqi people, for the economic reconstruction and repair of Iraq's infrastructure, for the continued disarmament of Iraq, and for the costs of Iraqi civilian administration, and for other purposes benefiting the people of Iraq;

15. Calls upon the international financial institutions to assist the people of Iraq in the reconstruction and development of their economy and to facilitate assistance by the broader donor community, and welcomes the readiness of creditors, including those of the Paris Club, to seek a solution to Iraq's sovereign debt problems;

16. Requests also that the Secretary-General, in coordination with the Authority, continue the exercise of his responsibilities under Security Council resolution 1472 (2003) of 28 March 2003 and 1476 (2003) of 24 April 2003, for a period of six months following the adoption of this resolution, and terminate within this time period, in the most cost effective manner, the ongoing operations of the "Oil-for-Food" Programme (the "Programme"), both at headquarters level and in the field, transferring responsibility for the administration of any remaining activity under the Programme to the Authority, including by taking the following necessary measures:

(a) to facilitate as soon as possible the shipment and authenticated delivery of priority civilian goods as identified by the Secretary-General and representatives designated by him, in coordination with the Authority and the Iraqi interim administration, under approved and funded contracts previously concluded by the previous Government of Iraq, for the humanitarian relief of the people of Iraq, including, as necessary, negotiating adjustments in the terms or conditions of these contracts and respective letters of credit as set forth in paragraph 4 (d) of resolution 1472 (2003);

(b) to review, in light of changed circumstances, in coordination with the Authority and the Iraqi interim administration, the relative utility of each approved and funded contract with a view to determining whether such contracts contain items required to meet the needs of the people of Iraq both now and during reconstruction, and to postpone action on those contracts determined to be of questionable utility and the respective letters of credit until an internationally recognized, representative government of Iraq is in a position to make its own determination as to whether such contracts shall be fulfilled;

(c) to provide the Security Council within 21 days following the adoption of this resolution, for the Security Council's review and consideration, an estimated operating budget based on funds already set aside in the account established pursuant to paragraph 8 (d) of resolution 986 (1995) of 14 April 1995, identifying:

(i) all known and projected costs to the United Nations required to ensure the continued functioning of the activities associated with implementation of the present resolution, including operating and administrative expenses associated with the relevant United Nations agencies and programmes responsible for the implementation of the Programme both at Headquarters and in the field;

(ii) all known and projected costs associated with termination of the Programme;

(iii) all known and projected costs associated with restoring Government of Iraq funds that were provided by Member States to the Secretary-General as requested in paragraph 1 of resolution 778 (1992); and

(iv) all known and projected costs associated with the Special Representative and the qualified representative of the Secretary-General identified to serve on the International Advisory and Monitoring Board, for the six month time period defined above, following which these costs shall be borne by the United Nations;

(d) to consolidate into a single fund the accounts established pursuant to paragraphs 8 (a) and 8 (b) of resolution 986 (1995);

(e) to fulfil all remaining obligations related to the termination of the Programme, including negotiating, in the most cost effective manner, any necessary settlement payments, which shall be made from the escrow accounts established pursuant to paragraphs 8 (a) and 8 (b) of resolution 986 (1995), with those parties that previously have entered into contractual obligations with the Secretary-General under the Programme, and to determine, in coordination with the Authority and the Iraqi interim administration, the future status of contracts undertaken by the United Nations and related United Nations agencies under the accounts established pursuant to paragraphs 8 (b) and 8 (d) of resolution 986 (1995);

(f) to provide the Security Council, 30 days prior to the termination of the Programme, with a comprehensive strategy developed in close coordination with the Authority and the Iraqi interim administration that would lead to the delivery of all relevant documentation and the transfer of all operational responsibility of the Programme to the Authority;

17. Requests further that the Secretary-General transfer as soon as possible to the Development Fund for Iraq 1 billion United States dollars from unencumbered funds in the accounts established pursuant to paragraphs 8 (a) and 8 (b) of resolution 986 (1995), restore Government of Iraq funds that were provided by Member States to the Secretary-General as requested in paragraph 1 of resolution 778 (1992), and decides that, after deducting all relevant United Nations expenses associated with the shipment of authorized contracts and costs to the Programme outlined in paragraph 16 (c) above, including residual obligations, all surplus funds in the escrow accounts established pursuant to paragraphs 8 (a), 8 (b), 8 (d), and 8 (f) of resolution 986 (1995) shall be transferred at the earliest possible time to the Development Fund for Iraq;

18. Decides to terminate effective on the adoption of this resolution the functions related to the observation and monitoring activities undertaken by the Secretary-General under the Programme, including the monitoring of the export of petroleum and petroleum products from Iraq;

19. Decides to terminate the Committee established pursuant to paragraph 6 of resolution 661 (1990) at the conclusion of the six month period called for in paragraph 16 above and further decides that the Committee shall identify individuals and entities referred to in paragraph 23 below;

20. Decides that all export sales of petroleum, petroleum products, and natural gas from Iraq following the date of the adoption of this resolution shall be made consistent with prevailing international market best practices, to be audited by independent public accountants reporting to the International Advisory and Monitoring Board referred to in paragraph 12 above in order to ensure transparency, and decides further that, except as provided in paragraph 21 below, all proceeds from such sales shall be deposited into the Development Fund for Iraq until such time as an internationally recognized, representative government of Iraq is properly constituted;

21. Decides further that 5 per cent of the proceeds referred to in paragraph 20 above shall be deposited into the Compensation Fund established in accordance with

resolution 687 (1991) and subsequent relevant resolutions and that, unless an internationally recognized, representative government of Iraq and the Governing Council of the United Nations Compensation Commission, in the exercise of its authority over methods of ensuring that payments are made into the Compensation Fund, decide otherwise, this requirement shall be binding on a properly constituted, internationally recognized, representative government of Iraq and any successor thereto;

22. Noting the relevance of the establishment of an internationally recognized, representative government of Iraq and the desirability of prompt completion of the restructuring of Iraq's debt as referred to in paragraph 15 above, further decides that, until December 31, 2007, unless the Council decides otherwise, petroleum, petroleum products, and natural gas originating in Iraq shall be immune, until title passes to the initial purchaser from legal proceedings against them and not be subject to any form of attachment, garnishment, or execution, and that all States shall take any steps that may be necessary under their respective domestic legal systems to assure this protection, and that proceeds and obligations arising from sales thereof, as well as the Development Fund for Iraq, shall enjoy privileges and immunities equivalent to those enjoyed by the United Nations except that the above-mentioned privileges and immunities will not apply with respect to any legal proceeding in which recourse to such proceeds or obligations is necessary to satisfy liability for damages assessed in connection with an ecological accident, including an oil spill, that occurs after the date of adoption of this resolution;

23. Decides that all Member States in which there are:

(a) funds or other financial assets or economic resources of the previous Government of Iraq or its state bodies, corporations, or agencies, located outside Iraq as of the date of this resolution, or

(b) funds or other financial assets or economic resources that have been removed from Iraq, or acquired, by Saddam Hussein or other senior officials of the former Iraqi regime and their immediate family members, including entities owned or controlled, directly or indirectly, by them or by persons acting on their behalf or at their direction,

shall freeze without delay those funds or other financial assets or economic resources and, unless these funds or other financial assets or economic resources are themselves the subject of a prior judicial, administrative, or arbitral lien or judgement, immediately shall cause their transfer to the Development Fund for Iraq, it being understood that, unless otherwise addressed, claims made by private individuals or non-government entities on those transferred funds or other financial assets may be presented to the internationally recognized, representative government of Iraq; and decides further that all such funds or other financial assets or economic resources shall enjoy the same privileges, immunities, and protections as provided under paragraph 22;

24. Requests the Secretary-General to report to the Council at regular intervals on the work of the Special Representative with respect to the implementation of this resolution and on the work of the International Advisory and Monitoring Board and encourages the United Kingdom of Great Britain and Northern Ireland and the United States of America to inform the Council at regular intervals of their efforts under this resolution;

25. Decides to review the implementation of this resolution within twelve months of adoption and to consider further steps that might be necessary;

26. Calls upon Member States and international and regional organizations to contribute to the implementation of this resolution;

27. Decides to remain seized of this matter.

Bibliographic Note

I have always enjoyed thumbing through a book to find, at the end, a bibliographic section that gives relative weight to the sources that have been used. With this in mind, and hoping that the reader will enjoy the exercise, I have decided to divide this Note into two sections. As this study examines international law from the perspective of the Middle East, the first part highlights the various sources of international law used, while the second deals with sources related to the Middle East. What I have sought to do, while drafting this monograph, is to bring my knowledge of international law to bear on the factual history of the evolution of the modern Middle East.

I. Sources of International Law

In drafting this study I was acutely aware that it is the first monograph to consider the Middle East from the perspective of international law. Other studies which have focused on the greater Middle East have been edited works, such as John Halderman (ed.), *The Middle East Crisis: Test of International Law*, 1969, which is, in fact, a collection of papers from an American Society of International Law symposium; or Majid Khadduri, (ed.) *Major Middle East Problems in International Law*, 1972. Though obviously dated, both deal with selected issues primarily centred on the Arab-Israeli conflict. Beyond these two edited works that focus on the Middle East generally, international law monographs that have appeared have sought to deal with specific issues within the meta-narrative of the Middle East. For instance, Moustapha El-Hefnaoui, *Les problèmes contemporains posés par le canal de Suez*, written in 1951, is almost palatable in expressing its frustration at the British occupation of Egypt and the manner in which the Suez Canal was managed in contradiction to the principles outlined in the 1888 Constantinople Convention. Other works, such as Henry Cattan's 1973 *Palestine and International Law: The Legal Aspects of the Arab-Israeli Conflict*, are so polemic as to render their legal analysis beyond consideration in an academic work. Which, in the case of Cattan, is a shame, as when not discussing the tragedy which has befallen the Palestinians—he was part of the Palestinian delegation that witnessed the passing of UN General Assembly Resolution 181, partitioning Palestine in November 1947—his writing has been quite rigorous. Consider, for instance his 1967 *The Law of Oil Concessions in the Middle East and North Africa*. Less passionate is Mallison and Mallison's 1986 *The Palestine Problem in International Law and World Order*, though often times the analysis is stretched. Other books that provide more value are often works undertaken by individuals whose work has brought them to the region. One such study is Lex Takkenberg's 1998 *The Status of Palestinian Refugees in International Law* which, while filling a gap, provides a traditional reading of the status of Palestinian Refugees much in line with the manner in which UNRWA has acted on the ground for more than fifty years. Edited works have also appeared which, while being grounded in international law, seek to focus on a specific Middle East issue. Worth paging through are John Norton Moore (ed.), *The Arab-Israeli Conflict: Readings and Documents*, 1977; or Ige Dekker and Harry Post (eds.), *The Gulf War of 1980– 1988: The Iran-Iraq War in International Legal Perspective*, which call on noted international legal scholars and set parameters of discussion which touch the salient issues at play.

Before highlighting the works related to the specific topics considered in this study, it is worth considering general pieces that allowed me to ground myself in international law. While Ian Brownlie's, *Principles of Public International Law*, 1990, has been praised, as a student textbook or a starting place to consider issues of international law it leaves one perplexed. Having been immersed in international law for many years now, I find myself having to page the index then go to the text two or three times before coming to the passage I seek. For students new to the discipline, it must be truly inaccessible. In truth, I have failed to find an English-language text that comes close to the mastery of Dailler and Pellet's *Droit international public*, which is now in its sixth edition. In both its breadth and structure it is a marvel, although recently I have noted Antonio Casesse's *International Law* which is eloquently written; and Malcolm Shaw's, *International Law*, 2003 which I assign to my students. Likewise, given a choice, I would shy away from Brownlie's *Basic Documents in International Law*, instead referring readers to Eric Suy's *Corpus Iuris Gentium: A Collection of Basic Texts on Modern Interstate Relations* to be used as a desk reference. Although it is difficult to obtain (it is published by Acco, in Leuven, Belgium), it is worth purchasing as it gives a nice balance of texts. It includes all those instruments one might expect (the UN Charter, the Vienna Convention on the Law of Treaties, Vienna Convention on Diplomatic Relations, as well as sections related to internationalised areas—Law of the Sea, Antarctica, *etc.*—human rights, and international criminal law, but also important primary documents including the 1970 Friendly Relations Declaration (UNGA Resolution 2625); the 1974 Definition of Aggression (UNGA Resolution 3314), and the Draft Articles on State Responsibility.

Going one step further in setting the groundwork for this study or, for that matter, any international study where one must consider the obligations of States is, of course, the United Nations' *Multilateral Treaties Deposited with the Secretary-General: Status as at 30 April 1999* (UN. Doc. ST/LEG/SER.E/17) which establishes not only which States are party to various international instruments, but sets out the extent to which they have accepted or modified those obligations by way of declarations or reservations. One might also mention here in protest, that the UN Secretariat offers limited access to such information via the internet by requiring individuals and institutions to pay an annual fee to gain access to their UN Treaty Series database—a situation which is thoroughly unacceptable. One final work which, although sorely outdated, is worth having in one's law library is Shabtai Rosenne's 1984 *Practice and Methods of International Law*. This slim volume is truly a road map for international jurists, providing much practical advice on seeking out sources, on citations, *etc.* One small example chosen at random, demonstrates my point: Rosenne, in speaking of citations, states, 'No hard-and-fast rules for the citation of doctrine can be given. If a publisher or the periodical in which a publication is to appear does not have house rules, the international character of the intended readership is to be remembered, and what is a familiar method of citations in one country may be almost unintelligible in another' (p. 121).

As far as international instruments are concerned, a number of texts come to mind that are worthy of mention. I would highlight Guy Goodwin-Gill's *The Refugee in International Law*, which is a masterpiece. Used as a text in a refugee law course, or simply sitting down to read through it, the book is unrivalled. As a resource book, it is easily accessible, reads eloquently, and has included the primary texts as appendices. As a leading authority, no other book I know has cornered the market as this one has; it is indispensable and worth emulating if one seeks to write on a specific subject of international law. Handy as references are also William Schabas' 2000 *Genocide in International Law*, Cherif Bassiouni's 1999 *Crimes against Humanity in International Criminal Law*, Leslie Green's 2000 *The Contemporary Law of Armed Conflict*, J.G. Merrills' 1998 *International Dispute Settlement,* and Jean Salmon's 1994 *Manuel de droit diplomatique*. As for basic documents texts related to a specific field of international law, Adam Roberts' and Richard Guelff's 2000 *Documents on the Laws of War* is worth having in one's private collection, while Brownlie and Goodwin-Gill's 2002 *Basic Documents in Human Rights* gladly replaces previous efforts.

With regard to the various chapters, works worth emphasizing in Chapter 1 with respect to issue of self-determination include Antonio Cassese's 1995 treatise, *Self-Determination of Peoples: A Legal Appraisal*. With respect to Kurdish issues: Richard Falk's article 'Problems and Prospects for the Kurdish Struggle for Self-Determination after the End of the Gulf and Cold Wars', which originally appeared in 1994 in Volume 15 of the *Michigan Journal of International Law* does well to bring forward the salient issues. I should, at this point, lay my cards on the table by noting that I have included this piece in a book I have edited of the works of Richard Falk related to the Middle East, entitled *Unlocking the Middle East: The Writings of Richard Falk*, Olive Branch Press, 2003. As I have noted in the introduction to that work, whether one agrees or disagrees with Falk's writings, one would be a lesser international scholar for not reading his work. In this case, Falk does well in highlighting the very political nature of the right of self-determination and its applicability to the Kurdish situation.

With respect to Chapter 2, which relates to the Suez Canal, Mohamed Olwan gives a fundamental understanding of such waterways in his 'International Canals', which appears in the very impressive M. Bedjaoui (ed.), *International Law: Achievements and Prospects*, 1986. Hoskins' 1943 'The Suez Canal as an International Waterway', gives an overview of the regime, while Leo Gross' 1957 'Passage Through the Suez Canal of Israel-Bound Cargo and Israeli Ships', reiterates the Israeli position. Both appeared in the *American Journal of International Law*. As for Chapter 3, regarding the formation of the State of Israel, much 'legal analysis' has been clouded by vested interests which renders much of it unfit for consumption. By contrast, James Crawford's study which appears in the 1999 Brownlie *Festschrift* 'Israel (1948–1949) and Palestine (1998–1999): Two Studies in the Creation of States', does well to set out the basic framework. Monographs such as W. F. Boustani, *Palestine Mandate, Invalid and Impracticable*, 1936; or J. Stoyanovsky's *The Mandate for Palestine: A Contribution to the Theory and Practice of International Mandates*, 1928, however, go too far in pressing their case.

With respect to Palestinian Refugees, the basis of the study of Chapter 4 reflects work that I undertook which was, unbeknownst to me at the time, running parallel to the work of Susan Akram. It must be said that her work, as reflected, for instance, in the *Brief Amicus Curiae*, which was presented by her and Guy Goodwin-Gill, to the United States Board of Immigration Appeals, along with 'Reinterpreting Palestinian Refugee Rights under International Law', which appears in Naseer Aruri (ed.), *Palestinian Refugees: The Right of Return*, 2001, is much more in-depth and thorough than what is presented within the pages of this study. However, the fundamental understanding remains constant—that Palestinian Refugees are entitled to international protection which they have been denied for more than fifty years.

With Chapter 5, which deals with the two Gulf Wars and Israel's occupation of Lebanon, not much of the *doctrine* was relied upon as the study considered the response of the UN Security Council to these various acts of aggression. Indispensable was the work by Anjali Patil, *The UN Veto in World Affairs, 1946–1990: A Complete Record and Case Histories of the Security Council's Veto*, 1992. Bailey's and Daws' classic, appearing in its third edition in 1998, *The Procedure of the UN Security Council*, as well as Bruno Simma (ed.), *The Charter of the United Nations: A Commentary*, 1995, were likewise essential. Regarding aggression, consider Yoram Dinstein, *War, Aggression and Self-Defence*, 2001, and Brownlie's 1964 publication of his doctoral dissertation reprinted in 1991 as *International Law and the Use of Force by States*. Readers might well be interested in Julius Stone's scathing critique of Benjamin Ferencz, *Defining International Aggression: The Search for World Peace—A Documentary History and Analysis*, 1975, which appeared in 1977 in the *American Journal of International Law*, as 'Hopes and Loopholes in the 1974 Definition of Aggression'.

While much has been written about the deadly effect of United Nations-imposed sanctions against Iraq, which is at the heart of Chapter 6, very little of substance has come out regarding the international implications of the sanction regime. Roger Normand and Chris af Jochnick's 1994 'The Legitimation of Violence: a Critical Analysis of the Gulf War', which appeared in the *Harvard International Law Journal*, lays out nicely the critical issue of the controls on the means and methods of warfare which lay at the heart of the suffering which would transpire in the following decade under UN sanctions. A fundamental question regarding the applicability of Hague Law remains open as neither the Yugoslavia or Rwanda tribunals have sought to take such violations seriously, instead they have been willing to defer to military planners' explanations regarding the military necessity of their targeting strategies.

As to the issue of states of emergency, which is the focus of Chapter 7, a number of general studies have appeared, including the International Commission of Jurists' 1993 *States of Emergency: Their Impact on Human Rights*, and Joan Fitzpatrick, 1994 Human *Rights in Crisis: The International System for Protecting Human Rights during States of Emergency*; though Jaime Oraá's *Human Rights in States of Emergency in International Law*, 1992 remains the text of preference. The work of the Special Rapporteur of the UN Human Rights Committee dealing with States of emergency, Leandro Despouy is invaluable. His ten years of study which resulted in 'General Comment Number 29—States of Emergency (article 4)' (UN. Doc. CCPR/C/21/Rev.1/Add.11) is masterly and deserves wider circulation. With respect to Chapter 8 of this study, regarding the peaceful settlement of disputes in the Middle East, I would be failing in my duty of self-promotion if I did not mention, in a general manner, Jean Allain, *A Century of International Adjudication: The Rule of Law and its Limits*, 2000. Beyond that, the reports of the International Court of Justice, the Permanent Court of Arbitration and the *International Law Reports* along with the *International Legal Materials* are the bread and butter for locating cases. With respect to the decolonization process, consider both Milan Bulajić, *Principles of International Development Law: Progressive Development of the Principles of International Law Relating to the New International Economic Order*, 1993, and Mohammed Bedjaoui, *Towards a New International Economic Order*, 1979.

One item is worth mentioning in closing this section devoted to international legal sources, and that is in regard to the *Encyclopaedia of Public International Law* edited by Rudolf Berhardt et al. The *Encyclopaedia* is an essential tool and should, perhaps have been mentioned earlier in this Note.

II.   Sources Related to the Middle East

While this study has brought to bear the insights of international law, my primary aim has been to get the facts right. This has meant much cross-referencing and seeking to ensure that sources (and authors) were both trustworthy and accurate. While one can never deny a bias in undertaking a project, I have sought to mitigate the extremes and, as much as possible, provide insights in following the path on which my analysis of the international legality of events has taken me. This has often times meant that I had to consider sources that went against the orthodoxy but were, in essence, portraying the events as they took place and not necessarily as States sought to have them understood.

The starting point, as I mentioned in the Introduction is Edward Said's 1995 *Orientalism: Western Conceptions of the Orient*. This work, more than any other, has radically altered the perception of Middle East studies, providing a voice for 'the other'. It is what Fanon's *The Wretched of the Earth* was to the decolonization process. The only significant general text I found regarding the establishment of the Middle East is David Fromkin's *A Peace to End All Peace: Creating the Modern Middle East, 1914–1922*, which gives much coherence to what transpired in the wake of the defeat of the Ottoman Empire and the emergence of a European imposed States system after the First World War.

With regard to Chapter 1 and issues Kurdish, for lack of material, much reliance was made on David McDowall's *A Modern History of the Kurds*, 1996, a work that seeks to bring together many primary sources in an accessible manner. Beyond it, Salah Jmor's 1994 published doctoral dissertation from the Graduate Institute of International Studies of the University of Geneva, *L'Origine de la question Kurde*, nicely lays out the rise and fall of the fortunes of a Kurdish State in the aftermath of the First World War. With respect to human rights violations perpetuated against Kurds, consider the annual reports of both Amnesty International and Middle East Watch, which is now known as Human Rights Watch (Middle East), including the following reports prepared by Human Rights Watch in the mid-1990s: *Weapons Transfers and Violations of the Laws of War in Turkey*; *Iraq's Crime of Genocide: The Anfal Campaign against the Kurds*; and the *Bureaucracy of Repression: The Iraqi Government in its Own Words*.

As for the factual history of issues surrounding the Suez Canal, D. A. Farnie's 1969, *East and West of Suez: The Suez Canal in History, 1854–1956*, remains in a class of its own. Charles Beatty's *Ferdinand de Lessep*, 1956 is the quintessential biography, which brings to life the zealot nature of de Lessep's personality. Regarding the events of 1956, consider Anthony Gorst's and Lewis Johman's *The Suez Crisis*, 1997, which compiles relevant historical documents and is an interesting piece of historiography. The United States Department of State provides more documentation in *The Suez Canal Problem: A Documentary Publication*, 1956; as do Boutros Boutros-Ghali and Youssef Chlala in *Le Canal de Suez: 1854–1957*, 1958; while Elihu Lauterpacht edits documents pertaining to the settlement of the fiasco in, *The Suez Canal Settlement*, 1960.

With respect to issues regarding the formation of the State of Israel dealt with in Chapter 3, two basic historical documents texts are worthy of mention. They are Walid Khalidi (ed.), *From Haven to Conquest: Readings in Zionism and the Palestine Problem Until 1948*, 1987; and Walter Laqueur, (ed.), *The Israel-Arab Reader: A Documentary History of the Middle East Conflict*, 2001. In many ways, these two texts, while presenting basic historical documents, demonstrate the great divide between supporters of Arabs and Israelis. Khalidi's text has the added benefit of providing more background on the texts in an attempt to give them context. For studies of the Arab-Israeli conflict consider Benny Morris, *Righteous Victims: A History of the Zionist-Arab Conflict, 1881–1999*, 1999, and Alvi Shlaim, *Iron Wall: Israel and the Arab World*, 2000. For historical studies that deal with the period in the lead-up to the creation of the State of Israel consider the ground-breaking Alvi Shlaim, *Collusion across the Jordan: King Abdullah, the Zionist Movement, and the Partition of Palestine*, 1988; and more recently Eugene Rogan and Avi Shlaim (eds.), *The War for Palestine: Rewriting the History of 1948*, 2001. I would recommend the latter as it brings one up-to-date not only on the discourse of the lead-up to the establishment of Israel, but also on the influence that has been made evident by the 'new historiography' movement which has transpired since the late 1980s when documents from both the British and Israeli archives became available, thus allowing scholars to consider the historical record for the first time. Read for instance Benny Morris, 'The New Historiography: Israel and its Past' in Rogan and Shlaim.

Shlaim's *Collusion across the Jordan* is worthy of note. Not so much for the fact that the author is a Professor of International Relations at Oxford University, but because the text derails many myths surrounding the movement to create the State of Israel and paves the way for what comes later. That the 1948 War was a monolithic struggle between Arab States and the newly established State of Israel is put to rest as Shlaim demonstrates that, in essence, there were two partition plans, one fostered by the United Nations as expressed in Resolution 181, the other—which ultimately transpired—tacitly agreed to by Great Britain, Israel, and Jordan which called for the infanticide of a nascent Palestinian State in exchange for Jordan receiving the West Bank.

What follows Shlaim are the 'new historians', such as Benny Morris and Ilan Pappé who do much to demystify the events of 1948 and beyond. Within this vein is a history developed from secondary sources which I relied on: Tom Segev, *One Palestine, Complete: Jews and Arabs under the British Mandate*, 2000. My willingness to rely on this work is based on the fact that Segev is a respected journalist for the leading Israeli daily *Ha'aretz*, and thus well within the Israeli mainstream. Thus, his criticisms of Jewish actions during the British Mandate are well within the parameters of intellectual discourse.

With respect to Chapter 4, the leading historian on Palestinian Refugees is Benny Morris, whose work 1987 *The Birth of the Palestinian Refugee Problem, 1947–1949*, is much to be praised, though it has been criticised for drawing the wrong conclusions from the evidence presented. See his response to his critics in 'The Cause and Character of the Arab Exodus from Palestine: The Israel Defence Forces Intelligence Service Analysis of June 1948', in Rogan and Shlaim. A valid criticism which has been leveled against States of the Arab world has been their unwillingness to open their archives, thus any historical narrative that emerges from Arab authors is either in the form of journalism—consider the works of Mohamed Heikal—or is based on the same Israeli or Western sources. Having said that, Naseer Aruri's 2001 edited piece entitled *Palestinian Refugees: The Right of Return* brings together much of writing favouring the Palestinian perspective regarding the 1948 Refugees.

Sources for Chapter 5, which deals with the Iraqi wars and the Israeli occupation of Lebanon include, for the latter, Edgar O'Ballance, *Civil War in Lebanon, 1975–92*, 1998, but more impressive is the journalistic account by Robert Fisk, entitled: *Pity the Nation: Lebanon at War*, 2001. For insights into *Hizballah*, consider Amal Saad-Ghorayeb's 2002 *Hizbu'llah: Politics and Religion*. For the wars involving Iraq see generally Charles Tripp's *A History of Iraq*, 2000; with regard to the specific issues surrounding the Tanker War, see Nadia El-Sayed El-Shazly's *The Gulf Tanker War: Iran and Iraq's Maritime Swordplay*, 1998. For the 1991 War Arthur Blair's *At War in the Gulf: A Chronology*, 1992; Dilip Hiro's *Desert Shield to Desert Storm: The Second Gulf War*, 1992, as well as United Nations, *The United Nations and the Iraq-Kuwait Conflict, 1990–1996*, which provides the basic UN documents related to the conflict and its aftermath.

Valuable sources used related to the UN Sanctions regime for Iraq (Chapter 6) include David Cortright's and George Lopez's *The Sanctions Decade: Assessing UN Strategies in the 1990s*, 2000, generally; and with respect to the Sanction Committee of the United Nations, Paul Conlon's *United Nations Sanctions Management: A Case Study of the Iraq Sanctions Committee, 1990–1994*, 2000. As to the effects of the sanctions on the health and lives of Iraqis, no one source deals adequately with the subject, though the 2000 Working Paper prepared by Marc Bossuyt for the Commission on Human Rights, entitled 'The Adverse Consequences of Economic Sanctions on the Enjoyment of Human Rights' (UN Doc. E/CN.4/Sub.2/2000/33), highlights many of the issues. Documentation regarding the suffering of Iraqis comes from various sources, including individual writers, organizations such as Human Rights Watch and the International Committee of the Red Cross/Red Crescent, as well as from both the United Nations humanitarian agencies and the UN Security Council itself. I would refer readers back to the footnotes in that chapter.

Chapter 7, dealing with states of emergency in Egypt and Syria, relies heavily on reports emanating from the UN human rights system, including treaty monitoring bodies and Special Rapporteurs, as well as findings by Egyptian, Syrian, and international human rights NGOs. Of note has been the work of the UN Special Rapporteur on issues of torture, Sir Nigel Rodley, who has been firm in his stand regarding the highlighting of the systematic use of torture in both Egypt and Syria. Middle East Watch's work entitled, *Syria Unmasked: The Suppression of Human Rights by the Asad Regime*, 1991 and Amnesty International's *Syria: Torture, despair and dehumanization in Tadmur Military Prison*, are worth reading; as is the Syrian Human Rights Committee's *Report of the Human Rights Situation in Syria over a 20-Year Period: 1979–1999*, 2001, though more for its breadth than depth. The decoding of the closed society that is Syria was made easier by Patrick Seale, *Asad: The Struggle for the Middle East*, 1988, and Daniel Pipes, *Greater Syria: The History of an Ambition*, 1990.

The final chapter does not lend itself to identifying historical sources as it is an examination of legal cases, reference to which has already been made in the previous section: reports of the International Court of Justice, the Permanent Court of Arbitration and, as secondary sources, the *International Law Reports* and *International Legal Materials*. With respect to the level of armaments and armed forces, the publications of the Stockholm International Peace Research Institute, including its *SIPRI Yearbook*, are indispensable; as is the annual *Military Balance* published by the London-based International Institute for Strategic Studies.

Where the Middle East is concerned, one often feels like one is walking through a minefield with regard to sources. And yet, once one gets a sense of the historical record, the realities of the region start to come into focus. It is hoped that the reader will appreciate the critical nature of the study presented and, at least to some extent, gain insights from the manner in which this study has sought to weave together fact and law in an attempt to provide a coherent narrative of the manner in which international law has been applied and interpreted in the Middle East.

Index

and Iraq 157, 159
and Israel 232
proliferation of 11
Webster, Daniel 274
Weizmann, Chaim 75 n4, 79 n17
Western powers, and international
law 2
Weston, Burns, and Israeli human
rights violations 114
Wilson, Woodrow
and San Remo Conference 82
and self-determination 5, 15, 81
World Bank, and Suez Canal
compensation 59, 70
World Court 241
World Health Organization 258
and sanctions against Iraq 180
World Jewish Congress 97

Yemen 4, 11
and United Arab Republic 233

Yemeni War 230
Yugoslavia
and Badinter Commission 37–8
and NATO intervention 272–3
and self-determination 36–7

Zionism
and Balfour Declaration (1917) 73,
77–9
British support of 74, 76–7
and administration of Palestine
87–9
establishment of 74–6
and Palestine 6–7
and Palestine Mandate 83
and possible homelands 75
support for 76–7
and war with Arabs 90
Zionist Congress, First (Basle, 1897)
74–5